D0643451

Attention and
Cognitive Development

Attention and Cognitive Development

Edited by

Gordon A. Hale

Psychological Development Research Division
Educational Testing Service
Princeton, New Jersey

and

Michael Lewis

Institute for the Study of Exceptional Children
Educational Testing Service
Princeton, New Jersey

Plenum Press · New York and London

Library of Congress Cataloging in Publication Data

Main entry under title:

Attention and cognitive development.

   Includes bibliographical references and index.
   1. Cognition in children. 2. Attention in children. I. Hale, Gordon A. II. Lewis,
Michael, 1937 (Jan. 10)-
BF723.C5A84   155.4'13   79-14518
ISBN 0-306-40234-3

First Printing — October 1979
Second Printing — February 1985

© 1979 Plenum Press, New York
A Division of Plenum Publishing Corporation
233 Spring Street, New York, N.Y. 10013

Printed in the United States of America

Contributors

LINDA F. ALWITT, *University of Massachusetts, Amherst, Massachusetts*

DANIEL R. ANDERSON, *University of Massachusetts, Amherst, Massachusetts*

NANCY BALDINI, *University of Rochester, Rochester, New York*

WILLIAM A. BALL, *Swarthmore College, Swarthmore, Pennsylvania*

ROBERT CALFEE, *Stanford University, Stanford, California*

JOHN T. COLLINS, *University of Michigan, Ann Arbor, Michigan*

VIRGINIA I. DOUGLAS, *McGill University, Montreal, Quebec, Canada*

ELEANOR GIBSON, *Cornell University, Ithaca, New York*

JOHN W. HAGEN, *University of Michigan, Ann Arbor, Michigan*

GORDON A. HALE, *Educational Testing Service, Princeton, New Jersey*

WENDELL E. JEFFREY, *University of California, Los Angeles, California*

MARCEL KINSBOURNE, *Hospital for Sick Children, Toronto, Ontario, Canada*

STEPHEN R. LEVIN, *University of Massachusetts, Amherst, Massachusetts*

MICHAEL LEWIS, *Educational Testing Service, Princeton, New Jersey*

ELIZABETH PUGZLES LORCH, *University of Massachusetts, Amherst, Massachusetts*

PATRICIA H. MILLER, *University of Florida, Gainesville, Florida*

KENNETH G. PETERS, *University of British Columbia, Vancouver, British Columbia, Canada*

DOROTHY PIONTKOWSKI, *Stanford University, Stanford, California*

NANCY RADER, *University of California at Los Angeles, Los Angeles, California*

JAMES M. SWANSON, *Hospital for Sick Children, Toronto, Ontario, Canada*

ELIANE VURPILLOT, *Université René Descartes, Paris, France*

TAMAR ZELNIKER, *Tel Aviv University, Ramat Aviv, Israel*

Preface

"My experience is what I agree to attend to," wrote William James (1890) nearly a century ago in his *Principles of Psychology*. Although certainly not the first to recognize the importance of attention in man's experience—poets and philosophers throughout history have touched upon the concept in one way or another—James deserves credit for having accorded attention a central role in the systematic study of the mind. With the advancement of psychology since that time, except during the behaviorist digression, the concept of attention has been an integral part of many prominent theories dealing with learning, thinking, and other aspects of cognitive functioning.

Indeed, attention is an important determinant of experience from birth throughout development. This has been an implicit assumption underlying our view of cognition since the writings of Charles Darwin (1897) and Wilhelm Preyer (1888) as well as James, all of whom offered provocative insights about the developing child's commerce with the environment. Although systematic research on attention in children was slow to pick up during the early part of this century, interest in the developmental study of attention has expanded enormously in recent years.

This book is an effort to bring together some of the important ideas and findings that have emerged from current work in the area. Our aim was to present a broad perspective on the topic, stressing the relation of attention to widely varying aspects of the developing child's cognition. Within this framework we had two principal objectives in compiling the book. First, we wished to emphasize the importance of attention in several basic cognitive processes. Much work has been devoted to the study of attention in relation to processes such as visual scanning, memory, problem solving, and others. We sought to present current research and thinking in many such areas and thus to highlight the variety of ways in which attention plays a role in children's cognition. Our second objective was to look at attention as a factor in the child's everyday functioning. Recent years have witnessed a growing interest in attention as an integral part of the child's behavior in real-life situations and as a key concept underlying certain individual differences in children's functioning. Thus, for example, researchers are currently studying attention in common activities such as television viewing and are examining attentional factors in conditions of impaired individual functioning such as hyperactivity. By presenting research in a variety of such topics we hoped to emphasize the importance of attention, and attentional problems, in the everyday functioning of the child. Recognizing, of course, that the term *attention* has been used in several different senses in the literature, we have not tried to impose any single definition of the term here. Rather, we have selected chapters that would reflect the diversity of ways that investigators have chosen to define and study attention in the developing child.

The book is outlined in accord with the two objectives just discussed. Following the introductory chapter by Gibson and Rader, which presents an overview of issues in the definition and assessment of children's attention, the chapters fall into two major groups. The five chapters in the first group deal with the role of attention in a variety of basic cognitive processes. Included here are chapters on visual scanning (Vurpillot and Ball), stimulus identification (Hale), perception and memory (Collins and Hagen), problem solving (Miller), and lateralization of function (Kinsbourne and Swanson). The remaining chapters deal broadly with the role of attention in the child's everyday functioning, and are further divided into two subgroups. Four of them have to do with individual variation in functioning associated with infant mental handicaps (Lewis and Baldini), hyperactivity and learning disabilities (Douglas and Peters, Swanson and Kinsbourne), and cognitive style (Zelniker and Jeffrey). The final two chapters deal with the role of attention in two prominent areas of the child's daily life—the school classroom (Piontkowski and Calfee) and television viewing (Anderson, Alwitt, Lorch, and Levin).

In short, the book is concerned with the role of attention in many different aspects of the child's cognition, with representation from a variety of experimental approaches. By thus presenting a broad view of the topic we hope to stimulate readers to consider interrelations among the various lines of evidence, to think about how this evidence contributes to understanding children's everyday functioning, and to ponder directions for further study of attention in the life of the developing child.

GORDON A. HALE
MICHAEL LEWIS

References

James, W. *The principles of psychology.* New York: Henry Holt, 1890.
Darwin, C. *The descent of man and selection in relation to sex* (New ed.). New York: Appleton, 1897.
Preyer, W. *The mind of the child.* New York: Appleton, 1888.

Contents

CHAPTER 8

Toward a Clearer Definition of the Attentional Deficit of
Hyperactive Children 173

Virginia I. Douglas and Kenneth G. Peters

CHAPTER 9

The Cognitive Effects of Stimulant Drugs on
Hyperactive Children... 249

James M. Swanson and Marcel Kinsbourne

1

Attention

The Perceiver as Performer

ELEANOR GIBSON AND NANCY RADER

Some Examples of Attending

A mountain climber is ascending a high cliff. He searches for handholds, checks the adjustment of his rope, the position of the person above and below him, and looks for signs of ice that will make a foothold dangerous. He carefully avoids any patch of gravel. Meanwhile, the view around him may be breathtakingly beautiful, but we say that he is paying, for the moment at least, no "attention" to it. He has a task (self-set) at hand, and to perform it adaptively he must perceive the affordances for climbing in footholds, handholds, surface conditions, and the state of his companions. Otherwise, disaster awaits them. Optimal pickup of information of this sort requires experience and skill in detection of the affordances involved. The same degree and quality of selection of information would not be found in the same man performing a task like walking along a sidewalk. Walking along a sidewalk does not require careful inspection; such a task allows a search for information relevant to tasks other than locomotion. Indeed, sidewalks are built to make the job of walking easier, to put fewer demands on the system to search for information to locomote.

When one performs a very familiar task of a predictable nature or any undemanding task, a second task may be taken on. When walking along a sidewalk, one is very likely to observe the view or the passersby. If the neighborhood is strange, one can look for landmarks or street signs. All the while perception of the sidewalk continues. But this perception goes on so economically that one's mind is not taken up by the task. One can still search for other information as well—for information about the people (are they pickpockets?) and about the route (is this the corner where I turn?). The affordance of the sidewalk for walking is observed at a glance, but that

ELEANOR GIBSON • Cornell University, Ithaca, New York 14850. NANCY RADER • University of California at Los Angeles, Los Angeles, California 90024.

does not mean it is unattended to. Knowledge breeds efficiency of information pickup in many ways, making environmental affordances for very practiced actions easy to pick up and leaving the observer more leisure for pickup of new, potentially useful information.

A small child, on the other hand, must attend solely to information for walking to remain upright when he first experiments with walking. He must search for footholds and handholds as he staggers around the room clutching pieces of furniture and occasionally tumbling between handholds. He, like the mountain climber, searches carefully; the task is new, difficult, and all-demanding.

In all three of our descriptions of people on the move, the mover is attending to information for support, but there are important differences. Our mountain climber must attend only to the information relating to climbing; attending to any other information may result in catastrophe. His desire to get to the top alive sustains his singularity of purpose; interesting scenes external to his purpose such as the beauty of the landscape must be ignored. Only information essential for climbing can be attended to until he reaches the top or a safe plateau along the way. The infant is more open to outside intrusions; should an object or event catch his attention, his task of walking will simply come to an end; attention to a kitten approaching and the continuation of walking are unlikely given that the walking requires so much cognitive involvement for success. Our sidewalk stroller, however, is free to continue his walking and to attend to a kitten frisking in someone's yard, storm clouds gathering overhead, or store windows. Walking is not an all-demanding task and other things may be attended to at the same time.

What is needed to understand such common human experience is an insight into how the cognitive system operates in what is commonly recognized as attentive behavior. First, we shall try to describe attentive behavior, or "attending." We shall consider what it is and what it is not, and then what variables distinguish behaviors that are more or less attentive. We shall see what we can say about its development and consider how tasks and expectations control attending.

What Is Attention?

"Attending" refers to perceiving in relation to a task or goal, internally or externally motivated. To be described as attending, a person must be set to do something, be motivated to perform a task or to achieve some end. When information for an event is picked up during performance, we say that he attends to that event. His goal may be amusement, problem solving, or locomotion—whatever fits his needs or desires in a particular state and situation. In judging a person's attention, attention is spoken of as "good" when perception fits well with the demands of performance. The initiation of a task may be the result of innate, species-specific programs (cf. Mayr, 1974) or it may be self-set or set by another person such as a teacher.

Attention, then, relates perception to action and to a person's needs and motives. Let us consider this relationship further. Attention points to perceiving as an active process, a process of extracting information from ongoing events in a selective, active, economical way. Perception is not always equally active, selective, and economical as regards performance. It is this variable aspect of perceiving that we refer to as more or less attentive. At its epitome, attending is the perceptual pickup of information that has optimal utility for the task at hand, resulting in perception that is efficient and economical for performance. Selection of information from ongoing events and utility of that information for performance ideally coincide.

What of human infants who can do little by way of problem solving or motor performance for 5 months or so? Can we say that they attend, that their perception is task-motivated? Certainly no one who observes them carefully would describe them as inattentive. Their perception seems often to be active and searching, although in a more exploratory and less specific sense than it will later become. The environment presents them with one big question, and their "purpose" is so huge and diverse it does not usually strike us as a "task": to sample all the ongoing events they can before they become overt performers, to discover invariant relationships in the world, to discover the uses of things in the world, and to develop ways of operating most adaptively in the world.

The motivation for this task appears to derive from the species-specific characteristics of human infants. For the most part, evolution seems to have equipped human infants, not with innately structured fixed action patterns, but with what Mayr (1974) calls "open programs." Closed programs produce fixed responses to certain information; no experience is necessary for the response and experience cannot change the response to the information even should it become nonadaptive. Open programs, on the other hand, produce adaptive responses as the result of experience; open programs allow responses to be made to information that has no specifically programmed, *a priori* response. Organisms with open programs are able to respond to nonpredictable aspects of the world. For example, they are able to learn to differentiate their own offspring from other young of the species. However, such organisms must spend time learning about their world. They need to examine the surrounding environment in every way they can to develop adaptive ways of behaving. This, then, becomes a significant task for human young. Infants look at things, they listen, they put things in their mouths for tasting as soon as they discover their hands, and later they move their hands exploringly over textured surfaces and probe substances

and objects. There seems to be motivation for perception present from the
beginning, but it differentiates with development into more specific tasks,
as we shall try to show.

The attention of infants has sometimes been called involuntary or captured. Salient aspects of the environment appear to demand attention. Evolution has left us, it seems, with some closed programs that tune the perceptual system to certain strong stimuli. In this case the task set by the closed
program is to "look out." For example, if a brightly colored, flashing, or
moving object enters the field of vision, the visual system focuses on it
regardless of preceding activity. This type of attentive behavior is clearly
observed in infants. Such involuntary attention, however, is present in
adults, too. That warning light on your car's dashboard *flashes*—just to be
sure that you attend to it. Observers have also reported that the attention of
infants is often "caught" by a small part of a display. But this is a different
matter altogether. Infants do not search in the same way adults do; perceptual development must occur for systematic search. The difference seems to
be in the cognitive schemes that have developed for perceiving, not in
attention.

We have said that attending refers to perceiving in relation to a task or
goal and that the task may be set by oneself. In an adult attending often is
self-directed or voluntary; the adult determines what he will attend to much
of the time in conjunction with a task he has set for himself. Such self-
directed attending can be observed fairly early in life as well. Even infants
as young as 2 months learn relationships presented to them by the environment consisting of information contingent on their own actions, and then
proceed to recreate the contingency on their own, as if to expose themselves
again to the information they were given, and even to improve it. Contingent head turning that brings something interesting into view, and contingent sucking that produces interesting sounds have become classic methods
of studying infant perception within recent years. It has been suggested
that this re-creation of the contingency is the beginning of volition (Bruner,
1968). The example of infants "sucking into focus" a motion picture available to them contingent on appropriate changes in sucking rate (Kalnins &
Bruner, 1973) is a particularly dramatic example. The infants are seeking
expected information; is this not intention or voluntary attending?

According to Preyer (1888), an important factor in the development of
the feeling of self is the "perception of a change produced by one's own
activity" (p. 191). Infants observed re-creating a contingent event, according to Preyer, are developing their sense of self. Preyer emphasizes that the
"I"-feeling is "not first awakened by the learning of words. Many head-
strong children have a strongly marked 'I'-feeling without calling themselves by anything but their names," he said (p. 202). Note the "head-
strong!" Does not the term imply self-willed, that volition is already
burgeoning?

We hope that the reason for our title is becoming clear. Attention refers to the perceiver as a potential performer, to the relationship between his perception and his task. Ideally, "good" attention is perceiving what has utility for what the perceiver is doing or intends to do, as a performer. He perceives the affordance of information in the world for his own activity. Optimal self-directed attention is economical perception that has utility for adaptive action in the service of a self—an ego, a person.

But we must also consider those cases where someone is asked to attend to something that another person thinks important. Such is often the case with schoolwork. The unfortunate student may see no utility in the school tasks set for him; they do not serve his ego. Therefore he has no motivation to attend. What makes an attentive student? Attention to school tasks may be the result of intrinsic interest—a meeting of the ego and the task. Or, the student may be less "strongheaded"; his ego may be less formed and hence more open to externally assigned tasks. Such is the student whom a teacher can interest in virtually anything but who takes an interest in nothing—perhaps a good student but not an inspired one. Attention may also come about by virtue of a discipline that incorporates the habit of putting aside one's own desires for the sake of social rewards. But the sort of attention that comes from such discipline seems to have a quality different from self-generated attention. The lessons are slow and joyless, the learning not as complete. Attention slips often and has to be brought back to the task with effort. But it is misleading, we think, to say that the child's attention is faulty. The problem is not with the child's attention but with the relation between task and ego. These school tasks do not result in self-directed attention.

We have described three types of attention: the captured or involuntary attention that is often observed in the infant, the self-directed voluntary attention of the adult, and the other-directed attention of a student. Probably all three types of attention are present at any age; however, the types seem to vary in dominance with development and with the situation. Changes in attending from infancy to adulthood are not so much a development of attention as a development of perceptual skills and a change in the tasks that are set for oneself as knowledge grows and an ego develops. Later we shall try to illustrate this point by looking at a developmental study, and we shall consider if and how attentiveness does develop. Before doing so, however, let us try to get clear what attention is *not,* lest it get in the way.

What Attention Is Not

Is an experiential description of attention possible? Can it be described as an attribute of conscious content? Titchener characterized attention as the focus of awareness as opposed to the fringe. One could presumably describe what was at the focus as having qualities available to introspection such as "vividness," "sharpness," "clarity." A description of these qualities of a percept would describe attention. But such a description does not help us understand the attentive behavior of a motivated organism living in and adapting to an environment.

Before Titchener, attention was thought of by many philosophers as a mental faculty with which an organism was endowed—not just man, since a cat poised to spring upon its prey would probably have been considered to be an exemplar of that faculty. Psychologists have been accustomed for many years to sneer at the notion of faculties—Thorndike presumably having disposed of them once and for all. But the concept still lives, because it is responsible for a widely prevalent notion, that attention is limited or has a certain *capacity* (cf. Kahneman, 1973; Mackworth, 1976). There is just so much of it at the organism's disposal, and it can be channeled from the reservoir in various ways. These ways are often termed strategies, and attention is said to be "deployed," like troops in a battle. It may all be concentrated at the thick of the battle, or distributed among the flanks in various degrees. Numerous developmental assumptions go along with a capacity theory. The total capacity (size of the reservoir) of attention increases with age; young children have no strategies for deploying attention and it just floats about as environmental temptations or harassments determine (children are "distractible"); it is all distributed early in life and can only later be concentrated; or, just the opposite, it is always concentrated early in life and only later does one learn to distribute it, by performing certain skills "automatically" so that a lot of attention is left over to use for something else.

With respect to limits of the human organism it seems likely that the organism has limits in terms of the perceptual systems' ability to process information. But to say this does not imply that attention is some faculty that is measured out from a reservoir as though by a hardworking homunculus somewhere in the brain, a reservoir that increases in size with age. We shall argue that attention is not a capacity that increases with development but, rather, that our perception changes with increasing knowledge of oneself and the world, allowing us to pick up the information more and more economically to perform a specified task.

Some may consider attention a *process*, perhaps putting it in a flow chart. Do we conceive of it best by contrasting it with perceiving or remembering or thinking? We believe not. "Attention" implies an evaluation of some kind. It works well as an adjective or an adverb: "attentive listening" or "looking attentively about him." Attention is a relationship between process and task, an adaptive relationship between performing and procuring information to guide and support that performance.

Despite the inclusion of attention in even the earliest models of information processing (cf. *channels* and *channel capacity*), attention does not seem to have been defined by anyone as a specific mechanism or a construction process of any kind. As a matter of fact, in most information processors' flow charts there is a gating mechanism or some device that *shuts out*, accounting for inattention rather than attention. Yet most psychologists would deny that there is true inhibition, except, perhaps, specifically in habituation. Hypothetical "detectors" in one or more strata of the nervous system seem to be the nearest anyone has come to positing a mechanism for attention, but they remain hypothetical and fail completely to capture the essence of the concept.

What can be said of attention as a mental condition of more or less specific expectancy, or vigilance? Neisser (1976) has outlined such a position, and it seems intuitively closer to what we feel to be the core of the concept. Vigilance has often been thought of as the essence of attention, on the *qui vive*, adrenalin flowing, posture indicating alertness. But such a state can be provoked with drugs and have no reference to anything cognitive. Is it then a state of specific expectancy, as Neisser has suggested? Certainly, expectancy created by knowledge structures or "schemes" determines what we will attend to in large degree. And expectancy must be closely tied to the setting of tasks for ourselves. But to equate the two, we feel, blurs the issue. Specific expectancy refers to the state of being ready for something specific to happen or being ready to find something specific on the basis of what we know about the world. Good attention, on the other hand, refers to bringing our perception in line with our task, of efficiently picking up the information necessary to perform some task. Our expectations will affect our attention; we will need to consider how later.

Restatement of the Theme

Good attention refers to perception that meshes with performance by efficiently picking up the information that has utility for a particular task. We speak of attention when the task and the expectancy of impending information are relatively specific. We also speak of attention when expectancy is less specific but the perceiver appears to be on the lookout for information. It is evident that the attentiveness of behavior varies in many ways, since these aspects of attention are not necessarily at a high point all at once. We need a descriptive theory of attention, and we need a developmental theory. Descriptively, attention refers to a search for information that is necessary for performance. Many variables have served to amplify the description. We will discuss them presently. Developmentally, attention changes toward greater specificity of correspondence between information pickup and utility of that information (one learns to perceive affordances and to define tasks); and developmentally, attention tends toward economy. As affordances for action are perceived more efficiently, the perceiver's task can become more complex, more information can be picked up, and superficially speaking, the "span" of attention increases.

Classic Variables of Attention

Attentive behavior is generally thought of as "alert," nonattentive behavior as "nonalert." Alertness brings to mind the image of one of Pavlov's dogs, with head raised, ears pointed toward a sound source, limbs poised for action—an "orienting response" in traditional terminology. A number of psychologists would in fact leave it at that. But peripheral manifestations of attention such as turning the head and eyes toward the opening door, pricking up the ears at approaching footsteps, sniffing the brandy, rolling the wine over the tongue, however obviously useful and important, cannot be the whole story. Attention is not always overtly manifested by strategic operation of the pickup mechanisms. In fact, covert attention has received a great deal of attention in recent years, and paradigms such as the dichotic listening experiment have been devised to study it.

The overt–covert dichotomy cuts across another that psychologists have found interesting, the distinction between active and passive attention. This dichotomy has been used to indicate the difference observed between voluntary or self-directed attention and the involuntary or captured attention that has been ascribed to infants. The attention of the infant is said to be passive because it is caught, rather than voluntarily bestowed upon an event or a scene. It is quite easy to think, however, of examples of involuntary attention in adults. A screeching of brakes followed by a resounding crash will divert anyone. At the same time, it is impossible to observe infants carefully for any considerable period without concluding that they do a lot of looking around, appearing far from passive. The developmental line to be drawn here at best indicates relative dominance rather than a clear-cut division.

The active–passive dichotomy is often used to categorize differences in search behavior with development. Piaget (e.g., 1969) has said that infantile and childish perception is "centered" on gestalt aspects of a scene, with measurable consequences such as overestimation of whatever is centered on; but as intelligence develops decentration is achieved, resulting in more active perception. Gibson (1969) has commented on the increase in systematic search with development. However, we would not consider this development a change from passive to active attention. The difference is not so much the difference between involuntary and self-directed attention as a difference in what is looked at as the result of development of knowledge about the world.

William James also used the terms *passive* and *active* in talking about attention, but he used them to discuss what we have called self-directed and other-directed attention, respectively. James contrasted the attention that comes of intrinsic interest with that which comes through discipline. He refers to the latter as voluntary or active because of the will needed to maintain the attention. In his *Talks to Teachers* James (1899) describes the effort needed for active attention and warns teachers that they should rely on "passive" or self-directed attention as much as possible:

> When we are studying an uninteresting subject, if our mind tends to wander, we have to bring back our attention every now and then by using distinct pulses of effort, which revivify the topic for a moment, the mind then running on for a certain number of seconds or minutes with spontaneous interest, until again some intercurrent idea captures it and takes it off. Then the process of volitional recall must be repeated once more. Voluntary attention, in short, is only a momentary affair. (p. 101)

To keep the pupils "where you have called them, you must make the subject too interesting for them to wander again" (p. 103). This kind of attention is passive, in James's terminology, because interest is engaged spontaneously and without effort. It is intrinsic, coming from within, rather than compelled from outside.

James also talked about distractibility, another kind of oppositional variable. James considered that children were typically more distractible than grown-ups—a ubiquitous view. "This reflex and passive character of the attention which, as a French writer says, makes the child seem to belong less to himself than to every object which happens to catch his notice, is the first thing the teacher must overcome" (1890, p. 417). Here is another popular developmental hypothesis, then: With maturity, we become less distractible, and more capable of sustained attention to the task we have committed ourselves to. Note the reference to volition again. Must the ego develop in such a way that attention can be sustained for tasks that are considered necessary or appropriate by society? The implication of such an ego function sounds akin to the Freudian usage of the term. We have thought mainly of "ego" as a way of referring to a concept of oneself as a unitary object and as a person interacting with an environment.

It is extraordinary that psychologists have accepted such propositions as the greater distractibility of the child with, as far as we know, very little careful examination. We might consider other explanations for "childish distractibility." Perhaps a child has to develop into an adult before there is motivation for tasks that adults consider important. Or, perhaps psychologists go about their work in such a manner that they observe only other-directed attention in children, and hence, distractibility. A child absorbed in playing with dolls may be every bit as nondistractible as an adult planning a vacation. It may be simply that children are more likely to be in the role of students, and hence appear more distractible.

Let us turn to another classic variable of attention, again dichotomous —the "focus" of consciousness as opposed to the "fringe." "Consciousness in attention," according to Titchener (1924), "is patterned or arranged into focus and margin, foreground and background, centre and periphery. And the difference between the processes at the focus and the processes in the margin is, essentially, a difference of clearness: the central area of consciousness lies clear, the more remote regions are obscure. In this fact we have, indeed, the key to the whole problem of attention" (p. 267). Here, Titchener describes attending to an object as having it clear in one's consciousness. James, in describing attention, also discusses degree of awareness: "Attention to an object is what takes place whenever that object most completely occupies the mind." He used the phrases "mental focus" and "marginal consciousness" to describe the degrees of attentiveness.

Awareness and attention are certainly closely related but perhaps not inseparable. The sidewalk may slip in and out of the awareness of a window-shopper; usually attention is drawn toward it only when there is some danger. An icy spot or a curb ahead may claim full consciousness, and so attention is turned away from the newest fashions in the store windows to the problem of footing. It seems as though unconscious knowledge signals the conscious self to "look out." In fact, despite shifts in awareness, information specifying the spatial layout is constantly monitored by the perceptual-cognitive system. Should we say that attention to the sidewalk is continuous? The first temptation is to say no, yet this easy solution is unsatisfying. What is continuous then? The shopper is unaware of and yet responding to information necessary for walking. It seems that as long as the perceptual-motor act can continue at an automatic level it will. For this to occur, the motor function must be well practiced and the perceptual information very regular. As long as the regularity of information continues, awareness of it will be minimal. Such automaticity must indicate extremely efficient, well-organized perception since it allows the performer to fit in other tasks at the same time. Perhaps a fourth type of attention should be added to our list—"unconscious" or "automatic" attention—where the object or event perceived is not in full awareness.

A trend toward automaticity in development has sometimes been proposed (cf. Kahneman, 1973; La Berge & Samuels, 1974). On the other hand, there also seems to be an increase in awareness with development. Consider, for example, the trouble 5-year-old children have segmenting speech sounds. They comprehend elaborate sentences, produce them themselves, enjoy and sometimes spontaneously produce rhymes. But when they are asked to attend to the acoustic information in a spoken message, they find it hard to do so. The meaning is all they appear to be aware of, and when asked to segment the message, they tend to break it up into semantic units. Phonemic units and even syllable and word units are difficult targets for analysis at first. Rhyme, too, if the child is asked to make it the object of his attention, does not seem to be understood as an acoustic property, although we feel confident that the child enjoys it. It seems to be awareness of his own speech and others' as a physical thing that has not yet evolved. Such development of awareness may be the result of perceiving the utility of such information for activities that are important to him.

A current popular dichotomy related to attention contrasts "central" with "incidental" learning. "Central" refers to learning the relevant aspects of a task; "incidental" refers to learning irrelevant aspects of a task. This central-incidental contrast carries some developmental hypotheses with it (see Hagen & Hale, 1973). Various writers have suggested that children do more incidental learning at an early age than they do later when they have developed efficient strategies of attending. One wonders exactly what is going on in such instances, however. It is possible that the younger the child, the less he knows about what is relevant information for whatever purpose is at hand; therefore he picks up incidental information that appears totally irrelevant to one who is older and wiser (cf. Pick, Frankel, & Hess, 1975). It is not that he lacks the ability to focus his attention; he doesn't know what to focus it on! The "incidental" learning of the younger child may also be the result of a failure to understand the task clearly. As one gets older, one comprehends better what other people want.

Another variable of attentive behavior is the exploratory quality of observation, or of search, when some target or goal has been specified. Again, we have pairs of dichotomous adjectives to evaluate the behavior. The observation or search may be *strategic* or nonstrategic. A 3-year-old playing hide-and-seek will hide again and again in the same place; and he will look again in the same place, never varying his strategy. The ability to consider multiple alternatives seems to be a key factor here. In tests of object permanence, infants of 8 months or so typically search for an object wherever it was found last, even when they have watched it being hidden in a new place. Identifying objects by touch especially shows up differences in methods of exploration. A young child, when blindfolded and given an object to identify, is likely to clutch it, whereas a few years later the same child will expose himself to all the features of the object by manipulating it with his fingers in skillful ways. *Flexibility* and its opposite are akin to strategic search and its opposite. Ability to adjust and to change one's method as the circumstances require seems to improve with age, although we can easily think of situations in which adults find it difficult to be flexible in observation. We are all "blind" to some things sometimes. *Systematic* search, not necessarily flexible, gives us another contrast. Children often show changing behavior in searching, but the changes may appear random, unplanned. Systematic, planned search seems to us heavily dependent on experience and education. In fact, a systematic program for searching may be situational; it may not indicate growth in attentiveness at all. Infants exhibit little flexibility and system in searching for good reasons; what they are searching *for* is often not very well specified (or if it is, it is not to the adults who are watching them); and they have had very little opportunity to devise and try out varied programs for searching in any particular situation.

We have said nothing of physiological accompaniments of attention, having little specialized knowledge of them. There seem to be contrastive variables here too. A hyperactive internal state associated with secretion of adrenalin, producing fast respiration, accelerated heart rate and galvanic skin reflex (GSR) seems to indicate vigilance. And yet, deceleration of heart rate and lowered activity seem to accompany "orienting," covert focusing on some present object or event. We shall leave the resolution of the problems raised by this contrast to someone more expert, only noting that attentiveness seems as variable when looked at from the physiologist's standpoint as it does from the psychologist's. There is again no obvious reason to conceive of it as a capacity or a mechanism or a construct or a box in a flow chart.

Expectation

An important variable of attentive perception that is currently receiving considerable attention is relative specificity. This variable relates to the quality of someone's expectancy. Is attention a specific expectation, awaiting a well-defined event, or is it a condition of general vigilance, being "keyed up," awaiting something without very clear knowledge of what the event will afford? Some psychologists would identify attention with specific expectancy, which depends on the possession of schemes or certain structures of knowledge. The person with a given scheme would "take in" (attend to) what fits the scheme. Neisser (1976) says, for example, "Attention is nothing but perception: we choose what we will see by anticipating the structured information it will provide" (p. 87). More generally, as adults especially, we tend to notice events that fit our own knowledge structure, our attitudes and interests. Education and experience necessarily play a very important role here. Specificity of expectancy depends on knowledge of particular affordances. Coordinated knowledge structures must come from having perceived order and relations in events in the world. With knowledge of affordances and experience of predictable relations between performance and information, knowledge becomes more systematized and planning more viable. Preparedness or readiness to perceive can be, accordingly, more specific.

However, we would not identify attention with expectancy; too much of what is normally implied by the term is obscured. *Specific expectancy* refers to the state of being ready for something specific to happen or being ready to find something specific on the basis of what we know about the world; *attention* refers to bringing our perception in line with our task, of picking up more or less efficiently the information necessary to perform some task. Expectations motivate and affect our attentive behavior.

Unquestionably, expectations tune the perceptual system to search for certain information. When one knows the appearance of something he is looking for, the perceptual system searches for specific optical information. If one looks for his glasses, expecting them to be in an orange case, he may pass over the glasses entirely when they are in an obvious place but not in their case. Von Üexkull (1934/1959) described this type of attunement some years ago:

> When I spent some time at the house of a friend, an earthenware water pitcher used to be placed before my seat at luncheon. One day the butler had broken the clay pitcher and put a glass water bottle in its place. When I looked for the pitcher during the meal, I failed to see the glass carafe. Only when my friend assured me that the water was standing in its usual place, did various bright lights that had lain scattered on knives and plates flock through the air and form the water bottle. (p. 62)

Expectations also create economical pickup of information through the knowledge of critical information for a task. If one knows the task demands and exactly what information is necessary, he presumably won't waste his time or clutter his mind by picking up useless information. So expectations are tied to the central/incidental learning dichotomy. The more you know what is wanted, and where and how to look for it, the less you will bother with irrelevant and unhelpful information in performing a task.

As we come to know the world, we expect to find certain invariant information specifying categories in the world. People, for example, make up such a category. It may be that such knowledge creates attentional hierarchies that cause us first to perceive an object as belonging to a category and then to search for distinguishing features that identify that particular member of the set. We automatically perceive a stranger as a person but may only later notice the distinctive aspects of his appearance. With experience in the world, we may come to expect individual members of sets to vary in particular ways. For example, planes may or may not have tapered wings, short noses, or a beer-bottle fuselage (see Gibson, 1969, p. 83). If someone has never tried to identify planes and has never searched for the distinctive features that differentiate types of planes, there would be a pattern of perceptual search different from that of someone familiar with planes.

Expectations can also result in incomplete sampling of features. The complete set of critical features may not be picked up when a small sample of the most salient features fits expectations. For example, one of us was taking the elevator to "A level" from the seventh floor; after what seemed like an unusually fast trip, the doors opened, she checked the floor sign, got off, and proceeded to her destination; but the room was not to be found on this level, for the level was 4 and not A; the presence of the diagonal and horizontal in the 4 matched expectations and no closer look had been taken. This short-cut process is very common and may lead to error (the errors reveal the strategy), but it is likely to be correct a good deal of the time. A similar process may go on while skimming printed text. Readers may "cheat" on processing aspects of the text if the information that they do pick up allows sense to be made. There will be a more careful check if what is picked up contradicts expectations. Consider also the task of proofreading a manuscript one has carefully written and rewritten. There is a very high expectation of what will be said, and therefore there tends to be only a very cursory check of the text. Personal experience suggests that if the writer puts the paper aside so that the words he used are not fresh in his mind, the typographical errors will be better detected. Apparently, when there are expectations, a faster check process is initiated, despite oneself.

How Does Attention Develop?

The quality of attentiveness surely does change with development, but in far more subtle ways than has sometimes been asserted. To describe the change as increasing capacity to attend or as merely a shift from captive to intentional attending is inadequate. In the first place, alertness to what is going on (the first variable of attentiveness that we discussed) does not seem to us to change with development after a few months. Quite young infants are alert to events in their environment. Anyone who has worked with infants 3 to 4 months old is struck with the perceptual exploration that goes on. Curiosity about what is happening seems nearly as strong as it will ever be. What changes are other aspects of attentiveness. The child gains progressively in the specificity of correspondence between what information his perceptual processes are engaged with (what he is attending *to*) and its utility for performance in the service of his needs. He gains in flexibility because more alternatives become open to him. He gains in preparedness for events, in readiness for performance. And he gains in how much he can do because of the increasing economy of his pickup of information. We shall consider each of these trends.

Specificity

A well-documented trend in perceptual development is the increasing specificity of perception—the major point of a differentiation theory

(Gibson, 1969). Specificity increases in many ways—for example, in the degree of correspondence between information in stimulation and what is perceived. Stimulus generalization declines with age. Things once responded to as the same become differentiated on the basis of learned distinctive features. In this paper we are pointing to a different aspect of specificity. There is increasing specificity of correspondence between what is perceived and recognition of its utility for performance of some task. The task itself becomes more specific, in the sense that the person progresses in ability to define it more precisely; and the recognition of a relation between information in an event and its utility for the task (its "affordance") becomes more precise.

It is an open question whether information can be picked up at some level without recognition of its utility for any adaptive activity. There is some reason to think that it can, and that affordances are largely learned by members of the human species. Babies do a tremendous amount of looking around the world, and there is good reason to suppose that they are taking in a lot of information (cf. the large and increasing body of literature on habituation, summarized in Cohen & Gelber, 1975). Its utility for immediate performance is not always obvious. To take a case in point, it is likely that infants learn that a cliff affords falling and hence should be avoided. When tested on a "visual cliff" apparatus (Gibson & Walk, 1960), nonhuman animals such as rats (reared in the dark) and chicks (shortly after hatching) avoid the cliff without opportunity to learn its affordances. It must be perceived innately. Human infants avoid it when they are of an age to crawl. But prelocomotor infants placed over a cliff or its noncliff control show an interesting kind of differentiation. They notice a difference, as evidenced by deceleration of heart rate over the cliff (Campos, Langer, & Krowitz, 1970). But their recognition of the affordance of a drop-off apparently develops after this early manifestation of differentiation.

Another change toward specificity is a change toward more selective search for affordances that goes along with increasing perception of them. As growing motor development brings increasing and more varied opportunities for performance, so does one's observation of things and places and events. As many psychologists like to put it, children become progressively more "selective." But it appears that this selectivity is the result of several changes: change in ability to perform, change in ability to set a task more precisely, and change in ability to perceive a match between what is perceived and its utility for the task.

We conceive of performance as broader than mere motor performance such as grasping, eating with a spoon, walking, and so on. There is cognitive performance too, like making decisions about what to do, categorizing information usefully, and solving problems. As a child's cognitive and linguistic abilities increase, his ability to perceive the useful information in such tasks increases. An experiment by Gibson, Poag, and Rader (1972) demonstrates a change during 3 mid-childhood years in perceiving useful information in a simple cognitive task.

The experiment was planned to investigate the development of children's ability to utilize effectively a redundant rhyme and spelling pattern in a verbal discrimination task. Children from second and fifth grades were presented with a discrimination learning task in which each of four projected words was to be paired with a left or right response button. Within each grade there were two groups of subjects. One group (Group E) saw two words sharing common rhymes and spelling patterns (e.g., *king* and *ring*) that were to be paired with the same response button; the other two words similarly shared a rhyme and spelling pattern (e.g., *yarn* and *barn*) and were to be paired with the other response button. But children in the second experimental condition (Group C) saw four words that had no rhymes or spelling patterns in common, so that each word had to be paired with one of the two buttons in an arbitrary fashion.

The children were corrected and given continued practice until a criterion was reached (10 consecutive correct responses) or until 60 trials were completed. They could take as long as they needed to make a response, and the slide remained on for 2.5 sec after a choice was made and its correctness or incorrectness indicated. This procedure was followed by a second stage of the experiment. Children in both conditions were given a new set of four words to pair with one of the two responses and told to do the same thing as before—that is, figure out the correct button for each word. The four words had two rhyming pairs (*boat/coat* and *cake/rake*) for everyone.

We wanted to know whether children were more able, with age and school experience, to perceive and use the redundant information (rhyme and spelling pattern), and whether they would transfer the strategy directly to the second task. We considered that beginning a criterion run on the fifth trial (the first opportunity for transfer) indicated immediate detection of the usefulness of the common rhyme and spelling for an economical performance. Table I shows the percent of subjects who began a criterion run by the fifth trial.

As one would expect, children in the fifth grade perceived the utility of the rhymes significantly more often than children in second grade. The difference was not due to mere ability to remember what went with what, because the two grades did not differ significantly in Stage 1 of the control condition. An unexpected finding was the negligible increase of early solutions in Stage 2 in the experimental groups. In neither grade did the percent of economical solutions increase significantly as a result of performing the first task with common rhyme and spelling present. It seemed as though a child had developed the ability to perceive the utility of the rhyming information or he had not.

Was it possible that the children who did not perform economically

TABLE I
Percent of Children Reaching an Economical Solution by Trial 5

Grade	Condition	Stage	
		Stage 1	Stage 2
2	E	20%	26.6%
	C	0%	13%
5	E	53%	60%
	C	6.6%	53%

were totally oblivious to the rhymes and common spellings? The children were questioned after the experiment about how they "figured out" the task. The children who were successful on the transfer task almost invariably commented on the rhyme and spelling, although it was not suggested to them. Most of the second-graders said they "just remembered." However, when two words printed on cards were presented successively and the children were asked whether there was anything special about them, they nearly always commented at once on the rhyme. We cannot say for certain that the children noticed the rhyme during the experimental task and simply did not perceive its utility; yet we think it unlikely that they would fail to notice the similarity of some of the words during the task since they were able to do so promptly and without hesitation a few minutes later.

These results imply to us that one can perceive something, like the rhymes in the task, at some level, without "attending" in the sense of seeing the utility of the perceived information for performance. This relationship exemplifies good attention—perceiving what is relevant for economical performance of a task at hand. It calls for knowledge of what is relevant, it calls for a well-defined task, and it calls for appropriately structured organization of the two. That the latter ability is one that matures "across the board" may be doubted. It seems possible that it is situational, or specialized to a considerable extent, since very young children perceive affordances for grasping, walking, and playing with things. It takes time and practice to perceive affordances in games of skill and sports like tennis and skiing. For highly cognitive tasks involving symbolic material, especially rather artificial ones, education and experiences may be protracted over a long period. If this view is correct, it would be a mistake to explain the development of attentiveness as an increase in pure capacity.

Flexibility

Superficially, progressively greater "specificity" would seem to contradict an increase in flexibility with age, and perhaps there is a period when it does (cf. the "AB" error in object permanence tests around 9 months). But as affordances are learned, alternative means of acting to obtain them grow. Growth of alternative means requires prior maturation of exploratory and motor capacities for search, manipulation, and locomotion, and time to try them out. Strategies of attending (ability to choose between alternatives with regard to their utility) may well depend on such maturation for their development. Means to an end and strategies for selecting them stress the role of the perceiver as performer. There has been frequent reference to strategies of attention in recent years, but little discussion of just what is meant by a strategy. We can say little about it, except that it implies a decision among alternative modes of performance, options for action that rest on organized perception of information, and that this decision is based on perceived utility for a task. Studies directed at growth of alternative modes of performance, given potentially informative environmental situations and a task to provide a criterion for utility, seem indicated. Search of earlier literature might be instructive (e.g., the work of Lewin and his students).

Preparedness

A third aspect of growth of attentiveness may be found in progressive preparedness for expected events. It is not searching for something that is indicated by this term, but awaiting something. Experience is necessary to provide a person with attuned schemes (cf. Neisser's view of attention, 1976) that are ready to accept certain information. Development of preparedness occurs as one lives in and experiences the world. Knowledge is gained, differentiated, and systematized. To the extent that such development occurs, the person has more to attend *to*, and greater readiness to perceive and assimilate new knowledge that fits with his own organized knowledge structures. One can be more attentive as he knows what to expect and thus what to look for. We should remember, however, that this proposition is probably true for people of any age. Expectancy facilitates information pickup for adults and children alike.

An experiment by Condry, McMahon, and Levy (1979) examined the effect of blocked versus unblocked trials when subjects were asked to attend to one or another aspect of verbal information (graphic, acoustic, semantic) in sets of words. Blocked trials with one instruction facilitated reaction time for all the subjects, and did not interact with age. There were large age differences overall, because the older subjects were better prepared to attend to the information desired under all conditions; but foreknowledge of the type of target was useful at all the ages tested.

Economy

There is one more aspect of attention that has generally been considered to mature. That is breadth of attention, the ability to attend to more than one thing at a time. In contemporary terminology, this is sometimes referred to as a developmental shift from "single channel" processing to parallel processing (cf. Wickens, 1974). Wickens summarizes evidence from several experiments on development of information processing as follows: "It appears, then, that, while both adults and children manifest some degree of single channel behavior with respect to the release of unpracticed responses, children do so to a greater degree, and the ability to 'coordinate' the simultaneous release of responses seems to be one that improves with age" (p. 752). And again, "This may reflect the existence of a more limited attention mechanism" (p. 753).

It is curious that this view seems to be nearly the opposite of a view recently expressed that characterizes children's attention as generally divided or dispersed (Smith, Kemler, & Aronfreed, 1975, pp. 360 ff.). Perhaps we can clarify this dilemma by emphasizing again that attention is not a mechanism. It seems to us that the direction of growth in "processing" information (we would prefer to say simply perceiving) is toward picking up more information. But such an outcome may not be the result of a different mechanism but rather the result of increasing ability to find structure and order in what is perceived. Rydberg and Arnberg (1976) gave children and adults concept learning problems that involved active touch. When it was necessary to attend to four dimensions in the same trial, adults solved the problems but young children could not, although they could when only one dimension had to be evaluated. However, when 6-year-old children were given a special pretraining program that familiarized them with the material and gave them practice in discriminating, many of them solved the four-dimension problem as fast as or faster than adults.

If structure is found that organizes information within a task or organizes two tasks as one, the resulting improvement in economical perception and attentive behavior is not a "capacity" change or a stretching out of a span. The change does not depend upon a mysterious increase in a reservoir or power, but on cognitive growth: growth in knowledge of meaningful affordances and ordering of a knowledge system so as to use order and structure. One may dub the change a change in "span," but that would ignore what the locus of the development really is. There is indeed broadening of information pickup with age, but this change is not due to a metamorphosis from single channel processing to parallel processing. It is due to increasing economy of information pickup as the developing individual becomes capable of discovering invariants such as common structures in tasks, and perceiving the utility of using such structure.

Conclusion

The foregoing discussion of attention may seem to the reader to solve no problems, nor even to formulate a set of testable hypotheses. We do not, in fact, claim that it does, although some of the ideas can be put into the form of workable hypotheses. What we intended is to force some thinking about a concept that now carries an enormous burden of concealed assumptions. Let us try to make the assumptions explicit, and try not to emerge with a glib formula that can be pinned down to neither logic nor observed behavior. The term *attention* is unfortunately susceptible to reification, although anyone would be hard put to say what the "power" or the "capacity" or even the "state" is. Let us try instead to talk about "attentive behavior," or "attending." If we want to talk about its development, we should consider what the variables of attentive behavior are, because the development will very likely be found to coincide with development of these variables.

We have considered several possible variables, stemming largely from intuition about the commonsense connotative meaning of the term *attention*. Some that seemed to us worthy candidates as variables of attentive (rather than nonattentive) behavior are these: (1) the degree of match between the information extracted from ongoing events (what is picked up in perceiving) and its utility for the task of the perceiver; (2) the nature and specificity of the goals, task-sets, and expectations of the perceiver-performer; (3) the alternative means that are available and the strategic quality of choosing an alternative; (4) the extent to which the task of the perceiver is in tune with his needs; that is, the extent to which attention is self-directed and to what extent other-directed; and (5) the extent to which information, alternative modes of action, and task can be economically organized as a single structure. All of these variables have a developmental history. Correspondence between what is perceived and what has utility for performance increases with development; goals become better defined and thus so do tasks; expectations are formed and affect perceptual strategies in performing a task; as the ego develops its needs change and hence so does motivation; and as perceiving and performing a task are organized for optimal utility, so economy increases.

Other variables were considered, such as "awareness," and still others could have been, but the ones discussed seem to be at the core of the concept. Metaphors like "capacity," "flashlight," "span," "deployment of strategies" seem to cover up what is real in the concept. But it has been with us a long time, and everyone agrees on one thing—don't throw out the term.

References

Bruner, J.S. *Processes of cognitive growth: Infancy* (Heinz Werner Lectures Series, Vol. 3). Barre, Mass.: Barre, 1968.
Campos, J. J., Langer, A., & Krowitz, A. Cardiac responses on the visual cliff in prelocomotor human infants. *Science*, 1970, *170*, 196–197.

Cohen, L. B., & Gelber, E. R. Infant visual memory. In L. B. Cohen & P. Salapatek (Eds.), *Infant perception: From sensation to cognition* (Vol. 1). New York: Academic, 1975.

Condry, S., McMahon, M., & Levy, A. A developmental investigation of selective attention to graphic, phonetic, and semantic information in words. *Perception and Psychophysics,* 1979, *25,* 88–94.

Elliot, R. Simple reaction time: Effects associated with age, preparatory interval, incentive shift, and mode of presentation. *Journal of Experimental Child Psychology,* 1970, *9,* 86–104.

Gibson, E. J. *Principles of perceptual learning and development.* New York: Prentice-Hall, 1969.

Gibson, E. J., & Walk, R. D. The "visual cliff." *Scientific American,* 1960, *202,* 64–71.

Gibson, E. J., Poag, M. K., & Rader, N. The effect of redundant rhyme and spelling patterns on a verbal discrimination task. In Appendix to Final Report, Project No. 90046, Grant No. OEG-2-9-420446-1071(010), Cornell University and U.S. Office of Education, 1972, pp. 1–11.

Hagen, J. W., & Hale, G. A. The development of attention in children. In A. D. Pick (Ed.), *Minnesota symposium on child psychology* (Vol. 7). Minneapolis: University of Minnesota Press, 1973.

James, W. *The principles of psychology.* New York: Holt, 1890.

James, W. *Talks to teachers on psychology: And to students on some of life's ideals.* New York: Holt, 1899.

Kahneman, D. *Attention and effort.* Englewood Cliffs, N.J.: Prentice-Hall, 1973.

Kalnins, I. V., & Bruner, J. S. The coordination of visual observation and instrumental behavior in early infancy. *Perception,* 1973, *2,* 307–314.

LaBerge, D., & Samuels, S. J. Toward a theory of automatic information processing in reading. *Cognitive Psychology,* 1974, *6,* 293–323.

Mackworth, J. Development of attention. In V. Hamilton & M. D. Vernon (Eds.), *The development of cognitive processes.* New York: Academic, 1976.

Mayr, E. Behavior programs and evolutionary strategies. *American Scientist,* 1974, *62*(6), 650–659.

Neisser, U. *Cognition and reality.* San Francisco: W. H. Freeman, 1976.

Piaget, J. *The mechanisms of perception.* London: Routledge & Kegan Paul, 1969.

Pick, A. D., Frankel, D. G., & Hess, V. L. *Children's attention: The development of selectivity.* Chicago: University of Chicago Press, 1975.

Preyer, W. *The mind of the child.* Part I. The senses and the will. New York: D. Appleton Century, 1888.

Rydberg, S., & Arnberg, P. W. Attending and processing broadened within children's concept learning. *Journal of Experimental Child Psychology,* 1976, *22,* 161–177.

Smith, L. B., Kemler, D. G., & Aronfreed, J. Developmental trends in voluntary selective attention: Differential effects of source distinctness. *Journal of Experimental Child Psychology,* 1975, *20,* 352–362.

Titchener, E. B. *A textbook of psychology.* New York: Macmillan, 1924.

Von Üexkull, J. [A stroll through the worlds of animals and men.] In C. H. Schiller (Ed. and trans.), *Instinctive behavior: The development of a modern concept.* New York: International Universities Press, 1957. (Originally published, 1934.)

Wickens, C. D. Temporal limits of human information processing: A developmental study. *Psychological Bulletin,* 1974, *81,* 739–755.

2

The Concept of Identity
and Children's Selective Attention

Eliane Vurpillot and William A. Ball

Introduction

As a source of information, the environment is inexhaustible, but not all events are relevant to the individual's present and future activities. Selective processes are inevitably part of cognition, first in determining which information is registered and then in specifying what information will be retained. Thus an initial selection of information may have a spatial component: Sensory systems such as the eyes or hands are oriented to a particular location at a given time. Only a fraction of the information registered will receive further processing, however. This second selection involves active recoding of certain aspects of the perceptual input in order to facilitate subsequent recall and recognition. Both forms of selectivity can occur together, and selective processes obviously play an important role in determining what information about the world an individual will obtain. In selecting only a portion of the available information for detailed processing, people restrict what they can know about the environment. The developmental problem is to determine how children come to adapt their selectivity in ways appropriate to the requirements of their activities.

Among the factors affecting attentional processes are the properties of the stimulus itself, the importance or relevance of the stimulus to the individual, and the requirements of the task in which the person is engaged. When there is no explicit task (e.g., as in casual inspection of a stimulus), it is likely that the intrinsic interest value of the stimulus determines what is selected for detailed processing. The physical properties of the stimulus may have a constant effect across a wide age range, assuming developmental invariance in some fundamental perceptual and attentional processes.

ELIANE VURPILLOT • Laboratoire de Psychologie Expérimentale, Université René Descartes, 75006 Paris, France. WILLIAM A. BALL • Swarthmore College, Swarthmore, Pennsylvania 19081.

The effect of the stimulus may be quite different, however, when people are assigned a task. Indeed, with explicit tasks such as having to make same–different judgments of stimuli, an individual must use a set of rules specifying the quantity and type of information needed to solve the problem. Furthermore, there may be optimum strategies for obtaining the information as well as decision rules necessary for using the information actually registered and processed. Thus a general characteristic of attentional development in children seems to be what Wright and Vlietstra (1975, p. 136) have called a "shift from the control of attention by salient features of stimuli toward its control by logical features of the task." Individual differences and age-related changes would be expected to the extent that there is variability in the rules underlying the selection of information and its subsequent use.

The fundamental theme of this chapter is that children's selection of information for use in a given task cannot be divorced from development of decision-making processes. We will examine in detail the performance of children who must compare two complex visual displays in order to judge them the same or different. We believe that the acts of overcoming defective perception and eliminating misunderstanding of instructions are minor factors in age-related improvement in children's comparison of novel objects. Rather, developmental changes in what information is selected and the strategies used to do so will be shown to depend on changes in cognitive functioning—in particular, the emergence of an adequate set of rules of identity. We will argue that rules specifying the meaning of "sameness" play a crucial role in determining how children select and use information during comparison of two objects. We will further argue that the *development* of efficient strategies of selecting information depends in some cases on prior appearance of adultlike rules specifying identity. Children's selection of perceptual information becomes less bound by the properties of a stimulus display and more closely regulated by a mature concept of similarity (or "sameness").

The Task

The studies to be discussed all used similar experimental paradigms. The children's task usually consisted of making paired comparisons between objects or drawings and required a judgment of their identity or nonidentity. A series of pairs of stimuli were presented to a child, one at a time. For some of the pairs, the items were identical in all respects, while for the rest of the pairs, the items differed in one or more ways. Children were given the following instructions:

"I am going to show you drawings [photographs, etc.] of houses [or other stimulus materials]. There will always be two of them side by side, and they will look much alike. But sometimes they will be just the same and sometimes they will not be the same. I want you to look at them as well as you can, and, as soon as you know, tell me if they are just the same or not the same."

In most of the studies, eye movements were recorded from the onset of presentation of a stimulus pair to the utterance of the response.[1] Films of the eye movements were scored in order to determine the number of different elements fixated in the overall display as well as the order in which the fixations occurred.

In general, the type of answer given by the child ("same" or "not the same") was examined as a function of the properties of the pairs of stimuli. The children's definitions of "just the same" and "not the same" were inferred from the way in which these responses were distributed across identical pairs and pairs that varied in the number and kind of their differences. Additional information about the criteria used in making decisions was obtained in some experiments by asking for justifications of the responses. The adequacy of the answers was never questioned, and no reinforcement for correct responses was given. When eye movements were recorded, the analysis of the scan paths provided a means of measuring the quantity and type of information that children of different ages considered necessary to obtain in order to make their judgments of sameness. Finally, the ways in which the structure of children's scan paths differed according to the type of stimuli provided an indication of whether the basis for children's selection of information lay in the stimulus itself or in the child's notions of same or different.

In the paired-comparison task just outlined, two findings emerged consistently. Both of them suggested that preschool children took into account only a limited amount of the available information in making their

[1]With the exception of the first experiment (Vurpillot, 1968), the apparatus was patterned after the Eye Movement Recorder—Wide Angle Model V-1166 of the Polymetric Company (Mackworth, 1968). In this system, the stimulus and the luminous markers placed above and below it were all seen by the subject through a half-silvered mirror placed at a 45° angle with respect to the stimulus. Both the stimulus and the markers were reflected by the subject's cornea. The image of the stimulus, the markers, and the subject's right eye were in turn reflected by the mirror into the lens of a 16-mm Beaulieu reflex movie camera. When the eye moved, the position of the markers changed with respect to the pupil. The relation of the markers to the center of the pupil specified the location of successive ocular fixations on the stimulus.

Distortions of the corneal reflections were introduced by the eccentricity of the fixated points and individual differences. These errors were neutralized by having each child fixate successively targets on a standard slide and in a particular order. Given the known location of these fixations, a code was established for each child and applied to fixations of all slides. A certain relation between the center of the pupil and the markers in the standard slide thus corresponded to the location of a fixation on all test stimuli. Filming was done at eight frames per second with Kodak 4x negative film (A.S.A. = 400).

judgments of same or different. First, the extent of visual exploration of the two members of a pair of stimuli was restricted. Younger children scanned only a limited region before making their judgments of same or different, but older children tended to inspect most of the stimulus display. Next, with younger children not all of the properties of a stimulus were taken into account, whereas older children used any potential difference between the stimuli in making their judgments. For instance, younger children did not always "count" differences in spatial arrangement in making their decisions, but older children did. Thus, in the task employed here, there was a developmental shift from defining sameness on the basis of equivalence to understanding of logical identity. In other words, older children tended to explore the displays exhaustively in search of any potential differences. Younger children, however, failed to search thoroughly and did not consider all kinds of differences as relevant to their decision—even when the differences were noticed! The conclusions and the empirical basis for them will be elaborated in the sections to follow.

Extent of Visual Scanning

Do Young Children Scan Only Part of the Stimuli?

In one experiment (Vurpillot, 1968) children between 4 and 9 years of age were instructed to make same–different judgments of pairs of drawings of houses. No justification of their response was required. Houses had six windows, arranged in three rows and two columns, with each window of a given house containing a different item (shutters, pots of flowers, blinds, etc.). Each child saw six pairs of houses. In three of the pairs, the two houses were identical (identical contents in homologous places); in the other pairs, the two houses had one, three, or five differences between them. All differences were substitutions of content. For example, a shutter with a small heart could be found in the upper left window in the house on the left, whereas two pots of flowers appeared in the homologous window of the right-hand house. All differences were thus differences in the contents of the windows, not in the spatial location of the items in the houses.

Eye movements were recorded and the extent of scanning was measured by the number of *different* windows fixated at least once for each pair of houses.[2] The results were clear. Children aged 4 to 5 years looked at only a few different windows (a mean of 7 of the possible 12 windows). This number did not vary with either the nature of the pair (identical or differ-

[2]This method of calculating the extent of ocular scanning eliminated redundant eye fixations. For instance, a child who looked at six different windows but used only 5 eye movements was scored as having the same extent of scanning as a child who needed 12 movements to see six different windows.

ent), the number of differences between the houses, or the type of response given (same or different). For children between 6.6 and 9 years of age, however, the extent of scanning varied with the properties of the houses. They looked at 10 to 12 windows on identical pairs, but with "different" pairs the number of different windows fixated decreased as the number of differences increased.

This pattern of findings suggests two questions. First, why do young children restrict the extent of their exploration to a limited area of the stimulus? Second, is the limited extent of ocular exploration the major cause of poor performances in tasks of differentiation? In other words, young children may have performed poorly because in failing to scan an area, they failed to detect a difference. Answers to these questions turn on what factors influence the extent of ocular scanning and whether exhaustive scanning is sufficient to produce perfect performance in tasks involving judgments of identity.

What Factors Affect the Extent of Ocular Scanning?

The data of the first experiment (Vurpillot, 1968) were reanalyzed (Vurpillot, 1976). The degree of visual activity (measured by the total number of eye movements) and the extent of scanning (given by the number of different windows fixated at least once) were examined trial by trial, with each presentation of a pair of stimuli constituting one trial. In this experiment six pairs of stimuli and hence six trials were given to each child.

Children in all age groups displayed a strong effect of trials: The total number of eye movements made during inspection of a pair of stimuli declined over trials. For 4- and 5-year-old children, the number of *different* windows fixated per pair also decreased. In contrast, the number of different windows fixated at least once in a trial remained constant throughout the experimental session for 6.6- and 9-year-olds. Thus in both age groups the sheer amount of ocular activity declined over trials. But in younger children, this decline was accompanied by a decrease in the extent of visual scanning, whereas for older children the extent of scanning was independent of the total amount of ocular activity.

In a different experiment (Vurpillot, Castelo, & Renard, 1975) children aged 5 and 6.6 years were asked to make same–different judgments of pairs of houses varying in the number of windows present in a pair: 12, 16, or 20 (i.e., 6, 8, and 10 windows per house, arranged in two columns and three, four, or five rows). Different groups of children were assigned to the three conditions: W_{12}, W_{16}, and W_{20}. Each child saw an equal number of different and identical pairs. Only differences by substitution were used (as defined in the first paragraph of the preceding section), and the ratio of the average number of differences to the number of windows remained constant across conditions. The first two pairs seen by the children were eliminated from the analysis in order to reduce the influence of novelty. Eye movements were recorded, but justifications of the children's answers were not required.

The results showed clearly that the extent of scanning was limited in both age groups, but it was not constant across the conditions. For both age groups the number of different windows fixated (F) increased with the number of windows present (W), although older children looked at more windows than did younger children in all conditions.

It should be noted, however, that the 6-year-old group was composed of two distinct types of individual: those who looked at virtually all of the different windows and those who did not. Children were divided into two groups according to the extent of their scanning with identical pairs of stimuli: Exhaustive scanners (W=F<1.5) and nonexhaustive scanners (W-F > 2). At 5 years of age, there was only 1 exhaustive scanner out of 36 children; at 6.6 years there were 16 out of 36. When the ratio of collected information to available information was computed for nonexhaustive scanners, no difference was found between the two age groups.

Children between 4 and 9 years of age can apparently be divided into two groups according to the amount of information they needed to decide whether two objects were identical. Some children always considered it necessary to scan a stimulus exhaustively before answering "just the same." For others, the extent of ocular scanning varied, often as a function of the number trials. The 4-year-olds' decline in the number of different windows fixated over trials has already been cited in this regard. By 9 years, however, nearly all the children used a criterion of exhaustive search in all trials (Vurpillot, 1976)—at least with the kind of task and type of material described in the present set of studies.

The general implications of these studies can be easily summarized. In a task requiring same–different judgments about pairs of stimuli, children's performance reflected implicit criteria of identity. When the criteria of decision included a specification of exhaustiveness of search before answering "just the same," the children inspected nearly all of the items composing each number of a stimulus pair. The number of different windows scanned was determined by a rule for exhaustiveness, not merely by the nature of the stimulus material. When the criteria of deciding same or different did not include a specification for exhaustiveness, children varied the extent of their scanning.

Can Insufficient Scanning Explain Poor Performance in Differentiation Tasks?

Young children make many errors in tasks of differentiation, and such errors are observed much more often with different than with identical pairs. Children seldom maintain that identical pairs differ in some respect, but different pairs of stimuli are frequently said to be the same. It is possible to argue that this pattern of results merely reflects a strong response bias to answer "same," and the problem then becomes one of accounting for the existence of the bias. Another possibility, however, is that with scanning restricted to a small area of a stimulus, the probability of not detecting a difference is high. Therefore young children might call different pairs "just the same" only because they did not happen to look where the differences were located. That the number of correct answers of "not the same" was positively related to the number of differences between drawings lends some support to such an interpretation (Vurpillot, 1969). But the real test of the hypothesis of deficient scanning is to induce the child to scan exhaustively. If the children's difficulty in correctly labeling different pairs were simply due to their not having seen the differences, then their performance should be perfect when they are induced to scan exhaustively.

Berthoud and Vurpillot (1970) presented 10 pairs of three-dimensional toy houses to children 3, 4, and 5 years of age. Each house had four windows, arranged in two rows and two columns. Pairs varied in the number of differences: zero (identical pairs), one, two, three, or four differences. All differences consisted of substitutions, i.e., differences in the contents of the windows belonging to the two houses. Eye movements were not recorded. The children were given the usual instructions for responding "just the same" or "not the same." They were also told to point to each window of each house in any order they chose and to describe the contents so that it was certain that the child had seen the eight windows before responding.

After inspection of the data, children were divided into three groups according to their pattern of responses. Children in Group A were those who only answered "same" to all of the stimulus pairs. In Group B were children who judged some pairs as "just the same" and some as "not the same," where some of the judgments were incorrect. Finally, children of Group C were always correct, responding "different" to pairs that were objectively different and "same" only to identical pairs. Table I gives the distribution of children according to age and group. For children in Group B, the percentage of correct responses to different pairs increased linearly with the number of differences between the stimuli. Despite the fact that scanning was always systematic and exhaustive, the greater the number of differences between the houses, the more likely it was that children responded correctly. Thus, limited scanning of the displays could not have been the cause of the children's failure to report that different stimuli were in fact different.

It might be argued that with eight windows for each pair, the children had forgotten the contents of the first windows inspected. In this case, the relationship between number of correct responses and the number of differences between the houses could simply have reflected mnemonic limitations. Therefore, a new set of toy houses was constructed such that the

TABLE I
Distribution of Children According to Age and Pattern of Responses[a]

Ages (years)	Groups[b]			
	A	B	C	Total
Experiment I[c]				
3, 4	9	—	—	9
4, 0	4	9	5	18
5, 0	—	6	12	18
Experiment II				
4, 6	10	15	11	36

[a]Data are expressed in number of children.
[b]Group A: stereotyped response "same"; Group B: some errors on different pairs; Group C: all responses are correct.
[c]Experiment I: Berthoud and Vurpillot (1970); Experiment II: Vurpillot (1976).

houses had only one, two, or three windows each. Houses were either the same or differed in one, two, or three windows. This new material was then presented to a new group of 4-year-olds in a procedure identical to that of the previous study (Vurpillot, 1976). The children in this experiment were distributed among groups A, B, and C in approximately the same way as the 4-year-olds of the initial study (see Table I). Ratios of the number of differences to the number of windows were also calculated for both studies. For children belonging to group B in both experiments, the percentage of correct responses increased with an increasing ratio of the number of differences to the number of windows. Even with a limited number of windows to be compared, the larger the number of differences, the more likely it was that young children would respond correctly. Mnemonic limitations, therefore, probably did not play a crucial role in determining the pattern of responding.

Thus, the origins of young children's difficulties in making correct same–different judgments about novel objects seemed to lie in the criteria they used to make their decisions, not in the limited extent of their ocular activity. Of course, some errors probably were attributable to poorly adapted scanning, but merely forcing children to scan exhaustively and systematically did not guarantee improved performance. Identical scanning activity led to varied patterns of judgments. This is a central finding of the research, for which an explanation must be sought.

An explanation may lie in the patterns of responses displayed by children in groups A, B, and C. These patterns were indicative of what decision rules children actually employed. The use of patterns of responses to infer criteria for same and different seemed preferable to obtaining only the children's verbal accounts of their answers. It is not always possible to obtain justifications from 3- and 4-year-olds, and their answers are often far from clear. Verbal justifications were, therefore, used sparingly in the analysis of the children's performance.

For Group A, the meaning of *same* seemed restricted to semantic equivalence of the two stimuli. They both represented houses; they both had windows. Each stimulus perhaps "meant" the same thing, meaning being relative to their "houseness" or the property of having windows. In short, identity might have been defined in terms of belonging to equivalent global categories of objects. Children were likely responding on the basis of their classifications of the types of objects involved without including in the definition of sameness the internal features of the object.

With children in Group B, two interpretations are possible, and the evidence does not at present support one over the other. In the first, it is assumed that children considered two houses the same when the houses were fairly similar, but not the same when they were very different. A dichotomous judgment was based on a global appraisal of similarity. The more numerous the differences, the less similar the houses appeared. Children may, in effect, have rated the displays according to the number of differences, and their judgment of same may have been based on an implicit cutoff point defined by a subjective criterion of "not too many differences."

A second interpretation of the responses of Group B was suggested by spontaneous remarks made by some children during the sessions. These children uttered a series of contradictory responses about the same pair of stimuli. For example, one child said, "Yes, the two are the same, see, here is a pot of flowers, and here is also one (on the other house). Oh, no—they are not the same because here are shutters, and here there are none . . . etc." It should be noted that such responses clearly indicated that not only were the contents examined but also they were often correctly detected as different. Comparisons were made between pairs of windows; each comparison of two windows led to a judgment of same or different that was independent of judgments about other pairs. There seemed to be a confusion between judgments concerning the properties of the parts of the houses and decisions relevant to the global judgment of identity of the whole houses. Children whose criteria for identity included independent comparison of constituents of the two stimuli may simply have based their same–different judgments on the last comparison of individual elements. These children failed to coordinate the relation between the whole houses and their windows. Comparisons made prior to the last one would have been irrelevant to the final decision. Thus, the more numerous the differences, the higher the probability for a difference to be found during the last comparison. Hence, it would follow that the number of correct responses of "not the same" should increase with an increasing number of differences between the stimuli, which was the result that was obtained.

Although the definitions used by children in Group B are somewhat in doubt, the criterion used by Group C seems straightforward. Two houses were considered just the same if and only if the contents of a window on one house were also found on the other house. The houses were not called the same if any difference in content was noticed. Such a criterion seemed to be adopted by the majority of the 5-year-olds. It is important to note, however, that the differences between stimuli in the present set of experiments involved only substitution of contents, not other types of differences such as putting the same contents in different locations. Thus, even though the criterion of the 5-year-old children seemed to be like that of adults, it is not obvious that the criterion used by the children was identical to that which an adult would use. Studies reported later, in which stimulus differences other than substitutions were examined, suggested that, in fact, 5-year-olds' decision criteria are not exactly the same as those of an adult.

In brief, children's criteria for identity seemed to change with age from one based on global equivalence to one requiring that stimuli have the same internal contents. Exhaustive scanning was not itself a sufficient condition for the appearance of the new rules because even when forced to scan systematically, children made errors. It is possible to speculate that exhaustiveness of search appears after the emergence of a criterion of sameness that requires that there be no differences in contents. Age-related improvement in scanning strategies would thus result from developmental changes in decision-making processes. This idea will be elaborated below.

Relevance of Perceived Differences to Judgments of Identity

Clearly the problem of what dimensions children use in solving tasks cannot be entirely reduced to difficulties of discrimination. Preschool children may be well able to detect differences among stimuli but still ignore the differences. The question is why some properties of stimuli are ignored and others attended to carefully.

We argue that what the child selects to look at and retain varies according to the nature of the task, and in many cases, according to the children's criteria for identity. Children choose dimensions that are pertinent to them, and the same dimension may be relevant for a child in one task but not in another. The relevance of a particular dimension for the children will depend on the rules that they use to make decisions about, for example, the identity of two stimuli. In the absence of an explicit task to perform, and a set of criteria for making a decision, attention will be directed to dimensions that are merely perceptually salient.

A recent set of experiments was performed to show that a refinement of certain spatial abilities was a necessary but not a sufficient condition for the development of a logical definition of identity. A task was first devised to determine the capacity of children between 3.6 and 5.6 years of age to localize discrete elements of a simple structure (Berthoud, 1973). Children were presented with toy houses, placed side by side. Each house had eight windows arranged in four rows and two columns. All windows were closed by identical shutters, and they could be identified only by their location. When the experimenter opened one shutter on "her" house, a light came on in the window. The child was told that if he opened a shutter at the homologous ("same") place on "his" house, there would also be a light in his window, but that no light would come on if any other window were opened. In short, the child's attention was directed to a single property of the windows, their places, and reinforcement by a light followed all correct responses.

At 3.6 years of age, the children localized "their" place on the appropriate horizontal row in 95% of the cases, but homologous windows were not differentiated from symmetrical windows. For instance, a child might have noted correctly that a window was located on the second row from the top but might have mistakenly opened the left window of his house instead of the right window. It should be noted that the expression "symmetrical windows" in this context refers to a pair of windows such that the left window of one house is paired with the right window of the other house. By 5.6 years of age, 80% of the children correctly localized windows in both horizontal and vertical dimensions, i.e., the correct rows and columns were used. Thus, when the instructions of the task clearly specified the pertinence of the location of an element and when location was the only cue to the identity of a window, position became a relevant attribute for the child, and partial information about position was used by even young children. Errors in the study resulted not from a total absence of a concept of place but from use of an incomplete or inadequate set of spatial references. Suppose, however, that the task was to make same–different judgments about pairs of stimuli—in the absence of any explicit reference to location. The pertinence for the child of the location of the elements and their precise details would then be determined chiefly by the child's definition of "just the same." A new set of studies demonstrated that the criteria for identity changed with age, the property of place being increasingly taken into account.

The new studies were undertaken in order to assess explicitly the role of spatial location in children's definitions of identity. Unless otherwise specified, the procedures all involved the standard task requiring same–different judgments of pairs of stimuli. Children's judgments were examined (a) when the stimulus differences were created by substitution of elements, as defined above, and (b) when the differences were created by permutation or rearrangement of the same set of elements. One consistent finding was that preschool children took differences of substitution of contents into account before they used spatial location in their criteria of decision. Vurpillot and Moal (1970) found that 55% of the 4-year-olds in their study correctly called pairs of houses "not the same" when the houses differed in the contents of their windows. Only 9% of the children said "not the same" when the same contents were simply found in different spatial locations within the two stimuli. Vurpillot, Lecuyer, Moal, and Pineau (1971) replicated the finding that 4-year-olds did not take permutations of elements into account. Employing circular or irregular figures as stimuli, they showed that 3- to 4-year-olds failed to take into account changes in which the individual elements composing the stimuli were *displaced* so as to modify the overall configuration. Spontaneous remarks by the children suggested that the differences were noted but not considered relevant to the decision.

Findings with older children confirmed this latter conclusion. Fewer than 50% of the 5- to 6-year-olds took differences in place (permutations of elements) into account in making their judgments of same or different. At this age the children were well able to localize objects as shown in the study by Berthoud (1973), in which children matched by spatial position of window. So the difficulty was clearly not attributable to perceptual confusion among spatial positions. Rather, spatial location was less pertinent to the children's definition of identity than others aspects of their decision criteria. This separation of perceptual and conceptual effects was further illustrated by many 9-year-olds who were able to distinguish homologous pairs of windows from symmetrical pairs on the standard houses but still considered them to be the same for purposes of making a judgment about identity! Thus, even some older children answered "just the same" when asked to compare identical houses and houses that were mirror images of each other (Vurpillot, 1977a).

These puzzling observations concerning features that are perceived but not used in children's decision criteria will not be pursued here. What is important, however, is the developmental progression revealed by the set of studies. There are at least three successive steps in the evolution of the influence of differences in location of elements on children's performance. In an early period (up to about 4 years), children show some ability to localize features according to the vertical dimension where stimuli are presented in the manner employed here, but homologous locations are confused with symmetrical places on the same row of windows. During a second period, differences in place are perceived accurately, but the children do not take them into account in making judgments of identity. For example, some permutations may be noted but not considered pertinent. Third, differences in location are included in the children's decision rule about sameness, although places seen to be different can occasionally be called "the same."

In this stage, confusion between locations in mirror-image pairs of stimuli occur not at the level of perceptual confusion among spatial locations but at the level of the children's definition of identity.

Criteria of Identity Judgments and Scanning Strategies

Much of the discussion so far has centered on how children between 4 and 7 years of age could be classified according to their definition of "just the same." Some of them used the logical definition of identity: Two objects were considered the same if, and only if, identical details or elements occupied corresponding places on both objects. If the "same places" were occupied by nonidentical details, then the objects were "not the same" even though the same contents appeared on both objects. For other children (mostly 4 to 5 years old), differences in spatial location (permutation of elements) were not taken into account. Furthermore, 5-year-old children often called objects the same when a detail was present twice on one object and only once on the other object (Vurpillot & Taranne, 1974, 1975). Only if a detail present on one were absent on the other (differences by substitution) were the two objects correctly judged "not the same." Thus, the data indicate a shift in definition of identity from one in which place is irrelevant to one in which place is pertinent.

One important issue is whether this conceptual development affects the ways in which children select information in stimulus objects. More specifically, is there a lessening in the degree to which stimulus configurations determine how children direct their perceptual activity? The result of a recent set of studies suggested that a shift does occur and that visual attention becomes less constrained by the stimulus. To anticipate the findings, definitions of identity in which location was not relevant led to different ocular scanning strategies from those for a definition in which place was taken into account. The former resulted in a scanning strategy of linking identical details while the latter was accompanied by a strategy of examining identical locations.

In the first study (Vurpillot, 1977a), 54 children aged 4.1 to 9.4 years of age made same–different judgments of pairs of houses, each house having six windows (Figure 1). The same set of six items was used in the windows of all houses, so that the two houses differed only in the positions of identical contents. Two identical and six different pairs of houses were used; both eye movements and verbal justifications of responses were recorded.

After the experiment was over, children were classified as belonging to one of four groups according to their definitions of the "same house" and the "same place." The definitions were inferred from the patterns of iden-

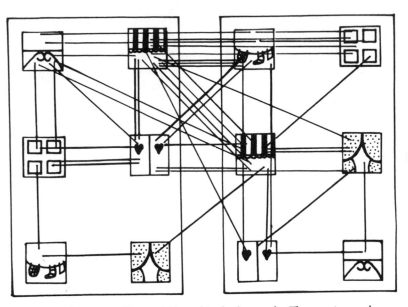

FIGURE 1. One of the pairs of houses (P₁) used in the first study. The superimposed scan path has been obtained from a child of group 1.

tity judgments and the justifications of these decisions. Children in group 1 never took place into account and called the houses the same when in fact they differed in the locations of identical items. Roughly 50% of the 5- to 6-year-olds but none of the 9-year-olds belonged to this group. In group 2 were children who occasionally used place information in making their judgments but did not do so systematically. These children had no consistent definition of "same place." Children in groups 3 and 4 always used location in their judgments, and at a minimum their criteria for "same place" involved the correct horizontal row of windows. For children of group 3, *both* symmetrical and homologous places were considered the same. In group 4 however, either symmetrical or homologous locations— but not both—were part of the definition of identical locations.

Once the children were divided into the four groups, their ocular scan paths were examined. The children's definition of identity was expected to affect the structure of their ocular scan paths. The most efficient means of finding out whether the same contents appeared in homologous locations was to compare directly the corresponding locations. It was expected that the children for whom place was relevant (groups 3 and 4) had made the greatest number of organized horizontal eye movements along rows of windows. Organized horizontal scans were defined as those in which at least three elements of the houses were linked in consecutive movements remaining in the same row. In other words, given a row of four windows, an organized horizontal scan involved fixating one window, then another, and then a third window. All three windows had to be different. Short horizontal scans were those movements linking only two elements of a given row before another row was examined.

Children in group 1, who defined "same" in terms of identical contents, were expected to have shown a different strategy. The most reliable way to locate the same contents would have been to start from a window on one house and then compare it successively to all the windows of the other house. After encountering a content identical to the starting window, the children could have repeated the process for each of the other windows. Children would have said "not the same" only if identical contents had not been found on the houses. This strategy of iterative search is, of course, very demanding and cumbersome; it is reliable only when all partial comparisons are effected systematically. No 5- to 7-year-old would actually have been capable of sustaining it. It should be clear, however, that approximations to the strategy were possible. For example, children could have compared a given window to any other without examining all the windows of the other house in succession. Because the children were only searching for identical contents, there was no advantage to using organized horizontal eye movements linking at least three elements of the same row rather than eye movements in other directions (e.g., oblique). Therefore, it was expected that children of group 1 had displayed relatively fewer instances of

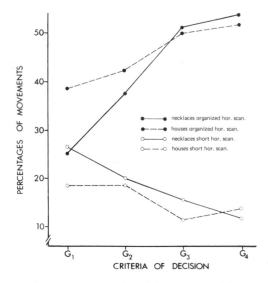

FIGURE 2. Percentage of eye movements classified as organized horizontal scans and short horizontal scans, according to patterns of responses: G_1—place is not relevant; G_2—place begins to be relevant; G_3—the "same place" is on the same horizontal row; G_4—the "same place" is the homologous place.

organized horizontal scanning than children in groups 3 and 4 for whom place was relevant to their criteria for identity.

The predictions were confirmed. The proportion of organized horizontal eye movements was larger in groups 3 and 4 than in group 1 (Figure 2). Children in groups 3 and 4 tended to examine identical locations, whereas the children in group 1 showed a lesser tendency to link homologous places. In fact, children in groups 3 and 4 seemed to show qualitatively comparable types of scanning, at least at the level of analysis permitted by the present techniques.

In a second experiment (Vurpillot 1977b) including 56 children, circular configurations (necklaces) of six stimulus elements (beads) were used in the standard task (Figure 3) in an effort to assess the generality of the above results. All of the necklaces were made of the same six beads. Children saw two pairs of identical necklaces and six pairs differing in the location of specific items in a manner analogous to that of the previous study. The results of this study were similar to those of the previous experiment. Groups 1, 3, and 4 were defined as before. Among children 5 to 6 years of age, one-half fell into group 1, those who failed to consider place in making their judgments. By 9 years most children belonged to groups 3 and 4. As in the first experiment, children in group 1 failed to show as much organized horizontal scanning as those in groups 3 and 4. Children for whom place was included in the definition of identity tended to compare the same places. Extensive horizontal scanning therefore was observed to a greater degree for these children than for children who did not include location in their criteria. The pattern of results thus replicated that obtained with houses as stimuli (Figure 2).

The crucial question is, of course, whether the differences in the physical characteristics of the stimuli affected children's performance. First, the

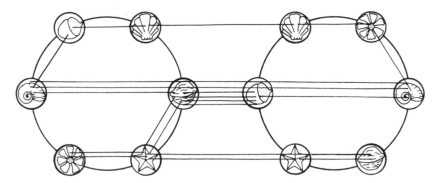

FIGURE 3. One of the pairs of necklaces used in the second study. The superimposed scan path has been obtained from a child of group 3.

amount of organized horizontal scanning shown with necklaces by children in group 1 was much less than that obtained with children in group 1 who saw houses. The rectilinear organization of the windows of the houses clearly favored horizontal scanning more than did the circular organization of the necklaces. That this was found in the data only for children in group 1 suggested that nonstimulus variables were determining scanning activity among children of groups 3 and 4. Thus, the consistent use of a strategy of comparing homologous locations despite variations in the structure of the stimuli depended on the appearance of a mature definition of identity in the older children. Taking place into account in the criteria for decision was crucial to the development of an efficient visual strategy of comparing homologous locations.

A second difference between the two studies was that children in groups 3 and 4 made fewer confusions between symmetrical and homologous positions with necklaces than with houses. Thus, even with older children, stimulus configurations affected performance. The role of stimulus organization in determining scanning strategies was relatively minor in these groups, however. The chief effects of the stimuli lay in influencing the final judgment of identity rather than in determining the scanning activity by which the information was selected.

Conclusion

In accounting for children's performance in perceptual tasks, a number of factors are relevant. Children must, of course, detect the stimulus information needed to perform the task. But merely having the ability to see the dimensions or features is no guarantee that they will be searched for in the first place or used appropriately if detected. The work outlined in this chapter underscores the necessity of examining conceptual development as a constraint on what children do in exploring and comparing novel objects.

In particular, the children's decision rules in making identity judgment were the focus of much of the work discussed. Children's definition of identity was shown to be a crucial factor in determining the amount of information sought, the strategies used to obtain it, and the way it was used once acquired. The criteria for identity underwent a change from a global impression of similarity to a requirement that any potential difference between stimuli was relevant (contents and their locations). Accompanying this change were an increase in the extent of children's ocular activity, the appearance of a strategy of visual comparison of homologous locations, and an increased willingness to consider any detected difference as supporting a judgment of "not the same."

This pattern of changes was consistent with what other authors have called a shift from associative or exploratory search to cognitive control of performance (Berlyne, 1960; Nunnally & Lemond, 1973; White, 1965; Wright & Vlietstra, 1975). The studies outlined in this chapter also documented a decline in the role of stimulus parameters in determining how information was selected. Children's perceptual activity became less constrained by physical characteristics of the stimuli such as spatial position. Rather, the appearance of a concept of logical identity—in which the same features must be found at the same location—resulted in a corresponding change in children's ocular activity. Older children came to exhibit a consistent strategy of horizontal comparisons of corresponding places on two stimuli. Furthermore, this strategy was consistently applied to both rectilinear and curvilinear displays by older children, whereas the latter type of stimulus configuration tended to disrupt the use of organized horizontal scans by younger children.

Perhaps the major issue yet to be addressed is that of causation. Simply put, does the development of scanning strategies produce change in children's criteria of identity or does development of mature decision criteria result in modified scanning strategies? We believe the latter is more likely the case for two reasons. First, forcing young children to engage in systematic comparisons of two houses did not automatically result in their considering such dimensions as spatial location or even content in making same–different judgments. Taking all potential differences into account was hardly an inevitable consequence of examining homologous locations. Next, there were several cases of children's exhibiting identical scanning strategies but not having identical definition of "just the same." For example, children who used either symmetrical or homologous locations (but not both) in their criteria for same place showed the same type of organized horizontal scanning as children who considered both symmetrical and homologous locations as the same place. Thus, similar types of scan paths did not invariably produce exactly the same criteria for identity.

Rather, it is more plausible that the older children selected a scanning strategy based on their criteria of same and different and that organized horizontal scanning was appropriate whenever location was taken into account. Comparing same places allowed immediate detection of a possible difference and hence allowed the fastest solution to the task consistent with exhaustive search for all relevant differences. Also, direct comparison of homologous places allowed children to ignore their contents subsequently. After the children maintained a representation of one item in memory for the short time needed to compare it with its corresponding element, the two *contents* would require no further processing. Children would only have to remember where they had looked, not the exact properties of the things seen, in order to avoid redundant eye movements.

To conclude, conceptual development is probably a precondition for efficient selection and use of some perceptual information, and the nature of ocular exploration of novel objects depends to some extent on cognitive functioning. The child's understanding of invariance—identity of features and spatial arrangement—plays an important role in the development of selective attention. Children come to fit what they choose to see and the nature of their exploration to the requirements of the task, not merely the organization of the stimulus. An important question concerns the factors underlying development of a concept of logical identity, but an answer awaits further research.

References

Berlyne, D. E. *Conflict, arousal, and curiosity.* New York: McGraw-Hill, 1960.

Berthoud, M. Les systèmes de référence spatiaux et leur interaction chez les enfants d'age préscolaire. I. Le degré de contrainte des données perceptives. *Année Psychologique,* 1973, *73,* 23–35.

Berthoud, M., & Vurpillot, E. Influence du nombre de différences sur les réponses "pas pareil" chez l'enfant d'âge préscolaire. *Enfance,* 1970, *23,* 23–30.

Mackworth, N. H. The wide angle reflection eye camera for visual choice and pupil size. *Perception and Psychophysics,* 1968, *3,* 32–34.

Nunnally, J. C., & Lemond, L. C. Exploratory behavior and human development. In H. W. Reese (Ed.), *Advances in child development and behavior* (Vol. 8). New York: Academic, 1973, pp. 60–109.

Sokolov, Y. N. *Perception and the conditioned reflex.* New York: Macmillan, 1963.

Vurpillot, E. The development of scanning strategies and their relation to visual differentiation. *Journal of Experimental Child Psychology,* 1968, *6,* 632–650.

Vurpillot, E. Contribution à l'étude de la differenciation perceptive chez l'enfant d'âge préscolaire. *Année Psychologique,* 1969, *69,* 37–54.

Vurpillot, E. *The visual world of the child.* New York: International Universities Press, 1976.

Vurpillot, E. *Some effects of stimulus structure and criteria of decision on visual scanning.* Paper presented at the biennial meeting of the Society for Research in Child Development, Symposium on Attention and Cognition, New Orleans, March 1977. (a)

Vurpillot, E. Définition du "pareil" ou "pas pareil" et stratégies d'exploration oculomotrice chez l'enfant. In G. Oléron (Ed.), *Psychologie expérimentale et comparée. Hommage à Paul Fraisse.* Paris: Presses Universitaires de France, 1977, pp. 339–352. (b)

Vurpillot, E., & Moal, A. Evolution des critères d'identité chez des enfants d'âge préscolaire dans une tâche de différenciation perceptive. *Année Psychologique,* 1970, *70,* 391–406.

Vurpillot, E., & Taranne, P. Jugement d'identité ou de non identité entre dessins et exploration oculomotrice chez des enfants de 5 à 7 ans. *Année Psychologique,* 1974, *74,* 79–100.

Vurpillot, E., & Taranne, P. Pertinence de différences et fréquence d'occurrence d'un élément particulier dans un jugement d'identité chez des enfants d'âge préscolaire. *Enfance,* 1975, *28,* 152–164.

Vurpillot, E., Castelo, R., & Renard, C. Extension de l'exploration visuelle et nombre d'éléments présents sur des stimulus dans une tâche de différenciation perceptive. *Année Psychologique,* 1975, *75,* 355–373.

Vurpillot, E., Lécuyer, R., Moal, A., & Pineau, A. Perception de déplacements et jugements d'identité chez l'enfant d'âge préscolaire. *Année Psychologique,* 1971, 71, 31–52.

White, S. H. Evidence for a hierarchical arrangement of learning processes. In L. P. Lipsitt & C. C. Spiker (Eds.), *Advances in child development and behavior* (Vol. 2). New York: Academic, 1965, pp. 187–220.

Wright, J. C., & Vlietstra, A. G. The development of selective attention: From perceptual exploration to logical search. In H. W. Reese (Eds.), *Advances in child development and behavior* (Vol. 10). New York: Academic, 1975, pp. 195–239.

3

Development of Children's Attention to Stimulus Components

GORDON A. HALE

Introduction

It is generally recognized that selective attention plays an important role in cognition (e.g., Broadbent, 1971; Gibson, 1969). People do not necessarily process or "take in" all of the sensory information to which they are exposed but often may select certain information on which to concentrate their attention. Among the ways in which selective attention functions is in the discrimination of objects. Typically, objects in the world differ in several components ("features," "dimensions"), such as their shape, color, or size. When differentiating among objects an individual may not make use of all these components but may attend only to a selected portion of them. Thus, for example, a person may distinguish an object from others principally on the basis of a single component, such as its shape, even though the objects may differ in a number of features.

A popular topic of developmental inquiry concerns children's ability to exercise selective attention. Research on this topic includes studies of children's concept identification (e.g., Zeaman & House, 1963), intra- and extradimensional shifts (e.g., Tighe & Tighe, 1972), and incidental learning (e.g., Hagen, 1972). These studies have shown that with increasing mental age, children become better able to detect and maintain an orientation to a task-relevant component of stimulus objects.

An issue that has largely been neglected concerns the way children typically approach stimulus objects. Much of the developmental research on selective attention has dealt with children's ability to attend to stimulus information that has been designated by an experimenter as task-relevant. It has generally remained to be determined how children of different ages identify multicomponent stimuli if allowed to discriminate among them

GORDON A. HALE • Educational Testing Service, Princeton, New Jersey 08541.

according to their natural inclination. Do children of a given age typically attend selectively to a single stimulus component, or do they attend to several components in combination? The issue is one of children's *disposition* or natural tendency to exercise selective attention and is quite distinct from the question of children's *ability* to attend selectively to a specified stimulus component.

This is a fundamental issue in the study of selective attention and its development. Theories of perceptual development (e.g., Gibson, 1969) place particular stress on understanding how the growing child normally perceives and interacts with the multicomponent objects that make up the environment. Furthermore, the study of children's tendency toward selectivity is essential for interpretation of much existing attentional data. If there is a developmental increase in children's natural disposition to attend selectively, then this trend could be largely responsible for previously observed age differences in selective attention; with age, children simply become more inclined to concentrate on a single component of a stimulus. However, if children's natural tendency toward selectivity does not increase with age, then previous findings likely reflect a developmental improvement in children's ability to deal with tasks that specifically require selective attention. In short, assessment of the way children typically attend to the components of a stimulus object (or "deploy attention" to stimulus components) is essential for interpreting the results of research involving experimentally imposed constraints on attention.

The stimulus information to which a person attends is often called the "functional stimulus," in that such information provides the basis on which he discriminates the stimulus from others in the environment. For example, if a person identifies an object by its shape, even though the object consists of information about color and other dimensions as well, then the functional stimulus in this case is the object's shape. The issue raised in the preceding paragraph has to do with the nature of the functional stimulus under nonconstrained circumstances, or circumstances in which children are allowed to discriminate among stimuli according to their natural inclination. Another important issue concerns children's flexibility of attention, or readiness to alter the functional stimulus when it is advantageous to do so. In a nonconstrained situation, if children of a given age attend to selected stimulus information, they may be doing so for either of two reasons. They may be identifying the stimuli the same way they would in all other situations, or they may be acting according to the decision that it is most useful to identify the stimuli in this way in this particular situation. To determine children's flexibility in controlling their manner of attention deployment, it is essential not only to examine the way they identify stimuli in a single-task situation but also to look at the way they respond to variation in the attentional demands of the task.

These two issues, development of children's disposition toward selectivity and development of attentional flexibility, have provided the focus of a series of studies that my associates and I have conducted. We have sought, in particular, to address these issues as they relate to children's discrimination among stimuli in learning, since discrimination of objects in everyday life usually occurs as an activity in service of learning—learning to associate objects with relevant actions or with relevant environmental cues. This chapter is an overview of our efforts to address these two issues, with discussion of selected studies in the literature that bear on these issues.

First there is a section on the method we have used to study these issues, the component selection task, including a general description of the task and discussion of some assumptions in use of this task for measuring attention. The main body of the chapter then follows and consists of sections dealing with the two major issues under study. At the end, an additional section is devoted to dicussion of a paradigm that has been widely used to assess attention to components in young children, the "dimension preference" matching task. In this section the basic issue is considered once again—whether there are developmental changes in the way children typically approach multicomponent stimuli—and the question is raised whether assessment of children's dimension preferences provides an appropriate test of this issue.

The Component Selection Task

To discover how children typically discriminate among stimuli in learning—that is, to determine the functional stimulus under nonconstrained circumstances—one must create a situation in which the children are free to distinguish among the stimuli in whatever way they choose. To devise such a situation we constructed a "component selection task" for use in developmental research that was analogous to the cue-selection paradigm used in verbal learning studies with adults (cf. Richardson, 1971).

The task consists of two phases, a learning phase with stimuli differing in two components, followed by a test to determine how the subjects had discriminated among the stimuli in learning. Specifically, the child was shown a row of (five or six) two-component stimuli, i.e., stimuli that contained two redundant components such as shape and color. In the first phase the child learned the spatial position of each stimulus in the row. Then test cards were held up, each containing information about only one of the components (e.g., a colorless shape, or a colored card). The child was asked in each case to point to the position of the stimulus in the row that had the same shape or color (or other attribute) as the card being shown. All 5 or 6 instances of each component were shown. Test scores were the total number correct for each of the two components separately.

The two test scores comprised the principal data from the task and were assumed to reflect the degree to which attention had been directed to each component. Thus, for example, if a child obtained a high score for one component along with a chance-level score for the other, presumably the child attended selectively to the first component in identifying the stimuli in learning. However, a high score for the second component as well as the first would show that the child had attended to both components in discriminating among the stimuli.

Attention is inferred from short-term memory scores in this task, and it is important to note why such an inference is reasonable. The question at issue is: To what information does a subject attend as a basis for distinguishing among stimuli? Information that serves this purpose must be retained during the time intervals between successive exposure to a stimulus in order for learning to occur. Such information can also be assumed to be retained for at least a short interval after the last learning trial. Thus, attention to stimulus components during learning is reflected in memory for component information after learning. Of course, in a broad sense the term *attention to a stimulus component* can have other meanings as well, such as the mere awareness of a component's presence at the moment of stimulus inspection. The research to be discussed here provides no information about children's awareness at this level. The term *attention* in the present context refers to a mechanism that continues to operate after the initial moment of stimulus inspection, causing selected information to be processed beyond a momentary storage register into memory (cf. Broadbent, 1971; Trabasso & Bower, 1968).

In order to infer attention from component selection data, it is also necessary to take note of two methodological points. First, one must be sure that results from the test phase are not due simply to differences among experimental conditions, or among age groups, in rate of learning on the initial phase of the task, since different learning rates would bring different amounts of stimulus exposure. Effects due to differences in learning rate can be ruled out in the research to be discussed. While analyses of the *test scores* showed several important effects of experimental treatments and interactions of these treatments with age, analyses of *learning rate* showed no significant (or near-significant) effects in these respects. The only significant effects involving learning rate were age differences, and these were in a direction opposite to that which could account for the observed age differences in test scores (i.e., 4- to 5-year-olds learned more slowly and thus received more stimulus exposure than did older children but still had lower test scores—cf. Hale & Morgan, 1973; Hale & Taweel, 1974a).

Second, it is of value to assess the relative difficulty of tasks that employ the individual components as stimuli—e.g., to examine how readily subjects learn a task with colors alone or with shapes alone as stimuli (Richardson, 1971). If differences observed in such an assessment are not sufficient to account for differential scores obtained on the component selection task, then the latter scores reflect the operation of attentional factors rather than merely differences in difficulty associated with the separate components. In two studies (Hale & Green, 1976; Hale & Taweel, 1974b) we assessed individual component difficulty for the principal stimuli used in our studies. We found that the components did not differ markedly in this regard, and where two components were expected to differ in difficulty, as a result of stimulus manipulations (Hale & Green, 1976), the difference was roughly the same at the two age levels studied. Therefore, component difficulty can likely be ruled out as a factor underlying the developmental trends to be discussed here.

Development of Children's Disposition toward Selectivity

Age Trends in Component Selection

Our initial objective was to address the basic developmental issue: Is there a change with age in children's disposition to exercise selectivity? To ask this question, we gave 4- and 8-year-olds the component selection task with stimuli differing in color and shape (Hale & Morgan, 1973). Also, to be sure that our conclusions could be generalized to other stimulus materials, we followed up with a more comprehensive study in which 5- and 8-year-olds were given a component selection task with one of three types of stimuli: colored geometric shapes, colored pictures (line drawings of objects), and shapes with patterns (Hale & Taweel, 1974a). The task was presented as described above: The subject performed an initial learning phase with one of these types of stimuli and then was tested for retention of each component separately. Test scores proved to be considerably higher for one component (shape or picture) than for the other (color or pattern), demonstrating the general dominance of the first component as a basis for identification of the stimuli. Developmental analyses revealed a trend that was consistent across studies and across types of stimuli. Whereas scores for the dominant component were relatively high for both the younger and the older children (e.g., 4.4 versus 4.6 out of 5 in the Hale & Taweel study), scores for the nondominant component showed a marked increase with age (from 3.0 to 4.0 in the Hale & Taweel study). These results suggest that there is indeed a developmental change in children's deployment of attention to stimulus components. With age, children attend to an increasingly greater amount of information in the stimulus, thus showing a developmental decrease in selectivity.

Although few other developmental studies have been done with component-selection types of tasks, the evidence from these few studies appears to be consistent with our own in indicating a developmental increase in the amount of stimulus information to which children attend. Eimas (1969) gave kindergarten, second-grade, and fourth-grade children a component selection task with colored shapes and found an increase with age in the children's total scores on the test for individual-component learning. Using comparable stimuli, Solso (1970) observed an increase from ages 5 to 9 in total test scores. A task with stimuli differing in shape, color, and size was employed by Schrover and Newsom (1976), who found a relation between mental age and total test scores, both in a group of normal children and in a group of autistic children (MA range 3 to 9 years in each group).

Comparisons between normal and retarded children also bear on the relation between mental age and selectivity. Wilhelm and Lovaas (1976) used a component-selection type of task in which the components of each stimulus were three pictures in a configuration. Comparing severely retarded, moderately retarded, and normal children, these investigators found a positive relation between mental age and total scores on the test for individual-component retention. Using stimuli consisting of nonsense syllables surrounded by color, Baumeister, Berry, and Forehand (1969) found that their normal subjects obtained higher total test scores than did their retarded subjects, although Berry and Baumeister (1973) failed to observe such a difference. While reasons for the discrepant results of this last study are unclear, in general the data from these studies and those cited earlier tend to support an interpretation similar to that put forward above: With increasing age and/or level of intelligence there is an increase in amount of stimulus information to which children attend in discriminating among learning stimuli.

In theoretical analyses of attention development, much emphasis has been placed on the idea that young children attend to a wide range of information in the stimulus and that with maturity, children become increasingly more selective. Yet evidence from the component selection research discussed here seems to indicate that as children develop, they become less rather than more selective, attending to an increasing amount of stimulus information. To understand this apparent discrepancy, it is important to bear in mind the distinction between children's *ability* to exercise selectivity and their *disposition* to do so. Where developmental increases in selectivity have been found, the tasks used have been ones in which selectivity of attention is required for successful performance; these tasks tap children's ability to attend selectively to specified information. In the component selection task, on the other hand, subjects are basically free to discriminate among stimuli according to their natural inclination; hence, data from this task reflect children's disposition or natural tendency to exercise selection. The fact that parallel developmental trends have not been observed with these two types of task suggest that different functions describe development of the ability to exercise selective attention and development of the disposition to do so. Where children's natural disposition is concerned, there is a developmental trend, not toward greater selectivity but toward increasingly broader attention deployment.

Overtraining Effects

According to a recent hypothesis (James & Greeno, 1967), a subject will attend selectively as he learns a task and then, when given additional trials after learning the task, or overtraining, he will relax the selective mechanism and distribute attention more broadly. In a sense, an overtraining period is an occasion in which the information load in the task is reduced, in that the subject no longer need devote his energies to mastering the task but need only continue to emit already learned responses. If the above hypothesis is true, we reasoned, then the degree to which children in our earlier studies had exhibited selective tendencies may have been partly due to the demands associated with attaining task mastery. A period of overtraining should give them an excellent opportunity to attend to a broad range of information in the stimuli if they are inclined to do so.

To examine this possibility we gave 4-, 8- and 12-year-old children a component selection task with stimuli differing in shape and color, either with or without extensive overtraining before the test (Hale & Taweel, 1974b). We found that the children did not avail themselves of the opportunity provided by overtraining. The children at all age levels failed to acquire additional stimulus information with training beyond criterion, indicating that they did not broaden their attention during the overtraining period as hypothesized but continued to attend to the same stimulus information. Thus, the basic results we had observed in the earlier studies were not due to factors related to the amount of stimulus exposure or to demands uniquely associated with mastery of the learning task. Rather, there appears to be a fundamental developmental change in children's attention deployment such that, as children grow older, they become less selective and attend to an increasingly greater amount of information in the stimulus.

Other component selection studies with children are consistent with our own in failing to show an attention-broadening effect of overtraining. Eimas (1969) obtained no effect of overtraining on attention to color and shape in kindergarten children and second- and fourth-graders. Similarly, overtraining has been found to have no effect on second-graders' performance with stimuli whose components were a word and a nonsense syllable (Ellis & Thieman, 1976). (Schrover & Newsom, 1976, also examined overtraining effects, but their data are not directly pertinent to the discussion since their overtraining trials were preceded by an initial test of component selection.) Thus, although there are only a few relevant studies of overtraining in children's component selection, the little evidence that has been obtained supports the view that children's scope of attention is not broadened by overtraining. Rather, their behavior seems to conform more closely to the hypothesis that a learner will not alter his manner of attention deployment once he has attained essentially errorless performance (Trabasso & Bower, 1968). Children apparently continue to attend to the information that had served as a functional stimulus during learning; simply receiving stimulus exposure beyond task mastery apparently is not enough in itself to make children alter the way in which they attend to the components of stimuli.

It should be noted that several studies with adults using comparable tasks and stimuli have obtained positive effects of extended training on acquisition of individual-component information (Berry, Joubert, & Baumeister, 1972a,b; Houston, 1967; James & Greeno, 1967; Trabasso & Bower, 1968; Wichawut & Martin, 1970). It is possible that overtraining has developmentally changing effects, tending to produce an attention-broadening effect only for subjects beyond a certain age (perhaps mediated by age changes in component salience, a key factor in overtraining effects according to Shepp, Kemler, & Anderson, 1972).

Stimulus Integration and Integrality

Our research has been concerned primarily with stimuli containing integrated components, such as color within shape, since these are the kinds of dimensions on which objects in the world differ from each other. Nevertheless, the general category "multicomponent stimuli" contains other subclasses as well. One such subclass is nonintegrated stimuli whose components form a figure–ground relationship, such as shapes on colored backgrounds. In order to develop theories about the general concept of attention to stimulus components, it is useful to examine effects obtained not only with the standard integrated stimuli but with nonintegrated stimuli as well. We (Hale & Green, 1976) hypothesized that there would be a difference in the way subjects would deploy attention with these two types of stimuli in a component selection task. Specifically, we thought that, due to the natural tendency to contrast figure and ground, subjects would be more likely to attend selectively to a single component if the components formed a figure–ground relationship than if they were integrated. Evidence for a functional difference between these two types of stimuli came from an earlier study of children's incidental learning (Hale & Piper, 1973); between ages 8 and 12 there was a developmental trend toward selection of the relevant shape component when the stimuli were shapes on colored backgrounds but not when they were colored shapes. When we examined performance on the component selection task with these two types of stimuli, however, we found that stimulus integration had little influence upon the children's tendency to exercise selective attention or upon developmental changes in this tendency from ages 5 to 12 (Hale & Green, 1976). It is possible that stimulus integration affects children's attention when selectivity is required for successful task performance, as in an incidental learning task, but not when a selective approach is nonessential, as in a component selection task. Such a hypothesis is purely tentative, however, and would need to be tested through direct assessment of the interactive effects of task and stimulus types.

Another key aspect of stimulus structure is stimulus "integrality" as described by Garner (1974). A stimulus is said to be integral if, according to performance on certain tasks, subjects treat it as a unitary whole rather than as a conjunction of individual components. As an example, the components' hue and brightness are typically seen by adults as integral, whereas size and brightness are seen as nonintegral. The developmental importance of this type of variable is apparent in the writings of Gibson (1969) and Tighe and Tighe (1972), who posited that children become more aware of the dimensional structure of stimuli with increasing age and experience; that is, they become more aware that complex stimuli are composed of several independent dimensions or components. Shepp and Swartz (1976), using sorting tasks like those of Garner, obtained evidence consistent with this position. First-grade children, unlike fourth-graders and adults, responded to stimuli with nonintegral components (shape and colored background) in the same way that they responded to stimuli with integral components (hue and brightness), suggesting that the young children perceived the nonintegral stimuli as if they were integral. Smith and Kemler (1977) employed a stimulus-matching paradigm and got results suggesting that size and brightness are perceived as integral by kindergartners but as nonintegral by fifth-graders. These findings support the view that there is a developmental change toward increased perception of the dimensional structure of stimuli. This developmental change in perceived stimulus structure may be at least partly responsible for the developmental trend toward greater selectivity observed in studies of attention to experimenter-designated information.

Development of Flexibility in Attention to Components

In the research discussed thus far we examined the nature of the functional stimulus for children under nonconstrained circumstances, or circumstances in which the children could discriminate among the stimuli according to their natural inclination. Just as important for understanding development of attentional capabilities is the study of children's flexibility of attention—the ease with which children alter the functional stimulus in response to varying task demands. The child who is inflexible tends to discriminate among stimuli in the same way in a variety of situations, whether or not it fits the specific requirements of the task to be performed. The child who is flexible, on the other hand, readily varies the manner in which he identifies the stimuli in accord with changing task demands. The research to be discussed in this section bears on the hypothesis that, as children grow older, they become more flexible in their manner of attention deployment.

Variation in Task Structure

The study by Hale and Taweel (1974a) was designed to find out not only how children would perform on the standard component selection task but also how they would perform on variants of this task that called for selective attention to a single component. The task variants were similar to the standard task in all major respects except that in the learning phase, the dominant component (shape or "picture") was defined as relevant, in that the subject was required to attend to this component in order to learn the first phase of the task. Labeled "incidental learning tasks," these two variants were structured in such a way that learning of information about the nondominant component (color or pattern) would be incidental, or nonfunctional, for successful performance of the learning phase. The test phase, identical for all groups, assessed retention of the individual stimulus attributes—i.e., each shape, color, picture, or pattern—in the manner described earlier.

Test scores for the dominant component proved to be relatively high and to show no consistent variation. The effects of greatest interest involved variation in scores for the nondominant component, color, or pattern. In the standard component selection task these scores increased with age. However, in the incidental learning tasks these scores generally remained constant across ages. (A comparable experimental manipulation in the study by Hale and Morgan, 1973, yielded similar developmental results.)

It will be recalled that in the incidental learning tasks the children had to attend to the dominant component in order for learning to occur. It would have been maladaptive for them to attend to more than this component. However, in the component selection task the two components were redundant and the children were free to discriminate among the stimuli in whatever way they chose. In this case it would have been adaptive for them to attend to both components, since discrimination among stimuli can be facilitated by utilizing all the redundant information available in the stimuli. The results indicate a developmentally increasing tendency for children to differentiate between these situations. While the younger children exercised selectivity in both situations, the older children tailored their manner of attention deployment to the task at hand. With age, children apparently develop increasing flexibility in the sense that they exercise selective attention when a selective approach is called for but exercise broader attention deployment when it can be advantageous to do so.

Instructional Effects

In the study just discussed we were interested in children's response to variation in attentional demands that were implicit in the structure of the tasks. We found that young children were relatively unresponsive to such variation and attended primarily to the dominant component of the stimuli, whatever the nature of the task. But while young children are not as responsive as older children to variation in attentional demands implicit in the task structure, we thought they might be just as capable of altering their approach to the stimuli in response to variation in explicitly stated attentional requirements. As part of a study on this issue (Hale, Taweel, Green, & Flaugher, 1978), we inquired whether children of various ages would increase their attention to the nondominant component of stimuli if specifically instructed to do so. We gave children a component selection task with colored shapes either according to the standard procedure or with instructions to attend to the nondominant color component in preparation for a test.

Results of the main study with 5- and 9-year-olds are depicted in Figure 1 (a separate substudy showed that 12-year-olds responded similarly to 9-year-olds). The data of initial interest are scores reflecting atten-

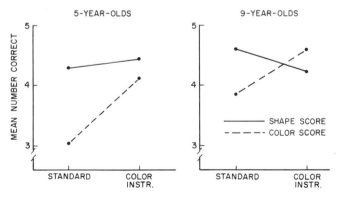

FIGURE 1. Mean correct responses to shapes and colors in test phase for each Age × Instruction subgroup. From study by Hale, Taweel, Green, and Flaugher. Copyright (1978) by the American Psychological Association. Reprinted by permission.

tion to the nondominant color component. As expected, the children increased their attention to this component in response to instructions emphasizing it. Especially notable is the fact that this effect was as great for the 5-year-olds as for the older children. It is clear, then, that young children are not totally lacking in attentional flexibility. Rather, they have control over their manner of attention deployment at least to the extent that they are capable of varying their attention to nondominant stimulus information if explicitly instructed to do so.

There was, nevertheless, a qualitative difference in the way the younger and older children responded to the instructions, as evidenced in scores for the dominant shape component. For the younger children, attention to this component was essentially unaffected by the instructions. For the older children, however, attention to shape decreased significantly in response to the instructions emphasizing color. It appears, therefore, that the older children employed a type of attentional "trading," in that they decreased attention to the dominant component along with increasing attention to the nondominant, or secondary, feature. Apparently, although both younger and older children can increase their attention to nondominant information emphasized by instructions, older children withdraw attention from the dominant component as they do so. They alter the functional stimulus to the extent that they adopt the secondary feature as the principal means of identifying the stimuli. This trend and its relevance to development of flexibility will be discussed further after consideration of some related evidence.[1]

Manipulation of Component Salience

Attentional flexibility can also be examined through manipulation of the stimuli themselves. The notion of developmentally increasing flexibility implies that, with age, children should become more responsive to

[1]The development of attentional trading has been discussed before (Hagen, 1972; Hagen & Hale, 1973) but in context of an individual-difference phenomenon: Beyond early adolescence, those individuals who showed a relatively high degree of attention to one stimulus component in incidental learning devoted relatively little attention to the other component, and vice versa. The general concept of "trading," however, also applies to children's response to changing task demands, where trading is defined as a reduction in attention to one component along with an increase in attention to another. According to the evidence considered here, this phenomenon becomes apparent with development, as does the phenomenon just discussed, but it emerges earlier—during the years between ages 5 and 9.

It is not claimed here that children below age 9 are totally incapable of attentional trading. To assess this possibility would require attempts to induce or to train such behavior in young children. But as a spontaneous reaction to varying task demands, trading of dominant for nondominant stimulus information is a response tendency that seems to appear between early and middle childhood.

TABLE I
Mean Test Scores for 5- and 9-Year-Olds under the Three Stimulus Conditions[a]

	5-year-olds			9-year-olds		
	S-S	S-F	N-F	S-S	S-F	N-F
Shape scores	4.6	4.4	2.9	4.7	4.7	1.8
Color scores	3.5	3.3	4.3	4.1	3.6	4.4

[a]Stimulus conditions are: (a) standard shapes with standard colors (S-S), (b) standard shapes with fluorescent colors (S-F), and (c) nonsense shapes with fluorescent colors (N-F). Data are for integrated stimuli in the study by Hale and Green (1976).

stimulus changes that make it advantageous to shift attention from one component to the other. As an example of such a change, it is possible to render the normally dominant component less salient than a secondary feature such as color, in the sense that shape is made a less useful cue for stimulus identification. To examine the developmental effects of such a manipulation, we gave children of various ages a component selection task under three stimulus conditions (Hale & Green, 1976). In the first condition, we employed the colored shapes from earlier studies. In the second, we used the same shapes but in fluorescent colors to make the color component stand out. In the third condition, we used nonsense figures in fluorescent colors (for comparison with the second condition), in order to render the shape component less useful as a cue for stimulus identification.

We found that, although fluorescence of color had little effect, replacement of the standard shapes with nonsense figures caused the children to adopt color as the primary cue for identifying the stimuli. As shown in Table I, scores for the color component increased from the second to the third stimulus condition, while scores for shape decreased. The result of greatest interest was a developmental change in response to the stimulus manipulation. The decrease in shape scores from the second to the third condition was about twice as great for the 9-year-olds as for the 5-year-olds, indicating a more pronounced reduction in attention to shape for the older than the younger children.

There is a striking parallel between this finding and the results of the instructional study. In that study, 9-year-olds showed a greater tendency than 5-year-olds to withdraw attention from shape when the instructions called for increasing attention to color. Here, the 9-year-olds showed a more marked reduction in attention to shape than did the 5-year-olds in response to a stimulus manipulation favoring a shift in attention toward color. Of course, there are differences in the nature of these two effects, but their similarities point to a general developmental phenomenon: With age, children become less reliant on the dominant component as the primary basis for stimulus discrimination when circumstances call for identifying stimuli by a secondary feature.

Related Literature

To our knowledge, effects of the above manipulations in component selection have not been examined in other developmental research. Although some studies have sought to determine the effects of salience manipulations on the way children discriminate among stimuli, these studies have used dimension preference tasks that, as will be argued below, often may be tapping nonattentional factors (see "A Further Issue . . .") Nevertheless, two indirectly related lines of research are worth looking at here, in that they bear on the general issue of flexibility in children's attention to components. One of these is the research of Pick and her associates on effects of instructional set in stimulus discrimination (Pick, Christy, & Frankel, 1972; Pick & Frankel, 1973, 1974). These investigators looked at second- and sixth-grade children's speed of responding when asked to indicate whether a pair of stimuli (animal pictures varying in shape, color, and size) matched on a component specified by the experimenter. The component was specified before the stimuli were presented in one condition, and afterwards in another, so that in the former condition it was advantageous for the subjects to attend selectively, whereas in the latter condition attention to all components was required at the time of stimulus inspection. The results suggested a greater tendency for the older than the younger children to vary their response speed across conditions. As Pick and her colleagues conclude, older children seem to adjust their attentional strategy to the demands of the task more readily than do younger children, thus evincing greater flexibility and adaptability of attention.

Another pertinent line of research involves the effects of component dominance in discrimination learning (here dominance or salience is usually defined for each subject individually). Odom and Mumbauer (1971) and Smiley (1973) used discrimination learning tasks with colored shapes and found that the rate of learning increased significantly between age 6 and adulthood when the *nondominant* feature was relevant for task solution but not when the dominant component was relevant. Using a memory task with four-component stimuli, Odom (1972) also found that after initial experience with this task, children showed developmental improvement in recall of task-relevant information only when a nondominant component was relevant. These results all suggest that early school-aged children as well as older children have relatively little difficulty performing tasks that call for attention to a dominant stimulus component. However, there is marked developmental improvement in performance when children must focus on the component to which they do not normally direct their attention.

General Conclusions on Development of Flexibility

Our own data and that just cited suggest that, with development, children become more flexible in attention deployment and that, in particular, they develop increasing flexibility in the way they distribute attention between dominant and nondominant stimulus information. To understand the significance of this trend it is important to consider the difference in functions served by the dominant and nondominant components of stimulus objects. A dominant component is the principal basis on which a stimulus object is normally identified. A nondominant or secondary feature, on the other hand, can aid in, but is not integral to, identification of the stimulus. The evidence discussed here bears on how readily children counteract their natural inclination to identify stimuli by a normally dominant component. Apparently children around age 5 rely on this component as the principal basis for stimulus identification, despite changing task demands. With age, however, children become less rigidly reliant on the dominant component, more readily withdrawing attention from this component when it becomes adaptive to identify stimuli by another feature.

It has often been said that young children seem to be "stimulus bound," and that, as children grow older, their behavior is guided to a greater extent by their thought processes and to a lesser extent by the specific stimuli put before them. However, we would agree with Gibson (1969) that the developmental changes lie not so much in the degree to which behavior is controlled by the stimulus as in the child's ability to extract the most useful information from the stimulus. If young children can be said to be bound by anything, it is not the stimulus as a whole but its *dominant aspect*—the feature that normally serves as its chief defining characteristic. As children grow older they can more readily redefine the functional stimulus, reversing the roles of the stimulus components and adopting a secondary feature as the principal identifying characteristic of the stimulus when it becomes useful to do so.

A Further Issue in Measuring Attention to Components: Dimension Preferences

It is of value to return to the question posed at the outset of this chapter: How do children typically discriminate among multicomponent stimuli? It was noted above that relatively little research had been devoted to this question. There is, however, one line of research that has often been cited as bearing on this issue, particularly in relation to studying developmental changes during the preschool years. This is the research falling under the rubric "dimension preferences." Since there is a quite substantial literature on this topic, it is important to look into this body of research and to consider how it relates to the issue of interest here.

In the most commonly used dimension preference task, a child is shown three stimuli, one of which is identical to the second stimulus on one component (dimension) and identical to the third stimulus on another component. He is asked to identify two stimuli that are most alike. Subjects generally match on the same component across several stimulus presentations (e.g., Suchman & Trabasso, 1966a), so that most subjects can be classified as showing a consistent preference for one component over another. The result of particular interest here is an often-reported developmental effect: With stimuli differing in shape and color, there is a shift from matching on color to matching on shape during the 3-to-6-year age period (Brian & Goodenough, 1929; Corah, 1966; Harris, Schaller, & Mitler, 1970; Suchman & Trabasso, 1966a). It has frequently been concluded that over the preschool years there is a fundamental change in the way children deploy attention in discriminating among stimuli.

It will be argued here that the dimension preference matching task may not be suited to testing hypotheses about attention development. It is acknowledged that attentional factors play some role in the matching response, as shown in the observed relationships between the matching task and such attention-related measures as concept identification (Suchman & Trabasso, 1966b; Trabasso, Stave, & Eichberg, 1969) and optional shift tasks (Brown, 1970; Trabasso et al., 1969). But it is our contention that as children grow older their performance on the matching task comes to be determined not only by their natural inclination to attend to a particular component but also by nonattentional factors related to decision processes and interpretation of task demands. Such factors, we feel, play a major part in children's increasing preference to match stimuli by shape rather than color or other features.

Before further discussion of this point, it is necessary first to consider three studies in which we have examined children's stimulus-matching behavior, as well as to consider some related literature. In the first study (Hale & Lipps, 1974) we sought to determine whether the matching and component selection tasks would elicit similar developmental results, by giving both tasks to children $3^1/2$ to $6^1/2$ years of age. We did find a relation between tasks for children below the median age of 4.8 years; shape-matching subjects showed higher scores for shape than color on the component selection task, while color-matching subjects showed slightly higher color than shape scores. However, when we examined developmental changes in performance we found that, while a shift from color to shape dominance was clearly evident in the dimension-preference data, no such shift was apparent in the component selection results. The shape scores averaged higher than the color scores, and the degree of difference between these two scores did not change with age. We concluded that somewhat different factors must underlie the developmental functions observed with these two measures.

A second piece of evidence comes from supplementary analyses in the salience study discussed above (these analyses are reported in Hale & Green, 1974). Recall that subjects were given a component selection task with stimuli consisting of (a) standard shapes and colors, (b) standard shapes and fluorescent colors, or (c) nonsense shapes and fluorescent colors. Immediately following this task, each group was given a dimension-preference matching task in which the stimuli consisted of the shapes and colors that were encountered in the component selection task. We found that, while the stimulus differences had a marked effect on scores in the component selection task (see above), those differences had little effect on the matching responses of children at either age 5 or age 9. The children matched stimuli predominantly on the basis of shape with all three types of stimuli. A separate sample of 5- and 8-year-olds given only the dimension preference task with the first and third types of stimuli also matched primarily by shape in both cases.

In a third study (Hale, n.d.) the effects of component salience on stimulus matching were examined and response latencies were recorded. Salience of shape relative to color was manipulated by varying the degree of difference between the shapes. In the standard condition the stimuli were a square and a circle; in another condition, they were squares with rounded corners, which differed in degree of curvature. The results showed no effect of the stimulus manipulation on the children's overt matching response, as both 5- and 8-year-olds matched stimuli primarily on the basis of shape regardless of the specific stimuli used. However, the latency of response was considerably longer in the condition in which the shapes were relatively similar than in the standard condition. Clearly, the children were affected by the manipulation of component salience, even though this effect was not manifested in their overt matching responses.

These last two studies suggest that color versus shape matching may be generally insensitive to manipulations of component salience for children of ages 5 and 8 or 9. Other researchers have also looked for effects of component salience on color versus shape matching but usually have not demonstrated, or have not assessed, such effects for children age 5 and older. Corah (1966) varied the complexity and degree of difference between shapes. Although he observed an effect of these manipulations for the younger children (mean age, $4^{1}/_{2}$ years) he found that in the older group (mean age, $8^{1}/_{2}$ years) all but 3 of the 144 subjects across all conditions matched exclusively by shape. In two other studies, shape–color preferences were found to be affected by the difference between levels of a dimension (Huang, 1945) and by the symmetry of the shapes (Suchman & Trabasso,

1966a); however, subjects in each of these studies ranged only from 3 to 6 years of age, and it was not possible to determine the effects for 5- to 6-year-olds alone. One study (Corah & Gross, 1967) did find that heightening the stimulus contrast by introducing brightness variation increased 5- to 7-year-olds' tendency to match stimuli by color. On the whole, however, there is little evidence to show that shape versus color matching in children age 5 and older is very sensitive to salience manipulations.

These various bits of evidence, we feel, raise some questions as to the meaning of shape versus color matching, particularly for drawing developmental conclusions about attention. We would hypothesize that the often-observed shift from color to shape matching does not reflect a basic developmental change in children's inclination to attend to one component rather than the other in discriminating among stimuli. Rather, it reflects a change in children's interpretation of the task demands, such that, for the older child more than the younger, the matching response is determined by a decision as to the kind of response he thinks the experimenter wants of him. As evidence for this point, consider the effects of the component-salience manipulations for children beyond age 5—manipulations that might be expected to make the stimuli more conducive to discrimination on one component or another. Such manipulations affected the way these children discriminated among the stimuli in the component selection task, and they influenced the latency of the children's response in the matching task. But they generally failed to affect the overt matching response itself. These findings suggest that beyond preschool age, children make the decision that the matching task requires a response to the shape component of the stimuli, and they act according to this decision whether or not the stimuli are readily conducive to discrimination by shape, and whether or not it takes some time to make such a response. That a considered decision enters into the matching response for an older child is also suggested in the fact that older children tend to respond more slowly than younger children in color and shape matching (Corah, 1964; Odom & Guzman, 1972). Further, informal observation shows that, when asked for a matching response, older children often ask a question such as "Do you mean the same color or the same shape?", then typically match on shape after the instructions are repeated (Hale & Lipps, 1974). It would appear that older children are very much aware of the possibility of matching on color as well as shape but interpret the instructions not as calling for an immediate, spontaneous reaction to the stimuli but as requiring them to make a carefully chosen response based on their assumptions as to the purpose of the task.

This is by no means an original conclusion. Indeed, Brian and Goodenough (1929) years ago said of the color–form shift, "Intellection rather than perception appeared to become more and more the dominant element in determining the choice" (p. 200). The intent here is simply to question a view implicit in many recent discussions of this finding, that the shift indicates a basic developmental change in the way children deploy attention when distinguishing among stimulus objects.

The question of whether there is such a developmental change, we feel, is more appropriately addressed with a task that allows subjects to discriminate among stimuli according to their natural inclination and minimizes the possibility of age differences in interpretation of the task instructions. One type of dimension preference task that does seem to meet these requirements is the opposed cues task, exemplified in the work of Sandra Smiley (1972a,b). It consists of two phases, a learning phase with stimuli containing two redundant components, followed by a test in which the attribute pairings are switched (e.g., yellow circle and blue square now become blue circle and yellow square); test responses indicate which component was dominant in learning. Unfortunately, the task has not, to our knowledge, been used to examine developmental shifts in attention during the preschool years, as it has been used primarily to study attention in older children (Brown, 1970; Gliner, Pick, Pick, & Hales, 1969; Smiley, 1972a, b; Smiley & Weir, 1966). Research using this type of task with preschoolers would be of great value in assessing early developmental changes in children's attention to stimulus components.

The component selection task was also designed to meet the requirements just specified. Observe that it is very similar to the opposed cues task, differing mainly in the fact that the test phase calls for a response to each component separately rather than a forced-choice response to the dominant component. To determine which component is dominant, scores for the two components can be compared. Toward this objective we gave a component selection task to children between 3 and 6 years of age in the above-mentioned study by Hale and Lipps (1974). We found that there was no appreciable age difference in the relative magnitudes of scores for shape and color, suggesting little developmental change during this age period in the way children distribute their attention between these two components. Additional work is needed before firm conclusions can be drawn. Preliminarily, these results give reason to question the view that around age 4 or 5, there is a basic change in the way children deploy attention when distinguishing among stimuli. Whether there is a developmental change in this respect during the preschool years is an issue that we feel is still very much open to investigation.

Concluding Remarks

Investigators of children's attention have often emphasized the development of children's ability to exercise selective attention, where such an ability is measured by tasks requiring attention to designated stimulus information. We believe that observed developmental changes on such tasks are best understood as part of a more general trend toward greater flexibility of attention. As children grow older they become better able to accommodate to the attentional requirements of a task, exercising selective attention when necessary, but also exercising broad attention deployment when it is advantageous to do so.

The development of attentional flexibility includes an increasing readiness to alter the functional stimulus. Typically, the dominant component of a stimulus serves as its principal identifying characteristic. With development, children more readily modify their manner of stimulus identification when it is useful to do so, withdrawing attention from the dominant component as they adopt another feature as the major identifying aspect of the stimulus. In short, children develop increasing flexibility to identify the stimulus in a manner that fits the demands of the task at hand.

In our research we have looked at how children attend to the components of stimuli and how they vary their attention with changing circumstances. In general, we conclude that a comprehensive view of attention development must take into account the variety of developing skills that contribute to flexible and efficient deployment of attention. Through continued research on important situational and stimulus variables, we hope to reach a better understanding of the factors underlying children's increasingly more efficient visual interaction with their world.

References

Baumeister, A. A., Berry, F. M., & Forehand, R. Effects of secondary cues on rote verbal learning of retardates and normal children. *Journal of Comparative and Physiological Psychology*, 1969, *69*, 273–280.

Berry, F. M., & Baumeister, A. A. Paired-associate learning by normal children and retardates with relevant redundant compound stimuli. *Journal of Experimental Child Psychology*, 1973, *15*, 63–76.

Berry, F. M., Joubert, C. E., & Baumeister, A. A. Single-letter selection in paired-associate learning by retardates as a function of degree of learning. *Journal of General Psychology*, 1972, *87*, 145–146. (a)

Berry, F. M., Joubert, C. E., & Baumeister, A. A. Stimulus selection and meaningfulness at different stages of paired-associate learning. *Journal of Experimental Psychology*, 1972, *95*, 189–194. (b)

Brian, C. R., & Goodenough, F. L. The relative potency of color and form perception at various ages. *Journal of Experimental Psychology*, 1929, *12*, 197–213.

Broadbent, D. E. *Decision and stress*. New York: Academic, 1971.

Brown, A. L. The stability of dimensional preference following oddity training. *Journal of Experimental Child Psychology*, 1970, *9*, 239–252.

Corah, N. L. Color and form in children's perceptual behavior. *Perceptual and Motor Skills*, 1964, *18*, 313–316.

Corah, N. L. The influence of some stimulus characteristics on color and form perception in nursery-school children. *Child Development*, 1966, *37*, 205–211.

Corah, N. L., & Gross, J. B. Hue, brightness, and saturation variables in color–form matching. *Child Development*, 1967, *38*, 137–142.

Eimas, P. Multiple-cue discrimination learning in children. *Psychological Record*, 1969, *19*, 417–424.

Ellis, J. A., & Thieman, T. J. Stimulus selection in children. *Bulletin of the Psychonomic Society*, 1976, *8*, 127–128.

Garner, W. R. *The processing of information and structure*. Potomac, Md.: Lawrence Erlbaum, 1974.

Gibson, E. J. *Principles of perceptual learning and development*. New York: Appleton-Century-Crofts, 1969.

Gliner, C. R., Pick, A. D., Pick, H. L., & Hales, J. J. A developmental investigation of visual and haptic preferences for shape and texture. *Monographs of the Society for Research in Child Development*, 1969, *34* (6, Serial No. 130).

Hagen, J. W. Strategies for remembering. In S. Farnham-Diggory (Ed.), *Information processing in children*. New York: Academic, 1972, pp. 65–78.

Hagen, J. W., & Hale, G. A. The development of attention in children. In A. D. Pick (Ed.), *Minnesota symposia on child psychology* (Vol. 7). Minneapolis: University of Minnesota Press, 1973, pp. 117–140.

Hale, G. A. *Children's dimension preferences: Effects of dimensional salience on latency of response*. Unpublished study, n.d.

Hale, G. A., & Green, R. Z. Children's attention to stimulus components with variation in relative salience of components and degree of stimulus integration. Research Bulletin 74–34. Princeton, N.J.: Educational Testing Service, 1974.

Hale, G. A., & Green, R. Z. Children's attention to stimulus components with variation in relative salience of components and degree of stimulus integration. *Journal of Experimental Child Psychology*, 1976, *21*, 446–459.

Hale, G. A., & Lipps, L. E. Stimulus matching and component selection: Alternative approaches to measuring children's attention to stimulus components. *Child Development*, 1974, *45*, 383–388.

Hale, G. A., & Morgan, J. S. Developmental trends in children's component selection. *Journal of Experimental Child Psychology*, 1973, *15*, 302–314.

Hale, G. A., & Piper, R. A. Developmental trends in children's incidental learning: Some critical stimulus differences. *Developmental Psychology*, 1973, *8*, 327–335.

Hale, G. A., & Taweel, S. S. Age differences in children's performance on measures of component selection and incidental learning. *Journal of Experimental Child Psychology*, 1974, *18*, 107–116. (a)

Hale, G. A., & Taweel, S. S. Children's component selection with varying degrees of training. *Journal of Experimental Child Psychology*, 1974, *17*, 229–241. (b)

Hale, G. A., Taweel, S. S., Green, R. Z., & Flaugher, J. Effects of instructions on children's attention to stimulus components. *Developmental Psychology*, 1978, *14*, 499–506.

Harris, L., Schaller, M. J., & Mitler, M. M. The effects of stimulus type on performance in a color–form sorting task with preschool, kindergarten, first-grade, and third-grade children. *Child Development*, 1970, *41*, 177–191.

Houston, J. P. Stimulus selection as influenced by degrees of learning, attention, prior associations, and experience with the stimulus components. *Journal of Experimental Psychology*, 1967, *73*, 509–516.

Huang, I. Abstraction of form and color in children as a function of the stimulus objects. *Pedagogical Seminar and Journal of Genetic Psychology*, 1945, *66*, 59–62.

James, C. T., & Greeno, J. G. Stimulus selection at different stages of paired-associate learning. *Journal of Experimental Psychology*, 1967, *74*, 75–83.

Odom, R. D. Effects of perceptual salience on the recall of relevant and incidental dimensional values: A developmental study. *Journal of Experimental Psychology*, 1972, *92*, 285–291.

Odom, R. D., & Guzman, R. D. Development of hierarchies of dimensional salience. *Developmental Psychology*, 1972, *6*, 271–287.

Odom, R. D., & Mumbauer, C. C. Dimensional salience and identification of the relevant dimension in problem solving: A developmental study. *Developmental Psychology*, 1971, *4*, 135–140.

Pick, A. D., & Frankel, G. W. A study of strategies of visual attention in children. *Developmental Psychology*, 1973, *9*, 348–357.

Pick, A. D., & Frankel, G. W. A developmental study of strategies of visual selectivity. *Child Development*, 1974, *45*, 1162–1165.

Pick, A. D., Christy, M. D., & Frankel, G. W., A developmental study of visual selective attention. *Journal of Experimental Child Psychology*, 1972, *14*, 165–176.

Richardson, J. Cue effectiveness and abstraction in paired-associate learning. *Psychological Bulletin*, 1971, *75*, 73–91.

Schrover, L. R., & Newsom, C. D., Overselectivity, developmental level and overtraining in autistic and normal children. *Journal of Abnormal Child Psychology*, 1976, *4*, 289–298.

Shepp, B. E., Kemler, D. G., & Anderson, D. R. Selective attention and the breadth of learning: An extension of the one-look model. *Psychological Review*, 1972, *79*, 317–328.

Shepp, B. E., & Swartz, K. B. Selective attention and the processing of integral and nonintegral dimensions: A developmental study. *Journal of Experimental Child Psychology*, 1976, *22*, 73–85.

Smiley, S. S. Instability of dimensional preference following changes in relative cue similarity. *Journal of Experimental Child Psychology*, 1972, *13*, 394–403. (a)

Smiley, S. S. Optional shift behavior as a function of dimensional preference and relative cue similarity. *Journal of Experimental Child Psychology*, 1972, *14*, 313–322. (b)

Smiley, S. S. Optional shift behavior as a function of age and dimensional dominance. *Journal of Experimental Child Psychology*, 1973, *16*, 451–458.

Smiley, S. S., & Weir, M. W. Role of dimensional dominance in reversal and nonreversal shift behavior. *Journal of Experimental Child Psychology*, 1966, *4*, 296–307.

Smith, L. B., & Kemler, D. G. Developmental trends in free classification: Evidence for a new conceptualization of perceptual development. *Journal of Experimental Child Psychology*, 1977, *24*, 279–298.

Solso, R. L. Stimulus selection by five-, seven-, and nine-year-old children. *American Journal of Psychology*, 1970, *83*, 216–221.

Suchman, R. G., & Trabasso, T. Color and form preference in young children. *Journal of Experimental Child Psychology*, 1966, *3*, 177–187. (a)

Suchman, R. G., & Trabasso, T. Stimulus preference and cue function in young children's concept attainment. *Journal of Experimental Child Psychology*, 1966, *3*, 188–198. (b)

Tighe, T. J., & Tighe, L. S. Stimulus control in children's learning. In A. D. Pick (Ed.), *Minnesota symposia on child psychology* (Vol. 6). Minneapolis: University of Minnesota Press, 1972, pp. 128–157.

Trabasso, T., & Bower, G. H. *Attention in learning: Theory and research*. New York: Wiley, 1968.

Trabasso, T., Stave, M., & Eichberg, R. Attribute preference and discrimination shifts in young children. *Journal of Experimental Child Psychology*, 1969, *8*, 195–209.

Wichawut, C., & Martin, E. Selective stimulus encoding and overlearning in paired-associate learning. *Journal of Experimental Psychology*, 1970, *85*, 383–388.

Wilhelm, H., & Lovaas, O. L. Stimulus overselectivity: A common feature in autism and mental retardation. *American Journal of Mental Deficiency*, 1976, *81*, 227–241.

Zeaman, D., & House, B. J. The role of attention in retardate discrimination learning. In N. R. Ellis (Ed.), *Handbook of mental deficiency*. New York: McGraw-Hill, 1963, pp. 159–223.

4

A Constructivist Account of the Development of Perception, Attention, and Memory

John T. Collins and John W. Hagen

Introduction

In their commerce with the world human beings come into contact with a seemingly endless array of people, objects, and events, some of which they notice and some of which they overlook, some of which they attend to and some of which they ignore, some of which they remember and some of which they forget. It is a truism to say that a great deal of perceptual/ cognitive work goes on in everyday existence. The nature of the processes involved in relating to the environment and the way they operate have, of course, long been issues of considerable interest among psychologists of many persuasions (see Kahneman, 1973; Keele, 1973; Klatzky, 1975; Turvey, 1975, for reviews of various positions).

In this chapter we are concerned with the development of memory and attention. These phenomena will be treated here not as independent entities but rather as integral and natural concomitants of the perceptual process. Our thesis is that perceptual development is characterized by two qualitative changes of process and that the development of memory and attention, in turn, is marked by two qualitative changes. The discussion will be limited primarily to the visual modality, although the implications no doubt extend beyond vision. Theory and research from both developmental and adult literature will be drawn upon. We begin with a statement of the thesis and then consider the rationale behind it, elaborating the proposed pattern of development.

John T. Collins and John W. Hagen • University of Michigan, Ann Arbor, Michigan 48109. This manuscript was prepared while both authors were supported in part by Grant 1T 32HD07109-01 United States Public Health Service.

The Thesis

Nonconscious versus Conscious Perception

Today few would endorse William James's famous description of the infant's world as a "blooming, buzzing confusion." From birth the human organism takes an active role in selectively attending to and organizing portions of the myriad of information that bombards the senses. The memorial consequences of the patterned interchanges with the environment, themselves influencing subsequent perceptual activity, are in evidence very early (see Cohen & Gelber, 1975; Frantz, Fagan, & Miranda, 1975; Haith & Campos, 1976; Salapatek, 1975, for reviews of infant perceptual/cognitive capabilities).

How, then, are we to describe the young infant's experience of the world, now that we have seen the early search for contour (Fantz *et al.,* 1975; Maurer, 1975) and are divested of the "preconception . . . that the visual field of the young infant [is] a formless blur" (Fantz *et al.,* 1975, p. 340)? Would the ascription of order and structure to early experience, albeit of a primitive sort, rectify our conception?

It is our contention that a qualitative change occurs during the course of perceptual development, before which all other changes, important though they may be, pale in significance: Perception becomes conscious. We shall argue that this major event occurs in the 8-to-12-month range. Until the infant has made the transition his or her experience is unimaginable. Nonconscious perception is by nature beyond imagination: Anything imaginable will necessarily incorporate conscious input and will, therefore, be totally inappropriate. Thus we ought to confine ourselves to a description of early infant processes and not try to describe, except perhaps metaphorically, early infant experience.

Conscious perception, we maintain, is the product of efferent motor processes. Infants are not born with such processes; they must acquire them. Once these processes are incorporated into the perceptual act, the course of the subsequent development of perception, memory, and attention is set. Before delineating the path from the nonconscious, primitive organism to the mature, conscious information processor, let us define several terms that will be used frequently in our discussion.

Under the rubric "conscious" we wish to include all perceptual processing for which there is the *slightest* awareness, however dim. A great deal of perceptual/cognitive processing that others often do not associate with the term falls into that category. Frequently the word is used to distinguish between limited-capacity, higher order processing that engages our selective attention, and low-level processing that is meted out to information for which we have only a very dim "background" awareness. This view proposes that there are levels of processing and of consciousness, and only the higher levels are referred to as conscious. In contrast, the distinction that we have in mind is much more basic. Rather than distinguishing among levels of awareness, it discriminates between awareness and nonawareness.

It will be helpful to contrast our intended dichotomy with Neisser's (1967) distinction between focal and preattentive processing (a distinction that has parallels in a number of attentional theories, e.g., Broadbent, 1958, 1970, 1971; Atkinson & Shiffrin, 1968; Norman, 1970; Treisman, 1969). According to Neisser, focal processes operate on a limited region of the visual field, usually serially, and most often require attention (and are thus often described as conscious in the sense in which the word is commonly used). Preattentive processes, on the other hand, operate upon large areas of the visual field (including the periphery), performing such basic tasks as the separation of figure from ground, and providing the aliment upon which the focal processes operate. They function automatically, in parallel, and usually without drawing attention to themselves (and so are often described as unconscious in the sense in which the word is commonly used). While preattentive processes were said to perform the low-level tasks that must precede the focal processes, Neisser did not set an upper limit to their processing potential. He left open the possibility that some preattentive processes are fairly sophisticated, perhaps involving conceptual processing. Not all preattentive processes are innate, then; experience and acquired knowledge can add to the repertoire.

Our use of the word *conscious* cuts across the focal/preattentive distinction. That is, while it is certainly true that not all of the information in the visual field receives the same amount of attention and subsequent processing, it is the case that there is awareness of considerable information in the field at any given time. The effects of context on visual perception have been substantiated many times. Objects that engage focal processes are not experienced as if in isolation, so that when one looks at a chair, for example, the wall behind it does not disappear. Clearly, then, there is some awareness—however slight—for objects outside of the focal processes. Thus, the preattentive processes, or at least a subset of them, must be included under our definition of *conscious*.

It will also be helpful to point out now how the notion that perception becomes conscious relates to another closely allied developmental accomplishment with which it might mistakenly be equated: the separation of the infant from the environment. This important early task has been recognized for some time, since the portrayal of the infant as united with the world is hardly new. Neonatal life is often depicted by both cognitive (e.g., Piaget) and affective (e.g., Freud) theorists as a state in which there exists a primitive psychological unity between the organism and the environment. According to such theorists the development of self-concept and the differentiation of that self from the physical and social environment are important tasks on the agenda of the neonate. Those tasks constitute major developmental hurdles, the successful completion of which takes years.

Werner and Kaplan (1963), in a representative statement, describe the early stages of such development in terms of "distancing." Among the different kinds of distancing discussed is one between person and object. They write:

> The early objects, even on the human level, are probably much like the "things-of-action" characteristic of the infra-human level, that is, they are things of momentary affective striving and of biologically directed action. Perceptual presentations are assimilated to the ongoing, rapidly changing states and are apprehended in terms of those states. . . . In the initial phases of the transition from the apprehension of presented contents as pragmatic things-of-action to their comprehension as cognitive objects, the degree of subject–object differentiation remains relatively slight. . . . Gradually, however, a fundamental transformation in the relation of person and object occurs with the shift from ego-bound things-of-action to ego-distant objects-of-contemplation. . . . Implied in this change is the functional shift wherein the externalized sensory-motor pattern by which an object is initially grasped is transformed into an internalized schema. (p. 44)

According to this conceptualization there is a growing realization that there exist stable objects, enduring over time, localized in space, interacting and relating among themselves, independent of the self and of the action of the self, that, finally, can be contemplated.

The transition that is described in such accounts is the result of the organism's actively constructing and internalizing more knowledge *about* what has been perceived for some time beforehand. The infant comes to contemplate the environment as he or she gains and stores information that indicates that there are things to know about it. What we are suggesting goes further than that. Rather than being simply a further accretion of knowledge about what the infant is perceiving, the transition to which we have alluded, while dependent upon learned and internalized information such as Werner and Kaplan discuss, constitutes a change in the act of perceiving itself. Nonconscious perception becomes, to coin a term, *perception of contemplation*. Prior to this transition, primitive perceptual processes are manifested in infants' responses to stimulation. However, we would argue that this responsiveness is without awareness. The infant processes information without consciously experiencing it, just as a computer may be said to process without experience.

Another term that will be used extensively in the ensuing discussion is *efferent*. A rough equivalent to it is *outgoing*. In terms of information flow within the organism, it refers to that which originates within and moves outward, and it is to be contrasted with information that flows inward through afferent mechanisms.

Efferent motor commands are, in accordance with this definition, centrally innervated instructions to act. Efferent motor acts are centrally innervated action sequences. However, a refinement in this definition is imperative. The simple fact that efferent motor processes are involved in some way in a particular motor task does not necessarily imply that the task is being performed in an essentially efferent manner. If that were the case, few acts would be excluded. Indeed, even the reflexes that Piaget (1952) describes operate spontaneously. An action sequence will be considered efferent here if, in its interaction with the environment, a substantial portion of its accommodation to that environment is performed according to inner specifications. In other words, a motor sequence will be considered efferent insofar as it is based upon stored accommodations to the environment. While no act in a world of variation and particularity will be free from accommodation to immediate circumstances, only if stored accommodations play a significant role in a particular action will it be considered efferent.

A simplified version of a task used in an experiment by Festinger, Burnham, Ono, and Bamber (1967) will help clarify our use of the term. Let us suppose that subjects are asked to move a stylus several times between two curved metal rods, which are placed parallel and close together on a board, under either of two sets of instructions: (1) the leaning condition—the subject is to move quickly, resting the stylus upon, and being guided by the inside surface of one of the two rods; (2) the free movement condition—the subject is to move the stylus fluently and quickly, attempting to avoid contact with the rods, but without being unduly concerned if contact is made. The latter task, but not the former, will yield efferent processes according to our definition. In the leaning condition the accommodation to the curve is externally effected by the rod. Very little learning will be expected to result, as proprioceptive feedback will always suffice in task performance. A change in the configuration of the rods after several runs would pose very little problem for the subject. The free movement condition, in contrast, will encourage the learning and storage of accommodations for use in subsequent task performance. If, after practice, the arrangement of the rods is changed, the subject will experience difficulty and will be forced to slow down and learn the new pattern.

The important point here is that two movements, which look very much alike to an observer and yield very similar proprioceptive feedback, are very different acts in terms of the degree to which they can be considered efferent. The extent to which inner accommodations are formed and utilized is the distinguishing feature. It is clear that toward that end the subjects' level of active involvement in the respective tasks is different from the beginning. The leaning condition encourages a mere guided tracing action, while the free movement condition encourages a far more active imitation and results in robust stored accommodations.

Two Qualitative Transitions of Development: From Nonconscious to Focal Processing

The development of perception, attention, and memory is characterized by two important qualitative transitions. The first occurs around 8–12 months of age, as a result of the incorporation of the emerging ability to imitate accommodatively into the processes of perception, attention, and memory. At that time perceptual processing becomes motor-efferent and, as a result, conscious. Following shortly thereafter is the use of full representation in the Piagetian sense—that is, information that is the fruit of internalized motoric imitation and that can be elicited in the absence of the environmental counterpart. The second transition occurs more gradually, over a period of years, and serves to resolve a processing burden introduced by the first transition. It consists of a shift from inefficient, scattered processing to more efficient, automatized processing that makes focal attention possible. These transitions are best conceptualized within a constructivist model of development that emphasizes the interrelations among perception, attention, and memory as aspects of a unified cognitive system.

From Nonconscious to Conscious Perception. The first transition does not occur in a vacuum. Rather, it entails the incorporation of motor-efferent processes into a perceptual system that is already the product of prior developmental changes. While a number of unresolved issues remain in the study of early infancy, it is possible to summarize several major trends that have been discovered by a number of researchers in early (i.e., pretransitional) visual processing. We do so here not to offer a quick review of a complex literature—several reviews of which have already been written (e.g., Cohen & Gelber, 1975; Fantz et al., 1975; Haith & Campos, 1976; Salapatek, 1975)—but to provide a more complete picture of the development of visual perception and related attentional and memorial processes.

Visual attention and information processing in the young infant have been shown to be stimulus-bound, that is, dominated by the salience of various dimensions of stimuli—contrast, contour, movement, and the like (e.g., Fantz, 1958, 1961, 1963; Kessen, 1967). Visual accommodation is thus externally governed. Attention is usually focused on a narrow portion of the visual sensory input, and on parts rather than wholes (Salapatek, 1975). Visual memory capacities, difficult to assess in the very young infant, are certainly primitive. By about the 3rd month infants begin to exhibit a preference for novelty when given the choice of looking at either of two stimuli, one of which has already been viewed (Fantz, 1964). This preference, of course, implies memory (and is, in fact, an important diagnostic measure of infant memory capacities). In subsequent months a gradual improvement in visual memory capabilities occurs, reflecting, perhaps, greater neurological stability as well as more practice interacting with the environment. The available set of memory encodings increases, according to Eleanor Gibson (1969), as the infant learns to differentiate the various aspects of the stimuli he or she encounters. Visual attention becomes somewhat less bound to stimuli as "decision rules" develop (Olson, 1976) and are stored in long-term memory, making such determinations as whether a global or sequential analysis of a stimulus will be performed. These rules are strategies of information analysis (nonefferent) that give the system a more varied capability. Perceptual/cognitive development between 3 months and approximately 8 months can be characterized as gradual improvement, largely quantitative.

The transition that occurs at this point—as perception becomes conscious through the incorporation of accommodative imitation—is more than simply quantitative. Taken from the vantage point of the visual processing system, it is a discontinuous transition. While primitive oculomotor processes may already have played a role in visual processing, now sophisticated motor processes are put at the very center. Further, accommodative motor imitation is not a simple derivative of the visual perceptual system. While visual perceptual experience is normally very important to the development of imitative skills, vision stands as only one of the sense modalities providing afferent stimulation upon which the motor system operates. Imitative behavior is distinctly motoric, and it transcends particular modalities. Hence the introduction of accommodative imitation (and, subsequently, representation) into the perceptual processes may be regarded as the intrusion of one system into the affairs of the other.

It is also possible to characterize this transition as a move from a "bottom-up" orientation to perceptual processing (in which perception determines conception, or is primary) to a "top-down" orientation (in which conception determines perception). The use of stored accommodations and representations implies such a change. To characterize subsequent perceptual processing in this way is not to remove the perceiver from contact with the environment, however. Such a state of affairs would clearly be maladaptive. The move to top-down processing entails a subordination of afferent information to constructive processes, which come to play a primary role in perceptual processing. Although some processing of afferent information still must occur before efferent ascriptions are made, such processing yields no conscious perceptual experience.

Posttransitional attentional patterns and memories are likewise very different from preceding ones. They, too, undergo a transformation to top-down status as efferent motor processes come to govern the way in which the environment is attended to and remembered. Attention becomes more holistic. Memory traces that issue from perceptual experience are now mediated by motor processes that, in all probability, must also be brought to bear in later recognition or recall.

Memory may also be expected to become more robust, according to a "levels-of-processing" analysis (Craik & Lockhart, 1972). As accommodative imitation yields representations that can be elicited in the absence of the environmental counterpart, single representations may be formed that combine information from present stimulation with information elicited from memory. Such representations may contain information that is related conceptually or affectively without the prior stipulation that the information be received in spatial and temporal contiguity. They may also contain information as to the contrasts among objects of experience widely separated in space and time. If, as this model of memory claims, stimuli are remembered according to the depth to which they are processed, then the efferent application of these representations to afferent perceptual input, which is characteristic of posttransitional perception, will result in more robust memories.

From Scattered to Focal Processing. The second qualitative transition is of a more continuous nature and occurs over a long period of time. The major task accomplished is the resolution of problems of perception created by the first transition. We begin our discussion of this second transition by considering in some detail the problems that the earlier transition poses and the way the successful perceptual system copes with them. Then we shall be able to profile development schematically.

The breadth of the processing demands that are visited upon the perceptual system by the earlier transition is at the heart of the difficulties. The world, quite obviously, is not constituted of only a single object to be perceived, recognized, and remembered. Human beings live amid a multiplicity of objects and events, and each glimpse normally brings into consciousness a large amount of information. If efferent motor processing underlies *all* conscious perception, then clearly a mass of efferent information must be ascribed to afferent sensory input.

The mature perceptual system must do more than simply create a conscious perception of the visual field, however. The capacity to select a limited portion of that field for special (i.e., focal) attention and processing is ultimately essential for effective adaptation of the organism, and it must be supported by the perceptual system. But this requirement creates conflicting processing demands. On the one hand, the perceptual system is asked to perform widespread processing on sensory data (to create a conscious perception of the visual field), while on the other hand, it is asked to perform deeper processing on a more limited portion of the perceptual input. The conflict is exacerbated by the fact that extrafocal efferent ascription is not innate but learned. It may draw upon the processing resources of a limited capacity system, thus decreasing that system's capability for the more effortful focal processes.

This problem is compounded by the fact that perception is continuous over time and occurs amid the movement of both the perceiver and the environment. The perceiver, to remain attuned to reality, must continually update and renew the conscious visual field through efferent ascription. Efforts to specially process subsets of the visual field must be made while this updating is taking place. They will depend upon the functioning of extrafocal processes in such a way as to demand very little attention.

Extrafocal perceptual activity is most likely carried on in the mature system by multiple processing units acting in parallel. The positions of objects in the natural environment are often changing (consider, for example, the experience of walking in a crowd), and even the positions of stationary objects appear to change relative to one another as the observer moves. Thus, constant updating of perceptual representations seems to be necessary. While a single, unitary representation of all the information in a visual field might be useful as an initial means of making the perceiver conscious of the entire visual field, such a representation is unlikely to be of continuing value for perceptual processing. Instead, we believe that the processing demands created by constantly changing perceptual input can be met only through the functioning of multiple, parallel processing units. They must operate "silently," i.e., must not draw attention to themselves, or focal processing will be disrupted.

Visual attention can thus be seen as a function of the way in which extrafocal processing is performed, and focal processing, in turn, is contingent upon the way in which attention is allocated. How must extrafocal processing be performed so as to permit volitional, focal attention? Norman and Bobrow (1976) state:

> A task that is practiced for a sufficiently long period appears to become "automated": it can be performed with little or no conscious [i.e., focal, as we have used the term] attention. Novel tasks or unexpected aspects of familiar tasks demand conscious attention, and whatever demands are placed on conscious processing resources tend to cause severe interference with whatever other cognitive task is going on at the same time. (p. 115)

Perceptual processing, as it has been described here, is a complex task, a problem to be solved—or, more properly, many tasks and many problems to be solved simultaneously. The efferent matching of acquired motor information to sensory data is, moreover, a learned task, and it can be expected, according to this conceptualization, to call upon focal resources unless it has become automatic. The multiplicity of parallel processing units thus creates a situation in which numerous calls for focal processing resources are being made at once. The result is reciprocal interference among these units and immature focal processing potential. Even under conditions in which a unitary ascription of motor information to sensory data is feasible, no focal processing can be performed until the two are reasonably matched across the entire visual field. Until this matching process is practiced and efficient, focal processing is slow and difficult. Attention is scattered.

The degree to which efferent motor information is matched to sensory data varies according to where the information falls on the retina and whether it is in focus. If information is fixated and is of sufficient quality, the matching process is fairly complete: Efferent motor information is adapted and closely accommodated to the particular environment. The same is true for information outside, but in the vicinity of, the point of fixation. If, however, sensory information is of poor quality, falls on the periphery of the retina, or is sufficiently out of focus, then the degree to which the match can be made is limited. Under such circumstances motor information will be ascribed without much externally effected accommodation. The viewer either assigns motor information to the impoverished sensory data without checking its veracity or ascribes motor information that is so gross as to be unamenable to discreditation (e.g., "there is a 'thing' off to my right"). The fact that such processing is not veridical does not mean that it is maladaptive, since the information is of peripheral interest to the viewer. Moreover, important dimensions of the peripheral stimulation, such as movement, could be coded to call upon focal processes. Thus, the burden of the perceptual system to accurately ascribe motor information to sensory data is not as onerous as might be expected.

Consideration of all of the difficulties involved in conscious perceptual processing and of the sophistication of the measures required to resolve them suggests that infants undergo a difficult transitional period of development. Much of effortful perception becomes automatic and scattered attention becomes focused during this time, gradually yielding the capacity for more sophisticated focal processing. While the changes that effect the second of these transitions are largely quantitative, the organism comes to apprehend the world in a qualitatively different fashion: more selectively, as attention becomes progressively less scattered, and in greater depth, as focal attention comes to enhance processing capabilities.

Development proceeds as follows (several points made earlier are reiterated here to present a more complete picture): Visual attention and information processing in the earliest days of life are stimulus-bound, dominated by the salience of various dimensions of stimuli (e.g., contrast and contour). Attention is focused on limited subsets of the sensory input, on parts rather than wholes, and becomes less stimulus-bound as "decision rules" develop. These nonefferent strategies of information analysis give the system greater versatility, such as the option of holistic or sequential analysis, without burdening it.

Between 8 and 12 months the situation changes dramatically. As perception becomes conscious an explosion of processing demands occurs. The infant is for the first time pressed to analyze sensory data extensively, efferently ascribing motor information to it. The task is a new one for the infant, and one for which the necessary perceptual/cognitive equipment is

at best immature. Accommodative imitation has been added only recently
to the repertoire of infant capacities. The art of matching stored imitative
responses to sensory data is undeveloped. Furthermore, the repertoire of
stored imitations will at first be limited and therefore in need of constant
revision and updating, posing additional processing difficulties. Hence the
infant must use immature, ever-changing cognitive structures to perform *en
masse* processes that are new. The result is scattered attention, inefficient
perceptual processing, and an inability to sustain focal processes. If ever
there is a period of development that fits James's description of a
"blooming, buzzing confusion," it is here. The infant has acquired conscious visual experience but cannot control it, as processing demands divert
attention in various directions.

Upon the incorporation of imitative motor processes into visual perception the infant again becomes stimulus-bound, but in a different sense.
Assuming that the perceptual system from that point on attempts to bring
conscious life to all sensory data that it receives (though not focal attention), the infant will be forced to engage in extensive ascription and matching of motor information to it, depending upon the resolvability of the
sensory information. The accommodation of the motor information to the
particular environment is an ever-present and time-consuming task for the
infant. In this sense the infant is stimulus-bound.

Scattered attention and inefficient processing will be the norm until
such time as perceptual processing becomes well practiced and largely
automatic. Only then, after attention has been withdrawn from the ever
more efficient processes distributed about the visual field, will volitional,
focal attention add practical new processing capacities to the child's repertoire. The enhancement of memory capacities that occurs upon the acquisition of the ability to process information in more depth will reach fruition at
that time.

The development of automaticity is thus the primary task of the second
transition. While it depends upon practice and the stabilization of motor-
efferent information, the dynamics of the process remain to be further specified. Language and other perceptual/cognitive capacities may well play
roles in this move toward automaticity.

The development of the visual perceptual system to the point at which
it can practicably sustain focal processes resolves processing demands
without eliminating them. The perceptual system's first task is always to
make perception of the visual field conscious. Thus, even in mature perceptual processing the initial stages will be devoted to those global efferent
motor ascriptions that are maximally inclusive of sensory data, thereby
quickly bringing large amounts of information to consciousness. Following
closely thereafter are the more limited, precise ascriptions that were said to
function in parallel. The degree to which the processor is aware of the

preliminary global ascriptions is contingent upon the level of automaticity in their use.

Empirical and Theoretical Underpinnings

The whole of the thesis just outlined revolves around the belief that motor efference is central to conscious visual experience. Further, in our specification of the developmental pattern accommodative imitation was identified as the key motor component. In this section we attempt to support our position vis-à-vis these issues.

Motor Efference as the Key to the Conscious Experience of Perception

The notion that motor efference is central to the conscious experience of perception is not new. Because of the importance of this point to the whole thesis, we begin with a summary of its history. Festinger *et al.* (1967) have provided a thorough review of the relevant literature. We shall summarize their major points here.

Near the beginning of this century several theorists proposed that afferent stimulation (not necessarily visual) was made conscious by outgoing motor innervation. Münsterberg (1899), for example, claimed that afferent and efferent information flow were part of a continuous, unitary neural process, with no clear demarcation between them. Motor discharge was seen as indispensible to conscious perception. Montague (1908) wrote: "Perceptions are presumed to arise synchronously with the redirection in the central nervous system of afferent currents into efferent channels" (p. 128, cited in Festinger *et al.*, 1967, p. 2).

Such views fell into disrepute for several reasons. First, the rise of behaviorism eclipsed the scientific inquiries into consciousness of which these theories were part and parcel. In addition, the theories seemed unable to cope with certain data. For example, Münsterberg's (1900) claim that vividness of experience is a function of the freedom of the motor pathway to discharge was contradicted by the fact that well-practiced skills, such as violin playing, yield progressively less focal awareness of movement. Washburn (1916) thus later offered the alternative suggestion that an optimal amount of interference with motor discharge creates the most vivid experience. Whatever the case, a very important problem with such theories lay in the fact that conscious perceptual experience is clearly not always accompanied by observable movement. The absence of overt action sequences forced the postulation of rudimentary or tentative movement. Festinger *et al.* (1967) describe the situation at this point: "The relationship between the conscious experience of perception and such motor move-

ments . . . remained hypothetical and, to modern psychologists, implaus-
ible" (p. 2).

Yet another factor probably contributed to the abandonment of these
theories. Until the end of the 19th century many psychologists accepted
Helmholtz's (1856) view that centrally innervated motor commands can be
consciously experienced. Then James (1890), and later Sherrington (1900),
argued successfully that such is not the case, and that only afferent sensory
input yields consciousness. With this resolution of the issue, interest in the
contribution of efferent processes waned. Recent evidence, however, summarized by Merton (1964) and Festinger and Canon (1965), indicates that
James and Sherrington were wrong. The organism apparently can be consciously aware of efferent commands without concomitant afferent
information.

An incidental observation made by Campbell, Sanderson, and Laverty
(1964) supports the notion that one can have conscious experience of limb
movement via efferent motor commands alone. In an experiment reported
by these authors five subjects received a drug that paralyzes the skeletal
musculature but does not anesthetize or eliminate awareness for surrounding events. The experimenters observed:

> The subjects described their movements (during the paralysis) as part of a
> struggle to get away from the apparatus and to tear off the wires and electrodes.
> Though in fact their movements were small and poorly controlled the subjects
> were under the impression they had been making large movements. (p. 632,
> cited in Festinger et al., 1967, p. 5)

Their conscious experience was apparently based upon efferent output.

In a less traumatic situation, without the use of a paralyzing agent,
Merton (1964) showed that a subject whose thumb has been anesthetized
by the application of a tourniquet around the wrist, but who can still move it
with approximately the same accuracy as before, believes that he or she has
moved it when, in fact, it has been restrained. Again, efferent output to the
motor system seems to be the source of conscious experience.

J. J. Gibson (1933) also made an observation that seems to indicate the
central role of efference. He investigated the possible role of kinesthesis in
visual adaptation. Previous research had shown that subjects who wore
wedge prism spectacles, which caused vertical straight lines to appear
curved, adapted over time, and the lines began to appear less curved. Gibson hypothesized that this adaptation results from a conflict between vision
and kinesthesis, with kinesthesis predominating and correcting vision. According to the hypothesis, if visually curved lines *feel* straight the visual
system is corrected. To test the hypothesis, Gibson asked spectacled subjects to run their hands along vertical edges. The result:

> It was discovered . . . that in actual fact the kinaesthetic perception, in so far as it
> was consciously represented, did *not* conflict with the visual perception. When a

> visually curved edge such as a meter stick was felt, it was felt *as curved.* This
> was true as long as the hand was watched while running up and down the edge.
> If the eyes were closed or turned away, the edge of course felt straight, as it in
> reality was. This dominance of the visual over the kinaesthetic perception was so
> complete that when subjects were instructed to make a strong effort to dissociate
> the two, *i.e.,* to "feel it straight and see it curved," it was reported either difficult
> or impossible to do so. (pp. 4–5, cited in Festinger *et al.,* 1967, p. 4)

An explanation of these results can be found within the context of efferent
theories of perception: The subject does not experience the externally effected kinesthetic accommodations. Rather, the subject experiences the internal accommodations that form in response to the visual input and are efferently issued to the limb.

In regard to visual perception, which is of foremost concern here,
efference theories run into difficulties. How, for example, is color vision to
be explained? Even if we are willing to ignore that issue there is another
important problem: It is clear that actual eye movements are not necessary
for perceptual experience. Contours, for example, can be perceived even
when a steady point of fixation is maintained. How then can a motor theory
be viable?

The answer that has been suggested by a number of theorists throughout the century is that "readiness" to issue motor-efferent commands underlies visual perception. As early as 1899 Breese offered that view, and
more recently Sperry (1952) wrote:

> If there be any objectively demonstrable fact about perception that indicates the
> nature of the neural process involved, it is the following: Insofar as an organism
> perceives a given object, it is prepared to respond with reference to it. This
> preparation-to-respond is absent in an organism that has failed to perceive. . . .
> The presence or absence of adaptive reaction potentialities of this sort, ready to
> discharge into motor patterns, makes the difference between perceiving and not
> perceiving. (p. 301, cited in Festinger *et al.,* 1967, p. 6)

Taylor (1962) evaluated existing data and concluded that all conscious
visual perception consists of learned motor responses to sensory input. The
developing organism gradually learns to make appropriate eye movements,
almost automatically taking into account head and body position. Over
time, well-learned response tendencies, referred to as "engrams," are
formed, and when well practiced, are automatically activated by sensory
input. A number of engrams are said to be activated at any given time. A
person thus experiences readinesses to respond that have been learned and
automatized.

Several other theorists implicated efference in perception. Hebb (1949)
attributed a central role to eye movements in learning to perceive contour
and the like, and in building cell assemblies for perception of geometric
patterns. Von Holst (1954) posited the importance of efference in distinguishing between self-produced and externally produced movement. Held

(1961) extended Von Holst's theory of "reafference," according to which the mature organism matches efferent output to reafferent input and responds to a lack of the expected correlation by perceptual and behavioral changes.

A variety of data led these theorists to their respective theories. Breese (1899) came to his conclusion upon investigating the conditions that determine how long each of two pictures in binocular rivalry is seen. (Normally such rivalry causes a fluctuation between the pictures.) He discovered that an effort on the part of the subject to prolong conscious awareness of either picture was successful only if eye movements were made when it was being "seen," and were suppressed when the other was being "seen." If subjects were trained not to make eye movements, their intentions made no difference. Note that eye movements, or lack thereof, are the same for both eyes, whichever picture is being experienced. Breese was led by these findings to emphasize motor-efference in the conscious experience of perception.

Data collected by Kohler (1951/1964) was of primary importance to Taylor's theoretical formulation. Kohler had subjects wear for several days wedge prism spectacles, which made vertical lines appear curved. They reported that the curves became straighter, and they were again thrown into visual confusion when the glasses were removed. About one subject Kohler observed:

> After ten days of continuously wearing the spectacles, all objects had straightened out and were no longer distorted. The subject then removed the spectacles. Immediately, impressions of curvature, distortions, and apparent movement set in. The subject complained: "What I experienced after I took off the spectacles was much worse than what I experienced when I first started wearing them. I felt as if I were drunk." Aftereffects continued for four days. (p. 34, cited in Festinger et al., 1967)

A retinal pattern that had been "seen" as straight thus came to be "seen" as curved. These observations are supported by the work of others. Wundt (1898), Gibson (1933), and Pick and Hay (1964) reported similar occurrences. Held and Rekosh (1963) and Cohen (1963) further showed that motor movements are required for visual adaptation to curvature brought about by the lenses.

It was Taylor's (1962) view that new motor movements were learned in response to sensory input, that subjects either activated these movements or held them in readiness to be activated, and that this process determined conscious experience. He further modified the basic paradigm by mounting the prisms on contact lenses. Under such conditions, in order to scan a contour the eye must move in accordance with the objective contour, and not with that received by the retina via the lenses. The eye must thus respond to a curved distortion of a straight object with a straight movement response. The prediction was that quick adaptation would result, as a

straight object was being met with a straight efferent pattern. Using himself as a subject, Taylor confirmed the prediction.

Festinger *et al.* (1967) conducted a series of four experiments. One was
a successful replication of Taylor's (1962) study under more controlled
circumstances. The others were designed to ascertain whether encouraging
a subject wearing prism spectacles to learn new afferent-efferent associations would aid visual adaptation. In the latter three experiments spectacled
subjects were asked to perform manual tracing tasks that either discour-
aged or encouraged learning and storage of the pattern they traced. (Recall
our earlier description of the "leaning" vs. "free movement" conditions
used in this paradigm, corresponding to discouragement and encourage-
ment, respectively.) It was found that those who were encouraged to learn
new efferent motor tracing patterns in response to visual input tended more
than the others to correct their vision to conform to objective reality. Arm
movements were not involved when perceptual adaptation was measured.
Thus the experiments were interpreted to support the view that readiness to
issue preprogrammed motor commands, activated by sensory input, is at
the heart of conscious visual experience.

Motor-efferent theories provide an extremely interesting interpretation
of the situation that is created when images are, with the appropriate use of
lenses, maintained at the same point on the eye, so that movement of the eye
does not change the position of visual sensory input on the retina. Under
such circumstances shapes and contours disappear. The most frequently
offered explanation is that the eye becomes fatigued or satiated by constant
stimulation of the same nerves. However, another explanation of these
observations is suggested by a motor-efferent conceptualization: The correlation between eye movements and movement of the stimulation across the
retina has been obliterated. Because eye movement has ceased being relevant to the position of retinal stimulation, the observer ceases responding,
or even readying a response, and the stimulation disappears. A strong
prediction of the motor-efferent conceptualization is that such a disappearance will occur not only under conditions of a stopped retinal image but also
when the movement of an image across the retina is rendered unrelated to
eye movements. Such a situation would discourage motor activity and
cause an apparent disappearance of visual information. Campbell and Robson (1961) produced the required circumstances and confirmed this
prediction.

Recently, Walter Weimer (1977) reviewed a wide variety of psychological and physiological data and concluded that a motor metatheory, not only
of perception but of all of cognition, is not merely viable but is indispensa-
ble. Of this conception he writes:

> What the motor metatheory asserts is that there is no sharp separation between
> sensory and motor components of the nervous system which can be made on

> functional grounds, and that the mental or cognitive realm is intrinsically moto-
> ric, like all the nervous system. The mind is intrinsically a motor system, and the
> sensory order by which we are acquainted with external objects as well as
> ourselves, the higher mental processes which construct our common sense and
> scientific knowledge, indeed everything mental, is a product of what are, cor-
> rectly interpreted, constructive motor skills. (p. 272)

Sensation, perception, conception, feeling, emotion, and action are all motor functions. The organism is characterized as a "generator of not only its
output but also its input" (p. 275). He cites Piaget's genetic epistemology
as a motor theoretic approach to knowledge. Constraints of space prohibit a
recapitulation of Weimer's arguments here. For an interesting and provocative discussion of the empirical and theoretical support for a motor metatheory, the reader is referred to his work.

Accommodative Imitation as the Key to Efference

The act of accommodative imitation of environmental objects and
events is the organism's efferent response to afferent sensory input that
underlies conscious perception. It is the action sequence through which
essential motor accommodations are made and stored for subsequent evoca-
tion. In our view, it lies at the heart of the learning process that motor-
efferent theorists have postulated for perception.

Piaget (1962) has provided a comprehensive theoretical description of
the development of imitation through infancy, which we review here. In his
account the infant progresses through a series of six stages of imitative
activity, closely linked to the stages of sensorimotor intelligence (Piaget
1952, 1954). At first (Stage 1: 0–1 month), only preimitative behaviors,
such as an infant's being stimulated to cry by the crying of another, bear
any resemblance to imitation. These actions are speculatively said to result
from a confusion between inwardly and outwardly produced sounds. In the
next stage (Stage 2: 1–4 months), still considered by Piaget to be preimitative, the infant initiates or repeats a recently performed habitual behavior
upon witnessing that behavior in another. Later (Stage 3: 4–8 months), a
more concerted effort is made to imitate observed behaviors, with two limitations: The infant only mimics actions that can be seen when performed by
himself or herself, excluding acts such as tongue protrusion; and, importantly, he or she imitates only conservatively, that is, through assimilation.
Acts that are not already part of the infant's behavioral repertoire, and that
thus predominantly require accommodation, are not normally imitated.

Only at the next stage of development (Stage 4: 8–12 months) does
imitation with unseen movement begin and is it appropriate to characterize
imitation as "the active, accommodatory replication by the subject of some
external event serving as model" (Flavell, 1963, p. 152) in which "the
paramount object is to adapt the self to reality" (p. 66). For the first time

imitation can be an act in which "All energy is focused on taking exact account of the structural niceties of the reality one is imitating and in precisely dovetailing one's schematic repertoire to these details" (p. 66). At this stage, "Imitation is . . . beginning to detach itself from adaptations-in-general to become a specialized tool of acquisition" (p. 125). As Piaget (1962) states:

> Now since in the fourth stage there is the beginning of dissociation between subject and object, the assimilating schemas through which the child adapts himself to things and persons must necessarily be gradually further and further differentiated. The way in which the child then views the situations with which he is confronted is quite different from that of the earlier stages. Instead of appearing to be the continuation of his own activity, they are now partially independent realities which are analogous to what he himself can do and yet distinct from it. Then and only then do new models have interest for the child and imitation follows accommodation. (p. 50)

Development during the next stage (Stage 5: 12–18 months) is predominantly quantitative. The infant refines the earlier acquired ability to imitate accommodatively. Representational thought—that is, thought that utilizes information that is evoked in the absence of the environmental counterpart—emerges only in the last major developmental phase (Stage 6: 18 months on). It issues directly from imitative behavior. The infant internalizes, schematizes, and abbreviates the motor code involved in imitation until it can function without the environmental referent and without overt behavior. [An image, in this conceptualization, is merely a "covert but active accommodation on 'tracing out' by the subject of the object or event imagined" (p. 83)]. The most reliable behavioral indicator of true representation is *deferred* imitation—the fact of imitative behavior occurring after a delay indicating the internal storage of information that can be evoked. Flavell (1963) describes the significant consequences of this developmental achievement:

> Sensory-motor intelligence is capable only of linking, one by one, the successive actions or perceptual states with which it gets involved. Piaget likens it to a slow-motion film which represents one static frame after another but can give no simultaneous and all-encompassing purview of all the frames. Representational thought, on the other hand, through its symbolic capacity has the potential for simultaneously grasping, in a single, internal epitome, a whole sweep of separate events. It is a much faster and more mobile device which can recall the past, represent the present, and anticipate the future in one temporally brief, organized act. (pp. 151–152)[1]

Research conducted subsequent to Piaget's publications has yielded results that both support and conflict with his initial formulation. The most

[1]From *The Developmental Psychology of Jean Piaget* by John H. Flavell, copyright 1963 by Litton Educational Publishing, Inc. Reprinted by permission of D. Van Nostrand Company.

notable conflict centers around behaviors that infants cannot see themselves perform. Contrary to Piaget's belief, infants apparently do mimic acts that they may not see themselves perform (Brazelton & Young, 1964; Gardner & Gardner, 1970; Meltzoff & Moore, 1977). The important corroboration, for our purposes, is the delay of accommodative imitation until at least 7–8 months, when it is acquired possibly as a result of the development of a means–end differentiation (Abravanel, Levan-Goldschmidt, & Stevenson, 1976; Hursch & Sherman, 1973; Litrownik, 1972; McCall, 1977a,b; McCall, Eichorn, & Hogarty, 1977; McCall, Parke, & Kavanaugh, 1977; Uzgiris, 1972, 1976).

As we have said, accommodative imitation, which arises in Stage 4 (8–12 months), provides the learning experience that yields efferent motor information such as has been postulated to underlie conscious perception. Through it the required motor accommodations are made and stored for future use. In prior stages, imitative actions are essentially conservative—assimilative. While they are, of course, accommodated to the environment during their performance and may bear some permanent effects of their encounters, they do not actively replicate the idiosyncratic environment or subordinate themselves to details sufficiently to become a "specialized tool of acquisition." Thus they cannot create and store efferent motor accommodations of such precision and quality as to be useful in perception. Conscious perception must then await further development.

Festinger *et al.* (1967) attempted to explore the developmental implications of an efferent theory of perception in a very brief consideration of neonatal visual perception. They write:

> If we wish to say that this visual perception of contour is determined by efferent readiness, then we must postulate that the efferent readiness appropriate to a given visual input must, to at least some extent, be learned and modifiable. This would make it likely that visual perception of contour and shape must be learned, or at least in part. We might imagine that the visual experience of a newborn infant has no sharp contours of definite shapes but consists entirely of fuzzy blotches of brightness and color differentials. Perhaps more than this is innately built into the organism but we need not concern ourselves with the problem. Even if only this much is built in, mature visual perception based on efferent readiness can easily develop. (p. 11)

In our view, this characterization seems to presuppose conscious perception, however amorphous, in the neonate. We have suggested that conscious perception is beyond the infant's capacities. This view is based on the fact that the learning process underlying conscious perception—the acquisition and storage of accommodative information pertaining to the environment—relies upon perceptual/cognitive development. While these authors are not to be criticized for what is clearly not intended as a precise developmental statement, their suggestion also conflicts with the picture of the very young infant that has emerged from certain studies conducted over the last decade (summarized by Salapatek, 1975; Fantz, *et al.*, 1975). In this research a high degree of selectivity in attention to features of the environment such as contour has been observed. Are we then forced to attribute to the neonate efferent motor patterns that mimic the environment? If so, how many? There is evidence against attributing such patterns to the newborn. Fantz *et al.* (1975), for example, write:

> The limited response capabilities during the early months of life had in earlier decades led to the assumption of a visual-perceptual void until the infant was able to interact actively with the environment and so "learn to perceive." In place of this view that action precedes perception, recent findings give further basis for the assertion that in humans perception precedes action.

In our view the apparent contradictions are resolved if we recall that motor efference has been said to underlie only conscious perception and that nonconscious perception presupposes no such underpinning. Theorists of early infant perception are then talking about nonconscious perception, which is totally different from that which concerns Festinger *et al.*

While accommodative imitation may be said to underlie conscious visual perception, it does not follow that accommodative imitation *is* consciousness. All that may be said is that it is a part of the process that yields conscious awareness for visual stimulation. Possibly both consciousness and conscious visual perception are contingent upon the emergence in development of a processing system capable of sustaining them (to be discussed in the next section).

Several other points related to the involvement of imitative processes in visual perception are important. First, the use of accommodative imitation ought not to be construed as limited to ocular movement. Infants imitate objects and events with many parts of their body. An example offered by Piaget (1962) illustrates this point quite nicely:

> At 1;0(10) T. was looking at a box of matches which I was holding on its end and alternately opening and closing. Showing great delight, he watched with great attention, and imitated the box in three ways. 1. He opened and closed his right hand, keeping his eyes on the box. 2. He said "tff, tff" to reproduce the sound the box made. 3. He reacted . . . by opening and closing his mouth. It seemed to me that these reactions were much more concomitants of perception than attempts to act on the object. (p. 66)

Eye movement, or readiness to execute eye movement, is thus only a subset of imitative activity. An intermodal conception of efference has been demonstrated by Festinger *et al.* (1967), who found that a manual tracing task could be used as a means of correcting vision.

A second point concerns the "readiness" to execute motor commands that has been said to underlie conscious visual perception. In Piagetian terms, such readiness may well correspond to internalized, and therefore unobservable, imitation. If so, the perceiver does not merely prepare motor commands; rather, he or she actually internally executes them.

Lastly, we may well ask whether the Stage 4 infant is capable of the ultimate in imitation behavior—representation. Such is not Piaget's opinion; he considers the acquisition of representation to occur in Stage 6 (18 months on). Yet, given that accommodative imitation—the basic cognitive requisite—is present much earlier, the delay of representational ability may seem problematic. Also, if we have been correct in attributing conscious perception to the earlier stage, the young infant appears to be not only unpracticed but also virtually powerless in trying to meet the widespread, simultaneous processing demands, unless he or she is credited with capacities associated with representation. Recall Flavell's (1963, pp. 151–152) contrast between prerepresentational and representational intelligence. The former is "a slow-motion film which represents one static frame after another but can give no simultaneous and all-encompassing purview of all the frames." The latter, by virtue of its symbolic capacity, "has the potential for simultaneously grasping, in a single, internal epitome, a whole sweep of separate events. . . . a faster and more mobile device which can recall the past, represent the present, and anticipate the future in one temporally brief, organized act." Is the ascription of representation to Stage 4 infants plausible?

The data are as yet inconclusive. Because representation is assumed to be necessary for object permanence, most relevant studies have centered on the infant's acquisition of object permanence. Bower and his co-workers (Bower, 1966, 1967, 1972, 1974; Bower & Paterson, 1972, 1973; Bower & Wishart, 1972; Bower, Broughton, & Moore, 1971; for a review see Gratch, 1977), working from a nativist position, have tried to demonstrate that even very young infants perceive a world of stable objects. Research with older infants has examined the processes underlying the infant's ability to find hidden objects. Much of this research has been devoted to specifying in detail the nature of the limitations on object permanence observed in Stage 4 infants.

According to Piaget, the infant in Stage 4 has developed the object concept to the point at which a search can be initiated for an object after it disappears from view. This effect has been corroborated many times (see Gratch, 1975, 1977, for reviews). While this seems to be compelling evidence of object permanence, Piaget contends that full object permanence has yet to be achieved. He cites two types of evidence in support of this position. First, he notes that infants at this age lack the capacity to infer invisible movements. Second, he points to the well-known "A$\overline{\text{B}}$ error" in which the infant, after having successfully found an object hidden under A a few times, again searches for it under A even when it has been viewed being placed under B. Piaget's interpretation is that the infant is still confusing an egoistic action-based experience of the object with the notion of the object as real and independent of self. However, the complexity of the results from recent work on the A$\overline{\text{B}}$ error (reviewed by Gratch, 1977) has cast some doubt on its status as evidence against full representation. Modifications of the paradigm (e.g., substitution of objects, delay of search, use of transparent covers) have yielded a maze of puzzling data that make interpretation tenuous at this time. Both Stage 4 limitations are also open to explanation by appeal to the infant's immature spatial coding system. Thus, Harris (1976) argues that the $\overline{AB}$ error occurs not as the result of lack of object permanence but rather due to an inability to find an object. He makes the case that the infant's predicament is similar to that in which an adult is placed when a magician makes an object disappear; he or she knows the object still exists but does not know where.

Researchers have differed on their interpretation of the evidence concerning object concept. Yet it seems at least plausible, for the present, to attribute object permanence—and thus representation—to the infant who initiates a search for a hidden object.

According to our conceptualization, interference is a reason why deferred imitation would not be expected until later in development even if representation were acquired at about the same time as accommodative imitation. Representation, in our view, utilizes the imitative process as does perception. Because of the widespread perceptual processing demands that the child faces and the immaturity of the system that resolves them, processing resources are already severely taxed. The addition of processing demands to an already overburdened system is impractical at best and unfeasible at worst. Just as visual-perceptual processing has been shown to interfere with tasks involving visual imagery (e.g., Brooks, 1968; Segal & Fusella, 1970), perceptual processing may be expected to interfere with cognitive functions based on representation. Thus, while representation may be achieved at an early age, the demonstration of that capacity will await more efficient perceptual processing.

A General, Unified Cognitive System?

A theory of perception that posits the centrality of efferent motor information belongs to a class of theories that has been referred to broadly as "constructivist." Of the alternative accounts offered on visual perception from within this school, Turvey (1975) writes:

> Only relatively superficial differences divide the various theories of visual perception with which we are most acquainted. With respect to the basic postulates on which each is founded there is an overwhelming consistency of opinion: they all concur to a greater or lesser degree that perception begins with retinal data that related imperfectly, even ambiguously, to their source—the world of objects, surfaces, and events.
>
> Consequently, it is customary to liken the task of the perceiver to that of a

> detective who must seek to determine what transpired from the bits and pieces of
> evidence available to him. (pp. 131–132)

Constructivists have long held that visual stimulation is impoverished, that it underdetermines perceptual experience, thus necessitating enrichment through processes dependent upon memory-inference, hypothesis testing, and the like. The tenet of these theorists is that conception determines perception.

The major alternative view holds that perception is primary, that it determines conception and not the reverse. Here visual stimulation is the sufficient source of information and does not require supplementation by the observer. J. J. Gibson (e.g., 1950, 1966), in his theory of "ecological optics," argues that classical theories have incorrectly conceptualized the issues by not recognizing which aspects of the visual stimulation are important (e.g., movement over stasis) and by not appreciating the rich supply of information within ambient light.

In our view, while sufficient information to perceive veridically may be available in ambient light, conscious perceptual experience is not possible without the enrichment provided by motor processes. This view is based upon the evidence that was cited earlier and does not rest upon the notion that visual information is deficient. It is consonant with that of Weimer (1977), who writes:

> The contructivist must realize that no construction can occur in any mental realm
> unless there is information available upon which constructive processes operate.
> The slogan, "everything is a construction" is a contradiction in terms: unless
> there is an informational basis available, no construction can occur. Similarly,
> the Gibsonian must realize that pointing out that the information necessary to
> account for perception is specified in the optic array (or the speech signal, etc.)
> says nothing about how we perceive. An adequate theory of perception must
> include not only a specification of what is perceived but also an account of how it
> occurs. (p. 285)

Turvey (1975) also notes of constructivism:

> This is a significant feature of constructivism: it encourages us to examine the
> possibility that psychological processes such as thought, language, and seeing,
> are more similar than they are different. The kinds of knowledge, heuristics,
> algorithms, and so on, that permit thought may not differ significantly from
> those that permit language, and these in turn may be equivalent to those that
> yield visual perception. Paraphrasing Kolers, Katz, Sutherland and others, there
> is nothing that would suggest to a constructivist different kinds of intelligence
> underlying these apparently different activities. (p. 133)

We have dealt primarily with visual perception and the attentional and memorial activities related to it. However, the implications of the constructivist perceptual model presented here and of the hypothesized qualitative transitions very likely extend beyond vision. As we have seen, Weimer relates his motor metatheory to all facets of the mind and supports his position with evidence that cuts across a variety of domains. He cites speech perception as an area in which motor theories have long been prominent (Liberman, 1959; Liberman, Cooper, Shankweiler, & Studdert-Kennedy, 1967; Halwes & Wire, 1974). Similarly, efferent imitation was said to be a general behavior, transcending particular modalities. The emergent capacity of efferent imitation may well mediate the development of a general, unified cognitive system. If so, the qualitative transitions that have been suggested here may be substantially more than modifications of the visual processing system. The first transition may, in fact, mark the birth of a system that comes to fruition in a unified processing structure of mature cognition. If so, processing systems that were relatively independent, though perhaps already coordinated, for the first time come under the aegis of a developing total cognitive system.

Norman and Bobrow (1976) offer a conceptualization of a cross-modal perceptual processing structure that embodies several features earlier said to be necessary for a viable perceptual system. It also helps begin to concretize these speculations about the notion of a general processing structure. In their view, perception involves a convergence between bottom-up and top-down processes, the latter revolving around active memory "schemata." "A schema consists of a framework for tying together the information about any given concept or event, with specifications about the types of interrelations or restrictions upon the way things fit together" (p. 125). Stimulation is said to be interpreted through the mediation of these active frameworks, born of experience and stored in memory. The perceptual task for the organism is to select appropriate schemata to make matches with current information. A number of them can act semi-independently, automatically, and in parallel, to process the output of the sensory information store. There are many schemata, automatically triggered by sensory stimulation (or "data-driven"), operating at a conceptual level, each semi-independently processing a portion of the visual field. The perceiver directs focal attention to that schema that accounts for the largest amount of information in the field, or that encounters information that is optimally discrepant from its expectations.

With the stipulation that the information underlying memory schemata be motor-efferent, this model meets many of the specifications noted earlier, particularly the demand for widespread processing. Here awareness of that part of the field that is not receiving focal attention is created by those schemata that function independently of the higher processes. The proposed processing structure is perhaps best viewed as one important facet of a total cognitive system that embraces the bulk of all perceptual/cognitive phenomena, a core element of a "central processing unit." If we have been accurate in ascribing a pivotal role to accommodative motor imitation, there is no reason to expect such a unifying processing structure until 8 to 12 months.

Concluding Remarks

Our foremost concern in this chapter has been to raise an issue that is by and large ignored in today's developmental literature: whether a viable account of development can be rendered without a careful consideration of the role of conscious processes. In our view, it cannot. Neither the complexities that are ushered in by the broader conceptual framework nor the difficulties involved in operationalizing key notions nor the vestiges of behaviorism ought to deter an effort to understand those processes.

We have further suggested a scheme of development that takes cognizance of the issue, drawing out some of the implications for perception, attention, and memory. The value of this depiction rests upon the degree to which it organizes data and accounts for research findings, present and future. While we cannot provide an extensive review of the literature here, several observations will indicate at least a *prima facie* concordance between the developmental scheme outlined here and what is already known. The first transition described above is consistent with that recently proposed by several researchers. McCall, Eichorn, and Hogarty (1977), for example, note qualitative changes at both the 8th and the 13th month, finding Piagetian theory the most satisfactory conceptual framework to account for these changes. They point out the emergence of a significant role for imitation within that period and describe development in terms of the progressive distancing of the infant from the environment and the separation of means from ends. Zelazo and Kearsley (1977) recently presented evidence for a cognitive "metamorphosis" in the 9-to-12-month range, citing the abrupt emergence of functional play at 11½ months. In general, there seems to be agreement among researchers that major changes occur near the end of the 1st year, though the nature of the changes is not clear. The enhancement of memory capacities by that time, possibly due to the development of recall memory (Schaffer, 1974), is often cited as a possible cognitive underpinning.

The proposed second transition—centered upon the task of consolidating a new perceptual system—is also consonant with recent research in cognitive development. Studies by Hagen and his collaborators (see Hagen & Hale, 1973) and Smith and her colleagues (see Smith, Kemler, & Aronfreed, 1975; Smith & Kemler, 1977) are particularly relevant. Hagen's work with school-aged children has used a central-incidental memory task. In this paradigm children are presented with pictures that contain two items, one of which is designated as the to-be-remembered (central) item. At the end of presentation the child is asked to recall both the central and the peripheral items. The youngest children as well as older children recall significant amounts of both types of information. The younger children seem to ignore instructions to focus only on central items and process both types of information. While recall for central items improves substantially with increasing CA level from ages 5–6 through ages 14–15, recall of peripheral items improves little and eventually even drops off. In terms of the analysis presented here, the younger children, due to their dispersed mode of perceptual processing, distribute attention between the two sets of pictures, thereby enhancing memory for both. Older children, on the other hand, may be better at directing attention because of the degree to which much of their perceptual processing has become automatic, thus requiring less focal effort. It may be expected that the more processing is automatized and performed without focal involvement, the less it will be accessible for effortful recall.

In other work, Smith and Kemler (1977) investigated the reason why, in tasks involving speeded responses, 5- and 6-year-olds were significantly more disrupted by the presence of irrelevant information than were children 4 to 5 years older. They found, surprisingly, that spatially separating the relevant information from the irrelevant actually *interfered* with the kindergartners' performance. This manipulation had no effect on fifth-graders' performance. The findings were interpreted to mean that the younger children, as compared to the older, actively distributed attention between relevant and irrelevant information, regardless of instructions to attend selectively. The younger children did not process poorly, but rather they processed differently:

> Specifically, the younger children's poorer performance appears due to an actual attempt on their part, to take in all the stimulus information. It should be noted, however, that the distribution hypothesis does not imply that young children are incapable of responding selectively. . . . Rather, by the distribution hypothesis, we are claiming that at the initial stages of information pick-up, young children distribute their attention where focusing would be more appropriate. . . . This conclusion is consistent with Pick and Frankel's (1974) proposal that one major trend in the development of selective attention is increasing flexibility in the use of attentional strategies. (pp. 8–9)

We would argue that the younger children are bound to distribute their attention until automaticity relieves the burden on attention.

Recognition that there is a difficult period in which a new perceptual system must be consolidated also helps explain data that have heretofore remained somewhat enigmatic. It has been known for some time, for example, that certain "competence–performance" discrepancies exist in which already acquired abilities are not utilized. One well-known finding is the lag between the acquisition of the ability to label verbally and the use of that ability in tasks where it is clearly advantageous (Flavell, 1970; Hagen, Jongeward, & Kail, 1975). We would suggest the following explanation. Verbal processes are primarily serial; however, until perceptual processing has been consolidated, the child is in a state in which attention is scattered and distributed over the visual field in a kind of clumsy attempt at parallel processing. Hence the verbal mode is simply inappropriate. Serial processing is only functional at a practical level when parallel processing—that is, the simultaneous processing of many semiautonomous schemata in Norman and Bobrow's terms—is efficient and does not overburden focal resources.

Certain research implications emerge from the developmental model presented here. In particular, the 8-to 12-month age range appears crucially in need of further study. We may expect in that period perhaps a slight falling off of visual recognition memory capacity (with the introduction of a new perceptual system), followed by a dramatic increase in capacity with enhanced levels-of-processing potential (as the new system is consolidated). A change in visual preferences may also occur at this point, depending upon the motor information that becomes available to the infant. The ability to focus on any one part of the visual field for an extended period of time may also be expected to diminish as the tendency toward global, distributed, scattered attention appears. If there is merit to the notion of a general, unified cognitive system, then a similar, simultaneous developmental shift ought to be observed in other modalities as well. Transformations in the social sphere would also be expected. For example, an attachment based upon nonconscious processes is likely to differ significantly from one that is subject to conscious scrutiny.

The present effort may be viewed as an attempt to sensitize researchers to the possibility of important transformations in both perception and cognition brought about by intervention of motor processes in ongoing functions. It is important both to identify the onset of the various perceptual/cognitive capacities as early as they appear and to determine when these processes begin to resemble those of the mature cognitive system. According to our thesis the two occurrences are temporally quite distinct in the visual modality, and perhaps in others. While language acquisition is often seen as the "great divide of development," an even more basic transformation may have already occurred before language becomes a significant factor on the cognitive scene.

ACKNOWLEDGMENTS

Special thanks are extended to Catherine Sophian, who read and commented on each draft. We also acknowledge the helpful comments received from Gary Olson, Tracy Sherman, Scott Miller, and Barbara Zimmerman.

References

Abravanel, E., Levan-Goldschmidt, E., & Stevenson, M. B. Action imitation: The early phase of infancy. *Child Development*, 1976, *47*, 1032–1044.
Atkinson, R. C., & Shiffrin, R. M. Human memory: A proposed system and its control

processes. In G. H. Bower & J. T. Spence (Eds.), *The psychology of learning and motivation* (Vol. 2). New York: Academic, 1968.

Bower, T. G. R. The visual world of infants. *Scientific American,* 1966, *215,* 80–92.

Bower, T. G. R. The development of object-permanence: Some studies of existence constancy. *Perception and Psychophysics,* 1967, *2,* 441–418.

Bower, T. G. R. Object perception in infants. *Perception,* 1972, *1,* 15–30.

Bower, T. G. R. Repetition in human development. *Merrill-Palmer Quarterly,* 1974, *20,* 303–318.

Bower, T. G. R., & Paterson, J. G. Stages in the development of the object concept. *Cognition,* 1972, *1*(1), 47–55.

Bower, T. G. R., & Paterson, J. G. The separation of place, movement and object in the world of the infant. *Journal of Experimental Child Psychology,* 1973, *15,* 161–168.

Bower, T. G. R., & Wishart, J. G. The effects of motor skill on object permanence. *Cognition,* 1972, *1,* 165–172.

Bower, T. G. R., Broughton, J. M., & Moore, M. K. Development of the object concept as manifested in the tracking behavior of infants between seven and twenty weeks of age. *Journal of Experimental Child Psychology,* 1971, *11,* 182–193.

Brazelton, T. B., & Young, G. An example of imitative behavior in a nine-week old infant. *Journal of Child Psychiatry,* 1964, *3,* 53–58.

Breese, B. B. On inhibition. *Psychological Review Monograph Supplement,* 1899, *3*(1, Whole No. 11), 1–65.

Broadbent, D. E. *Perception and communication.* London: Pergamon, 1958.

Broadbent, D. E. Stimulus set and response set: Two kinds of selective attention. In D. I. Mostofsky (Ed.), *Attention: Contemporary theory and analysis.* New York: Appleton, 1970.

Broadbent, D. E. *Decision and stress.* New York: Academic, 1971.

Brooks, L. R. Spatial and verbal components of the act of recall. *Canadian Journal of Psychology,* 1968, *22,* 349–368.

Campbell, D., Sanderson, R. E., & Laverty, S. G. Characteristics of a conditioned response in human subjects during extinction trials following a simple traumatic conditioning trial. *Journal of Abnormal and Social Psychology,* 1964, *68,* 627–639.

Campbell, F. S., & Robson, J. G. A fresh approach to stabilized retinal images. *Proceedings of the Physiological Society,* 1961, 11P–12P.

Cohen, L. B., & Gelber, E. R. Infant visual memory. In L. B. Cohen & P. Salapatek (Eds.), *Infant perception: From sensation to cognition* (Vol. 1). New York: Academic, 1975.

Cohen, M. *Visual curvature and feedback factors in the production of prismatically induced curved-line after-effects.* Paper presented at the meeting of the Eastern Psychological Association, New York, April 1963.

Craik, F. I. M., & Lockhart, R. S. Levels of processing: A framework for memory research. *Journal of Verbal Learning and Verbal Behavior,* 1972, *11,* 671–684.

Fantz, R. L. Pattern vision in young infants. *Psychological Record,* 1958, *58,* 43–47.

Fantz, R. L. The origin of form perception. *Scientific American,* 1961, *204,* 66–72.

Fantz, R. L. Pattern vision in newborn infants. *Science,* 1963, *140,* 296–297.

Fantz, R. L. Visual experience in infants: Decreased attention to familiar patterns relative to novel ones. *Science,* 1964, *146,* 668–670.

Fantz, R. L., Fagan, J. F., & Miranda, S. B. Early visual selectivity. In L. B. Cohen & P. Salapatek (Eds.), *Infant perception: From sensation to cognition* (Vol. 1). New York: Academic, 1975.

Festinger, L., & Canon, L. K. Information about spatial location based on knowledge about efference. *Psychological Review,* 1965, *72,* 373–384.

Festinger, L., Burnham, C. A., Ono, H., & Bamber, D. Efference and the conscious experience of perception. *Journal of Experimental Psychology*, 1967, *74*, 1–36. (Monograph supplement)

Flavell, J. H. *The developmental psychology of Jean Piaget*. New York: Van Nostrand, 1963.

Flavell, J. H. Developmental studies of mediated memory. In H. W. Reese & L. P. Lipsitt (Eds.), *Advances in child development and behavior* (Vol. 5). New York: Academic, 1970.

Gardner, J., & Gardner, H. A note on selective imitation by a six-week-old infant. *Child Development*, 1970, *41*, 1209–1213.

Gibson, E. J. *Principles of perceptual learning and development*. New York: Appleton-Century-Crofts, 1969.

Gibson, J. J. Adaptation, after-effect and contrast in the perception of curved lines. *Journal of Experimental Psychology*, 1933, *16*, 1–31.

Gibson, J. J. *The perception of the visual world*. Boston: Houghton Mifflin, 1950.

Gibson, J. J. *The senses considered as perceptual systems*. Boston: Houghton Mifflin, 1966.

Gratch, G. Recent studies based on Piaget's view of object concept development. In L. B. Cohen & P. Salapatek (Eds.), *Infant perception: From sensation to cognition* (Vol. 2). New York: Academic, 1975.

Gratch, G. Review of Piagetian infancy research: Object concept development. In W. F. Overton & J. M. Gallagher (Eds.), *Knowledge and development* (Vol. 1). New York: Plenum, 1977.

Hagen, J. W., & Hale, G. A. The development of attention in children. In A. D. Pick (Ed.), *Minnesota symposia on child psychology* (Vol. 7). Minneapolis: University of Minnesota Press, 1973.

Hagen, J. W., & Kail, R. V., Jr. The role of attention in perceptual and cognitive development. In W. M. Cruickshank & D. P. Hallahan (Eds.), *Perceptual and learning disabilities in children. Vol. 2: Research and theory.* Syracuse: Syracuse University Press, 1975.

Hagen, J. W., & Stanovich, K. E. Memory· Strategies of acquisition. In R. Kail, Jr., & J. W. Hagen (Eds.), *Perspectives on the development of memory and cognition*. Hillsdale, N.J.: Lawrence Erlbaum, 1977.

Hagen, J. W., Jongeward, R. H., Jr., & Kail, R. V., Jr. Cognitive perspectives on the development of memory. In H. Reese (Ed.), *Advances in child development and behavior* (Vol. 10). New York: Academic, 1975.

Haith, M. M., & Campos, J. Human infancy. In M. R. Rosenzweig & L. W. Porter (Eds.), *Annual review of psychology*. Palo Alto: Annual Reviews, 1976.

Halwes, T., & Wire, B. A possible solution to the pattern recognition problem in the speech modality. In W. B. Weimer & D. S. Palermo (Eds.), *Cognition and the symbolic processes*. Hillsdale, N.J.: Lawrence Erlbaum, 1974.

Harris, P. L. *Subject, object and framework; a theory of spatial development*. Unpublished manuscript. Amsterdam, Free University, 1976.

Hayes-Roth, F. Critique of Turvey's "Contrasting orientations to the theory of visual information processing." *Psychological Review*, 1977, *84*, 531–535.

Hebb, D. O. *Organization of behavior*. New York: Wiley, 1949.

Held, R. Exposure-history as a factor in maintaining stability of perception and coordination. *Journal of Nervous and Mental Disease*, 1961, *132*, 26–32.

Held, R., & Rekosh, J. Motor-sensory feedback and the geometry of visual space. *Science*, 1963, *141*, 722–723.

Helmholtz, H. von. *Handbuch der physiologischen Optik*. Hamburg and Leipzig: Voss, 1856.

Helmholtz, H. von. [*Physiological optics*] (J. P. C. Southall, Trans.). New York: Dover, 1962.

Hursch, D. E., & Sherman, J. A. The effects of parent-presented models and praise on the vocal behavior of their children. *Journal of Experimental Child Psychology*, 1973, *15*, 328–339.

James, W. *The principles of psychology* (Vol. 2). London: Macmillan, 1890.

Jeffrey, W. E. The orienting reflex and attention in cognitive development. *Psychological Review*, 1968, 75, 323–334.

Jeffrey, W. E., & Cohen, L. B. Habituation in the human infant. In W. H. Reese (Ed.), *Advances in child development and behavior* (Vol. 6). New York: Academic, 1971.

Kahneman, D. *Attention and effort*. Englewood Cliffs, N.J.: Prentice-Hall, 1973.

Keele, S. W. *Attention and human performance*. Pacific Palisades, Cal.: Goodyear, 1973.

Kessen, W. Sucking and looking: Two organized congenital patterns of behavior in the human newborn. In H. W. Stevenson, E. H. Hess, & H. L. Rheingold (Eds.), *Early behavior: Comparative and developmental approaches*. New York: Wiley, 1967.

Kessen, W., Haith, M. M., & Salapatek, P. H. Human infancy: A bibliography and guide. In P. H. Mussen (Ed.), *Carmichael's manual of child psychology* (3rd ed., Vol. 1). New York: Wiley, 1970.

Klatzky, R. L. *Human memory: Structures and processes*. San Francisco: W. H. Freeman, 1975.

Kohler, I. [The formation and transformation of the perceptual world] (H. Fiss, Trans.). *Psychological Issues*, 1964, 3(4), 173. (Originally published, 1951.)

Liberman, A. M. Some results of research on speech perception. *Journal of the Acoustical Society of America*, 1959, 29, 117–123.

Liberman, A. M., Cooper, F. S., Shankweiler, D. P., & Studdert-Kennedy, M. Perception of the speech code. *Psychological Review*, 1967, 74, 431–461.

Litrownik, A. J. Observational learning in retarded and normal children as a function of delay between observation and opportunity to perform. *Journal of Experimental Child Psychology*, 1972, 48, 117–125.

Maurer, D. Infant visual perception: Methods of study. In L. B. Cohen & P. Salapatek (Eds.), *Infant perception: From sensation to cognition* (Vol. 1). New York: Academic, 1975.

McCall, R. B. *Stages in mental development during the first two years*. Paper presented at the Society for Research in Child Development Symposium on Qualitative Transitions in Behavior during Infancy. New Orleans, March 1977. (a)

McCall, R. B. Challenges to a science of developmental psychology. *Child Development*, 1977, 48, 333–344. (b)

McCall, R. B., Eichorn, D. H., & Hogarty, P. S. Transitions in early mental development. *Monographs of the Society for Research in Child Development*, 1977, 42, (3, Serial No. 171).

McCall, R. B., Parke, R. D., & Kavanaugh, R. D. Imitation of live and televised models by children one to three years of age. *Monographs of the Society for Research in Child Development*, 1977, 42 (5, Serial No. 173).

Meltzoff, A. N., & Moore, M. K. Imitation of facial and manual gestures by human neonates. *Science*, 1977, 198, 75–78.

Merton, P. A. Human position sense and sense of effort. Society of Experimental Biology Symposium XVIII, *Homeostasis and feedback mechanisms*. Cambridge: Cambridge University Press, 1964, pp. 387–400.

Moltz, H. Imprinting: An epigenetic approach. *Psychological Review*, 1963, 70, 123–138.

Montague, W. P. Consciousness: A form of energy. In *Essays, philosophical and psychological, in honor of William James*. New York: Longmans, Green, 1908.

Münsterberg, H. The physiological basis of mental life. *Science*, 1899, 9, 442–447.

Münsterberg, H. *Grundzuge der Psychologie* (Vol. 1). Leipzig: J. A. Barth, 1900.

Neisser, U. *Cognitive psychology*. New York: Appleton-Century-Crofts, 1967.

Neisser, U. *Cognition and reality: Principles and implications of cognitive psychology*. San Francisco: W. H. Freeman, 1976.

Norman, D. A. *Models of human memory*. New York: Academic, 1970.

Norman, D. A., & Bobrow, D. G. On the role of active memory processes in perception and cognition. In C. N. Cofer (Ed.), *The structure of human memory*. San Francisco: W. H. Freeman, 1976.

Olson, G. M. An information processing analysis of visual memory and habituation in infants. In T. Tighe & R. Leaton (Eds.), *Habituation: Perspectives from child development, animal behavior, and neurophysiology*. Hillsdale, N.J.: Lawrence Erlbaum, 1976.

Paivio, A. *Imagery and verbal processes*. New York: Holt, Rinehart & Winston, 1971.

Piaget, J. *The origins of intelligence in children*. New York: International Universities Press, 1952.

Piaget, J. *The construction of reality in the child*. New York: Basic, 1954.

Piaget, J. *Play, dreams, and imitation in childhood*. New York: Norton, 1962.

Pick, A. D., & Frankel, G. W. A developmental study of strategies of visual selectivity. *Child Development*, 1974, *45*, 1162–1165.

Pick, H., & Hay, J. Adaptation to prismatic distortion. *Psychonomic Science*, 1964, *1*, 199–200.

Rosch, E., Mervis, C. B., Gray, W. D., Johnson, D. M., & Boyes-Braem, P. Basic objects in natural categories. *Cognitive Psychology*, 1976, *8*, 382–439.

Salapatek, P. Pattern perception in early infancy. In L. B. Cohen & P. Salapatek (Eds.), *Infant perception: From sensation to cognition* (Vol. 1). New York: Academic, 1975.

Salzen, E. A. Imprinting and fear. *Symposia of the Zoological Society of London*, 1962, *8*, 197–217.

Schaffer, H. R. *The growth of sociability*. Baltimore: Penguin, 1971.

Schaffer, H. R. Cognitive components of the infant's response to strangeness. In M. Lewis & L. A. Rosenblum (Eds.), *The origins of fear*. New York: Wiley, 1974.

Scott, J. P. Critical periods in behavioral development. *Science*, 1962, *138*, 949–958.

Segal, S. J., & Fusella, V. Influence of imaged pictures and sounds on detection of visual and auditory signals. *Journal of Experimental Psychology*, 1970, *83*, 458–464.

Shaffer, W. O., & Shiffrin, R. M. Rehearsal and storage of visual information. *Journal of Experimental Psychology*, 1972, *92*, 292–296.

Shepard, R. N. Recognition memory for words, sentences, and pictures. *Journal of Verbal Learning and Verbal Behavior.* 1967, *6*, 156–163.

Shepp, B. E., & Swartz, K. B. Selective attention and the processing of integral and nonintegral dimensions: A developmental study. *Journal of Experimental Child Psychology*, 1976, *22*, 73–85.

Sherrington, C. S. The muscular sense. In E. A. Schafer (Ed.), *A textbook of physiology*. Edinburgh and London: Pentland, 1900.

Smith, L. B., & Kemler, D. G. *A developmental study of attentional strategies*. Paper presented at the Biennial Meeting of the Society for Research in Child Development, New Orleans, March 1977.

Smith, L. B., Kemler, D. G., & Aronfreed, J. Developmental trends in voluntary selective attention: Differential effects of source distinctness. *Journal of Experimental Child Psychology*, 1975, *20*, 352–362.

Sokolov, E. N. *Perception and the conditioned reflex*. New York: Macmillan, 1963.

Sperry, R. W. Neurology and the mind-brain problem. *American Scientist*, 1952, *40*, 291–312.

Strutt, G. F., Anderson, D. R., & Well, A. D. A developmental study of the effects of irrelevant information on speeded classification. *Journal of Experimental Child Psychology*, 1975, *20*, 127–135.

Taylor, J. G. *The behavioral basis of perception*. New Haven: Yale University Press, 1962.

Treisman, A. M. Strategies and models of selective attention. *Psychological Review*, 1969, *76*, 282–299.

Turvey, M. T. Perspectives in vision: Conception or perception? In D. Duane & M. Rawson

(Eds.), *Reading, perception and language: Papers from the World Congress on Dyslexia.* Baltimore, Md.: York, 1975.

Turvey, M. T. Contrasting orientations to the theory of visual information processing. *Psychological Review,* 1977, *84,* 67–88. (a)

Turvey, M. T. Preliminaries to a theory of action with reference to vision. In R. Shaw & J. Bransford (Eds.), *Perceiving, acting, and knowing: Toward an ecological psychology.* Hillsdale, N. J.: Lawrence Erlbaum, 1977. (b)

Uzgiris, I. C. Patterns of vocal and gestural imitation in infants. In F. Monks, W. Hartup, & J. deWit (Eds.), *Determinants of behavioral development.* New York: Academic, 1972.

Uzgiris, I. C. Organization of sensorimotor intelligence. In M. Lewis (Ed.), *Origins of intelligence.* New York: Plenum, 1976.

Von Holst, E. Relations between the central nervous system and the peripheral organs. *British Journal of Animal Behavior,* 1954, *2,* 89–94.

Washburn, M. F. *Movement and mental imagery.* Boston: Houghton Mifflin, 1916.

Weimer, W. B. A conceptual framework for cognitive psychology: Motor theories of the mind. In R. Shaw & J. Bransford (Eds.), *Perceiving, acting, and knowing: Toward an ecological psychology.* Hillsdale, N.J.: Lawrence Erlbaum, 1977.

Werner, H., & Kaplan, B. *Symbol formation: An organismic developmental approach to language and the expression of thought.* New York: Wiley, 1963.

Wundt, W. Zur Theorie der Raumlichen Gesichtswarnehmungen. *Philosophical Studies,* 1898, *14,* 11.

Zelazo, P. R., & Kearsley, R. B. *Functional play: Evidence for a cognitive metamorphosis in the year-old-infant.* Paper presented at the Biennial Meeting of the Society for Research in Child Development, New Orleans, March 1977.

5

Stimulus Dimensions,
Problem Solving, and Piaget

PATRICIA H. MILLER

Introduction

There is a tremendous amount of stimulus information in the child's world. Children develop a number of methods for reducing the complexity of the environment to a more manageable level. One of these methods is to analyze stimuli into dimensions such as color, size, and shape. This process of extracting dimensions will be labeled "dimensionalization." A definition of dimensionalization will be the focus of the final section of this chapter. In brief, dimensionalization refers to any process that provides the child with information about properties that can be ordered dimensionally. Dimensionalization helps the child both gather information about objects and solve problems that involve objects, such as discrimination learning tasks.

Most of the research on dimensionalization in children has been concerned with attention, which is one aspect of dimensionalization. This research usually examines attention in the context of common problem-solving tasks, e.g., discrimination learning, reversal shift, and sorting tasks. In these tasks attention is typically defined as the selection of one dimension while ignoring other dimensions. A common finding is that the more salient the relevant dimension (the dimension whose levels are associated with reward or nonreward), the more likely a child is to attend to it, and the faster learning will be (e.g., Suchman & Trabasso, 1966b).

This research on children's attention during problem solving has rarely been related to another area of current interest, Piaget's theory of cognitive development. However, recent research suggests that certain stimulus variables affect performance on Piagetian tasks much as they affect problem solving (Miller, 1975). One goal of this chapter is to examine the role of attention in Piaget's theory. A second goal is to develop a broader view of the development of dimensionalization than has been provided by either the

PATRICIA H. MILLER • University of Florida, Gainesville, Florida 32611.

Piagetian or problem-solving approaches alone. This view encompasses both attention and the "higher order" mental abilities described by Piaget. The discussion will draw on the most relevant studies in the problem-solving literature and the Piagetian literature. Piaget's concept of conservation will be emphasized because of the importance he assigns to it and the large amount of research on this concept. Piaget believes that conservation is important because it reflects the acquisition of cognitive operations.

Before discussing how the two approaches converge, a brief description of the most common paradigms is in order. In the problem-solving approach, investigators have most commonly used some version of the discrimination learning paradigm. A particular dimension is designated as relevant (e.g., color; red is rewarded, blue is not) and all other dimensions are irrelevant. Typically, there are many trials, and two stimuli are presented simultaneously on each trial. Attentional theories, such as that of Zeaman & House (1963), propose that learning involves two stages. First, the child learns which dimension is relevant through a trial-and-error selection of dimensions. Second, he learns which stimulus cue (e.g., red) within that dimension is associated with reinforcement. Attentional theories have been offered to explain the results obtained with variations of the discrimination learning task, such as discrimination shifts, oddity learning, transposition, and sorting tasks. More recently, attention to dimensions has been examined in other paradigms such as tasks measuring selective memory (e.g., Odom, 1972) and tasks requiring children to switch attention from one dimension to another when judging whether two objects have the same color, shape, etc. (e.g., Pick & Frankel, 1974).

The conservation task begins with two identical stimuli (e.g., balls of clay, lines of objects, glasses of water). After the child agrees they are equal in amount (or number), he watches as one of the stimuli is transformed (e.g., rolled out, bunched up, poured into a glass of a different shape). If the child still thinks the two stimuli have the same amount or number he is considered to be a conserver. Some investigators, in addition, require the child to give a logical explanation before classifying the child as a conserver. If, however, the child believes that the transformation has altered the number or amount of material, he is said to be a nonconserver.

The organization of this chapter is as follows. First, there will be a description of Piaget's four-step model of the development of conservation. This will include Piaget's cognitive interpretation of developmental changes in the use of dimensions. Second, an alternative interpretation of the development of conservation will be offered. It will be proposed that the development of attention to dimensions contributes to the development of conservation. Third, it will be argued that the performance of young children who do not consistently conserve is very much affected by how dimensions are presented and processed during testing or natural experiences with objects.

Finally, there will be a discussion of how a consideration of differences between the conservation and problem-solving tasks can produce a broader view of the development of dimensionalization.

Developmental Relationships between Conservation and Attention to Dimensions

Piaget's Model of Conservation

Piaget discusses children's dimensionalization in his four-step model of the development of conservation (Piaget, 1960, 1970). The model is exemplified in a test of conservation of substance in which one of two identical balls of clay is rolled out into a longer and longer snake. At various points the child is questioned about the equality of the two objects. In Step 1 a nonconserver centers on one dimension—either length or width. Centering seems to be both perceptual (e.g., looking at the length of the snake and ignoring the width) and conceptual (e.g., reasoning only on the basis of the length). If the child centers on length he thinks the snake has more clay than the ball because it is longer. In Step 2 the child centers on the other dimension (e.g., width) and consequently makes the opposite nonconservation error (the ball has more because it is fatter). By the end of Step 2 there may be centering first on one dimension, then on the other, and so on back and forth. In Step 3 the child begins to deal with both dimensions at the same time. He has some awareness that the changes in the two dimensions are related. Also, the child is increasingly aware of the transformation rather than only the static states. In Step 4 the child acquires the compensation operation, the knowledge that an increase in one dimension is *exactly* corrected by a decrease in the other dimension. Compensation, along with certain other mental operations, leads to conservation.

There are three major problems with Piaget's model. One is that research has only partially confirmed the sequence of steps (see Miller, 1975). A second problem is that there is no satisfactory account of the processes involved in the movement through the four steps. Piaget's position is that changes in the use of dimensions result from the underlying cognitive development. According to Piaget, nonconservers believe that length and height are accurate measures of amount. This belief is based on a more general use of ordinal comparisons of points of arrival; longer means going further (Piaget, 1968). The subsequent change to a focus on width and eventually both dimensions reflects a number of cognitive processes such as equilibration, decentration, and compensation. Unfortunately, these processes are vaguely defined and only loosely tied to observable behavior. Piaget also claims that movement through the steps is partially caused by more specific factors, such as (a) the increasing perceptual contrast between dimensions as the stimulus object is subjected to further transformation and (b) dissatisfaction with giving the same answer repeatedly when it is not accompanied by certainty and when perceptual conditions are changing. These factors, however, appear to have little or no empirical support.

A third problem is that the model is tied to a limited and artificial situation—repeated questioning as one of two balls of clay is rolled out further and further (Flavell, 1963). It is difficult to imagine that some of the proposed factors, e.g., dissatisfaction with always giving the same answer to repeated questioning, are important bases for switching dimensions in natural situations.

An Attentional Interpretation of Piaget's Model

Research on children's attention to stimulus dimensions in problem-solving situations can provide an empirically supported, process-oriented version of Piaget's model. This attentional model takes into account both the characteristics of the stimuli and the level of development of the child, but emphasizes the former more than Piaget does. The attentional model does not contradict Piaget's model as much as it adds to and further specifies it. The interpretation offered here is that changes in the dimensions that are selected and in how they are used during the development of conservation may be due not only to the development of abstract cognitive processes (e.g., ordinal comparisons of points of arrival, compensation), as claimed by Piaget, but also to the development of processes such as attention and perception that are associated with stimulus input. It is proposed that there is a complex, continuing interaction between these two levels of processing, with progress in one level facilitating progress in the other. Since Piaget has described how cognitive processes might facilitate attention to dimensions, the other half of the interaction will be emphasized here. It will be argued that developmental changes in attention to dimensions may be partly responsible for the child's movement through the steps of Piaget's model.

Piaget's Step 1 may reflect a child's dimensional preference. There is a large literature that indicates that children have a hierarchy of preferences for dimensions. That is, they are more likely to attend to some dimensions than to others. In a typical test of such preferences a child is shown a standard object and two comparison objects. Each comparison object is the same as the standard along one dimension and different along another dimension. The child is asked which comparison object is the same as, or most like, the standard. For example, a red square might be compared with a red triangle and a green square. The choice of the green square would indicate a preference for shape over color, whereas choice of the red triangle would indicate a preference for color. It is usually assumed that a child's preference indicates the dimension to which he is attending.

The preference studies, for the most part, have examined the color, form, size, and number dimensions. A common finding is that attention preferences can facilitate or retard problem solving, depending on whether the preferred dimension is relevant or irrelevant for solution (e.g., Suchman & Trabasso, 1966b). Thus, the exclusive selection of a dimension in Step 1 of Piaget's model may simply reflect the child's dimensional preference rather than factors posited by Piaget, such as a belief in ordinal comparisons of points of arrival. It is not clear what causes dimensional preferences, but some of the variables that appear to be involved are task requirements and discriminability of the stimuli (Fernandez, 1976), complexity (Corah, 1966), and prior experience with the dimensions (Medin, 1973). An examination of these variables could clarify causes of preferences in the conservation task.

There is evidence that most nonconservers attend to height or length rather than width or density on dimensional preference tasks (Henry, 1976; Miller, 1973; Miller & Heller, 1976). This attentional bias may be due to certain characteristics of the conservation task that make these dimensions salient—the greater change in length than width as the clay ball is rolled into a snake, the rapid rise of the water as it is poured, etc.

It should be mentioned that the extraction of dimensions could occur both during the transformation and when there is no movement of the stimuli. Although Piaget used to claim that the transformation was the crucial phase of the conservation test, he more recently proposed (in an address to the Jean Piaget Society, Philadelphia, 1975) that the static states are also quite important.

There is some doubt whether Piaget's Step 2 even exists. Nonconservers seldom base their answers on the width dimension in conservation tasks (e.g., Miller, Grabowski, & Heldmeyer, 1973) and seldom attend to width on dimensional preference tasks (Miller, 1973). If Step 2 in Piaget's model is to be retained, it is necessary to make one or perhaps both of the following modifications in the description of this step. First, Step 2 may exist, but for such a brief period of time that few children tested happen to be in Step 2. In this case the attentional interpretation would be that the change from centration on one dimension to centration on the other dimension reflects a developmental change in the dimension to which the child prefers to attend. Developmental changes in preferences, especially change from color to form, are well documented (e.g., Brian & Goodenough, 1929; Suchman & Trabasso, 1966a).

A second possible modification of Step 2, probably more reasonable than the first modification, is that the child does not switch to centration on, or preference for, width but does become much more aware of width than in Step 1. That is, the child is now able to break away from the perceptual pull of the preferred dimension but does not necessarily switch his preference to width. This ability to direct one's attention away from one's preferred dimension is gradually acquired during the preschool and early elementary school years. As evidence for this developmental trend, Kofsky and Osler (1967) found an increase with age in the number of reclassifications of stimuli in a sorting task. Young children found it very difficult to stop using a preferred dimension. As children grow older their attention becomes more flexible. They can select one dimension, reject it when it is advantageous for problem solving to do so, and select another dimension (Hale & Green, 1976; Pick & Frankel, 1974).

In Step 3, the child can attend to two dimensions at the same time. In situations in which it is useful to attend to several dimensions, there is a developmental increase in the tendency to do so (Hale, this volume). The ability to attend to two dimensions may facilitate movement to Step 3 in the following way. As the child becomes skillful at attending to both dimensions and switching from one dimension to the other, he is increasingly likely to notice that a change in one dimension is related to a change in the other dimension. For example, when a child switches back and forth between the length and width of clay as it is rolled out into a snake, he begins to notice that as the snake becomes longer, it also becomes thinner. This can lead to conflict between the outcomes of each dimension; longer means more and thinner means less. This awareness of a relationship between the dimensions can be the beginning of what eventually becomes the compensation operation. Thus, the ability to attend to dimensions may develop to the point where higher order concepts take over.

If the first three steps in Piaget's model can be interpreted in relation to the development of attention to dimensions, then training children to attend to dimensions might move certain nonconservers closer to compensation. Perceptual training studies by Tighe and Tighe (e.g., 1969) suggest a procedure that might be effective. Their training consisted of same–different judgments about objects that varied in one or several dimensions. This training facilitated performance on a subsequent reversal shift task. Using a similar training procedure, Timmons and Smothergill (1975) obtained seriation in children who originally were unable to seriate height and brightness. Such data suggest that the procedure may have promise for teaching compensation. In a liquid conservation problem, for example, training might involve same–different judgments with liquid height differences, then with width differences, then with both. The training might include both static presentations (as in the Tighe studies) and dynamic presentations (e.g., pouring liquids). The latter technique would involve greater similarity between training and the subsequent test of conservation. Such training should teach the following: (a) stimuli can and should be broken down into dimensions, (b) dimensions can change independently (if the liquid is not simply poured), and (c) changes in the dimensions are correlated if the liquid is poured from one container to another.

Step 4, in which compensation and conservation are developed, involves abstract thought beyond that which can be tied to attentional processes. Developments in the child's attention to dimensions in the first three steps may set the stage for the transition to Step 4 by providing the child with information concerning changes in two dimensions. However, simultaneous attention to two dimensions is not sufficient for making the inference that the two quantities are equal. This inference requires the development of mental operations that can relate information about changes in the stimulus dimensions to questions concerning the equality or inequality of two quantities. In addition, there may be other cognitive changes within Step 4 that carry the conservation concept even further from its dimensional origins. These cognitive changes may include the integration of compensation with other operations such as reversibility, the notion that the transformation can be reversed. It is necessary to hypothesize that conservation involves more than just attentional factors because many conservation tasks include stimulus transformations that are not easily broken down into dimensions, e.g., dividing a ball of clay into several pieces, arranging a line of objects into a circle.

According to this reanalysis of Piaget's model, the child's growing ability to attend efficiently to dimensions partially underlies the movement through the steps leading to conservation. There are also related developmental changes in the information-processing system that may underlie the development of attention and, consequently, attention to dimensions in quantity problems. For example, Pascual-Leone (1970) suggests that an increase in the amount of information the child can process makes progress through the Piagetian stages possible. The information-processing demand of a task is defined as the number of schemes that the child must activate simultaneously, via attention, in the course of solving the problem. Pascual-Leone's hypothesis implies that the child becomes increasingly able to attend to two dimensions simultaneously and to compare changes within each dimension. Another relevant model of information processing comes from Schaeffer, Eggleston, and Scott (1974), who propose that practice with component skills causes them to become automated. Automation reduces the information load, which in turn makes it possible to integrate the component skills. If attention to each dimension eventually becomes automatic, part of the information-processing capacity is freed to integrate the dimensions. In still another model of information processing, Klahr and Wallace (1976) stress the elimination of redundant processing by discovering consistent sequences. In the four-step model, then, the child widens the range of dimensions he will consider in the search for consistent indicators of quantity. Finally, the recent finding that children have a growing understanding of the process of attention to dimensions (Miller & Bigi, 1977) raises the possibility that children's understanding of the information-processing system may affect their strategies of attending to dimensions.

In conclusion, the Piagetian model can be enriched by examining the four steps in light of evidence concerning the development of attention in several kinds of problem-solving tasks. In contrast to Piaget's emphasis on changes in cognitive structures, the attentional model emphasizes processes closely tied to stimulus input, for example, selective attention and attentional capacity. There is, of course, continual interaction between these "higher" and "lower" levels during development.

The Role of Attention to Quantity

In the reanalysis of Piaget's four-step model, the dimensions considered to be relevant were those having a relationship in which an increase in one dimension (e.g., height) is compensated for by a decrease in another dimension (e.g., width). Thus, the appropriate strategy was to attend simultaneously to the two dimensions. However, there appears to be yet another way in which the development of attention could contribute to the development of conservation. The child may become increasingly adept at attending to the quantity dimension itself. Although a preoperational child, by definition, cannot conserve, he is developing some understanding of quantity, especially number, and is increasingly able to direct his attention to that dimension. There are several sources of evidence for this claim. Preschoolers can directly perceive without counting (subitize) a collection of up to three objects (Chi & Klahr, 1975). Klahr and Wallace (1976) claim that subitizing is necessary (but not sufficient) for the eventual development of conservation. There is evidence that preschoolers can correctly judge the number of objects in static arrays under certain conditions (e.g., Gelman, 1972). Furthermore, nonconservers often can attend to number on dimensional preference tasks (Miller & Heller, 1976). The ability to judge the number of objects, estimate numbers or amounts, and attend to number or amount increases during development (Miller, 1975).

The development of the ability to attend to the quantity dimension may facilitate the development of conservation by helping the child select out the quantity dimension from the other dimensions, keep track of it over time and events (the transformation), and resist distracting irrelevant dimensions, such as length on number conservation tasks. The ability to keep track of the number dimension may be necessary for the child to develop the concept of reversibility, notice that the number of objects is the same before and after the transformation, etc.

The close relationship between attention and conservation appears to continue even as conservation appears. As conservation develops and stabilizes, attention to number or amount becomes more frequent (Henry, 1976; Miller, 1973). Also, certain stimulus variables such as number of objects and type of array affect attention to number and conservation of number similarly (Miller & Heller, 1976).

One issue that should be raised is whether one can attend to number or amount in the same way that one can attend to dimensions such as color or height. The present author has discussed this issue elsewhere (Miller, 1975). Briefly, there are both similarities and differences. Quantity is a dimension like color and height in that it consists of physical values along a scale. There is perceptual information about this dimension, such as that available when a child sees a group of objects or containers of water. However, it should be emphasized that quantity is more abstract, in that it is less directly available from direct perception than are dimensions such as color and length. Consequently, the notion of "attention to quantity" should be used with some caution, recognizing that the notion is a departure in some ways from the usual use of the term *attention*.

To summarize this section, there is some evidence that children's growing ability to attend to dimensions is intimately related to the development of conservation. Most of the research thus far demonstrates a relationship between attention and conservation but does not identify how the developing processes affect each other. There are several ways in which these developing abilities could interact. In general, it is hypothesized that an advance in attention to dimensions paves the way for compensation and conservation, which in turn facilitates attention to dimensions, and so on. At some points in development the two systems may lead to the same behavior. For example, the choice of the elongated dimension could be based on both the perceptual salience of that dimension and the child's knowledge that long things and tall things usually have more than short things. In other cases there may be conflict at first, as when attention to length competes with a rudimentary notion of number.

How Attention to Dimensions Affects Conservation Performance

It has been argued thus far that developmental changes in attention are partly responsible for the steps leading to conservation. However, even after conservation is first developed, attention to dimensions continues to play a role. Until the concept of conservation is strong enough to be demonstrated in all situations, the child's tendency to attend to salient or preferred dimensions affects whether his understanding of conservation is expressed in his performance. The child's attention either facilitates or interferes with the demonstration of his new, fragile concept of conservation. This interference is similar to that which occurs when a child does not solve a discrimination learning task because of his tendency to respond to an irrelevant dimension and his inability to switch to the relevant dimension (e.g., Suchman & Trabasso, 1966b). If the child is trained to respond to the relevant dimension, performance on a subsequent learning task is facilitated (e.g., Caron, 1969).

That attention can interfere with conservation performance is seen in a study by Gelman (1969). She presents the following argument: Five-year-olds understand conservation but often are unable to demonstrate it because of attention to salient dimensions that are irrelevant to quantity (e.g., a horizontal versus a vertical orientation) or imperfect indicators of quantity (e.g., length in the case of number). In fact, when the experimenter manipulates the material during the transformation, these misleading dimensions may be further emphasized. It should be possible to redirect the child's attention to quantity and thereby allow the understanding of conservation to be expressed in performance. Gelman used learning-set training with feedback to achieve this. Attention to the quantity dimension was reinforced and attention to other dimensions was not. Her attentional training was highly successful, producing conservation not only on the number and length conservation tasks on which subjects were trained but also on mass and liquid quantity conservation tasks. Conservation was still demonstrated 2 to 3 weeks later. Subsequently, Boersma and Wilton (1974) found that this attentional training also advanced the children's visual activity; they looked at more parts of the stimuli than they did before training. They no longer centrated on a single stimulus dimension.

Gelman's interpretation of the improvement of conservation performance is that the training did not teach conservation *per se*. Rather, the training taught the children which dimension was relevant to the solution of the problem. This interpretation is supported by two aspects of the results. First, the children quickly mastered the training tasks. If a full understanding of conservation had actually been taught, the children would have required a much longer time to master the training tasks. Second, on certain trials in which quantity was the only possible basis of response, children had little or no difficulty in selecting the quantity dimension. When irrelevant dimensions were added, children switched their attention to them in the early part of training.

Gelman's results are impressive, but two issues concerning the interpretation of the results should be raised. First, an attentional interpretation is not the only one that can be offered (see Miller, 1975, for a discussion of this point). It has been suggested that more general mechanisms believed to underlie conservation could explain improvement after "attentional" training. For example, Beilin (1971) suggests that the training may have caused cognitive conflict, which led to a new level of equilibrium. The second issue is whether Gelman's training is effective with children younger than age 5. Vadhan and Smothergill (1977) found little improvement in conservation performance as a result of attentional training in 4-year-olds.

Although the way in which the child attends to dimensions seems to affect his performance on conservation tasks, it is not clear what the locus of this influence is. The conservation task consists of three parts, a static presentation of identical objects or groups of objects, a transformation that involves movement of the stimuli, and a final static state in which the two arrays are no longer perceptually identical. These three phases differ from each other in the type of information about dimensions they present. The child's attention to dimensions in any or all of these phases could influence whether the child gives a nonconservation or a conservation answer. Furthermore, the nature of the dimensions in the first phase may determine what dimension the child attends to in the later phases. That is, the first phase may create a bias or "set" for attending to a particular dimension (e.g., length or number) over the later phases. For example, in a number conservation task two rows with equal numbers of objects are *the same length* in the first phase. This physical arrangement may draw attention to length or imply to the child that the length dimension is relevant. Since young children find it difficult to switch attention from one dimension to another (Kofsky & Osler, 1967), they may simply attend to length in later phases as well and therefore fail to conserve. Similarly, in the case of liquid quantity, the identical heights of liquids in containers may create a bias for attending to height. There is as yet no experimental evidence that provides an unambiguous test of this hypothesis. However, there is evidence that an attentional set can be created over a series of conservation of number trials. Miller, Heldmeyer, and Miller (1975) found that giving conservation tasks in order from easiest to hardest elicited more conservation responses than giving them in the opposite order. The number dimension was perceptually accentuated on the easiest trials by presenting a small number of objects with matching corresponding pairs (two zebras, two turtles, etc.). Apparently, this facilitated the child's attention to the number dimension and the child continued to use this dimension. In contrast, beginning with the most difficult trial (a larger number of objects placed in rows with no emphasis on correspondence) may have created a set for attending to length.

Bryant (1974) presents an argument similar to Gelman's claim that improper attention leads some children with knowledge concerning conservation to give nonconservation answers. Bryant, however, stresses the conflict of strategies. He suggests that young children who have some understanding of invariance may give a nonconservation answer because they use different dimensions as a basis for their response on the first and last phases of a number conservation task. The number dimension, based on the spatial correspondence of the objects, is used in the first phase. The length dimension is attended to in the last phase and, because it is the dimension to which attention has most recently been directed, forms the basis for the nonconservation answer. Bryant's experiments show that when the perceptual basis for the length bias is removed the child can apply his strategy of using correspondence cues and consequently give a conservation answer. Bryant also demonstrated that children can be taught which dimension is

relevant for the conservation problem. As in the Gelman experiment, training allows conservation competence to be expressed in conservation
performance.

The literature on the role of attention in problem solving suggests
several ways to increase conservation performance besides training children
to attend to quantity. For example, in a test of conservation of number,
conservation should be more likely to be expressed if one removes irrelevant, salient dimensions such as length (Lubker, 1967), fades in the irrelevant dimensions (Caron, 1968), or increases the salience of the relevant
dimension, number (Trabasso, 1963), by emphasizing the correspondence
of pairs or de-emphasizing length.

If attention to dimensions does affect conservation performance, then
knowing the salience of each dimension for a particular child in a given
situation should allow one to predict whether that child will conserve in that
situation. However, the evidence only partially supports this view. In apparent support of this position, Henry (1976) and Miller (1973) report that
kindergarten nonconservers are more likely to attend to length and height
than to number and liquid quantity on dimensional preference tests. Furthermore, kindergarten conservers, if probed, reveal more awareness of
both height and width, or length and density, than kindergarten nonconservers. In addition, attention to quantity subsequently increases as conservation stabilizes. On the other hand, kindergarten conservers as well as
kindergarten nonconservers are more likely to attend to length and height
than to number or liquid quantity on dimensional preference tests (Henry,
1976; Miller, 1973) unless small numbers of objects and nonlinear transformations are used (Miller & Heller, 1976). Thus, although it has been shown
that attentional factors are involved in conservation, prediction of conservation performance on the basis of the child's attention to dimensions is by no
means perfect. Either attention underlies only part of the variance in conservation performance or attentional assessment is not refined enough at
present.

Recent research on another Piagetian concept, double classification,
demonstrates that the salience of dimensions can predict performance. Performance is better when the two relevant dimensions are high in the child's
preference hierarchy than when one dimension is high and one is low
(Odom, Astor, & Cunningham, 1975).

A recent review (Miller, 1978) documents the fact that a number of
stimulus variables affect the performance of transitional conservers. For
example, perceptual supports for one-to-one correspondence (e.g., matching colors for corresponding pairs) improve performance in conservation of
number tasks (Miller et al., 1975) unless the number of objects is too large
(Miller & West, 1976). Removing salient irrelevant dimensions such as
height (Miller & Heldmeyer, 1975) and using certain types of transforma-

tions such as spreading objects out randomly rather than in a line (Miller & Heller, 1976) also facilitate conservation. The effect of these stimulus variables may be due in part to their effects on attention. The one study that has examined this hypothesis demonstrated that the number of objects and the type of transformation have similar effects on conservation of number and attention to number as measured on dimensional preference tasks (Miller & Heller, 1976).

Since information about the effect of attention to dimensions on conservation performance is only beginning to accumulate, an evaluation of the attentional approach would be premature at present. It is the author's view that attentional factors should be explored further because they are of particular importance for two areas of concern to those studying cognitive development—cognitive assessment and a performance model of cognition. If attention to dimensions is, in fact, important, it is clear that an accurate assessment of conservation would require a cognizance of attentional factors. For example, if salient or preferred dimensions are present and they are irrelevant, conservation ability would be underestimated. The second area of concern is the construction of a performance model, a model of how the child's knowledge about conservation is expressed in a particular situation. The expression of this knowledge involves a chain of interrelated psychological events, such as the interpretation of instructions, attention to certain aspects of stimuli while ignoring other aspects, retrieval of certain information from memory, activation of logical structures, etc. Attention to stimulus dimensions is one factor in an adequate performance model. Although Piaget has primarily been concerned with a competence model of conservation, a model specifying cognitive structures that describe the child's knowledge, a performance model is equally important for describing and explaining cognitive development.

Implications for an Understanding of the Development of Dimensionalization

This discussion began with a definition of dimensionalization as any process that provides the child with information about properties that can be ordered dimensionally. One aspect of dimensionalization has been discussed thus far—attention to stimulus dimensions. A common operational definition of attention is the selection of a particular dimension in a dimensional preference task. Research on attention to dimensions has been fruitful and, as argued in this chapter, appears to have implications for Piaget's theory of cognitive development. However, Piaget's theory, in turn, has implications for research on attention. Of particular interest here is the fact that the attentional approach appears to be too narrow an approach to

studying dimensionalization in two ways. First, dimensionalization involves more than simply attending to dimensions, in that there are several
levels of dimensionalization. Second, dimensionalization occurs not only
with static objects that do not change their appearance within a particular
trial, as in attentional tasks, but also with events in which there is perceptual change and even correlated change between dimensions, as in conservation tasks. An examination of the conservation and attentional paradigms
together gives a broader view of how children extract and use dimensions
during development. The following discussion will describe this broader
view of dimensionalization.

Levels of Dimensionalization

A comparison of various problem-solving and Piagetian tasks suggests
that there is a continuum of dimensionalization abilities, ranging from those
involving attention to a distinctive feature, such as straight versus curved,
during perceptual discrimination to Piaget's concept of seriation, an abstract mental operation. Thus, "dimensionalization" can have varying degrees of completeness, depending on the developmental level of the child's
thinking and the particular stimulus situation. The processes involved in
dimensionalization can include those usually labeled perceptual, attentional, or cognitive. This continuum of processes will now be examined in
more detail.

In the tasks examined in this chapter, the first and simplest dimensional information extracted during development seems to be distinctive
features (Gibson, 1969). A minimum of two points along a dimension defines a distinctive feature, for example, line versus curve, jagged versus
smooth, tall versus short. The extraction of a distinctive feature requires
only a very primitive notion of a dimension. For example, recognizing that
one object is taller than another or attending to height on a discrimination
learning task with two objects need not imply a fully developed notion of a
dimension of tallness. Gibson (1969) presents evidence that very young
children can perceive distinctive features. Some of the training studies (e.g.,
Caron, 1969) and conservation-related studies (e.g., Gelman, 1972) mentioned earlier in this chapter also indicate that even young children can
detect distinctive features.

The next levels of dimensionalization are not easily identified from
research conducted thus far. Thus, to some extent their nature must be
predicted on a logical basis. Dimensionalization no longer involves a simple
two-choice judgment but rather a judgment about the relative lengths of
rows of objects, sizes of objects, etc. The research reviewed earlier identifies
several developmental changes in dimensionalization. First, the child's notion of a relatively undifferentiated, qualitative dimension changes into the
concept of a differentiated, quantitative dimension. Second, the child grad-

ually comes to understand that each dimension is separable from other dimensions. Third, there is an increase in the number of dimensions the child can attend to simultaneously. Fourth, the child comes to exercise more control over his dimensionalizing behavior. For example, the dimension to which a child attends becomes determined less by stimulus characteristics such as the salience of the dimension and more by a tendency to engage in active search for dimensions that are relevant to the task. In addition, the child decides whether attention to one or several dimensions is more efficient in a particular task. Fifth, the child's notion of a dimension becomes more conceptual. Whereas earlier the child merely perceived differences in the height of objects, later he develops an abstract concept of height that can be evoked even when no stimuli are present. Sixth, a general "set" to dimensionalize may develop; a child tends to analyze stimuli into dimensions when it is useful to do so, even when dimensionalization is not suggested by the experimenter or the type of stimuli. In addition, dimensionalization would come to occur in a wide variety of settings, with various types of stimuli. These six trends that emerge during the middle levels of dimensionalization are probably related in their development. The exact nature of their interconnection must be identified in future research.

The final level of dimensionalization refers to the concept of seriation. Inhelder and Piaget (1964) define seriation as "the product of a set of asymmetrical transitive relations connected in series" (p. 6). There is a logical addition (and subtraction) of these ordered differences. When the child is able to seriate he grasps the fact that a dimension is a continuum, with each point being "more than" the point below it and "less than" the point above it with respect to some property such as height, brightness, or number. In a test of seriation, the child might be given a set of 10 sticks varying in length and asked to put them in order. Piaget contrasts true seriation of the sticks with an earlier perception-based ordering that relies on a perceptual "good form" and the proximity of the members of the series. True seriation is a mental operation that does not need perceptual supports.

The acquisition of seriation in the middle years of childhood is the culmination of the six trends described above. The child now has a differentiated, quantitative concept of a dimension *per se* as well as many specific dimensions. This concept is applied in the child's active problem solving in a wide variety of situations.

After the early levels of dimensionalization are developed, children are capable of applying any of these levels of dimensionalization to a task. Which level is most appropriate depends on whether a perceptual or conceptual judgment is required, whether stimuli are presented in a static or dynamic manner, whether the dimensions are independent or dependent, etc.

The developmental changes in dimensionalization described here are closely related to three trends in perceptual development identified by Eleanor Gibson (1969). These trends are (a) an increasing specificity of correspondence between information in stimulation and the differentiation of perception, (b) an increasing optimization of attention, largely through the improvement of strategies of extracting the relevant information and ignoring the irrelevant information, and (c) an increasing economy in the perceptual process of information pickup, e.g., extracting and processing higher order structure. Gibson's theory is especially suitable for the tasks considered here because she includes the perception of both static objects (as in problem-solving tasks) and events over time and space (as in the conservation task, object concept task, etc.).

The proposal that the ability to dimensionalize develops through several levels can help account for Piaget's notion of horizontal décalage, the fact that some cognitive structures are first successfully applied to one content area and only later to another content area. As an example of a horizontal décalage, Piaget finds that conservation of mass precedes conservation of weight, which in turn precedes conservation of volume (Piaget & Inhelder, 1962). Genevans claim that the reason conservation of mass, weight, and volume are not acquired at the same time is that the child encounters specific "resistances" from the physical reality (Inhelder, Sinclair, & Bovet, 1974). The nature of these resistances, however, is not specified. It may be that this décalage is due to the relative ease with which the materials can be dimensionalized. How difficult it is to extract a dimension may be determined by the materials themselves. For example, displaced volume may be a more abstract dimension (less directly tied to sensory input) than weight, which in turn may be more abstract than substance. The more abstract the dimension, the later one would expect it to be developed. The way the tests for the different materials are presented also may affect the difficulty of dimensionalizing. In support of this claim, Baylor and Lemoyne (1975) found that the décalage between length and weight seriation nearly disappeared when the information-processing demands of length and weight seriation tasks were made more similar than they are in typical tests of seriation. Simultaneous viewing and comparing of the various sticks, normally a part of the length seriation task but not the weight seriation task, was not allowed. Thus, the kind of information about the dimension that is available to the child may affect the ease with which the dimension can be extracted, which in turn may contribute to the décalages. Odom (1978) found that manipulating the salience of dimensions removed or greatly diminished differences in performance related to age on several types of cognitive tasks. For example, 4-year-olds performed nearly as well as 6-year-olds on a double classification matrix problem if both of the dimensions were very salient for the younger children.

Since the various conservations appear over a wide age range (from about 6 to 13) and dimensionalization is also developing at the same time, it is likely that the relationship between conservation and dimensionalization changes throughout this period. The early conservations such as number and liquid quantity probably would be more affected by the child's perception of distinctive features and attention to stimulus dimensions, which are developing rapidly during the preschool and early elementary school years, than by the more advanced dimensionalization abilities, which are developed later. The conservations developed later, such as displaced volume, are probably more influenced by the development of the most advanced levels of dimensionalization.

Relationships between Dimensions

As discussed in the previous section, an implication of Piaget's work is that there are several levels of dimensionalization. A second implication is that the research on attention to dimensions has had too narrow a focus by using only stimulus materials that do not move or change and that present only a small subset of the dimensions that could be presented, such as color, shape, and size. Drawing on the Piagetian tasks, the present section and the following section will present a broader view of the nature of dimensions than is found in either the Piagetian or the attentional approaches alone.

During development, children learn about relationships between dimensions as well as about single dimensions. Dimensions are related to varying degrees. In a conservation task the two dimensions that have a compensatory relationship are completely interdependent, i.e., there is a correlation of -1.00 between changes in the two dimensions, if the quantity is unchanged. Height and width in liquid quantity and length and density in number have this relationship. Other dimensions in the conservation tasks, such as color or orientation, are not correlated with each other or with height, width, or quantity, and thus are independent. Between these two extremes are dimensions that have a moderate correlation in real life. For example, tall things often, but not always, have more than short things, as when milk is poured into a glass and the level rises or when a stick of candy is eaten and becomes shorter.

In contrast, the dimensions in common problem-solving tasks are independent. That is, objects can be constructed from any combination of values of shape, size, and color. Any correlation between dimensions is artificial; the experimenter can arbitrarily create a correlation between two dimensions by making them relevant and redundant, e.g., by reinforcing responses to red squares. This artificial dependency contrasts with the necessary and natural dependency between dimensions in the conservation task and between dimensions found in certain natural situations.

Thus children must learn the degree of correlation between dimensions and the situations in which that correlation holds. This knowledge can be rather complex. For example, changes in height and width are correlated when the amount of liquid remains the same, but not when two different amounts are involved. In the latter situation, height and width are analogous to color, shape, and size in problem-solving tasks in that the dimensions are independent.

Dimensionalization of Changing Stimuli

One important difference between the conservation and problem-solving tasks lies in the amount and type of information provided about each dimension. Since the conservation task involves movement, it presents the child with changes in the values within dimensions. In fact, in some transformations, such as rolling a ball of clay into a snake, there is an infinite number of values in two dimensions (length and width). The child must deal with simultaneous changes within two dimensions in addition to the static arrays before and after the transformation. Also, during the transformation he must integrate the values in two dimensions over many points in time. Thus there is both spatial and temporal integration. Gibson (1969) suggests that part of the development of conservation involves the perception of invariance over time and over an event sequence. The child eventually can perceive the transformation as a unitary happening and extract perceptual structure from the change. In short, there is much more perceptual information about dimensions in the conservation task than in common problem-solving tasks. In fact, this large amount of information may increase the demands on the child's information-processing system and make it more difficult to extract dimensions and see the relationship between dimensions in conservation situations.

In contrast, in common problem-solving tasks the values are static and only a small number of values along each dimension are presented. In addition, the variety in the values usually comes from a large number of trials rather than from a single trial. Elkind (1969) points out that the conservation concept has to do with variation *within* things, while multidimensional problem solving has to do with variation *between* things.

In short, children encounter stimulus dimensions in the world in many different ways. Materials may be stationary or have varying degrees of movement or perceptual change. It is likely that the type of information that a task gives about dimensions affects whether a child dimensionalizes the stimuli, selects one dimension over another, extracts one or several dimensions at a time, and sees relationships between the dimensions.

Implications for Research on Dimensionalization

Based on the analysis of dimensionalization in this chapter, there are three general recommendations for future research. First, the development of dimensionalization *per se* should be examined. The vast majority of research on dimensionalization in children has examined this ability within the context of a problem-solving task. Dimensionalization could certainly be studied more directly. There is little information about (a) how children dimensionalize stimuli, (b) what causes improvement in dimensionalization during development, (c) why some dimensions are more difficult to extract than others, and (d) how the ability to attend to dimensions is related to the abilities to construct them (put stimuli in order), remember them, and use them to solve problems.

Second, the relationship between dimensionalization and cognitive performance at different levels of dimensionalization should be examined. One might inquire, for example, whether a 5-year-old's dimensionalization ability affects his problem solving in the same way that a 10-year-old's does. Also, one might ask how advanced the ability to extract a particular dimension must be before a child can use that dimension in a problem-solving or conservation task.

Third, it is important to separate a child's *ability* to dimensionalize from his *tendency* to dimensionalize. Ability and tendency have often been confused in past research. In many studies the child has had a choice of whether or not to select a particular dimension. It often is erroneously inferred that the child *cannot* dimensionalize if he *does not* dimensionalize during such tasks. In fact, there may be a "production deficiency" similar to that observed in the area of memory (Flavell, 1970). The child may not select a particular dimension or may not even dimensionalize at all because he does not yet realize that such a strategy is relevant to the solution of the problem. The child, however, can be encouraged to select an appropriate dimension through training (e.g., Gelman, 1969). With development, the strategy of dimensionalizing is quickly and reliably evoked and applied to many types of stimuli and situations. Also, there is an improvement in the choice of the correct dimensionalizing strategy. For example, children learn that whether one or several dimensions should be selected depends on the situation (e.g., Hale, this volume). Some organization and planning on the part of the child is necessary to use the dimensionalizing strategy efficiently. Also, the child may need some understanding of cognitive and perceptual processes in order to use dimensions appropriately. For example, there appear to be developmental changes in children's understanding of how stimulus dimensions affect problem solving (Miller & Bigi, 1977). All of these factors involved in moving the child from the ability to dimensionalize to the application of this ability are important subjects for future research.

Summary

This chapter has discussed the importance of children's extraction and use of stimulus dimensions, activities that play a role in a wide variety of problem-solving and learning situations. It was proposed that the development of attention to dimensions contributes to the development of conservation and helps determine whether a child's conservation competence will be reflected in his performance. It was also noted that the development of conservation, in turn, may affect the development of attention to dimensions. Thus, there may be mutual facilitation between the development of attention and conservation. In a discussion of differences between conservation and common problem-solving tasks, several issues were raised about the development of dimensionalization *per se*. It was proposed that as children develop they acquire a variety of dimensionalization abilities, learn about relationships between dimensions, and learn to extract dimensions from both static and changing stimuli.

References

Baylor, G. W., & Lemoyne, G. Experiments in seriation with children: Towards an information processing explanation of the horizontal décalage. *Canadian Journal of Behavioural Science,* 1975, *7,* 4–29.

Beilin, H. The training and acquisition of logical structure. In M. F. Roskopf, L. P. Steffe, & S. Taback (Eds.), *Piagetian cognitive-developmental research and mathematical education.* Washington: National Council of Teachers of Mathematics, 1971.

Boersma, F. J., & Wilton, K. M. Eye movements and conservation acceleration. *Journal of Experimental Child Psychology,* 1974, *17,* 49–60.

Brian, C. R., & Goodenough, F. L. The relative potency of color and form perception at various ages. *Journal of Experimental Psychology,* 1929, *12,* 197–213.

Bryant, P. E. *Perception and understanding in young children.* New York: Basic, 1974.

Caron, A. J. Discrimination shifts in children as a consequence of dimensional training. *Journal of Experimental Child Psychology,* 1968, *6,* 522–542.

Caron, A. J. Discrimination shifts in three-year-olds as a function of dimensional salience. *Developmental Psychology,* 1969, *1,* 333–339.

Chi, T. H., & Klahr, D. Span and rate of apprehension in children and adults. *Journal of Experimental Child Psychology,* 1975, *19,* 434–439.

Corah, N. L. The influence of some stimulus characteristics in color and form perception in nursery-school children. *Child Development,* 1966, *37,* 205–211.

Elkind, D. Conservation and concept formation. In D. Elkind & J. H. Flavell (Eds.), *Studies in cognitive development: Essays in honor of Jean Piaget.* New York: Oxford University Press, 1969.

Fernandez, D. Dimensional dominance and stimulus discriminability. *Journal of Experimental Child Psychology,* 1976, *21,* 175–189.

Flavell, J. H. *The developmental psychology of Jean Piaget.* New York: Van Nostrand, 1963.

Flavell, J. H. Developmental studies of mediated memory. In H. W. Reese & L. P. Lipsitt (Eds.), *Advances in child development and behavior* (Vol. 5). New York: Academic, 1970.

Gelman, R. Conservation acquisition: A problem of learning to attend to relevant attributes. *Journal of Experimental Child Psychology,* 1969, *7,* 167–187.

Gelman, R. The nature and development of early number concepts. In H. W. Reese (Ed.), *Advances in child development and behavior* (Vol. 7). New York: Academic, 1972.

Gibson, E. J. *Principles of perceptual learning and development.* New York: Appleton-Century-Crofts, 1969.

Hale, G. A., & Green, R. Z. Children's attention to stimulus components with variation in relative salience of components and degree of stimulus integration. *Journal of Experimental Child Psychology,* 1976, *21,* 446–459.

Henry, D. E. Interrelationships among attentional preferences, cardinal-ordinal ability, and conservation of number. *Child Development,* 1976, *47,* 750–758.

Inhelder, B., & Piaget, J. *The early growth of logic in the child.* New York: Norton, 1964.

Inhelder, B., Sinclair, H., & Bovet, M. *Learning and the development of cognition.* Cambridge, Mass.: Harvard University Press, 1974.

Klahr, D., & Wallace, J. G. *Cognitive development: An information-processing view.* New York: Halsted, 1976.

Kofsky, E., & Osler, S. F. Free classification in children. *Child Development,* 1967, *38,* 927–937.

Lubker, B. J. Irrelevant stimulus dimensions and children's performance on simultaneous discrimination problems. *Child Development,* 1967, *38,* 119–125.

Medin, D. L. Measuring and training dimensional preferences. *Child Development,* 1973, *44,* 359–362.

Miller, P. H. Attention to stimulus dimensions in the conservation of liquid quantity. *Child Development,* 1973, *44,* 129–136.

Miller, P. H. *The development of attention and conservation* (Report No. 73). Ann Arbor: University of Michigan, Developmental Psychology Program, 1975.

Miller, P. H. Stimulus variables in conservation: An alternative approach to assessment. *Merrill-Palmer Quarterly,* 1978, *24,* 141–160.

Miller, P. H., & Bigi, L. Children's understanding of how stimulus dimensions affect performance. *Child Development,* 1977, *48,* 1712–1715.

Miller, P. H., & Heldmeyer, K. H. Perceptual information in conservation: Effects of screening. *Child Development,* 1975, *46,* 588–592.

Miller, P. H., & Heller, K. A. Facilitation of attention to number and conservation of number. *Journal of Experimental Child Psychology,* 1976, *22,* 454–467.

Miller, P. H., & West, R. Perceptual supports for one-to-one correspondence in the conservation of number. *Journal of Experimental Child Psychology,* 1976, *21,* 417–424.

Miller, P. H., Grabowski, T., & Heldmeyer, K. H. The role of stimulus dimensions in the conservation of substance. *Child Development,* 1973, *44,* 646–650.

Miller, P. H., Heldmeyer, K. H., & Miller, S. A. Facilitation of conservation of number in young children. *Developmental Psychology,* 1975, *11,* 253.

Odom, R. D. Effects of perceptual salience on the recall of relevant and incidental values: A developmental study. *Journal of Experimental Psychology,* 1972, *92,* 285–291.

Odom, R. D. A perceptual-salience account of décalage relations and developmental change. In L. S. Siegel & L. J. Brainerd (Eds.), *Alternatives to Piaget.* New York: Academic, 1978.

Odom, R. D., Astor, E. C., & Cunningham, J. G. Effects of perceptual salience on the matrix task performance of four- and six-year old children. *Child Development,* 1975, *46,* 758–762.

Pascual-Leone, J. A. A mathematical model for the transition rule in Piaget's developmental states. *Acta Psychologica,* 1970, *32,* 301–345.

Piaget, J. Equilibration and the development of logical structures. In J. M. Tanner & B. Inhelder (Eds.), *Discussions on child development* (Vol. 4). New York: International Universities Press, 1960.

Piaget, J. Quantification, conservation, and nativism. *Science,* 1968, *162,* 976–979.

Piaget, J. Piaget's theory. In P. H. Mussen (Ed.), *Carmichael's manual of child psychology.* New York: Wiley, 1970.

Piaget, J., & Inhelder, B. *Le développement des quantités physiques chez l'enfant* (2nd rev. ed.). Neuchâtel: Delachaux and Niestlé, 1962.

Pick, A. D., & Frankel, G. W. A developmental study of strategies of visual selectivity. *Child Development*, 1974, *45*, 1162–1165.

Schaeffer, B., Eggleston, V. H., & Scott, J. L. Number development in young children. *Cognitive Psychology*, 1974, *6*, 357–379.

Suchman, R. G., & Trabasso, T. Color and form preference in young children. *Journal of Experimental Child Psychology*, 1966, *3*, 177–187. (a)

Suchman, R. G., & Trabasso, T. Stimulus preference and cue function in young children's concept attainment. *Journal of Experimental Child Psychology*, 1966, *3*, 188–198. (b)

Tighe, L. S., & Tighe, T. J. Transfer from perceptual pretraining as a function of number of task dimensions. *Journal of Experimental Child Psychology*, 1969, *8*, 494–502.

Timmons, S. A., & Smothergill, D. W. Perceptual training of height and brightness seriation in kindergarten children. *Child Development*, 1975, *46*, 1030–1034.

Trabasso, T. Stimulus emphasis and all-or-none learning of concept identification. *Journal of Experimental Psychology*, 1963, *65*, 395–406.

Vadhan, V. P., & Smothergill, D. W. Attention and cognition. *Cognition*, 1977, *5*, 251–263.

Zeaman, D., & House, B. J. The role of attention in retardate discrimination learning. In N. R. Ellis (Ed.), *Handbook of mental deficiency*. New York: McGraw-Hill, 1963.

6

Developmental Aspects of Selective Orientation

Marcel Kinsbourne and James M. Swanson

In addition to its general alerting effect, the orientation response (OR) has a selective component (Sokolov, 1963). In its most overt form the selective OR consists in turning (of gaze, head position, and body) toward the source of stimulation. For all bisymmetrically organized species (Bilateria) this lateral orienting is the point of departure for the adaptively crucial choice—to approach or to withdraw (Schneirla, 1959). It is hardly surprising that newborn (and even premature) human infants are able to orient to either side. For the Bilateria this is, after all, perhaps the most ancient and basic behavior (Kinsbourne, 1974a). And inasmuch as neurological elaboration, and therefore behavioral elaboration, typically proceeds not by introducing new ("emergent") organizational principles but by refining existing ones, it comes as no surprise that a hierarchy of behaviors culminating in ones that are quite abstract are stacked upon and modify this primitive response.

From Selective Orienting to Mental Representation

In this section we will first discuss the overt orienting of the infant, then the internalization of orientation for purposes of mental representation, and finally how organized orienting patterns become possible.

Neurologists describe in young babies the asymmetrical tonic neck *reflex* (Gesell, 1938). The baby lies on his back. One turns his head to the right. The right arm extends, the left arm flexes, right leg extends, and left leg flexes. The baby assumes a position of pointing and turning to the right. The behavioral counterpart of this item in the neurological examination is the asymmetrical tonic neck *response,* which is something babies do in real

Marcel Kinsbourne and James M. Swanson • Neuropsychology Research Unit, Hospital for Sick Children, Toronto, Ontario M5G 1X8 Canada.

life. A spot check on a series of newborn babies would find many of them in some positional variant of the asymmetrical tonic neck response.

The tonic neck response is no mere neurological curiosity. It is a highly organized lateral orienting response, providing the basis for the earliest form of selective attention. The newborn infant is capable both of "anticipatory" and "reactive" orientation (Kinsbourne, 1978). He will orient sidewards in anticipation of a stimulus. When laterally stimulated, be it in the auditory, visual, or tactile modality, he will react by orienting toward the source of stimulation. The baby looks where he points and points to where he is looking. His body is posed for possible movement toward the focal point of attention. The tonic neck response is most obvious in young infants (less than 28 weeks of age) who cannot yet walk, so the bodily rearrangements are not yet used as a point of departure for locomotion toward the target (Gesell & Ames, 1950). However, as is typical in behavioral development, the bodily arrangements that are a vehicle for behavior become apparent well before the behavior itself can be implemented through the maturation of additional relevant parts of the brain. (Other examples include interactional synchrony between speaking adult and attending baby—Condon & Ogston, 1971—and babbling, which is "free floating phonology" awaiting organization.) Indeed, looking and pointing where one is looking are so closely intertwined in the young that it is probably not possible for an infant to do one and at the same time restrain himself from doing the other. Furthermore, much of early babbling, and of subsequent naming of objects occurs in the context of this orienting synergism (Kinsbourne & Lempert, in press). One might question whether at the earliest stage of language development a child is able to name an object without looking and pointing at it (or at where it was). Only as motor maturation proceeds and differentiation of component responses becomes possible do children become able to dissociate their verbal responses from these physical readjustments, which are their earliest accompaniment and vehicle (Greenfield & Smith, 1976). Even then, they map their early syntax on the sequence of perceived action. Only after further maturation and increase in ability to dissociate internal representation from observed reality can they manipulate syntax into variants such as the passive form, which violate the sequence in which children orient to features of the action represented (Lempert & Kinsbourne, in press).

Naturally, the propensity to orient away from the point of regard is not limited to turning strictly right and strictly left. Even terrestrial animals can orient in both the lateral and the vertical plane and along any oblique that is the vector resultant of interacting vertical and lateral turning tendencies (and for fish and birds that move freely in both planes, this must be adaptively even more essential). But the central organization of vertical turning is by no means independent from that of turning sideways. Rather, symmetrical action of (right-sided) left turning centers and (left-sided) right turning centers, be it at cerebral or at brainstem (Kinsbourne, 1974a) levels, results in orientational shifts along the vertical plane. Thus the lateral turning tendencies that we are examining are not mere behavioral fragments but are the building steps for selective orientation toward any point in actual (and probably also in representational) space.

It is apparent, therefore, that differentiation of components of the selective orienting response may underlie much of the sophisticated behavior that develops later. A young child noticing some item of interest can hardly help but point to it (to the chagrin of those who would impose on young children conventional standards of courtesy that call for unrealistic levels of brain maturation). But this orienting response is not purely childish behavior. In more subtle form, it is observable in adults also (Fukuda, 1961; Hirt, 1967). A dramatic demonstration is reported by Berntson and Torello (1977). They measured normal adults' strength of grasp (squeezing a dynamometer) and found it greater if the subject held his head rotated away from the active hand. This is consistent with the synergy of head turning and contralateral finger flexing of the tonic neck reflex. A more casual instance is the observation, at the dinner table or committee meeting, of an involuntary glance toward the person who is being discussed (or the chair that everyone knows he has already vacated). When we internalize a representation of ambient space and let our attention range across that map, our eyes move, although they would have to gaze inward rather than outward to make any useful observation. This is because the selective orienting response does not disappear as the ability to abstract and internally represent space develops. It has merely become easier to suppress. Any change in mental set or problem-solving mode, unless it is purely symbolic (verbal, mathematical, etc.), has an imaginative spatial component. When the thinker changes what he is thinking about, that internal reorganization of spatially distributed attention is reflected by a visible and measurable shift in the postural orientation of the body.

How blatant that shift is depends both on the maturity of the observer's nervous system and on the degree of his determination to suppress that telltale response. But a completely unrevealing "poker face" is hard to attain; perhaps it is impossible for a child. The more frequent the shift in mental focus, the more frequent the motor displacements—giving, in the impulsive and "hyperactive" individual, an impression of "restlessness" (Swanson & Kinsbourne, 1978).

Lateral orienting can also be differentiated into modality-specific components. The more mature the observer, the better he can, when necessary, limit selective orientation to one mode only, overtly or covertly. But even in adults traces of the synergic organization of orientation can be observed. Subjects wearing earphones are instructed to attend selectively to one of two simultaneous auditory messages. As they attend to the input into one ear, their gaze can be observed to swivel in that direction (Kahneman, 1973) —although the configuration of the skull precludes them from seeing that ear, and it would avail them little if they could. The covert shift of auditory attention and the overt gaze shifts are synergically linked.

The limitations of young children's selective attention have been comprehensively discussed (e.g., Gibson, 1969; Jeffrey, 1968). Orienting will first occur to the most salient aspect of a situation. But the subsequent habituation of that OR effectively permits another stimulus attribute to become more salient and therefore produce a reorientation of attention. Such a hypothesis is capable of explaining even internalized problem solving at a high level. With repeated presentation of a stimulus complex, a well-integrated chain of response results. Whereas the older child can switch mental focus with celerity and ease down the perceptual hierarchy from salient to less salient feature till the relevant information has been gathered, young children tend to remain riveted to salient perceptual appearances. In Piagetian terms, they can only with difficulty "decenter" (Gelman, 1969). The behavior of immature humans (and of animals with less elaborate systems for behavioral control) is referenced to specific loci in external space. As higher mental function develops in humans, it gradually detaches from spatial reference, and in the form of symbolic behavior loses reference to outside locations altogether. This makes it possible for higher mental functions to be represented asymmetrically in brain—from whichever hemisphere the process is deployed, it serves the total organism (Kinsbourne, 1974b). But even then, its relationship to lateral orienting is not lost. The verbal behavior arises in an orienting context, and as orienting is rightward biased, it arises in left brain. Reciprocally, the verbal behavior itself can release secondary rightward orienting tendencies (see the final section).

Orienting Asymmetry and the Development of Handedness

In this section we will discuss how hand preference and language lateralization arise out of the asymmetrical tonic neck response.

Gazzaniga (1970) has suggested that handedness mediates hemispheric specialization. Early right hand preference in environmental exploration offers the left cerebral hemisphere prior access to information, and on account of the as yet unmyelinated state of the corpus callosum, the information is not automatically shared with the other side of the brain. That the left hemisphere does obtain exclusive tutoring by such a mechanism is unlikely, as it is now clear that myelination is by no means necessary for neuronal function in brain. Also, Gazzaniga's proposal is disconfirmed by the majority of left-handers who show left hemisphere dominance for language (Milner, 1974). But we may fare better if we think in terms not of manual but of lateral orienting (turning) asymmetry. Although human beings are roughly symmetrical around the saggital (front–back) plane, their preferred direction of action is not straight ahead but in most cases is subtly biased to the right. This effect is observable in many situations, ranging from obvious ones that call for use of a preferred hand (the right in 9 people out of 10) to less well-known effects like people's tendency to enter a public building by stairs leading to the center from the right rather than leading to the center from the left, or their tendency to drift rightward when walking on or swimming under surfaces devoid of landmarks (Ludwig, 1932). This overall rightward bias of motor behavior becomes apparent immediately after birth.

It was noted early that the tonic neck reflex in most babies can be more easily elicited by turning the head right rather than left. More importantly, if one observes the spontaneous positioning of infants, one finds most of them to be pointing (orienting) to the right. This was noticed early on by Gesell (1938) and has since been confirmed by Siqueland and Lipsitt (1966). They tried to use head turning as a conditioned response and found it much easier to condition head turning to the right than to the left. Indeed, they obtained so many spontaneous right head turns that they abandoned that particular response for purposes of their experimentation (e.g., Turkewitz, 1977). Turkewitz and his colleagues (Turkewitz, Gordon, & Birch, 1965) have performed a series of studies in the course of which they have repeatedly verified this phenomenon and we (Liederman & Kinsbourne, in press) have also found it to be the case.

Given that this lateral orienting behavior has such important implications for behavioral development, one cannot but be impressed by the blatant asymmetry that it exhibits from birth onward. Were the asymmetry known to be biologically preprogrammed, it might give us an important lead toward an explanation of that prime riddle of human brain organization, the lateralization of cerebral function (and notably of language to the left cerebral hemisphere in 19 people out of 20). Turkewitz (1977) has argued that the rightward bias of tonic neck response is due to a rightward bias in the way that nurses position babies after tending them. Nurses do indeed place babies more often on their right than on their left side. This, argues Turkewitz, shuts off the right ear from auditory stimulation. When the baby is then placed on its back, it is disproportionately sensitive to auditory stimulation coming from the right, which therefore exerts more control over behavior. The baby then preferentially turns toward the right-sided stimulus.

This argument does not survive inspection. Given simultaneous tactile stimuli to the two cheeks, newborns turn more to the right than to the left. When a baby lies on its right side, it is its right cheek that is subject to continuous tactile stimulation, while its left cheek remains untouched. By Turkewitz's logic, it should then be the touch to the left that is more effective and leftward turning bias should result. It does not. Further evidence against a situational mechanism for the rightward bias of turning comes from Turkewitz's own laboratory. Premature infants were followed longitudinally up to 39 weeks of conceptual age. It was only at 35 weeks that the right bias became apparent, and it reached the magnitude previously observed only at 39 weeks. Thus the right bias is due to aspects of brain organization that develop in the last 2 months of intrauterine life (Gardner, Lewkowitz, & Turkewitz, 1977).

In recent studies, Liederman & Kinsbourne (in press) addressed this issue by noting which way babies turn after being given midline tactile or gustatory stimulation (a puff of air or a bitter taste on a nipple). A rightward bias in turning away from these mildly noxious stimuli was apparent. In fact, it was somewhat more marked than the bias in turning *toward* one of paired milder stimuli similar to those used by Turkewitz. Now, if there is a rightward bias in turning away from a midline stimulus (as well as a bias toward choice of the right of two simultaneous stimuli competing for attention), then perceptual factors are ruled out as causing the bias. The asymmetry must reside in the motor control of turning tendencies. A newborn baby tends to turn to the right more than to the left in a perceptual field that is effectively symmetrical.

Why should right turning be innately favored? Of any lateralized phenomenon one can ask: (a) Why is the response lateralized at all? And given that it is, (b) why to a particular side? A simple response to the second question would invoke genetic diversity: An ancestor's genetic complement has become perpetuated throughout the species. The first question is less readily answered. Perhaps Corballis and Beale (1970) were right in supposing that in order to be able to respond differentially to right and left, an organism cannot be perfectly bisymmetrical, and perhaps the motor bias constitutes the adaptively effective deviation from bisymmetry.

One might expect such a bias, whatever its adaptive justification, to be potentially harmful if left unchecked once the organism becomes mobile—both because relevant events (potentially beneficial and potentially hazardous) would not be given an equal degree of attention and because cognitive biases of this kind would make the organism's behavior more predictable to predators and to prey, and thus less effective in dealing with either. Indeed, it is probably only because the precocial human infant is motorically so inert that motor biases are not selected against at that stage in the life-span. Biased or not, the infant is helpless, and the caretaker easily overrides asymmetrical biases to respond. So it comes as no surprise to learn that the rightward motor bias diminishes with central nervous system maturation and can be readily overcome by the time the individual is mature enough to be able to locomote in relation to external landmarks, or in relation to decisions arrived at by internal processes.

This rightward turning tendency could be a precursor of the customary right hand preference. Although it is usually supposed that people prefer the right hand because it is more skillful (dextrous) than the left in most cases, it could be that lateralized hand preference is a specific instance of a more general motor asymmetry, as here discussed. If newborn babies tend to turn more to the right than to the left, then by virtue of the nature of tonic neck response, the right hand, pointing to and approaching the target object, becomes the natural one to manipulate it. Indeed, the preferred direction of head position after birth predicts the hand used for visually guided reaching at age 12 weeks (Coryell & Michel, in press). The whole body turns in such a way that attention is readily focused to the right side of personal space, the field of action of the right hand. Thus we see in the tonic neck response the origin both of dextrality and of those subtle but pervasive rightward biases of behavior to which we alluded at the beginning and which we will discuss in more detail.

The gradation from tonic neck response to manual preference has not been systematically studied in the longitudinal fashion that is called for, although Gesell and Ames (1950) have claimed that it is the rightward-biased babies who become right-handers. Hand preference itself is rather hard to demonstrate before the 2nd year of life. An infant cannot spontaneously reach for things, and it is reaching behavior and its elaborations that are mostly used as criteria for hand preference. When the 9- or 10-month-old baby does begin to be able to reach, he shows a striking "reluctance to cross the midline." This means that he will use the hand on the same side as the object rather than a "preferred" hand for reaching and still not reveal in his reaching behavior what his manual laterality is or is going to be. However, if one uses a behavior that is more natural to young babies, one can reveal a striking asymmetry of performance as early as at 3 months of age. Caplan and Kinsbourne (1976) placed a rattle into either the right or the left hand of 3-month-old babies and timed how long the child would continue to clutch the rattle before dropping it. They found a striking asymmetry, with more prolonged grasp on the right (see also Halverson, 1937a,b; White, 1969). This asymmetry held only for children of right-handed parents, suggesting that it is related to handedness by virtue of a genetic mechanism.

This observation brings us into an area of current controversy. What is the origin of hand preference? Analogous to Turkewitz's view about rightward orienting, some have suggested that hand preference is learned or modeled from parents (Collins, 1970). Others fit genetic models to handedness distributions in families (Annett, 1967; Nagylaki & Levy, 1973). Others regard deviation from right-handedness as due to brain damage (with emphasis on the motor strip of the left hemisphere (Bakan, Dibb, & Reed, 1973). It has even been suggested that handedness is a consequence of oocytic (nongenetic) inheritance (Morgan, 1977).

In a cross-fostering study, Hicks and Kinsbourne (1976a) showed that hand preference cannot be regarded as a behavior that is modeled by the child based on his long-term observation of his parents' behavior. They studied children who lived with one biological and one adoptive parent and found that whereas there was a highly significant correlation of the child's with the biological parent's handedness, there was no correlation at all between the child's and the adoptive parent's handedness. It follows that if hand preference is the consequence of some form of learned behavior, then that learning must occur very early in life (i.e., during the period before the adoptive parents in the Hicks and Kinsbourne study has joined the probands' families). But studying hand preference in very young children, before even early learning could have occurred, is problematic. Infants do not manifest hand preference as tested for in the conventional way because the behaviors called for are not yet under their control. For this reason, Liederman and Kinsbourne (unpublished) used the asymmetrical tonic neck response as their preference indicator. They examined the prevalence of rightward turning bias in children of right-handed parents as compared to children with one parent who was not right-handed. They found that the rightward bias was confined to the group whose parents were both right-handed.

The preferred direction of turning of a newborn baby could hardly result from its imitation of preferential hand use by either parent. Young babies are quite unable to make the necessary discrimination and to perform the imitations that would be called for. Also, being in the hospital, they have little opportunity to be influenced by the mother's hand preference and even less by that of the father. Yet we were able to show that mothers' and fathers' hand preference exert equal effect on the newborn turning bias. If nonright-handedness in the parents were a brain damage effect, it is hard to see how this could have influenced the turning tendencies of these babies who were selected for their ability to meet stringent criteria of normality. As for oocytic inheritance (Morgan, 1977), this should show a maternal but not a paternal effect. Yet as we have mentioned, the two parents contributed equally in this study.

We cannot escape the conclusion that hand preference is genetically determined, that it is a component of a more general asymmetry of motor control as manifest in imbalance between the right and the left turning tendency, and manifest subsequently in different levels of development of right and left manual skills. The mature organism becomes increasingly able to override this rightward bias in behavior but it never disappears completely. Right hand preference in the adult emerges out of it.

Handedness may be viewed from two distinct viewpoints: preference and proficiency. Strictly speaking, the orientational mechanisms that we have considered so far address only the preference aspect of handedness. It is possible that a completely separate mechanism programs the gradual emergence of greater proficiency of one hand (usually the preferred hand) at a variety of tasks. But we cannot be sure of this, because no one has so far succeeded in deconfounding differential proficiency and differential practice between the two hands.

Given the rightward attending bias of most people, the right hand will usually be the first limb to approach, and therefore to grasp and manipulate objects. Over time, this will result in much greater practice for it than for the left hand in many manual manipulations, and the emerging greater proficiency ("dexterity") of the right hand will, for all we know, simply be a consequence of differential practice.

Two ways of addressing this issue experimentally are, at least in principle, possible. One is to equate practice between the hands from infancy on. This is not feasible. The other is to determine whether, given an established inequality in manual proficiency, the inequality disappears when both hands are practiced to asymptote. Evidence on the latter point is conflicting and in any case such evidence would be indirect and not totally unambiguous (Hicks & Kinsbourne, 1976b).

After the disappearance of the overt tonic neck response after an age of about 28 weeks, what developmental changes do we see in the phenomenon of laterally biased attention?

A relatively simple case is that of selective attention to one of the two inputs into dichotically stimulated ears. When preschool children were asked to report selectively the verbal message provided to one (specified) ear only, they could do so, but subject to intrusions from material presented to the other ear (Hiscock & Kinsbourne, 1977). Performance with the left ear was worse. Moreover, there was asymmetrical persistence of lateralized listening set. Those preschool children who were first asked to monitor the left ear switched readily to the right at the next session. Those who were asked to begin with the right ear message had great trouble making the change to the left ear selective listening, even if the two sessions were separated by a whole day.

A way to interpret the findings is to suppose that, within the dimension of lateral space, the right side is more salient for most young children, the left side less salient. The effect is not absolute: Children can attend selectively to the less salient side but suffer more intrusion from the more salient source of information. If the latter is the initial focus of attention, it is apt to carry over and obstruct a move down the perceptual hierarchy to a less salient input source.

Again, what is seen in major form in children can be seen in minor form in adults when one uses a more difficult task. Treisman and Geffen's (1968) subjects were better able to confine their attention to the right than to the left of two concurrent dichotically presented verbal passages.

Effect of Rightward Response Bias on Lateral Attending

When people sustain severe damage to one or the other cerebral hemisphere, typically after a stroke, they often show a phenomenon known as unilateral neglect of person and of space. Not only do they complain surprisingly little about the paralyzed and numb side of the body, they do not look at, touch, or move it to the extent expected; they neglect it to a degree beyond that accounted for by the fact that the bodily part is weak and difficult to use. Furthermore, they pay little attention to the side of space opposite their damaged side. They do not look in that direction, seem not to attend to sounds coming from there, and in general, fail to explore the side of space opposite the lesion. In contrast, they explore to an exaggerated degree perceptual changes occurring on the other side.

These phenomena of neglect are due to damage of the lateral orienting center of the affected hemisphere. There is normally a balance between right and left turning tendencies, each subserved by one hemisphere. When one hemisphere is appropriately activated (either by whatever neuronal changes underlie the decision to turn to the opposite side or by the stimulating electrode applied directly to brain), its turning tendency becomes more potent and the vector resultant of its influence and that of the opposing hemisphere plants attention in the desired direction (Kinsbourne, 1974a). When hemispheric disease implicates the lateral orienting center, then this may suspend action partly or completely, leaving the opponent process disinhibited and unchecked. This attentional imbalance accounts for the clinical manifestations of unilateral neglect (Kinsbourne, 1977). But although damage to either hemisphere is capable of generating a contralateral neglect syndrome, the effects of equivalent right- and left-sided lesions are not equal. By far the most striking neglect syndromes arise from right hemisphere damage. This suggests that the right and left turning tendencies did not, in the premorbid state, have equal force. The right turning tendency, produced by the action of the left hemisphere, is the more powerful and, when disinhibited, causes the more severe orientation bias in behavior.

However, the conclusion is not as simple as might so far appear. The rightward bias of attention in neglect and in the Treisman and Geffen study may be partly attributable to verbal aspects of the situation. We will now discuss how the adoption of particular cognitive sets interacts with the direction of attention.

Task-Related Attentional Biases

Even in infants there is some evidence for attentional biases that are categorically determined. Entus (1978) presented either music or speech and reported a categorical effect on habituation of nonnutritive sucking in infants. Her subjects dishabituated more rapidly to verbal change if it occurred on the right, and musical change if it occurred on the left (but see Varga-Khadem & Corballis, 1977). Glanville, Best, and Levenson (1977) reported similar findings using a cardiac orientation response as the dependent variable. Molfese, Freeman, and Palermo (1975) showed that average evoked potentials achieve greater amplitude over the left side of the skull when elicited by verbal stimuli (in the preverbal infant) and over the right skull to music. Gardiner and Walter (1976) reported analogous results using power spectrum analysis of the EEG. These data may be interpreted as revealing brain specialization at an early age. But what type of specialization? It hardly could be verbal processing or musical appreciation.

As Porter and Berlin (1975) have suggested, there may be several levels at which the auditory stimulus is processed—for instance, a level associated with phonetic, auditory memory of stimulus components or that associated with memory of temporal order in a stimulus set. The demonstrations of lateralized response in infants all could be related to the simplest phonological level. It might be that at deeper levels of processing, asymmetries would only be demonstrable in older children. If so, this would show not that the representation of function at such levels gradually lateralizes but merely that it gradually develops and when developed, is lateralized.

When one undertakes a cognitive task, one has both to adopt the appropriate verbal set and to implement the specific processing that the task and materials call for. In physiological terms, one has to activate the appropriate region of brain and it then has to function. Now, there is no necessary reason why these two stages must always be linked. Electrophysiological changes related to brain activity are cryptic. They may herald or coincide with processing, but we do not know exactly what they represent. Do they represent activation of the relevant brain area (in this case hemisphere)? If so, it is unnecessary to debate the existence in infants of cerebrally based verbal or musical skills. We know they can respond differentially to verbal versus nonverbal material, and we also know that double dissociation of function (language versus spatial skills) obtains—at least in the adult—at brain stem level (Ojemann, 1977). Perhaps we are witnessing a lateralized alerting response that, when the specialized hemisphere processing has later become available, will serve to implement the initiation of a categorically defined mental set.

These possibilities suggest that the lateralized response to categorical stimulation is linked to selective orienting. Rightward orienting is synergically linked with verbal preparedness, leftward orienting with preparation for processing nonverbal stimuli. As verbal behavior itself arises out of selective orienting and is, like selective orienting, specific and sequential, it might naturally evolve in the hemisphere that manifests an advantage in the control of lateral attending. To the right hemisphere would then remain the task of providing a simultaneous spatial framework for these specific acts.

In adults, cognitive-orienting relationships have been repeatedly demonstrated, initially by Kinsbourne (1972), who showed that subjects pondering verbal problems unconsciously look right, while when pondering spatial problems they look up and to the left. This is equally true for 6-year-old children (Kinsbourne & Jardno, unpublished). The reverse causal connection also holds: Looking right facilitates verbal decision making, looking left facilitates spatial decision making (Kinsbourne, 1975; Casey, 1977). This lateral orienting is associated with lateralized information processing, a relationship that suggests that the more recent functions are constructed not *de novo* but in some relation to the archaic orienting capability.

We may now reconsider the Treisman and Geffen (1968) finding of greater ease in shadowing the right than the left of two concurrent messages. This may have been due to the verbal nature of the task. If nonverbal messages had been used, the opposite attentional bias might have emerged.

With respect to the asymmetrical incidence of spatial neglect after lateralized cerebral damage, Kinsbourne (1977) suggested that verbal thoughts of the patient, and verbal interaction between patient and clinician, might account for at least some of the greater tendency for right hemisphere lesions to appear to generate the more severe lateral neglect. Verbal activation of a damaged left hemisphere could counteract a leftward attentional bias, but verbal activation of the left hemisphere when the right is damaged would further exaggerate the preexisting rightward attentional bias.

As has elsewhere been discussed (Kinsbourne, 1970, 1975), familiar paradigms such as hemifield viewing and dichotic listening also appear to generate task-specific performance asymmetries based on the attentional imbalance. This is due at least in part to the lateralized brain activation that underlies the cognitive processing demanded by the task. When subjects adopt a verbal mental set, in expectation of a verbal problem (as in the classical hemifield and dichotic situations), or on account of a verbal warning signal (Bowers & Heilman, 1976; Bowers, Heilman, Satz, & Altman, in press; Carter & Kinsbourne, in press), or persist in a verbal set engendered by a prior verbal task (Kinsbourne, 1970, 1975; Hellige & Cox, 1976), the left hemisphere is "primed" (i.e., activated) and this activation overflows more into the adjacent right turning center than into the contralateral left turning center. This biases attention (be it visual, in the hemifield situation, or in dichotic listening) in a rightward direction—i.e. contralateral to the more activated left hemisphere. In contrast, spatial priming (Goodglass, Shai, Rosen, & Berman, 1971), nonverbal auditory (Bowers & Heilman, 1976), and visuospatial (Carter & Kinsbourne, in press) engender leftward attentional shifts and the left ear and hemifield advantages reported for musical and spatial tasks (e.g., Spellacy & Blumstein, 1970; Kimura, 1964) may be so accounted for. The development of these perceptual asymmetries has been discussed in detail (Kinsbourne & Hiscock, 1977, 1978). In overview, the category-specific attentional biases are clearly present at least down to age 3 and when proper provision is made for the differing difficulty of a given task for differently aged children, there is little or no evidence of any change in the degree of this asymmetry from age 3 into adolescence (e.g., Hiscock & Kinsbourne, 1977, 1978; White & Kinsbourne, in press). The issue of whether the degree of lateral attentional bias (and by implication the degree of central lateralization) varies systematically with changing age during childhood will be addressed by longitudinal studies in progress in our laboratory. Probably there will turn out to be no significant change in degree of lateral bias of attention in association with tasks that rely on the specialized contributions of particular hemispheres. If so, we will be able to conclude that the development of selective lateral orientation consists essentially in a growth of the ability voluntarily to attend selectively in a manner adaptive to the changing needs of the moment (regardless of "prewired" task-related attentional biases). We will not need to postulate any change in the manner in which attentional biases arise out of brain organization.

References

Annett, M. The binominal distribution of right, mixed and left-handedness. *Quarterly Journal of Experimental Psychology,* 1967, *19,* 327–333.

Bakan, P., Dibb, G., & Reed, P. Handedness and birth stress. *Neuropsychologia,* 1973, *11,* 363–366.

Berntson, G. G., & Torello, M. W. Expression of Magnus tonic neck reflexes in distal muscles of prehension in normal adults. *Physiology and Behavior,* 1977, *19,* 585–587.

Bowers, D., & Heilman, K. Material specific hemispheric arousal. *Neuropsychologia,* 1976, *14,* 123–128.

Bowers, D., Heilman, K., Satz, P., & Altman, A. Simultaneous performance on verbal, nonverbal and motor tasks by right-handed adults. *Cortex,* in press.

Caplan, P. J., & Kinsbourne, M. Baby drops the rattle: Asymmetry of duration of grasp by infants. *Child Development,* 1976, *47,* 532–536.

Carter, G. L., & Kinsbourne, M. Spatial mental set and visual laterality: A developmental study. *Developmental Psychology,* in press.

Casey, S. M. The effect of lateral eye positioning on information processing efficiency. Ergonomics Program Report. Raleigh, N.C.: North Carolina State University, April 1977.

Collins, R. L. The sound of one paw clapping: An inquiry into the origin on left-handedness. In G. Lindzey & D. D. Tiessen, (Eds.), *Contributions to behavior—genetic analysis— the mouse as a prototype.* New York: Meredith Corporation, 1970.

Condon, W. S., & Ogston, W. D. Speech and body motion synchrony of the speaker-hearer. In M. David & J. Jenkins (Eds.), *The perception of language*. Columbus, Ohio: Merrill, 1971.

Corballis, M. C., & Beale, I. L. Bilateral asymmetry and behavior. *Psychological Review*, 1970, *77*, 451–461.

Coryell, J. F., & Michel, G. F. How supine postural preferences of infants can contribute towards the development of handedness. *Infant Behavior and Development*, in press.

Entus, A. K. *Hemispheric asymmetry in infants*. Doctoral dissertation, McGill University, 1978.

Fukuda, T. Studies on human dynamic postures from the viewpoint of postural reflexes. *Acta Otolaryngologica (Suppl.)*, 1961, *161*, 1–51.

Gardiner, M. F., & Walter, D. O. Evidence of hemispheric specialization from infant EEG. In S. Harnad, L. Doty, J. Goldstein, J. Jaynes, & G. Krauthamer (Eds.), *Lateralization in the nervous system*. New York: Academic, 1976, pp. 481–502.

Gardner, J., Lewkowitz, D., & Turkewitz, G. Development of postural asymmetry in premature human infants. *Developmental Psychobiology*, 1977, *10*, 471–480.

Gazzaniga, M. S. *The bisected brain*. New York: Appleton-Century-Crofts, 1970.

Gelman, R. Conservation acquisition: A problem of learning to attend to relevant attributes. *Journal of Experimental Child Psychology*, 1969, *7*, 167–187.

Gesell, A. The tonic neck reflexes in the human infant. *Journal of Pediatrics*, 1938, *13*, 455–464.

Gesell, A., & Ames, L. B. Tonic neck reflex and symmetrical behavior: Developmental and clinical aspects. *Journal of Pediatrics*, 1950, *36*, 165–176.

Gibson, E. J. *Principles of perceptual learning and development*. New York: Appleton-Century-Crofts, 1969.

Glanville, B. B., Best, C. T., & Levenson, R. A cardiac measure of cerebral asymmetry in infant auditory perception. *Developmental Psychology*, 1977, *13*, 1.

Goodglass, H., Shai, A., Rosen, W., & Berman, M. *New observations on right–left differences in tachistoscopic recognition of verbal and non-verbal stimuli*. Paper presented at the International Neuropsychology Society meeting, Washington, D.C., 1971.

Greenfield, P. M., & Smith, J. H. *The structure of communication in early language development*. New York: Academic Press, 1976.

Halverson, H. Studies of the grasping responses of early infancy I. *Journal of Genetic Psychology*, 1937, *51*, 371–392. (a)

Halverson, H. Studies of the grasping responses of early infancy II. *Journal of Genetic Psychology*, 1937, *51*, 393–424. (b)

Hellige, J. B., & Cox, P. J. Effects of concurrent verbal memory on recognition of stimuli from the left and right visual fields. *Journal of Experimental Psychology*, 1976, *2*, 210–221.

Hicks, R. E., & Kinsbourne, M. Human handedness: A partial cross-fostering study. *Science*, 1976, *192*, 908–910. (a)

Hicks, R. E., & Kinsbourne, M. On the genesis of human handedness: A review. *Journal of Motor Behavior*, 1976, *8*, 257–266. (b)

Hirt, S. The tonic neck reflex mechanism in the normal adult. *American Journal of Physical Medicine*, 1967, *46*, 362–369.

Hiscock, M., & Kinsbourne, M. Selective listening asymmetry in preschool children. *Developmental Psychology*, 1977, *13*, 217–224.

Hiscock, M., & Kinsbourne, M. Ontogeny of cerebral dominance: Evidence from time-sharing asymmetry in children. *Developmental Psychology*, 1978, *14*, 321–392.

Jeffrey, W. E. The orienting reflex and attention in cognitive development. *Psychological Review*, 1968, *75*, 323–334.

Kahneman, D. *Attention and effort*. Englewood Cliffs, N.J.: Prentice-Hall, 1973.

Kimura, D. Left-right differences in the perception of melodies. *Quarterly Journal of Experimental Psychology*, 1964, *16*, 355–358.

Kinsbourne, M. The cerebral basis of lateral asymmetries in attention. *Acta Psychologica, 33.* In A. F. Sanders, (Ed.), *Attention and performance III.* Amsterdam: North-Holland Publishing Company, 1970, pp. 193–201.

Kinsbourne, M. Eye and head turning indicate cerebral lateralization. *Science,* 1972, *176,* 539–541.

Kinsbourne, M. Lateral interactions in the brain. In M. Kinsbourne & W. L. Smith (Eds.), *Hemispheric disconnection and cerebral function.* Springfield, Ill.: Charles C Thomas, 1974. (a)

Kinsbourne, M. Mechanisms of hemispheric interaction in man. In M. Kinsbourne & W. L. Smith (Eds.), *Hemispheric disconnection and cerebral function.* Springfield, Ill.: Charles C Thomas, 1974. (b)

Kinsbourne, M. The mechanism of hemispheric control of the lateral gradient of attention. In P. M. A. Rabbitt & S. Dornic (Eds.), *Attention and performance V.* London: Academic, 1975.

Kinsbourne, M. Hemi-neglect and hemispheric rivalry. *Advances in Neurology,* 1977, *18,* 41–49.

Kinsbourne, M. The biological determinants of functional bisymmetry and asymmetry. In M. Kinsbourne (Ed.), *The asymmetrical function of the brain.* New York: Cambridge University Press, 1978.

Kinsbourne, M., & Hiscock, M. The development of cerebral dominance. In S. Segalowitz & F. A. Gruber (Eds.), *Language development and neurological theory.* New York: Academic, 1977.

Kinsbourne, M.; & Hiscock, M. Cerebral lateralization and cognitive development. In J. S. Chall & A. Mersky (Eds.), *Education and the brain, Yearbook of the National Society for Study in Education.* Chicago: University of Chicago Press, 1978, pp. 169–222.

Kinsbourne, M., & Jardno, R. Differential lateral gaze in six year old children while pondering verbal and spatial questions. Unpublished manuscript.

Kinsbourne, M., & Lempert, H. Naming while pointing: The orientational origin of speech and its control by the left brain. *Human Development,* in press.

Lempert, H., & Kinsbourne, M. Action as substrate for early syntax. In P. French (Ed.), *The development of meaning.* Tokyo, Japan: International Congress of Language Development, in press.

Liederman, J., & Kinsbourne, M. The mechanism of neonatal rightward turning bias: A sensory or motor asymmetry? *Infant Behavior and Development,* in press.

Liederman, J., & Kinsbourne, M. *Rightward motor bias in neonates depends upon parental right-handedness.* Unpublished manuscript.

Ludwig, W. *Das Rechts-Links-Problem: Im Tierreich und beim Menschen.* Berlin: Springer, 1932.

Milner, B. Hemispheric specialization: Scope and limits. In F. Schmitt & F. Worden (Eds.), *The neurosciences: Third study program.* Cambridge, Mass.: M.I.T. Press, 1974.

Molfese, D. K., Freeman, R. B., & Palermo, D. S. The ontogeny of brain lateralization for speech and nonspeech stimuli. *Brain and Language,* 1975, *2,* 356–368.

Morgan, M. Embryology and inheritance of asymmetry. In S. Harnad, R. W. Doty, L. Goldstein, J. Jaynes, & G. Krauthamer (Eds.), *Lateralization in the nervous system.* New York: Academic, 1977.

Nagylaki, T., & Levy, J. The sound of one paw clapping is not sound. *Behavior Genetics,* 1973, *3,* 279–292.

Ojemann, G. A. Asymmetric function of the thalamus in man. *Annals of the New York Academy of Sciences: Evolution and Lateralization of the Brain,* 1977, *299,* 380–396.

Porter, R. J., & Berlin, C. I. On interpreting developmental changes in the dichotic right-ear advantage. *Brain and Language*, 1975, *2*, 186–200.

Schneirla, T. C. An evolutionary and developmental theory of biphasic processes underlying approach and withdrawal. In M. R. Jones (Ed.), *Nebraska symposium on motivation*. Lincoln: University of Nebraska Press, 1959, pp. 1–42.

Siqueland, E. R., & Lipsitt, L. P. Conditioned head-turning in human newborns. *Journal of Experimental Child Psychology*, 1966, *3*, 356–376.

Sokolov, E. N. *Perception and the conditioned reflex*. New York: Macmillan, 1963.

Spellacy, F., & Blumstein, S. E. The influence of language set on ear preference in phoneme recognition. *Cortex*, 1970, *6*, 430–439.

Swanson, J. M., & Kinsbourne, M. Should you use stimulants to treat the hyperactive child? *Modern Medicine*, 1978, 71–80.

Treisman, A., & Geffen, G. Selective attention and cerebral dominance in perceiving and responding to speech messages. *Quarterly Journal of Experimental Psychology*, 1968, *20*, 139–150.

Turkewitz, G. The development of lateral differentiation in the human infant. *Annals of the New York Academy of Sciences: Evolution and Lateralization of the Brain*, 1977, *299*, 309–318.

Turkewitz, G., Gordon, E. W., & Birch, H. G. Head turning in the human neonate: Spontaneous patterns. *Journal of Genetic Psychology*, 1965, *107*, 143.

Varga-Khadem, F. W., & Corballis, M. C. *Cerebral asymmetry in infants*. Paper presented at the Biennial Meeting of the Society for Research in Child Development, New Orleans, March 1977.

White, B. The initial coordination of sensorimotor schemas in human infants: Piaget's ideas and the role of experience. In D. Elkind & J. Flavell (Eds.), *Studies in cognitive development: Essays in honor of Jean Piaget*. New York: Oxford University Press, 1969.

White, N., & Kinsbourne, M. Does speech output control lateralize over time? Evidence from verbal-manual time-sharing tasks. *Brain and Language*, in press.

7

Attentional Processes and Individual Differences

MICHAEL LEWIS AND NANCY BALDINI

Given the observable fact that infants attend to and explore their environments, it is valuable to ascertain what variables determine these behaviors. In this chapter we turn our effort toward examining attention in infancy, in the belief that attentional processes play an important role in the child's early cognitive development.

Both Piaget (1963) and Bruner (1966, 1973) have ascribed a sensorimotor form of stimulus processing and storage to the young organism. They contend that the infant comes to know or represent events through the motor schemata or enactive representations that give them meaning. According to Piaget (1963), it is through sensorimotor activity, or physical interaction with the environment, that the cognitive structure of the infant is formed. Implicit in Piaget's theory is the assumption that motor activity plays a vital role in cognitive growth. This conceptualization, while not precluding the possibility that sensory activity (as opposed to motor activity) contributes to cognitive growth, assumes an interaction between perception and action.

Lewis (1975), however, has reviewed evidence that indicates that infants can come to know or represent events perceptually, rather than strictly motorically. He concludes that the infant has a sophisticated sensory system capable of very complex sensory acts, while at the same time being an immature output system in terms of its motor or response behavior. Lewis argues that a meaningful conception of the infant's manner of representing the world must include more than motoric responses; that it is biologically advantageous for an organism, at birth, to be able to experience

MICHAEL LEWIS • Educational Testing Service, Princeton, New Jersey 08541. NANCY BAL-DINI • University of Rochester, Rochester, New York 14627. This research and review was supported by a grant from HEW Bureau of Education for the Handicapped, 300–77–0307.

the world around it and form cognitive structures from that experience, without being required to engage in sophisticated actions in that world. Support for this view comes from the work on habituation that demonstrates perceptual learning even during the newborn period, when physical interaction with stimuli in the environment is minimal (Friedman, 1975). In addition, data on handicapped infants suggest that physical inability to act does not necessarily prevent the organism from forming cognitive structures and from developing normally (Decarie, 1969). Thus, at least for some cognitive structures, a sensory interaction may be all that is necessary. Granted, the development of certain schemata clearly requires a motoric component, and the interaction between sensory and motor systems in the child's cognitive and social development needs further consideration. But it is Lewis's contention that motor activity has received too prominent a role in theory, especially in the sensorimotor stage of genetic epistemology. A consequence of this has been the strong tendency to focus on motoric behavior by those attempting to assess the intellectual ability of the newborn and young infant, as evidenced by the importance placed on motor functions in our standardized infant intelligence tests.

For all the work that has been and continues to be generated, attention is not easily definable. In a general sense, attention involves those processes by which an organism directs his sensory and elaborating cognitive systems. The direction of these systems is in the service of all subsequent action, thought, or affect. Researchers have attempted to define attention more specifically through the indices used to measure it, such as (a) receptor orientation; (b) decreases in such activities as moving, talking, vocalizing, and sucking; (c) autonomic nervous system changes such as heart rate decreases, galvanic skin resistance change, vasodilation in the head, vasoconstriction in the extremities, and changes in breathing rate; and, finally, (d) cortical changes.

Although there is a variety of parameters that may be used to assess attention, in order for these measurements to have meaning within the context of the developing organism, they need to be incorporated in a model of attention as it relates to cognitive processing. William James (1890) described two types of attending processes, "passive, immediate attention," by which the organism is drawn to attend to stimuli that are of interest in themselves, and "associational ('derived') voluntary attending," which is active attending to stimuli whose interest value is derived from their association with past experience.

A review of the research investigations bearing on these two types of attention reveals that a major distinction between them is the role of the infant's previous involvement with the stimuli. Whereas research on the first type of attention has to do with effects of such factors as stimulus complexity and intensity, research on the second involves effects of stimulus novelty and familiarity. One must take the developmental characteristics of the infant into consideration prior to defining scaling dimensions for constructs such as novelty or familiarity. Unlike intensity or complexity, novelty and amount of familiarity are completely dependent on the past experience of the organism. Hence the features of the environment that elicit associational attending are designated by the organism rather than being inherent in the stimuli; their effect is determined by the interaction between one's current cognitive set and past experiences or learning.

Research on associational attention and related memory processes can be further divided into two categories. The first category deals with the study of attention as a reflection of the organism's mental structures, these including not only schema acquisitions but also such basic processes as memory capacity. The second category focuses on attention as a measure of central nervous system functioning. This latter research rests on the assumption that attention and the memory processes upon which it depends are vital for the infant's intellectual development. Specifically, it is assumed that the rate of change in the organism's attention to an external stimulus is directly proportional to the rate at which an internal model of the stimulus is constructed. Based on this assumption, the reduction in attention that accompanies the repeated presentation of a stimulus, or habituation, can be viewed as a measure of cognitive functioning. Consequently, individual differences in the rate of habituation can be viewed as indicative of important differences in intellectual growth and capacity.

Distinctions involving other aspects of attention are also important. Cohen (1976) and Greenberg (1977) have reviewed the research on visual information processing during infancy. They note that researchers have made great advances beyond early attempts to identify the infant's perceptual abilities. They have proposed a conceptualization of information processing in terms of the four stages of perception that underlie the distribution of visual attention in infancy: attention getting, discrimination, attention holding, and memory processes.

A Review of Models of Attention and Memory

Through the study of infants' habituation of attention, it is possible to gain some understanding of the way infants acquire internal representations (Lewis, 1971). Habituation refers to a decrease in the strength of the attending response as a function of repeated presentations of a stimulus display. It is believed that as the organism repeatedly processes the information available in a particular display, an internal representation of the display is developed; as a consequence, the novelty of the observed stimulus is reduced and the attending response decreases.[1]

Central to the habituation paradigm is the assumption that the reduction in attention is a function of cognitive processing (Engen & Lipsitt, 1965; Sokolov, 1963, 1969; Thompson & Spencer, 1966). Therefore, it is important to demonstrate that the reduction in attention is not due to receptor, effector, or general organism fatigue, or to a progressive physiological loss of the ability to respond. That these alternatives can probably be ruled out is indicated by evidence that, following habituation, an organism will show renewed interest in response to the presentation of a novel stimulus. The possibility of physical restlessness has also been rejected by Cohen (1969), who showed that mere presence in the testing situation does not produce a decline in responsiveness. Also, there is considerable neurophysiological evidence (Rebert, McAdam, Knott, & Irwin, 1967; Walker, 1964) that strongly suggests that there are cortical changes such as negative slow potential change while the organism is showing response decrement, further supporting the view that reduction in attention reflects cognitive processing.

It then follows that if response decrement is a measure of the speed of model acquisition, then the amount or rate of this decrement should be associated with a more efficient system of forming representations such that those infants who show more rapid response decrement are those who build internal representations faster. Consequently, the infant is conceptualized as an active organism capable of building up an internal representation of an event, and of using this internal representation or memory trace to influence ongoing processing. In agreement with these assumptions, most

---

[1]The terms *habituation* and *response decrement* have been used interchangeably in the literature. Whether the subjects in most studies can be said to have habituated is in some doubt. Technically, to demonstrate habituation requires that a subject be shown a stimulus until he reaches a very low level of responding. Such has not been the case in most studies since the procedures do not allow for each subject to continue until he reaches a low level of responding. Typically, the criterion has been defined as a response level of about 50% of the original level of response. A drop of 50% may not be very substantial for some subjects. For example, subjects who initially fixate a stimulus for the full 30 seconds of a 30-second trial may only be on their way toward habituation upon reaching the trial in which they fixate for 15 seconds and thus have not yet formed a complete internal representation of the stimulus. There has been very little empirical work that has, in fact, tried to fully habituate the subjects' orienting response—that is, tried to get the subjects to stop or nearly stop attending. Moreover, there have been no studies looking at whether such factors as age or maturational status should play a role in deciding what percentage change should be used as a criterion of habituation. For these reasons the term *response decrement* may be the most accurate term to use, since it is a direct descriptor of the observed phenomenon, in contrast with the term *habituation,* which involves some inference. Nevertheless, we have followed custom and have used the term *habituation* in this chapter, along with the term *response decrement* in reference to the general phenomenon of a decrease in response to a repeated stimulus.

of the models of infant memory development are based on the notion that reduction in attention to a repeated stimulus reflects the formation of internal representations. In the following sections we summarize some of these models.

Sokolov

Sokolov (1963, 1969) proposed a model of habituation based on his investigations of the orienting reflex (OR) and the relationships of the OR to adaptive and defensive reflexes. The orientation of receptors toward the source of stimulation is the behavioral component of the OR. In addition, the OR includes several physiological responses, such as EEG activation and heart rate deceleration, which occur following the presentation of a novel stimulus. After several presentations of a stimulus, the behavioral and physiological responses habituate. However, an alteration in the originally presented pattern will elicit the OR again.

According to Sokolov, the decrease in response level is the result of the formation of a model of the repeated stimulus in the nervous system. The OR is the product of the discrepancy between current inputs and the neural traces established in memory from previous experience. Sokolov defines the internal model as an organization of neuronal cells in the cortex that retain and process characteristics of the repeatedly presented stimulus display. Encoded in the model are features such as intensity, duration, and quality of the stimulus. Information about such features is compared with incoming excitation; if the features match, attending is terminated; if not, an OR is activated and the organism continues to process the stimulus. These interactions eventually lead to the strengthening of the memory trace via reinforcement of neuronal excitation patterns or biochemical alterations.

The amount of activation of the OR is a function of the discrepancy between representations coded in memory and the stimulus being processed. Thus, information that is novel, and thereby highly discrepant from the mental representation, produces a relatively strong OR upon its initial presentation. After repeated presentation of the stimulus, the information becomes encoded as a neural trace. Consequently, the salience of the stimulus, or discrepancy from existing structures, will decrease, and habituation of the organism's response systems will result. Introduction of a new stimulus will produce increased attending.

Lewis (1971) takes issue with two aspects of this model. First, he argues that the internal representations of perceptual experience are not simply mirror images of events in the external world. Rather than constructing an exact internal copy of the external object, the organism creates a representation of the object that is a construction from multiple perspectives. This type of processing integrates past experience with current cognitive activities. The encoded internal representation remains invariant even though the sensory excitation pattern may change. Therefore, not all alterations of a stimulus will reactivate the OR.

The second criticism of Sokolov's position has to do with the time required for an organism to search internal structures to match external events. By Sokolov's formulation, which involves scanning all representations in memory, the attending process would be functionally inefficient. Lewis suggests that plans and intentions of the organism help to organize the perception, searching, or processing of external events in a manner that taps information in existing cognitive structures.

Lewis argues that one must posit such a hierarchy in order to account for the fact that attention is often directed to signal stimuli, or stimuli with meaning acquired from past experience. According to a simple match–mismatch model like that of Sokolov, meaningful stimuli that are familiar from past experiences should not be attended to. However, this is clearly not the case. Not only are signal stimuli attended to but they vary greatly in the magnitude of attention they elicit because of differences in their derived interest value.

Cohen and Gelber (1975) also find limitation in Sokolov's model. Their data from backward habituation curves indicate that attention may increase just prior to habituation, whereas Sokolov's model would predict a gradual decrease in attention across repeated exposures of a stimulus. In addition, they note that infants tend to look away from the stimulus on prehabituation trials, a phenomenon that Sokolov's model cannot explain.

Lewis

Lewis's model attributes a more active role to the organism than does the model of Sokolov and many others. It is based on a constructivist formulation of perceptual processing. In this model the infant is regarded as an active agent that seeks out meaningful stimulation in the environment, rather than a passive organism that simply processes stimulation provided by external sources. Consistent with other theorists, Lewis (1971) argues that the decrease in attention to repeatedly presented stimuli reflects the operation of cognitive processes, indicating formation of an internal representation of the stimulus. These processes are responsible for the organism's selective attention to aspects of the environment that contain new information.

According to Lewis, an adequate model of information processing must incorporate cognitive rules by which the relevant information is monitored and processed. In Figure 1 such a model is offered. In this model, cognitive decision rules form the basis for performance by the central processor. Incoming stimulus information is integrated with input from permanent

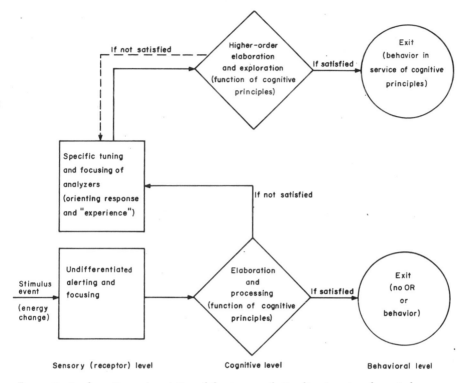

FIGURE 1. A schematic representation of the process of attending to external events by comparison with internal representations.

storage. Thus, past experience, which James (1890) contends is the basis for associational attention, comes into play. Passive attending, produced by intense stimulus, enters the system at the second level (specific tuning and focusing of analyses) and bypasses the first level, which involves past experience and simple cognitive principles.

As shown in Figure 1, the energy qualities of a stimulus event, or the change in energy caused by an event, are the initiators of perceptual processing and feature extraction. The receptors have a brief excitation period, during which time the stimulus may be further analyzed by the immediate processing system according to decision rules; if the stimulus is not analyzed during this brief period, the trace will decay, as represented by Exit. The immediate processing system plays an important role in cognitive development, as it serves to limit and direct the flow of incoming information. Once the stimulus event has been attended to by the system, it produces a general state of arousal or alerting whose function is to effect a change from totally unprepared, undifferentiated behavior to organized behavior—either internal behavior such as thinking or overt behavior such as motor responses. Concomitant with the increase in alertness is the start of analyzer tuning, stimulated by the energy change itself. This alerting-arousing function may be subcortical, located at the reticular level, and occurs in short time-spans.

At the next point in the information-processing sequence, the first type of elaboration operation occurs. Its outcome will determine whether the organism directs further attention to the stimulus event. This first elaboration operation could be either cortical or subcortical and may be initiated according to certain cognitive principles. These cognitive principles, as yet not fully understood, might consist of expectations or rules, innate releasing mechanisms, or specific mental structures. Moreover, these principles may involve the subject being programmed for specific events (as in the example of the mother programming herself to wake only when the infant cries) or for more general events (as in the case of a response set being developed in a learning problem). These principles will determine if attention is to be produced by match or mismatch between the internal representation and the stimulus event.

Two outcomes of this first type of elaboration are possible: (1) The elaboration operation may determine that the alerting event is unimportant and no further tuning or focusing is to occur, or (2) the operation may determine that the event is relevant to some cognitive principle and that the analyzers should therefore be tuned or focused for the next operation. In a sense, this operation can be thought of as a screen that omits from consideration those sensory events that are irrelevant to the various cognitive principles (although there are some classes of sensory events that impose themselves regardless of the desire or intent of the organism).

It is important to note that, with regard to the initial elaboration phase, no statement is made regarding the match or mismatch of the external event to any internal representation. Both may produce attention, and whether attention is produced by one or the other may depend on the nature of the external event and the particular cognitive principle involved. Thus, for example, the degree of match may determine amount of attention to signaled events, while the degree of mismatch may determine the amount of attention to nonsignaled events.

If the information is unimportant, inhibition occurs, alerting ceases, and the analyzers stop focusing and turn to alternative events. This is a continuous process. But if the information is important (as determined by the organism's cognitive principles), there is excitation and full tuning of the analyzers, preparing the organism for a second state of elaboration, exploration and processing. The second elaboration operation, like the first, is in the service of cognitive principles, such as the reduction of stimulus uncertainty (Lewis & Goldberg, 1969; Pribram, 1967). If the information supplied by the analyzers is insufficient, it might be necessary for the organism to refocus or utilize an alternative set of analyzers and then reconsider the elaboration step. Thus, oscillation takes place until a particular cognitive principle is satisfied.

In summary, the model proposes two levels of sensory analyzers and two levels of elaboration, all in the service of a set of cognitive principles. This model differs from most attentional models in that it contains a feedback loop. The model is analogous to Miller, Galanter, and Pribram's (1960) multiple-step information-processing (or TOTE) system, where the steps of the attending response here form what might be called a "tune-elaborate-tune-exit" system. The model is best viewed as specifying not a separate operation for each step but rather an interactive process whereby both the tuning and the elaborating function occur together, each necessary for the other. Thus, tuning and elaborating, operating in an oscillating fashion, transform the stimulus event from a general energy statement to a highly differentiated information statement sufficient for the organism to act upon.

McCall

Like Sokolov and Lewis, McCall also proposed that during habituation a neural trace or schema of the stimulus is established and that presentation of a novel stimulus produces recovery of the response. Based on a framework of complexity theory and motivation (e.g., Walker, 1964), McCall and his associates (McCall & Kagan, 1967, 1970; McCall & Melson, 1969) also have argued that attention in the human infant is governed by an interaction between stimulus factors and the infant's cognitive structures. Specifically, the infant attends to stimulation according to a function of its discrepancy from a familiarized standard, with novel and familiar stimuli being least attended to. More recently, McCall and McGhee (1977) have incorporated parameters of complexity theory—specifically, information potential and subjective uncertainty—within this discrepancy model in an attempt to more accurately predict developmental changes.

The discrepancy hypothesis has been criticized on theoretical and empirical grounds (Cohen & Gelber, 1975; Jeffrey & Cohen, 1971; Lewis, 1978). First, the model requires that the stimuli that are presented to the subject be scaled so that infants perceive them along a unitary dimension. Second, the discrepancy model fails to predict results prior to the subject's response. There is no a priori method of determining if the presented stimuli represent a sufficiently broad range of discrepancy to elicit the full inverted-U-shaped curve, and within a small range of discrepancy, it is possible to obtain an increasing linear, decreasing linear, or inverted-U-shaped curve, depending on the particular relationship between the stimuli presented and the infant's cognitive structures. Consequently, McCall, Kennedy, and Applebaum (1977) conclude that a perfect test of the discrepancy hypothesis is a methodological impossibility and that the only way to investigate it is to proceed to test the hypothesis by an analysis of converging trends. McCall *et al.* (1977) and McCall and McGhee (1977) have adopted this approach in reviewing the research on discrepancy and they conclude that most of the ambiguity in findings is a function of the different definitions of stimulus parameters used, rather than the construct investigated. In an attempt to isolate the factors responsible for variation in the infant's response to discrepancy, McCall and McGhee (1977) have analyzed the process that influences length of fixation to a particular target, independent of any effects related to the stimuli *per se*. According to the analysis, when an infant is presented with a stimulus, the initial phase of processing is concerned with categorizing it as familiar or not. If it is familiar, memory stores are then scanned for relevant engrams; concomitantly, comparisons are made between these existing structures and the perceived stimulus. McCall and McGhee assert that this comparison process creates subjective uncertainty, which in turn will determine the organism's attention response according to the discrepancy function. If the stimulus is categorized as completely unfamiliar, then no scanning or comparison with existing structures occurs. Instead, the stimulus information is processed according to the amount of new but assimilable information represented in its physical form; attention will increase linearly with the amount of information potential.

Discrepancy theory predicts a different sequence of information-processing events when the infant is presented with stimuli that are related to existing structures rather than to novel ones. In an attempt to clarify this situation, McCall and McGhee (1977) have made the following distinction between discrepancy and relative novelty:

> Discrepancy refers to the degree of physical similarity in the Gestalts of the two stimuli (e.g., pattern elements or basic stimulus attributes). In contrast, a stimulus is novel when it does not relate to anything in the infant's available experience; that is, it is totally unfamiliar. . . . Prolonged cognitive interaction with the memory store occurs only when the stimulus is judged to be familiar but not identical to existing memories, a condition that does not characterize relative novelty. (p. 189)

Based on this distinction, discrepancy theory predicts that the infant's attention will be an inverted-U-shaped function of discrepancy and an increasing linear function of relative novelty. When the stimulus represents a mixture of these two, the relationship between length of fixation and stimulus discrepancy may be characterized by two factors: (1) an attempt to retrieve from memory the standard stimulus and compare the new stimulus with this representation, and (2) an attempt to process the residual information in the new stimulus, which is different from the memory representation of the old stimulus. Consequently, for stimuli of this nature, the inverted-

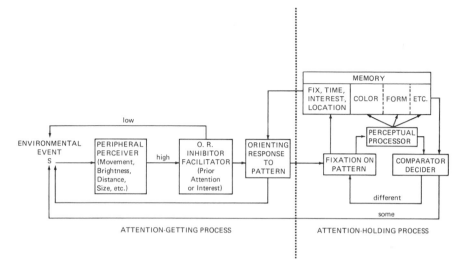

FIGURE 2. A schematic representation of Cohen's (1973) model of infant attention and habituation. Reproduced with permission.

U-shaped curve should be enhanced by increases but diminished by reductions in information potential while amount of discrepancy may be equated. More specifically, if the discrepancy is in the direction of increased complexity, both the attempt to make a comparison and the amount of residual information available will contribute markedly to the subjective uncertainty, resulting in a highly inflected inverted-U-shaped curve. On the other hand, if the discrepancy represents a lower level of complexity, the comparison will produce uncertainty, but the residual information is a subset of the familiarized standard and is easily assimilated into memory, resulting in a less inflected curve.

Finally, McCall and McGhee (1977) maintain that incorporating subjective uncertainty and information potential with discrepancy theory permits a developmental application of the model. Since stimulus discrepancy with increased information potential is more preferred by the system than reduced information potential, as the organism develops, selective attention will always be directed toward increasing levels of stimulus complexity.

Cohen

Cohen (1973) has developed a model of infant visual attention that integrates several processes determining the direction and duration of attention in the young infant. Consistent with existing formulations, this model is based on the assumption that attention is determined by a comparison of incoming perceptual excitation and the organism's cognitive structures, which must process the new stimulus information. Cohen's model differentiates between attention getting and attention holding. General stimulus factors, such as size, movement, or brightness, influence whether or not the infant will orient his head and eyes toward a visual display, while the specific informational content of the stimulus, such as complexity or familiarity, determines how long the infant will continue to look at the stimulus.

The parameters that influence processing during each of the stages are represented in the flow diagram in Figure 2 (Cohen, 1973, p. 176). Initially an environmental event occurs and if it is sufficiently stimulating to attract the *peripheral perceiver*, the attention-getting process is set in motion. If this is not terminated by the *inhibitor-facilitator*, low or high excitation values occur. If the event is of very low perceptual excitation, no orienting will occur; however, if the event is of high perceptual excitation, fixation of the stimulus will occur. The act of fixation represents the initial phase of attention-holding processes, from which three possible steps may follow. One, the stimulus information must be analyzed by the *perceptual processor* into relevant stimulus dimensions (e.g., color, form). The amount of information represented in the display will influence how long this phase of processing will take, that is, how long the infant will fixate the target. Two, from this dimensional analysis, abstract propositions of the stimulus information are formed and stored in memory. Concomitant with these processes, the *comparator decider* executes an analysis of the cognitive representations formed by the perceptual processor. When these representations match, fixation will terminate and the infant will look away. This describes the infant turning away from the stimulus prior to habituation. Three, the infant's fixation is a function of the operant conditioning mechanism, which influences attention through the OR inhibitor-facilitator. When an infant stores information about how interesting or reinforcing particular targets were, this information is incorporated in future attending behavior by either inhibiting or facilitating the speed or direction of subsequent orienting responses. The role of conditioning in attention has been demonstrated by Cohen (1973) and Deloache, Wetherford, and Cohen (1972).

Habituation occurs as each component of the stimulus is processed and the representation formed in LTM becomes increasingly accurate. In addition to comparing the STM representation produced by the perceptual processor to the stimulus observed, the comparator decider also compares the stimulus with the representation formed in LTM. When the LTM model matches the external stimulus, the infant will turn away and not process the stimulus further; he has habituated.

Cohen and Gelber (1975) point out that this model's strength rests on its specificity and ability to summarize a great deal of data. It provides an explanation for turning away from a visual display prior to habituation and is consistent with the observations reported from backward habituation curves. The model, like the others described above, is still incomplete. How to measure rate of habituation, or why infants increase their attention just prior to habituation, is not explained. Moreover, it is not a developmental model since it is based primarily on research with 4-month-olds.

Jeffrey

Jeffrey (1976) presents his model as an alternative to Cohen's (1973) position. He contends that his position, although similar, accounts for attention behavior during habituation more accurately. Based on data that Cohen (1976) reported from presentation of complex stimuli, Jeffrey argues that the habituation curve may be separated into two phases that represent two different types of habituation.

According to Jeffrey, the initial attending or orienting response to a stimulus is a targeting reflex. The targeting reflex is determined by general stimulus characteristics (e.g., size, color, or movement), as was true for the attention-getting response described by Cohen, or the tuning of the analyzers, as in Lewis's model. Jeffrey (p. 290) contends that the targeting reflex has an arousal component that is "related motivationally to basic alimentary and defensive systems." Independent of sensory or perceptual factors, arousal and perceptual or motivational factors determine if the orienting response will occur. Moreover, Jeffrey suggests that the rapid habituation of the targeting reflex is a function of the habituation of this arousal system.

With very simple stimuli (low in information content), the targeting reflex completely describes the cognitive processing executed by the infant. However, when a complex stimulus is introduced, much more than simple stimulus components must be processed so that a second system, one that takes over prior to habituation of the targeting reflex, is necessary to consider. Jeffrey refers to this system as an information-processing sequence that reflects the serial habituation process. He argues that the arousal mechanisms that influence this system are different from those that determine the targeting reflex. Based on Hunt (1963), Jeffrey suggests that the information-processing arousal system is related to the extraction of information from the environment rather than alimentary or defensive needs.

This model predicts that the information-processing phase of the habituation curve would be characterized by an increase in fixation as the infant begins responding to more than one cue, permitting spontaneous recovery of cue salience. The result of serial attention to multiple cues is an increased arousal level, which Jeffrey contends is reinforcing for the organism.

Jeffrey has proposed two systems, which interact as the organism attends to and processes different types of stimuli. Consequently, the shape of the habituation curve could be influenced by varying the stimulus parameters that are presented to the infant. For example, if the attention-getting characteristics of the stimulus display are low, the more rapidly the second information processing system will take over and the earlier will be the peak attention response. However, if the factors that determine the targeting reflex have a very high arousal value, this will delay the habituation of this phase and the beginning of the information-processing aspects of attention, thus retarding the peak attention response associated with actively processing information. With very simple stimuli or stimuli that are very familiar, the second stage of processing may never occur.

Jeffrey has also considered the mechanisms responsible for the final drop in attention associated with habituation. While processing the components of a stimulus and forming a percept, the stimulus cues of lesser salience are attended to after the most significant features are processed. Consequently, the cues initially perceived as most important would recover less and less across trials. The final cues to be processed are weak and require little attention so the entire scanning sequence would rapidly decrease to a single extended glance and the organism would be described as habituated to the stimulus.

In reference to the relationship between habituation and memory, Jeffrey proposes that the most important characteristic of what is stored is a neurological change that ultimately influences the organism's responsiveness. This is clearly distinct from the formation or encoding of a representation of the stimulus with meaningful labels associated with it. Jeffrey seems to be making a distinction between perception and memory, suggesting that the establishment of meaningful associations is not basic to perceptual processing. Rather than suggesting a model based on the formation of a memory trace (e.g., Cohen, 1973), Jeffrey argues that the sensory habituation characteristic of repeatedly attending to a stimulus display is a function of general inhibitory processes. He contends that the inhibition that determines habituation of the response system is the result of limbic system activities that block arousal of the targeting reflex, not the higher order recognition memory structures that memory theories have suggested. Jeffrey (1976, p. 294) concluded that "for simple perception or recognition to occur we need not propose anything so involved as a memory store or a neurological model. If the organism has had sufficient experience with the stimulus complex in the past he will spend little time with it, if he has not, or if there is a salient novel element, additional processing will automatically occur."

Jeffrey criticizes Cohen and Gelber's (1975) explanation that the two phases of the backward habituation curve represent short-term (looking away from the stimulus prior to habituation) and long-term (looking away when an internal representation has been established) memory processing. He argues that these complex memory functions are based on models of

adult verbal learning and are therefore not necessarily applicable to perceptual processing in infancy. Jeffrey suggests that the models proposed to
explain picture memory might prove more fruitful. With respect to these
comments, it should be recalled that current models of information processing (e.g., Pylyshyn, 1973) argue that perception may never be isolated from
memory or the cognitive structures of the organism processing the stimulus
and that visual as well as verbal information is processed in an analogous
manner and stored in abstract, neural propositions.

Olson

Olson's (1976) model of infant visual memory is based on a flow system of visual information processing (see Figure 3). This model assumes
that "the perceptual and memory encodings of events consist of a vector of
features that characterize the distinctive attributes of an event" (Olson,
1976, p. 267). Consistent with Gibson's (1969) position that perceptual
development may be characterized by an improved ability to detect the
distinctive features of information in the perceptual field, Olson conceptual-
izes these features as one of the primary determinants of developmental
change; the features that the organism will select to encode will vary as the
system learns to differentiate and assimilate different aspects of perceived
events.

As soon as a stimulus is processed at the receptor level, the pattern of
excitation is responded to by active or working memory. This interaction
determines the specific vector of perceptual features that will be maintained

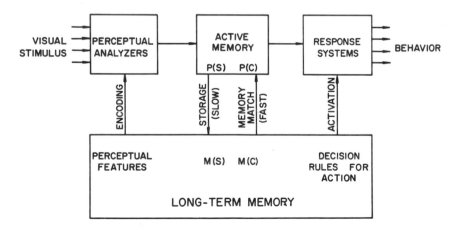

FIGURE 3. Flow diagram for infant visual information processing. P and M refer, respectively,
to perceptual and memory vectors; S refers to the target stimulus and C to the context. From
Olson (1976). Copyright 1976, Lawrence Erlbaum Associates. Reproduced with permission.

at this level of processing. The active processor maintains this information while there is concomitant input from permanent memory structures. A match process scans the existing network for a memory vector similar to the perceptual vector that has been encoded from the stimulus excitation pattern. The final result of this scanning process (a single valued match score) will be used to determine decision routines that control the direction and duration of subsequent eye movements.

The second stage of this model consists of the encoding or transfer of the information represented by the perceptual vector into abstract propositions that may be stored in permanent memory. According to this approach, this is accomplished by the transformation of a perceptual vector into a memory vector; that is, the information content of the perceptual vector must be acted on and integrated into existing, meaningful, cognitive structures. Olson assumes that what is stored is an associative representation of the perceptual features extracted from the stimulus pattern, as well as information concerning the context in which it was experienced. In contrast to the match processes that ultimately scan memory to retrieve information, the formation of meaningful propositions and storage in memory is a relatively slow process.

Olson proposes that decision rules (see Figure 4) that have been established in permanent memory are responsible for directing the activity of the central processor and therefore for reducing attention with repeated stimulus exposure. As the diagram in Figure 4 indicates, the first phase of processing the information in the stimulus pattern is a general check for match between the excitation pattern in active memory and relevant propositions in long-term memory. If the input from the existing cognitive structures fails to reach threshold, then the stimulus–excitation must be recirculated so that a more sequential, detailed, feature-by-feature analysis may be executed. Habituation will signal the completion of this phase of processing.

As soon as an adequate analysis has been completed, the infant will rapidly look away from the exposed pattern. However, prior to habituation, while active memory is maintaining the excitation pattern at a surface level of processing, the infant will attend briefly and then look away. This model accounts for the slow looking away from the target that is observed during prehabituation trials. During each of these exposures the infant reprocesses the pattern, at a deeper level of analysis, until an accurate trace has been established. Eventually, the excitation pattern represented in active memory will be immediately responded to by a concomitant input from memory structures and the infant will habituate.

Olson's position is consistent with Cohen's (1973) in that short-term memory processes are responsible for prehabituation turning away and long-term processes direct the final turning away, characteristic of habituation. However, Olson's position is distinct from Cohen's (1973) in that it

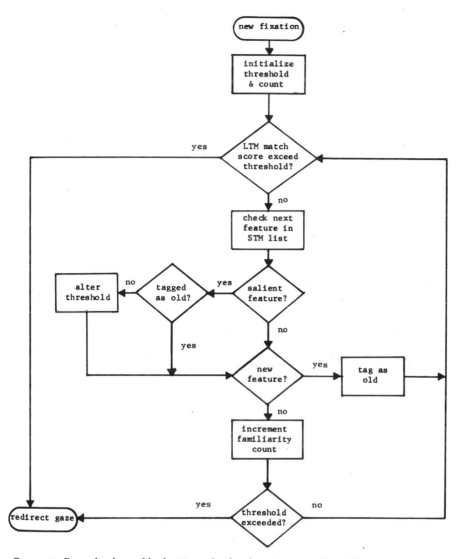

FIGURE 4. Example of possible decision rules for changing gaze. From Olson (1976). Copyright 1976, Lawrence Erlbaum Associates. Reproduced with permission.

assumes that propositions are being formed during the prehabituation exposure trials; that is, each stimulus exposure results in the formation of a stronger memory trace. This conceptualization is consistent with the levels of processing analysis of memory proposed by Craik and Lockhart (1972). During each presentation a more meaningful, deeper level of abstraction is reached as the infant slowly establishes a trace or proposition for the perceptual information. This implies that there is a steady increase in the strength of the trace during prehabituation trials.

With respect to the development of this system, Olson suggests two areas of developmental change. The first is in the set of perceptual features available for encoding stimulus information. This is exemplified by the developmental trends observed in the nature of the infant's scanning patterns (e.g., Salapatek, 1975). The second area of change is in the set of decision rules available for directing the activities of active or working memory. Clearly, the specific strength and direction of the infant's preference for novelty changes as his cognitive structures become more complex and, in turn, respond in a different manner to incoming stimulus information. However, Olson maintains that the basic organization of this processing system does not change over the course of development.

Fagan

Fagan (1977) has proposed a model of infant recognition memory based on the assumption that "the infant's recognition performance can be described in both qualitative and quantitative terms, by variants of attention theories of discrimination learning" (p. 345). Investigations have consistently demonstrated that infants will show differential attention to a novel target over a target previously viewed and this has been interpreted as indicating that the infant finds the two stimuli discriminable and that the standard stimulus is recognized as familiar, thereby defining the other pattern as novel or preferred. Researchers have systematically varied the relationship between the standard and novel targets presented, as well as the amount of study time prior to testing, in an attempt to draw inferences about the particular stimulus characteristics the infants have encoded. This type of approach typifies Fagan's interests in infant recognition memory. His investigations are designed to explore what the infant attends to in a particular display or, more specifically, what attributes of the presented target are selected for storage in the infant's memory, and how the abstraction and storage of features will influence subsequent recognition behavior.

In attempting to investigate these very specific questions, Fagan (1977) has found existing flow-diagram models of infant memory to be inadequate. He contends that these models (e.g., Cohen, 1973; Olson, 1976) are primarily based on adult models of verbal recall that rely heavily on transfer processes such as rehearsal and are therefore not applicable to picture processing in infancy. Fagan argues for the application of discrimination learning theory principles to analyze infant visual recognition memory.

Based on an attention model of discrimination learning (e.g., Zeaman & House, 1963), Fagan's model is an attempt to aid in a quantitative analy-

sis of selective attention in infants. Fagan reports that research on discrimination learning demonstrates that two components are necessary to solve a
discrimination problem: (1) An attentional response must occur in response
to a particular stimulus dimension, and (2) an instrumental response must
follow a particular feature of that dimension. Applying this type of analysis
to infant research, Fagan has argued that when exposed to a novel target
after familiarization to a standard, the infant's fixation response will be
characterized by two internal response systems: (1) an attentional-orient-
ing response to a dimension of the target and (2) an attending or fixation
response to a particular cue. Fagan's model is based on mathematical probability relationships that may be used to predict the chance that an infant
will observe a particular cue, given a specific novel-familiar cue relationship. Fagan (1977) discusses the specific mathematical relationships that
direct attentional processing; only a summary of the important concepts
will be presented. His model allows the researcher to establish probability
values of fixation duration to particular stimuli. These values may then be
used to derive an equation for estimating the probability that the infant will
encode the dimensions of the stimulus that define its distinctiveness relative
to previously viewed targets.

Based on these assumptions, Fagan conducted a series of experiments
to test the relationship between predicted and observed attention responses.
In one experiment, infants 22–30 weeks of age were observed in a typical
paired-comparisons task, requiring a distinction of novel from familiar cues
along the component dimensions of either color or form. The results indicated that the presence of the familiar compound yielded the most marked
novelty preference. Fagan interpreted this as indicating an attention response to a compound dimension, as well as to the specific components.
The data from this investigation were then used to estimate probabilities of
observing the component and compound dimensions, as sources of differential recognition. These estimates formed the basis of predicted novelty preferences for the infants, under three variations in familiarization time.
Fagan reported that in each condition the predicted and observed results
were in close agreement.

Fagan reviewed several areas of current research to which his model is
applicable. He discusses the value that the quantification of observing a
particular stimulus dimension would have for the discrepancy model of
attention. As discussed earlier, one of the major criticisms of the discrepancy position is the difficulty of making a priori predictions of the discrepancy function. Fagan argues that his model would be able to more specifically assess the predictions of this model. In addition, he has related his
position as an explanatory mechanism to two aspects of the model proposed
by Jeffrey (1976): serial processing of stimulus dimensions, and specific
dimensional preferences. Finally, Fagan contends that this model has im-

portant implications for the assessment of processes that determine individual differences in early perceptual development, and for analyzing the nature of visual-environmental stimulation that would prove profitable for retarded infants.

The seven models that have been discussed vary in their use of cognitive factors proposed for explaining infants' behavior to redundant information. Clearly, habituation behavior is a function of a variety of factors, some of which may be cognitive, others related to arousal levels, and still others involving maturational and biological variables. Most of these theories have been based on group data and relatively little effort has been given to individual differences.

Individual Differences in Information Processing

Based on the theoretical framework that earlier sections of this chapter have established, we will now examine evidence pertaining to individual variation in information processing within and across developmental levels.

Developmental Variation

Early work on habituation of sucking suppression in 2- to 4-month-old infants by Haith and co-workers (Haith, 1966; Haith, Kessen, & Collins, 1969) failed to find evidence for habituation of response to a repeatedly presented moving light. Meyers and Cantor (1967) using 6-month-olds and McCall and Kagan (1967) using 4-month-olds also failed to find response decrement. However, Kagan and Lewis (1965) were able to demonstrate habituation in 6-month-old infants. In two subsequent investigations, Lewis, Bartels, Fadel, and Campbell (1966) and Lewis, Goldberg, and Rausch (1968) assessed developmental changes in rate of habituation in infants ranging from 3 to 18 months of age. The infants were presented with four 30-second habituation trials with either a stationary or a moving, blinking light followed by four trials with the opposite type of light and finally a single presentation of the original stimulus. In this design, the stimuli presented on trials 5 and 9 differed from those of the preceding trials and may therefore be considered novel stimuli. As predicted, response decrement in both fixation time and heart rate response (deceleration) were obtained over the first four habituation trials; this decrement was directly related to age, such that the older the infant, the more rapid was the decrease in responding over trials.

In order to further explore the relationship between developmental level and response to repeatedly presented stimuli, Lewis, Goldberg, and Campbell (1969) conducted a series of investigations with infants, 3 to 44 months of age. The stimulus in some studies was a single blinking light, in another it was a light describing a square helix pattern, and in still others it was a slide of some geometric forms. The results consistently showed that the amount of habituation was a function of age. The 3-month-olds showed very little decrement in attention, whereas the older infants did habituate, and the degree of habituation showed an almost perfect relationship with age.

The failure of the 3-month-olds to show response decrement might be due to the long intertrial interval used in the studies by Lewis *et al.* (1969). Saayman, Ames, and Moffett (1964) used a single 4-minute presentation period (in effect a 0-second intertrial interval) and they were successful in demonstrating habituation, and response recovery to a novel pattern, in 3-month-old infants. Lewis *et al.* (1969) also varied the length of the intertrial interval in an attempt to ascertain the significance of this variable for the development of a memory trace by 3-month-olds. These researchers hypothesized that their 30-second interval may have been too long for a very young infant's memory storage system. Three lengths of intertrial intervals were used (0, 5, and 15 seconds) in a fixed-trial habituation paradigm. Although these 3-month-olds failed to show marked response decrement, the results indicated that the longer the intertrial interval, the less the decrement in attention. Lewis *et al.* (1969) suggested that use of a shorter intertrial interval facilitated the formation of memory in these young infants, as shown by the greater reduction in attention.

Lewis and Scott (1972) conducted a longitudinal analysis of habituation in the visual and auditory modality for infants at 3, 6, 9, 12, 18, and 24 months of age. As expected, the visual habituation data revealed an age effect, with the younger infants showing less response decrement than the older ones. Lewis and Scott also reported interesting findings that relate to the stimulus complexity variable. Since the subjects received a simple and a complex series (on different days and counterbalanced) the effects of complexity on habituation could be evaluated. The more complex stimuli proved to elicit less response decrement than the simple stimuli. Moreover, the relation of age to response decrement was demonstrated with two different visual stimuli that varied, at least, in complexity. This relation of age to response decrement therefore, may be invariant with respect to the nature of the stimulus.

Lewis and Scott (1972) found that response recovery was also related to age, with older infants demonstrating the greatest increase in attention in response to the introduction of the novel stimulus. Like habituation response, recovery was a perfectly ordered function of age. Moreover, the nature of the novel stimulus was varied. The four different stimulus discrepancies (size, color, form, and number) resulted in different degrees of response recovery, which varied as a function of age.

As would be expected, the data for the auditory stimulation trials paralled those for the visual modality. For a simple auditory signal, there was a systematic age effect in habituation such that, the older the infant, the greater the response decrement. For a complex auditory signal, the data were only suggestive of an age pattern, with the oldest infants showing the greatest decrement. A possible explanation of this last result is that the complex auditory stimuli may have been sufficiently interesting so as to mask the age effect. The data do reveal a complexity effect in the auditory mode, which parallels that found in the visual mode; there was less habituation for the complex than for the simple stimuli. If attention continues to be elicited longer by a complex than by a simple stimulus, one might expect to observe a relatively small amount of habituation to complex stimuli in a fixed trial procedure such as this.

Based on previous reports of a preference for familiarity in infants under 2 months of age, Greenberg, Uzgiris, and Hunt (1970) investigated habituation to stimuli exposed for long-term periods. They believed that if very young infants are provided with sufficiently long exposures they may eventually develop a preference for novel patterns. Starting at 1 month of age, infants viewed a stimulus daily for a half-hour period. At 2 months, preference was demonstrated for the familiar pattern, but 2 and 4 weeks later, after continued exposures, preference was clearly demonstrated to the novel display. In a similar long-term exposure design by Weizmann, Cohen, and Pratt (1971) similar results were obtained. Infants 1 month of age viewed a mobile for a half hour per day for a month. At 6 weeks of age the infants demonstrated a consistent preference for the familiar display. By 8 weeks of age, though, their preference shifted to the novel mobile. Although both of these investigations confounded amount of familiarization with age, in concurrence with earlier results, however, the data support the view that there is a change in preference for novelty at about 2 months of age.

Given the evidence for habituation in early infancy, Wetherford and Cohen (1973) combined cross-sectional and longitudinal methods in an attempt to ascertain what information was being processed by infants under 2 months of age and how the manner of information processing changed after 2 months. They presented infants, 6–12 weeks of age, with the same geometric form repeatedly and recorded fixation times. The procedure consisted of 17 15-second trials; on trials 2, 9, and 16, novel forms were shown while on all other trials the standard stimulus was presented. The 6- and 8-week-old infants failed to decrease fixation times across presentations of the standard form, but the 10- and 12-week-olds showed a marked decline in response to this stimulus. Analysis of fixation times to the novel form indicated that even though younger infants (8-week-olds) did not show habituation, they did remember something. The researchers concluded that a decrement in looking is a sufficient but not a necessary condition for concluding that information about the visual environment is being stored. Hunt (1963) proposed that as infants develop the ability to recognize repeatedly presented objects, the act of recognition is rewarding, so newly recognized patterns come to be preferred. Then, as the infant develops further, recognition becomes more "commonplace" and less rewarding, so novel stimuli come to be preferred. Hunt maintains the switch to preference for novel stimuli occurs at approximately 8 weeks of age.

Although others have had difficulty demonstrating habituation in infants under 2–3 months, Friedman and his co-workers have consistently reported habituation during the newborn period (Friedman, Nagy, & Carpenter, 1970; Friedman, Carpenter, & Nagy, 1970; Friedman & Carpenter, 1971; Friedman, 1972, 1975). Friedman (1972) used a counterbalanced design in which the habituated stimulus S_1 and the novel stimulus S_2 were equated for potency. He reported that neonates show the decrease in fixation associated with repeated presentation of a visual display (a 2 x 2 or a 12 x 12 checkerboard pattern). Consistent with research on more mature infants, the reduction in response was more marked for older than for younger neonates (Friedman & Carpenter, 1971). A developmental trend was also observed in the infants' renewed attention to the novel pattern (Friedman, 1972). Part of the difficulty in interpreting these results is the fact that in some of the studies cited more than half of the newborns tested failed to show habituation. Nevertheless, it appears that, as Friedman (1972) states, "some infants, soon after birth, are capable of storing simple visual information as reflected in their ability to detect and respond to change in the immediate environment" (p. 339).

In support of Friedman's conclusion, Milewski and Siqueland (1975) also report response decrement and recovery of attention to a novel target in infants 1 month of age, while Werner and Siqueland (1978) were able to demonstrate discrimination between a novel and familiar stimulus in preterm infants after removal from the intensive care unit (the mean gestational age of these infants was 35 weeks and the mean postnatal age was 6.5 days).

After reviewing research on developmental changes in information processing, Fagan (1975) contends that the age at which infants show immediate recognition is a function of the discrepancy of the previously exposed and novel stimuli. Consistent with research on habituation and on effects of complexity, Fagan's study showed that stimuli that differ along several dimensions were differentiated earlier than were stimuli that are more similar. Apparently recognition memory ultimately depends on the infant's ability to encode the discriminating features of a pattern and form a representative neural trace. As would be expected, more mature infants are more competent in their attempts to extract the relevant features of a stimulus and form a permanent trace.

In general, the research reviewed above suggests that the infant's preference for novel over familiar stimuli is gradually acquired around 2–3 months of age. Additional evidence for this premise was first reported by Fantz (1964). In his study two patterns were presented simultaneously for 10 successive 1-minute trials. One pattern was changed from trial to trial while the other remained constant throughout. The data revealed that as the task progressed, infants over 2 months of age tended to show a decrease in fixation time, with the most marked decrease demonstrated by the oldest infants. However, infants under 2 months of age showed no evidence of a preference for either novelty or familiarity. Thus, there was a consistent developmental trend toward increasing differentiation of, and preference for, novel stimuli.

We conclude that infant recognition memory must be considered within the context of the developing cognitive network. The differential levels of relevant feature detection reflect the perceptual and cognitive sophistication of the processor. As the child develops he learns which attributes of a stimulus carry the most relevant information while concurrently establishing a network of stored information within which new material may be integrated and made meaningful.

Individual Variation in Habituation

Individual differences in the rate of habituation have been examined from an information-processing viewpoint. Many studies have been undertaken to explore the hypotheses that amount of attention reflects the rate of information processing and that there are individual differences in the speed of formation of a memory trace.

McCall and Kagan (1970) hypothesized that infants who demonstrate rapid habituation should respond more positively to discrepancy than infants who fail to show habituation. Four-month-old infants were classified as rapid or slow habituators on the basis of their response pattern to a sequence of standard and discrepant stimuli. The results indicated that the slow habituators never really habituated and that they failed to respond differentially to the discrepant stimulus. On the other hand, the rapid habituators showed the typical decrease in fixation of the repeated standard and an increase in fixation of the discrepant pattern. Differential responsiveness of fast and slow habituators was also reported by McCall and Melson (1969) and Melson and McCall (1970). These investigations suggest that the slow habituators formed less complete memory traces; that is, these infants failed to discriminate between the familiar and novel stimuli because they had not adequately encoded the familiar pattern. An additional cate-

gory of individuals was established by Greenberg, O'Donnell, and Crawford (1973): erratic habituators, or infants who demonstrated erratic performance across stimulus presentations in a habituation task. These infants
were found to respond similarly to the slow habituators on a complex preference task.

Cohen and Gelber (1975) and Deloache (1976) caution against a simple
analysis of these findings. They discuss the problems in defining habituation that arise when the initial level of response to the stimuli differs between groups or individuals. Also, they argue that most of the early work
on habituation was based on a fixed-trial presentation method, which may
be an inadequate procedure for assessment of habituation. Since the slow
habituators require more time than other subjects to habituate, a fixed-trial
procedure will not permit equating fast and slow habituators for relative
amount of habituation. The use of arbitrarily picked criterion values for
habituation, such as a fixation time of 3 sec, is also criticized by these
writers. This practice fails to take into consideration the initial fixation
level; infants who show a short initial fixation may be classified as having
habituated without even showing a decrease in fixation time. A definition of
habituation based on proportional response decrement has been suggested,
i.e., amount of decrement as a proportion of initial response level. The use
of proportional criterion allows each infant to reach his own level of response in proportion to his initial level, thus making comparisons of rate of
habituation more meaningful, although the level of this proportion will still
markedly affect the results of any study (see footnote 1).

In an attempt to more carefully assess the relationship between rate of
habituation and the development of memory, McCall, Hogarty, Hamilton,
and Vincent (1973) presented 12- and 18-week-old infants with the same
vertical or horizontal arrow until they fixated 3 sec or less on two consecutive trials following the first five exposures. Response to discrepancy was
assessed by then presenting various rotations of the arrow. All infants
showed habituation to the standard and response recovery to the discrepant
designs. Individual subject analysis indicated that the slow habituators
fixated most on the most discrepant stimulus, while rapid habituators
showed an inverted-U curve as a function of discrepancy between the standard and novel stimulus. The use of an absolute criterion makes these
results difficult to interpret; however, McCall *et al.* (1973) concluded that
developmental differences are more apparent in encoding than in retrieval
processes. Thus, if rate of habituation is a reflection of cognitive development, the main difference between fast and slow habituators should be in
the formation of a memory trace; once the trace is established, differences
should be minimal.

Controlling for the methodological problems of earlier investigations,
Deloache (1976) investigated the influence of discrepancy on 17-week-old
infants' visual fixation, using a proportional criterion measure of habitua-

tion. Infants were considered to have habituated when their fixation of the display decreased to 50% of the initial fixation level. The infants were repeatedly presented with a display containing four geometric shapes until the criterion of habituation was reached. Based on duration of time required to reach criterion, the infants were divided into 2 groups: fast habituators, who took 8 trials or fewer to habituate, and slow habituators, who required 11 trials or more. Clearly, the slow habituators were capable of engaging in the cognitive processes that underlie habituation. Given sufficient exposure they eventually habituated and subsequently showed response recovery with the introduction of the novel stimulus. Following habituation, infants were presented with one of three novel stimuli, ranging from zero to high discrepancy. The results revealed a similar response for both groups of infants to both medium and high discrepancy, with no change in response for zero discrepancy. Although these two groups of habituators differed in the number of presentations required for them to form an accurate model of the stimulus, once that model was formed and further looking was inhibited, they were equally capable of discriminating a novel design from the familiarized pattern. Deloache concluded that fast and slow habituators probably do not differ significantly in the adequacy of their memory trace of the stimulus, or in their ability to retrieve the trace or to compare new information to it. The source of variation in rate of habituation seems to be related to the process of discriminating the relevant features of a display to be encoded and stored. One possible explanation, according to Deloache, is that a difference may exist in the speed at which the two groups begin to process the observed display. Another possibility is that the two groups may approach the environment differently and assess different aspects of the information in the display. Finally, Deloache suggests that slow habituators may process and store some information on every trial but a smaller amount per trial than their faster habituating counterparts.

Hoping to further isolate the variables that differentiate fast and slow habituators, Deloache has analyzed these data using backward habituation curves by which the subject's average level of response is determined for each trial, working backward from the point of habituation. The results of this analysis do not support the hypothesis that fast habituators encode information more rapidly than slow habituators, but reveal that both groups showed the same peak in fixation just prior to habituation. The primary difference between the two groups of infants was in the number of trials required to reach the beginning of the peak response level, not in the general mode of processing, a conclusion that is also supported in research by Cohen and Gelber (1975).

The meaning of these individual differences is not clear. Several investigators (Cohen, 1976; Cohen & Gelber, 1975; Lewis et al., 1966; Lewis, 1971; McCall, 1971) have suggested that early perceptual-cognitive abilities might be important predictors of later cognitive functioning. However, little systematic research aimed at assessing the predictive validity of such abilities has been conducted. Lewis *et al.* (1969) explored this issue in a normal population of infants; they reported a .50 correlation between the amount of habituation before 12 months of age and Stanford Binet IQ scores at 44 months of age. In addition, the amount of habituation has been shown to be related to other mental operations at concurrent stages of development, e.g., concept formation and discrimination learning (Lewis, 1971, 1975). Gelber (1972) reported that the degree of habituation in 4-month-old females predicted their later performance on a two-choice discrimination problem. In general, the infants who showed the greatest habituation were the same infants who later demonstrated faster learning.

Lewis and Brooks (1978) attempted to extend these findings. They examined the relationship between (a) different measures of cognitive functioning at 3 months of age including a habituation task and (b) intellectual ability at 12 and 24 months as measured by the Bayley Mental Development Index (MDI). Their results demonstrated that the adjacent-age MDI scores were significantly related (3→ 12 and 12→ 24), while the nonadjacent ones were not. Correlations between habituation and intelligence measures suggested that perceptual-cognitive ability at 3 months is related to later performance on intelligence tasks. Specifically, rate of habituation at 3 months was significantly related to 24-month MDI scores in part of the sample and degree of response recovery was related to 24-month MDI scores in the entire sample. Recently, Fagan (1979) has also shown a positive relationship between amount of response recovery (novelty) and IQ scores at 4 and 6 years of age.

While these results are in need of replication, they imply that habituation and recovery of attention may be one of the earliest predictors of an individual's intellectual capability. Standard infant IQ tests have generally been unable to predict later intellectual functioning. But the results reviewed here suggest that measurement of infant attention may provide a more suitable approach to assessment of intellectual functioning.

Clinical Applications of Individual Differences in Habituation

Extending this reasoning, we maintain that a habituation task can be a valuable clinical assessment tool for use in detecting central nervous system (CNS) dysfunction in infancy. Two lines of evidence for this position are those just discussed, showing that rate of habituation changes with developmental level, and performance on habituation and recovery tasks discriminates between individuals who differ on standardized measures of intellectual functioning. A third line of evidence is that derived from research on attention and habituation of attention as a function of variables assumed to be associated with mental impairment.

Several investigators (Bowes, Brackbill, Conway, & Steinschneider, 1970; Brackbill, 1971; Brackbill, Kane, Manniello, & Abramson, 1974; Conway & Brackbill, 1969; Stechler, 1964) have found that habituation of attention in the newborn was directly related (negatively) to the amount and type of medication given to the infant's mother during labor. For example, Bowes et al. (1970) presented auditory stimuli and measured heart rate deceleration in infants 2 days, 5 days, and 1 month after birth. The highly medicated infants required three to four times as many trials to habituate as did the lightly medicated or nonmedicated infants. Since the drugs themselves could not have been present in the infant's bloodstream at 1 month, yet effects of the drugs on responsivity to stimulation were still observed at this time, these results suggest that cortical structure may have been affected. These investigators concluded that the influence of the medication on the CNS of the infant was revealed in the differential attention behavior, though no clinical signs of dysfunction had been observed at birth.

Lewis, Bartels, Campbell, and Goldberg (1967) explored the relationship between an infant's Apgar Score at birth (a standard index of neonatal condition) and subsequent performance on a habituation task. Infants were presented with a redundant visual stimulus at 3, 9, and 13 months of age. The infants were divided into a group with perfect Apgar scores and a group with less than perfect scores (all infants were within the normal range). The results showed that at 3 months the two groups differed significantly in amount of habituation, with greater response decrement shown by the perfect scoring group.

In a review of the literature on individual differences in information processing, Lewis (1971) stressed that a relationship between habituation and cortical functioning has been observed in research on animals (Thompson & Spencer, 1966). He also noted that infants' habituation rate has been related to incidence of birth injury (Bronstein, Itina, Kamenet-skaia, & Sytova, 1958) and prematurity (Polikania & Probatova, 1958). Research on infants' preference for novelty also bears on infants' ability to encode and remember a repeatedly presented stimulus. Like the work on habituation, this research indicates marked differences as a function of factors associated with cognitive dysfunction. Sigman (1973) found that full-term infants preferred novelty more than did premature infants even when both groups were equated for conceptual age, or estimated age from conception. Werner and Siqueland (1978), also working with premature infants, found that visual exploration and responsiveness to novelty were positively correlated with maturational level, while they were negatively correlated with perinatal complications. Fagan, Fantz, and Miranda (1971) looked at full-term and preterm infants' responses to paired familiar and novel stimuli and examined effects of both conceptual and postnatal age. Both full-term and preterm infants showed a developmental trend toward increased preference for novelty. The term infants' developmental curve was a full month more advanced than that of the preterm group, when postnatal age was the independent variable. However, there was little difference between groups when performance was plotted as a function of gestational or conceptual age, as both groups began showing a preference for novelty at about 51 weeks of conceptual age. In contrast, Sigman (1973) and Sigman and Parmalee (1974) found that even by 59 weeks full-term infants showed a greater preference for a novel stimulus than did premature infants. In fact, the premature infants failed to demonstrate a reliable preference for the novel stimulus.

In general, these investigations demonstrate a relationship between CNS function and either rate of habituation to repeatedly presented stimulation or preference for novelty. These data would allow us to conclude that the effect of stimulus familiarization may be an important indicator of CNS integrity, and that individual differences in habituation to environmental stimulation should have important implications for predicting subsequent intellectual development. Several recent studies in our laboratory have been designed to further explore the notion that factors associated with cognitive dysfunction in infancy are related to habituation rate and response recovery.

Yoshida, Lewis, Schimpler, Ackerman, Driscoll, and Koenigsberger (1974) explored the relationship between an infant's condition at birth and his performance on a habituation task. A clinic population of infants was divided into high and low risk groups, with the high risk group divided further on the basis of their Apgar scores: those with scores of 8 or better (15 infants) versus those with scores of 7 or worse (15 infants) as assessed 5 minutes after birth. It was hypothesized that the infants in the low risk and high risk–high Apgar group would show more efficient response decrement and recovery patterns than infants in the high risk–low Apgar group; i.e., the low risk group would show the most efficient performance.

The infants were generally tested within the 1st week of life, with the high risk infants tested as soon as permission was granted. It was necessary for the high risk infants to remain under intensive care until they were no longer at risk for mortality. Although the high risk infants were thus tested slightly later than the low risk infants, the two groups were of roughly comparable gestational ages when tested, due to the greater incidence of premature births in the high risk group.

The infants were given 10 15-sec presentations of a human voice reciting a paragraph, followed by a single 15-sec presentation of a musical score (of a similar average decibel level). The infants' sucking behavior was recorded throughout the testing session. A decrease in sucking rate when the stimulus was presented, or sucking suppression, served as the index of attention.

The results, shown in Figure 5, indicated marked differences in the infants' attending behavior. The solid curves reflect the actual data while the dotted lines are best fit lines. The low risk group showed both sucking suppression and habituation of this response across trials. The high risk–high Apgar group showed little sucking suppression but did show a change in response over trials: increased sucking activation with increased redundancy. The sickest infants, the high risk–low Apgar group, showed no suppression and no evidence of habituation over the 10 presentations. On the 11th trial a novel stimulus was presented; it was predicted that this would elicit renewed attention in the infants. As can be seen in Figure 5, all groups did show sucking suppression or attentiveness on the final trial, even though there had been no habituation, at least in the high risk–low Apgar group. This fact suggests that infants may be capable of attending to novelty even though they may show few effects of familiarization (Wetherford & Cohen, 1973).

Still another area of study relevant to assessment of CNS dysfunction is the work with infants who have various types of intellectual handicaps. One such type of handicap is Down's syndrome, a condition that has recently received considerable study. Miranda (1970) investigated differential responsiveness to novelty in normal and Down's syndrome infants. He

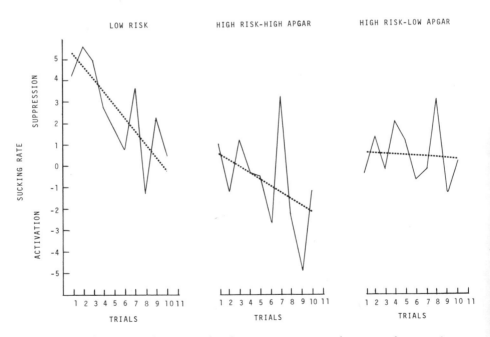

FIGURE 5. Habituation and recovery of sucking suppression to auditory stimulation in three groups of newborn infants.

reported that at 8 months of age, both groups of infants demonstrated a reliable preference for a novel design after familiarization to abstract black-and-white patterns. In a similar investigation, Fagan (1971) tested Down's syndrome and normal infants at 22 weeks of age. Again, the results indicated that both groups showed a preference for a novel display, both immediately and after a delay of several minutes. These two subject populations, therefore, did not appear to differ in recognition memory, as assessed by their response to novelty. These researchers suggested that their findings do not necessarily indicate identical cognitive functioning in normal and Down's syndrome infants, but may have been due to a ceiling effect. It is possible that their stimuli were not sufficiently complex to differentiate between the two groups.

Miranda and Fantz (1974) conducted an investigation to test this possibility. They used younger infants, shorter familiarization exposures, and memory problems that were more difficult, in that the novel stimulus in each recognition test was minimally discrepant from the familiarized stimulus. Three tasks that represented different levels of difficulty were used to assess the formation of a memory trace in normal and Down's syndrome infants. Infants were tested at 12, 24, and 36 weeks of age with a presentation exposure of only 30–60 sec, followed by a two-choice test of recognition memory. For each age level three tasks were given: In one the subjects were shown abstract patterns varying along a number of dimensions, in the second the stimuli varied in arrangement of the pattern elements only, and in the third the stimuli were face photographs. The fixation data from each task revealed a marked superiority in recognition memory on the part of the normal infants over those with Down's syndrome. Consistent with earlier data, the results indicated that by 5 months of age, Down's syndrome infants preferred a novel design after this short-term familiarization period, when the stimuli in the recognition test differed in several dimensions. This novelty preference was observed immediately and after a delay of several minutes. By 8 months of age, these infants were capable of discriminating face photographs, clearly demonstrating the ability to acquire, store, and retrieve visual information.

Of particular significance, however, is the fact that the above-mentioned abilities appeared at a later age in Down's syndrome than in normal infants, indicating a developmental delay in the former group. The delay across all three tasks was about 2 months. The patterns that most clearly revealed a difference between the two groups were the ones that were equated in area of black and white, shape of elements, and number of elements—patterns whose recognition required analysis of the relations among elements in the configuration. Also, the Down's syndrome infants had considerably more difficulty than normal infants with the face stimuli. Miranda and Fantz suggest that this reflects the need for a longer period of neural maturation and/or long-term exposure to faces. They concluded that both age and type of stimulus difference are central factors underlying the difference in recognition memory between normal and abnormal groups of infants.

A study of developmental changes in habituation from 3 to 36 months in normal and Down's syndrome infants was conducted by Hawryluk and Lewis (1978). Using a fixed-trial approach, in which six trials of a redundant visual stimulus were presented, followed by a seventh trial with a novel stimulus (each 20 sec in duration with a 20-sec intertrial interval), they obtained several interesting results. First, while normal infants have been shown to increase their amount of habituation as a function of age, Down's syndrome infants failed to show this pattern (see Figure 6). Of particular theoretical importance is the observation that differences between

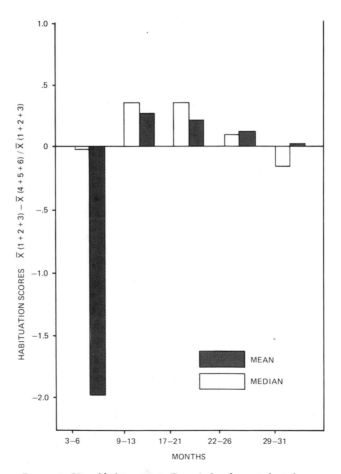

FIGURE 6. Visual habituation in Down's Syndrome infants by age.

these groups become apparent around 3 months. From studies using a variety of techniques, there is converging evidence for the belief that around 2-3 months there is a significant change in attentional and information processing ability in normal infants. Before this time infants show relatively little habituation and little preference for novelty, whereas after this time both habituation and novelty preference are in evidence. While this pattern has been found for the normal infants it has not been observed for Down's syndrome children. For these children, it was not until 2 or 3 months later that they showed a comparable developmental change (Miranda & Fantz, 1974). That even Down's syndrome children advance to a higher level of cognitive functioning, albeit later than normals, argues that their problem lies not so much in lack of ability to show normal functioning as in their delay in developing this ability. Individual differences obtainable at so early an age ultimately may have value for predicting later social and intellectual achievement.

One other area of research bearing on attention and CNS dysfunction is that on the effects of malnutrition, a condition often assumed to be associated with cognitive impairment. Lester (1975) used a habituation paradigm in studying infants suffering from malnutrition, hypothesizing that the basis for the poor intellectual performance of these infants is their general lack of responsiveness to stimulation. Well-nourished and malnourished infants, 12 months of age, were presented with 20 trials of a 90-decibel pure tone. As predicted, the normal infants showed a marked orienting response followed by rapid habituation to the repeatedly presented tone; however, the malnourished infants showed no orienting response to the tone and no evidence of habituation throughout the 20 presentations. Lester interpreted these results as indicating a substantial attention deficit attributable to nutritional insult to CNS development. Similar findings have been obtained in a nutritional study conducted in Bogota, Colombia (Herrera, personal communication, 1978). Infants were given a nutritional supplement at different ages: during the fetal period (through the mother), immediately after birth, and 3 months after birth. Amount of visual habituation to a repeated stimulus, as measured at 3 months, assessed via a fixed-trial sequence, indicated a direct and positive relationship between rate of habituation and timing of nutritional intervention; the earlier the intervention, the greater the habituation at 3 months.

Conclusion

The study of the relationship between attentional processes and both concurrent and subsequent intellectual status needs to be further explored. To date the evidence is encouraging and is consistent with theories of attention and information processing. What is needed is further study of the relationship between early attention and later development. One important issue in all of this research is that of how to measure infants' cognitive processes. The methods that have been used differ in several respects: first, the use of sequential or paired presentation; second, the use of a criterion of habituation or fixed number of trials; third, the use of absolute or proportional change for defining habituation; and fourth, the use of a fixed or variable trial length.

These and many more methodological issues confront the investigator. Yet even with the diversity of procedures that have been used, the data show remarkable consistency and allow us to offer several general conclusions:

1. During infancy, redundant information does not, in general, elicit a high degree of attention.
2. Novel information (perhaps of moderate discrepancy) is preferred and does elicit attention.
3. There are developmental changes in the process underlying these behaviors, with an important transition taking place at about 2 to 3 months of age.
4. Attentional processes are critical in the intellectual growth of the child.
5. There are marked differences among children in attention that appear to reflect individual differences in CNS integrity.

References

Bowes, W. A., Brackbill, Y., Conway, E., & Steinschneider, A. The effects of obstetrical medication on fetus and infant. *Monographs of the Society for Research in Child Development,* 1970, 35 (4, Serial No. 137).

Brackbill, Y. The role of the cortex in orienting: Orienting reflex in an anencephalic human infant. *Developmental Psychology,* 1971, 5, 195–201.

Brackbill, Y., Kane, J., Manniello, R. L., & Abramson, D. Obstetric premedication and infant outcome. *American Journal of Obstetrics and Gynecology,* 1974, 118(3), 377–384.

Bronstein, A. I., Itina, N. A., Kamenetskaia, A. G., & Sytova, V. A. The orienting reactions in newborn children. In L. G. Voronin, A. N. Leontiev, A. R. Luria, E. N. Sokolov, & O. S. Vinogradova (Eds.), *Orienting reflex and exploratory behavior.* Moscow: Academy of Pedagogical Sciences of RFGSR, 1958.

Bruner, J. S. On cognitive growth: I. In J. S. Bruner, R. R. Olver, & P. M. Greenfield (Eds.), *Studies in cognitive growth.* New York: Wiley, 1966.

Bruner, J. S. The growth of representational processes in childhood. In J. Anglin (Ed.), *Beyond the information given.* New York: Norton, 1973.

Cohen, L. B. *Alternative measures of infant attention.* Paper presented at a meeting of the Society for Research in Child Development, Santa Monica, March 1969.

Cohen, L. B. A two process model of infant visual attention. *Merrill-Palmer Quarterly,* 1973, 19, 157–180.

Cohen L. B. Habituation of infant visual attention. In R. J. Tighe & R. N. Leaton (Eds.),

Habituation: Perspectives from child development, animal behavior, and neurophysiology. Hillsdale, N. J.: Lawrence Erlbaum, 1976.

Cohen L. B., & Gelber, E. R. Infant visual memory. In L. B. Cohen & P. Salapatek (Eds.), *Infant perception: From sensation to cognition* (Vol. 1). New York: Academic, 1975.

Conway, E., & Brackbill, Y. *Effects of obstetrical medication on infant sensorimotor behavior.* Paper presented at a meeting of the Society for Research in Child Development, Santa Monica, March, 1969.

Craik, F. I. M., & Lockhart, R. S. Levels of processing: A framework for memory research. *Journal of Verbal Learning and Verbal Behavior,* 1972, *11,* 671–684.

Décarie, T. G. A study of the mental and emotional development of the thalidomide child. In B. M. Foss (Ed.), *Determinants of infant behavior IV.* London: Methuen, 1969, pp. 167–188.

Deloache, J. S. Rate of habituation and visual memory in infants. *Child Development,* 1976, *47,* 145–154.

Deloache, J., Wetherford, M., & Cohen, L.B . *The effects of motivation and conditional head-turning on infant attention to patterns of varying intensity.* Paper presented at the Midwestern Psychological Association meetings, Cleveland, Ohio, 1972.

Engen, T., & Lipsitt, L. P. Decrement and recovery of responses to olfactory stimuli in the human neonate. *Journal of Comparative and Physiological Psychology,* 1965, *59,* 312–316.

Fagan, J. F. Infants' recognition memory for a series of visual stimuli. *Journal of Experimental Child Psychology,* 1971, *11,* 244–250.

Fagan, J. F., Infant recognition memory as a present and future index of cognitive abilities. In N. R. Ellis (Ed.), *Aberrant development in infancy: Human and animal studies.* Potomac, Md.: Lawrence Erlbaum, 1975.

Fagan, J. F. An attention model of infant recognition. *Child Development,* 1977, *48,* 345–359.

Fagan, J. F. *Infant recognition memory and later intelligence.* Paper presented at a meeting of the Society for Research in Child Development, San Francisco, March 1979.

Fagan, J. F., Fantz, R. L., & Miranda, S. B. *Infants attention to novel stimuli as a function of postnatal and conceptional age.* Paper presented at a meeting of the Society for Research in Child Development, Minneapolis, April 1971.

Fantz, R. L. Visual experience in infants: Decreased attention to familiar patterns relative to novel ones. *Science,* 1964, *146,* 668–670.

Friedman, S. Habituation and recovery of visual response in the alert human newborn. *Journal of Experimental Child Psychology,* 1972, *13,* 339–349.

Friedman, S. Infant habituation: Process, problems and possibilities. In N. R. Ellis (Ed.), *Aberrant development in infancy.* Hillsdale, N. J.: Lawrence Erlbaum, 1975, pp. 217–237.

Friedman, S., & Carpenter, G. C. Visual response decrement as a function of age in human newborn. *Child Development,* 1971, *42,* 1967–1973.

Friedman, S., Carpenter, G. C., & Nagy, A. N. Decrement and recovery of response to visual stimuli in the newborn human. *Proceedings of the 78th Annual Convention of the American Psychological Association,* 1970, *5,* 273–274.

Friedman, S., Nagy, A. N., & Carpenter, G. C. Newborn attention: Differential response decrement to visual stimuli. *Journal of Experimental Psychology,* 1970, *10,* 44–51.

Gelber, E. R. *Habituation, discrimination learning, and visual information processing in infants.* Unpublished doctoral dissertation. University of Illinois, 1972. (Cited in Cohen & Gelber, 1975.)

Gibson, E. J. *Principles of perceptual learning and development.* New York: Appleton-Century-Crofts, 1969.

Greenberg, D. J. Visual attention in infancy: Processes, method, and clinical application. In I. Uzgiris & F. Weizmann (Eds). *The structuring of experience.* New York: Plenum, 1977.

Greenberg, D. J., O'Donnell, W. J., & Crawford, D. Complexity levels, habituation and individual differences in early infancy. *Child Development,* 1973, *44,* 569–574.

Greenberg, D. J., Uzgiris, I. C., & Hunt, J. McV. Attentional preference and experience: III. Visual familarity and looking time. *Journal of Genetic Psychology,* 1970, *117,* 123–135.

Haith, M. M. The response of the human newborn to visual movement. *Journal of Experimental Child Psychology,* 1966, *3,* 235–243.

Haith, M. M., Kessen, W., & Collins, D. Response of the human infant to level of complexity of intermittent visual movement. *Journal of Experimental Child Psychology,* 1969, *7,* 52–69.

Hawryluk, M. K., & Lewis M. *Attentional patterns in infants with Down's syndrome: A preliminary investigation.* Paper presented at the Eastern Psychological Association meetings, Washington, D. C., March 1978.

Hunt, J. McV. Motivation inherent in information processing and action. In O. J. Harvey (Ed.), *Motivation and social interaction.* New York: Ronald, 1963, pp. 35–94.

James, W. *The principles of psychology.* New York: Holt, 1890.

Jeffrey, W. E. Habituation as a mechanism for perceptual development. In T. J. Tighe & R. N. Leaton (Eds.), *Habituation: Perspectives from child development, animal behavior, and neurophysiology.* Hillsdale, N. J.: Lawrence Erlbaum, 1976.

Jeffrey, W. E., & Cohen, L. B. Habituation in the human infant. In W. H. Reese (Ed.), *Advances in child development and behavior,* (Vol. 6). New York: Academic, 1971.

Kagan, J., & Lewis, M. Studies of attention in the human infant. *Merrill-Palmer Quarterly,* 1965, *11,* 95–127.

Lester, B. M. Cardiac habituation of the orienting response to an auditory signal in infants of varying nutritional status. *Developmental Psychology,* 1975, *11,* 432–442.

Lewis, M. Individual differences in the measurement of early cognitive growth. In J. Hellmuth (Ed.), *Exceptional infant, Vol. 2. Studies in abnormalities.* New York: Brunner/Mazel, 1971, pp. 172–210.

Lewis, M. The development of attention and perception in the infant and young child. In W. M. Cruickshank & D. P. Hallahan (Eds.), *Perceptual and learning disabilities in children* (Vol. 2). Syracuse: Syracuse University Press, 1975.

Lewis, M. Attention and verbal labeling behavior: A study in the measurement of internal representation. *Journal of Genetic Psychology,* 1978.

Lewis, M. & Brooks, J. *Visual attention at three months as a predictor of cognitive functioning at two years of age.* Unpublished manuscript, 1978.

Lewis, M., & Goldberg, S. The acquisition and violation of expectancy: An experimental paradigm. *Journal of Experimental Child Psychology,* 1969, *7,* 70–80.

Lewis, M., & Scott, E. *A developmental study of infant attentional distribution within the first two years of life.* Paper presented at the Twentieth International Congress of Psychology, Symposium on Learning in Early Infancy, Tokyo, Japan, August 1972.

Lewis, M., Bartels, B., Campbell, H., & Goldberg, S. Individual differences in attention: The relationship between infants' condition at birth and attention distribution within the first year. *American Journal of Diseases of Children,* 1967, *113,* 461–465.

Lewis, M., Bartels, B., Fadel, D., & Campbell, H. *Infant attention: The effect of familiar and novel visual stimuli as a function of age.* Paper presented at the meetings of the Eastern Psychological Association, New York, April 1966.

Lewis, M., Goldberg, S., & Campbell, H. A developmental study of learning within the first three years of life: Response decrement to a redundant signal. *Monographs of the Society for Research in Child Development,* 1969, *34* (Serial No. 133).

Lewis, M., Goldberg, S., & Rausch, M. Novelty and familiarity as determinants of infant attention within the first year. Unpublished manuscript, 1968.

McCall, R. B. Attention in the infant: Avenue to the study of cognitive development. In D.

Walcher & D. L. Peters (Eds), *Early childhood: The development of self-regulatory mechanisms.* New York: Academic Press, 1971, pp. 107–140.

McCall, R. B., & McGhee, P. E. The discrepancy hypothesis of attention and affect in infants. In I. Uzgiris & F. Weizmann (Eds.), *The structuring of experience.* New York: Plenum, 1977.

McCall, R. B., & Kagan, J. Stimulus-schema discrepancy and attention in the infant. *Journal of Experimental Child Psychology,* 1967, 5, 381–390.

McCall, R. B., & Kagan, J. Individual differences in the infant's distribution of attention to stimulus discrepancy. *Developmental Psychology,* 1970, 2, 90–98.

McCall, R. B., & Melson, W. H. Attention in infants as a function of magnitude of discrepancy and habituation rate. *Psychonomic Science,* 1969, 17, 317–319.

McCall, R. B., Hogarty, P. S., Hamilton, J. S., & Vincent, J. H. Habituation rate and the infant's response to visual discrepancies. *Child Development,* 1973, 44, 280–287.

McCall, R. B., Kennedy, C. B., & Applebaum, M. I. Magnitude of discrepancy and the distribution of attention in infants. *Child Development,* 1977, 48(3), 772–786.

Melson, W. H., & McCall, R. B. Attentional responses of five-month girls to discrepant auditory stimuli. *Child Development,* 1970, 41, 1159–1171.

Meyers, W. J., & Cantor, G. N. Observing and cardiac responses of human infancy to visual stimuli. *Journal of Experimental Child Psychology,* 1967, 5, 16–25.

Milewski, A. E., & Siqueland, E. R. Discrimination of color and pattern novelty in one-month infants. *Journal of Experimental Child Psychology,* 1975, 19, 127–136.

Miller, G. R., Galanter, E. H., & Pribram, K. H. *Plans and the structure of behavior.* New York: Holt, 1960.

Miranda, S. B. Response to novel visual stimuli by Down's syndrome and normal infants. *Proceedings of the 78th Annual Convention of the American Psychological Association,* 1970, 5, 275–276.

Miranda, S. B., & Fantz, R. L. Recognition memory in Down's Syndrome and normal infants. *Child Development,* 1974, 45, 651–660.

Olson, G. M. An information-processing analysis of visual memory and habituation in infants. In R. J. Tighe & R. N. Leaton (Eds.), *Habituation: Perspectives from child development, animal behavior, and neurophysiology.* Hillsdale, N.J.: Lawrence Erlbaum, 1976.

Piaget, J. *The origins of intelligence in children.* New York: Norton, 1963.

Polikania, R. I., & Probatova, I. E. On the problem of formation of the orienting reflex in prematurely born children. In I. C. Voronin, A. N. Leontiev, A. R. Luria, E. N. Sokolov, & O. S. Vinogradova (Eds.), *Orienting reflex and exploratory behavior.* Moscow: Academy of Pedagogical Sciences of RSFSR, 1958.

Pribram, K. H. *The new neurology and the biology of emotion: A structural approach.* Paper presented at the Eastern Psychological Association Meeting, Boston, 1967.

Pylyshyn, Z. W. What the mind's eye tells the mind's brain: A critique of mental imagery. *Psychological Bulletin,* 1973, 80, 1–24.

Rebert, C. S., McAdam, D. W., Knott, J. R., & Irwin, D. A. Slow potential change in human brain related to level of motivation. *Journal of Comparative and Physiological Psychology,* 1967, 63, 20–23.

Saayman, G., Ames, E. W., & Moffett, A. R. Response to novelty as an indicator of visual discrimination in the human infant. *Journal of Experimental Child Psychology,* 1964, 1, 189–198.

Salapatek, P. Pattern perception in early infancy. In L. B. Cohen & P. Salapatek (Eds.), *Infant perception: From sensation to cognition* (Vol. 1). New York: Academic, 1975.

Sigman, M. *Visual preferences of premature and full-term infants.* Paper presented at meeting of the Society for Research in Child Development, Philadelphia, March 1973.

Sigman, M., & Parmalee, A. H. Visual preference of four-month-old premature and full-term infants. *Child Development*, 1974, *45*, 959–965.

Sokolov, E. N. *Perception and the conditioned reflex.* New York: Macmillan, 1963.

Sokolov, E. N. The modeling properties of the nervous system. In M. Coles & I. Maltzman (Eds.), *A handbook of contemporary Soviet psychology.* New York: Basic, 1969, pp. 671–704.

Stechler, G. Newborn attention as affected by medication during labor. *Science,* 1964, *144,* 315–317.

Thompson, R. F., & Spencer, W. A. Habituation: A model phenomenon for the study of neuronal substrates of behavior. *Psychological Review,* 1966, *173*(1), 16–43.

Walker, E. L. Psychological complexity as a basis for a theory of motivation and choice. In D. Levine (Ed.), *Nebraska symposium on motivation.* Lincoln: University of Nebraska Press, 1964, pp. 47–95.

Weizmann, F., Cohen, L. B., & Pratt, R. J. Novelty, familiarity, and the development of infant attention. *Developmental Psychology,* 1971, *4,* 149–154.

Werner, J. S., & Siqueland, E. R. Visual recognition memory in preterm infants. *Infant Behavior and Development,* 1978, *1,* 79–84.

Wetherford, M. J., & Cohen, L. B. Developmental changes in infant visual preferences for novelty and familiarity. *Child Development,* 1973, *44,* 416–424.

Yoshida, R. K., Lewis, M., Schimpler, S., Ackerman, J. Z., Driscoll, J., & Koenigsberger, M. R. The distribution of attention within a group of infants "at risk." Research Bulletin 74–41. Princeton, N.J.: Educational Testing Service, 1974.

Zeaman, D., & House, B. J. The role of attention in retardate discrimination learning. In N. R. Ellis (Ed.), *Handbook of mental deficiency.* New York: McGraw-Hill, 1963, pp. 159–223.

8

Toward a Clearer Definition of the Attentional Deficit of Hyperactive Children

Virginia I. Douglas and Kenneth G. Peters

Introduction

Over the past several years, acceptance of the central importance of an attentional deficit in hyperactive children has been emerging in the clinical, educational, and research literature. When we examine the definitions of *attentional deficit* being used by different authors, however, it becomes evident that a good deal of confusion and disagreement remains about the exact nature of the deficit being attributed to hyperactive children.

To complicate matters further, attentional deficits also are being emphasized as focal symptoms in children classified as "learning-disabled," a label that often has been used almost synonymously with "hyperactivity." Thus, the reader is left to sort out each author's method of defining his hyperactive or learning-disabled samples and, even if he is successful in achieving this, he must still discover whether the "attentional deficits" being attributed to the two groups of children are the same or different.

For some time, Douglas (1972, 1974, 1976a) has argued that the major disability of hyperactive children involves an inability to sustain attention and to inhibit impulsive responding on tasks or in social situations that require focused, reflective, organized, and self-directed effort. Unlike Ross (1976), who believes that the hyperactive child's impulsivity and hyperactivity are learned reactions to failure experiences resulting from a more

Virginia I. Douglas • Department of Psychology, McGill University, and Montreal Children's Hospital, Montreal, Quebec, Canada H3G 3G1. Kenneth G. Peters • Children's Hospital and Department of Psychology, University of British Columbia, Vancouver, British Columbia, Canada. The research on which parts of this report are based was supported by Grants S72-1398 and S74-0750 from the Canada Council of Canada and Grant MA-1577 from the Medical Research Council of Canada; principal investigator: V. I. Douglas.

basic selective attention problem, Douglas considers impulsivity, hyperactivity, and the inability to sustain and organize attention as intimately
related aspects of the same constitutionally determined problem.

In this chapter, we shall attempt to demonstrate how this attentional-
impulsivity deficit contributes to the hyperactive child's failure on tasks
that make special demands for concentrated, self-sustained, and self-directed effort. The range of tasks on which the deficit appears is very wide,
varying from simple vigilance and reaction time tasks of a dull, long, and
repetitive nature to perceptual tasks that require careful analysis of available (visual, auditory, or haptic) cues to complex problem-solving and
memory tasks that require a similar kind of self-directed and self-sustained
investment in the process of considering, rehearsing, and evaluating relevant information and knowledge.

We will try, as well, to convince the reader that the hyperactive child's
failure to sustain and direct attention in a disciplined manner cannot be
explained by theories based on filter models of attention (e.g., Broadbent,
1958; Moray, 1969; Treisman, 1969), and we shall point to some of the
more recent attentional theories (e.g., Bindra, 1976; Hebb, 1976; Kahneman, 1973; Neisser, 1976) as being more relevant to the problems of the
hyperactive child. Clinical descriptions that assume that hyperactive children have defective filter mechanisms and, consequently, are "stimulus
driven" or distractible will be questioned, and research investigations that
have attempted, usually unsuccessfully, to demonstrate abnormal distractibility in the hyperactive child will be reviewed. On the other hand, we will
suggest that similar studies involving children who demonstrate specific
learning disabilities leave open the possibility that at least some kinds of
learning-disabled children may be particularly vulnerable to the influence of
distracting stimuli.

It is important to mention one further source of confusion in the existing literature with which we shall attempt to deal. This arises from a failure
to differentiate between behavior that is "stimulus driven" and behavior
that is "stimulus seeking." Although we reject "stimulus driven" or "defective filter" explanations of the hyperactive child's deficiencies, we do
continue to entertain the possibility that these children show an unusual
inclination to seek out stimulation, particularly under conditions of stimulus deprivation. After reviewing the data available a few years ago, Douglas (1974) cautioned that "we should keep our minds open to the possibility
that the presence of stimulation and/or hyperactive behavior may sometimes help maintain alertness and thus improve attention" (p. 162). Similar
suggestions have been made by several other investigators working with
hyperactive children (e.g., Dykman, Ackerman, Clements, & Peters, 1971;
Satterfield & Dawson, 1971; Zentall, 1975). Similar notions appear, as
well, in the literature dealing with other groups, including impulsive, ex-

traverted, psychopathic, antisocial, and delinquent individuals (e.g., Farley & Farley, 1970; Quay, 1977; Skrzypek, 1969; Whitehill, DeMyer-Gapin, & Scott, 1976; Weisen, 1965).

In the present chapter, we will explore this hypothesis further. In anticipation of this discussion, however, the reader should be alerted to the fact that certain implications follow from acceptance of the notion that hyperactives have an unusual need for stimulation. Perhaps the most important of these is that, depending on the salience of the distractors, the nature of the task, and the motivational state or arousal level of the child, the presence of task-irrelevant stimuli might contribute to *either impaired or improved* performance. What is needed is a careful analysis of the effect of each of these situational, task, and distractor variables, as well as the interactions among them. Although no studies designed to directly test the stimulus-seeking hypothesis with hyperactive children are available at this time, we will point to findings bearing on this assumption as we discuss the attentional studies.

Confusion Caused by Current Diagnostic Labels

Like all reviewers in the area of childhood disorders, we have been continually hampered by the inconsistent and ill-defined methods used by investigators to select and label their subjects. Terms like *minimal brain dysfunction, learning disability,* and *hyperactivity* frequently are used vaguely and sometimes interchangeably. As a result, we have been forced to draw our own conclusions about the nature of subject samples, often from very incomplete descriptions.

We have made certain arbitrary decisions regarding the use of diagnostic labels. The first was to eliminate the label "minimal brain dysfunction" (MBD) from our review and to concentrate instead on the terms *LD* and *hyperactivity*. Our decision to avoid MBD as a diagnostic label was influenced by several recent investigations and reviews that have raised doubts about the validity and utility of this classification (e.g., Campbell, 1976; Crinella, 1973; Ross, 1976; Stine, Saratsiosis, & Mosser, 1975). Certainly, few would deny that attentional problems must ultimately be associated with some kind of dysfunction of the brain; however, no suitable criteria or norms are currently available for establishing neurological signs that could be used in applying the MBD label. Thus, although promising work on this problem is under way, we believe that use of the MBD classification at this time is premature and likely to lead to further confusion.

Whenever doubts arose about whether to classify a particular sample as learning-disabled or hyperactive, we looked at the authors' descriptions of their selection procedures. If hyperactive, impulsive behavior was emphasized in the selection process, we included the study in our discussion of hyperactive children; if these symptoms were not mentioned and the investigators seemed to be interested primarily in learning problems, the sample was considered learning-disabled. This differentiation was easier to make when a specific learning disability, such as a reading problem, was used in selecting subjects. However, as we shall discuss later, it appears likely that hyperactive children frequently have been included in LD groups, particularly in studies completed after hyperactivity achieved prominence in the educational and research literature.

We recognize that this procedure (like any other we might have adopted) is fraught with difficulties. Nevertheless, we believe that it comes closest to conforming with existing knowledge about the nature of hyperactivity and learning disabilities. In spite of the very loose and general use of the term *learning disability* in the literature, there is increasing evidence to suggest that individual children sometimes may demonstrate fairly specific deficits in the manner in which they process information. We believe, for example, that it is important to know whether the deficit is limited to the processing of visual, auditory, verbal, spatial, or kinesthetic information, and also whether the problem occurs at the level of encoding, decoding, or storage. Recent research developments, including current investigations of brain lateralization, offer considerable hope that these kinds of differentiation will become possible. If we accept the premise that specific learning disabilities exist, there is no *a priori* reason for associating these disorders with hyperactivity and its related symptoms. Although we (Douglas 1976b) and others have reported that hyperactivity and attentional-impulsivity deficits often accompany school failure, we did not intend to imply that these symptoms are always present in children demonstrating specific learning disabilities.

The need for considering the two labels separately also is evident from studies of the academic and learning problems of hyperactive children. Certainly, most hyperactive children receive poor marks in school, and many fail one or more grades (Minde, Lewin, Weiss, Lavigeur, Douglas, & Sykes, 1971). On the other hand, rather extensive assessments involving individually administered tests designed to tap learning disabilities and performance on standardized tests of academic achievement have yielded surprisingly weak or equivocal evidence of specific disabilities (Douglas, 1972; Hoy, Weiss, Minde, & Cohen, 1978). Thus, in diagnosing a child, it becomes important to make separate and independent decisions about the appropriateness of applying the hyperactivity and learning-disability label. This does not mean, of course, that a particular child could not be *both* learning-disabled and hyperactive; we simply are arguing that separate judgments be made on the basis of empirical evidence.

Description of Samples Used in the McGill Studies

Before describing our own method of choosing hyperactive samples, we should confess that we believe that the hyperactivity label may be outgrowing its usefulness. For some time now, investigators have recognized that measures of activity level often are unreliable and fail, as well, to capture the fragmented and disorganized quality of the hyperactive child's behavior (Cromwell, Baumeister, & Hawkins, 1963; Werry, Sprague, Weiss, & Minde, 1970). Douglas (1974) has argued that the inability of these children to organize and sustain attention and to inhibit impulsive responding are the qualities that differentiate them most clearly from other groups. If Douglas is correct in her belief that attentional and impulsivity problems usually accompany hyperactivity and are, in fact, more critical symptoms than the hyperactive behavior, then it follows that a more suitable label might be "attentional-impulsivity disorder," or possibly, "attentional-impulsivity-hyperactivity disorder."

Although we might wish, in hindsight, that we had recognized more of the complexities we have been discussing when we set out to study "hyperactive" children, it is probably true that samples of children studied at McGill have been somewhat more homogeneous and more clearly defined than those of other early investigators. Because of the prevalence of hyperactivity in boys, the samples typically have been limited to males. The age range included in the studies usually has been between 6 and 12 years, although 5- and 10-year follow-up investigations now have been completed on many of the children (Weiss, Minde, Werry, Douglas, & Nemeth, 1971; Hechtman, Weiss, Finkelstein, Werner, & Benn, 1976).

For a child to be included in our studies, hyperactivity had to be the major presenting complaint, and it had to be a chronic problem, present for at least several years. Because we felt it important to exclude children demonstrating "restless" behavior resulting from emotional causes, an attempt was made, through careful interviewing, to screen out children whose symptoms appeared to be a reaction to a disturbed home situation. Also excluded were neurotic, psychotic, or retarded children (WISC IQ had to be at least 80).

Another factor in the selection process, which probably serves to diminish the overlap between our samples and the learning-disability group, is the fact that no academic criteria were used in choosing our hyperactive subjects; in fact, our sampling techniques tend to minimize the number of children attending special classes. As mentioned previously, data later collected on our subjects revealed serious academic difficulties but only limited evidence of specific learning disabilities.

Also eliminated were children who had been diagnosed as brain-damaged and those whose histories strongly suggested brain injury. Subsequent studies in which we have searched diligently for more subtle neurological signs or evidence of abnormalities from birth history data have yielded relatively little indication of such abnormalities in our hyperactive samples (Minde, Webb, & Sykes, 1968; Werry, Weiss, & Douglas, 1964; Werry, Weiss, Dogan, Minde, & Douglas, 1969).

In our more recent studies, we have included the Conners Teacher and Parent Rating Scales (Conners, 1969, 1970) and the Matching Familiar Figures Test of Reflection-Impulsivity (Kagan, Rosman, Day, Albert, & Phillips, 1964) in our screening procedures, and we have experimented, as well, with statistical methods for weighting scores from these and other tests in order to sharpen and objectify our selection criteria (Douglas, Parry, Marton, & Garson, 1976; Garson, 1977).

Because of the importance of subject selection in the studies to be reviewed, we usually shall begin with a discussion of publications by either the first author or investigators who completed their doctoral dissertations with her (Campbell, 1969; Cohen, 1970; Firestone, 1974; Freibergs, 1965; Garson, 1977; Parry, 1973; Peters, 1977; Schleifer, 1971) or of work done by our psychiatric colleagues at the Montreal Children's Hospital (particularly Drs. Minde, Morgenstern, Weiss, and Werry), since we can be reasonably confident that all of these investigators selected their subjects according to the criteria just described. Our method of coping with diagnostic labels used by other investigators has already been outlined. Finally, it should be emphasized that, although we will draw comparisons from time to time with children in the learning-disabled group, our primary focus is on childhood hyperactivity.

Confusion Caused by Definitions of Attention

As several reviewers (e.g., Boring, 1970; Egeth & Bevan, 1973; Swets & Kristofferson, 1970) have reported, attention was a neglected topic within psychology for many years. As a result, only preliminary attempts have been made to label the various aspects of attention and to develop operational definitions of the processes involved in each. Moray (1969), for example, reminds us that "attention is a word with many varied meanings, applicable to a very wide range of phenomena" (p. 5). He produces a tentative list of seven different kinds of attentional processes, including mental concentration, vigilance, selective attention, search, activation, set, and analysis-by-synthesis.

It is probably reasonably accurate to say, however, that most of the available research on attentional deficits in hyperactive children has dealt either with the *selective* aspects of attention, as defined by filter theories, or with the *sustained* or *intensive* aspects, as defined by vigilance and related measures. Some investigators make no attempt to separate these two kinds of attention. Ross (1976), for example, speaks of the learning-disabled child's difficulty in "sustaining selective attention." In contrast, we believe that it is important to try to maintain this differentiation, particularly since there is evidence to suggest that some children may have a selective attention deficit while others have difficulty sustaining attention.

In the past few years, definitions have become even more confused because several recent theorists (e.g., Neisser, 1976; Wright & Vlietstra, 1975) use the term *selective attention* to describe processes that differ markedly from those posited by the filter theories. We shall be arguing that these processes, involving the use of sophisticated strategies to search for subtle clues, as opposed to having one's attention "captured" by salient features of a stimulus, share important characteristics with the processes involved in vigilance tasks.

Selective Attention as Defined in Studies of Stimulus Reduction, Distraction, and Incidental Learning

Most reviewers of the literature on attention (e.g., Berlyne, 1970; Kahneman, 1973; Posner & Boies, 1971; Solley & Murphy, 1960; Swets & Kristofferson, 1970) place heavy emphasis on the selective aspects of attention. Indeed, Berlyne (1970) suggests that the term *attention* be reserved for selective attention, which he describes as involving "how attention is distributed among elements of a stimulus field" (p. 29). Swets and Kristofferson (1970) define it as the "process of the organism's choosing to notice a particular part of his environment" (p. 53). Following the work of Broadbent (1958), theorists usually have thought of selective attention as involving some kind of filtering process. Broadbent believes that information enters the organism over many different parallel sensory pathways or channels. Man's ability to process information at any given time, however, is restricted by the limited capacity of a single central channel. Although Broadbent's original formulations have undergone several modifications (e.g., Broadbent, 1971; Deutsch & Deutsch, 1963; Moray, 1969; Treisman, 1969), the idea of a filtering or modulating mechanism, necessitated by a limitation in the capacity of the human nervous system to process information, has remained an essential aspect of these theories.

Several investigators in the area of childhood psychopathology have speculated that there may be important individual differences in children's ability to filter out or ignore irrelevant stimuli. Strauss and Lehtinen (1947), for example, believed that as a result of brain injury, the hyperactive child is "abnormally responsive to the stimuli of his environment, reacting unselectively, passively, and without conscious intent" (p. 129). Consequently, they recommended isolating such children in quiet, stimulus-reduced environments in order to protect them from being bombarded by stimulation.

Stimulus Reduction Studies with Hyperactive Children

In spite of the intuitive appeal of the Strauss and Lehtinen approach, most attempts to provide stimulus-reduced learning environments within school settings for children demonstrating symptoms of hyperactivity have found no evidence of improved academic performance (Cruickshank, Bentzen, Ratzeburg, & Tannhauser, 1961; Rost & Charles, 1967; Shores & Haubrich, 1969; Somerville, Jacobsen, Warnberg, & Young, 1974; Somerville, Warnberg, & Bost, 1973).

Although it can be argued that the research design of some of these studies does not provide a valid test of the stimulus-reduction hypothesis (Cruickshank, 1975; Shores & Haubrich, 1969; Hallahan, Kauffman, & Ball, 1974b), the results must be considered disappointing for those who believe that extraneous stimulation is particularly detrimental to the academic performance of hyperactive children. In addition, several investigations with retarded and nonretarded hyperactive children have yielded an intriguing finding: They have obtained *increases in activity level* when the children were placed in stimulus-reduced environments (Cleland, 1961; Cromwell *et al.,* 1963; Forehand & Baumeister, 1970; Gardner, Cromwell, & Foshee, 1959; Switzky & Haywood, 1973; Zentall & Zentall, 1976). This result is much more in line with the hypothesis that hyperactive children need and seek stimulation.

Studies of Distractibility with Hyperactive Children

Laboratory investigations of distractibility in hyperactive children have provided a more direct method of investigating the hypothesis that these children are unable to screen out task-irrelevant stimulation. As can be seen in the summary of studies of distractibility in hyperactive children presented in Table I (adapted from Peters, 1977), investigators have experimented with a wide variety of tasks and task-irrelevant stimuli (or potential distractors). Sometimes the distractor is in the same modality as the task (i.e., both the task and the task-irrelevant stimuli are visual or both are auditory) and sometimes they are in different modalities. Sometimes the distractors are presented close to the task or are embedded within it, and sometimes they occur at a distance from the task. Finally, in some studies the distractors are unrelated to the task, while in others they consist of contradictory or discordant cues that are introduced into the task.

In most studies, "distractibility" has been assessed by the differential deterioration in task performance of experimental and control groups in the distraction as opposed to the nondistraction condition. In a few recent studies (Bremer & Stern, 1976; Steinkamp, 1974; Sykes, Douglas, & Morganstern, 1973), a different kind of measure has been employed. This is a measure of the amount of time the child spends "off-task" (i.e., time during which observers note either that the subject is not working at the task or that he is looking at the task-irrelevant stimuli). It is important to distinguish between these two kinds of measures. As we shall see, the presence of task-irrelevant stimuli sometimes results in an increase in looking behaviors or time off-task in hyperactives, without producing a concomitant drop in performance. Thus, it may be misleading to interpret some kinds of "time-off" behaviors on the part of hyperactives as evidence of distractibility, at least as the term usually is understood. On the other hand, the fact that they sometimes pay more attention than normal children to extraneous events occurring in their environment may suggest stimulus-seeking behavior rather than an inability to ignore or screen out task-irrelevant stimuli.

Our research group at McGill University has carried out several investigations of distractibility in hyperactive children: they are included in the summary of studies provided in Table I. Sykes, Douglas, Weiss, and Minde (1971) piped white noise into the testing room at frequent random intervals while hyperactive children and a matched control group were performing on a vigilance task, which required monitoring a visual display for the appearance of a designated letter. Performance under a distraction and a nondistraction condition was compared. The results revealed that the presence of the white noise failed to produce a decrement in the performance of either group.

Sykes et al. (1973) used a Choice Reaction Time task (CRTT) to test the effects of contradictory color cues on the ability of hyperactive and normal children to make rapid discriminations among different geometrical figures. The child's task was to push buttons corresponding to figures appearing on the screen. In the nondistraction condition, shapes appearing on the screen and on the push buttons were presented as white figures against a black background. In the distraction condition, the shapes appeared against colored backgrounds and, in addition, the background colors for the figures on the push buttons were discrepant with the background colors appearing with those shapes on the screen. Although Sykes et al. found that the introduction of the color discrepancy increased reaction time for both hyperactives and normal controls, no differential effect was obtained between the two groups.

Campbell, Douglas, and Morgenstern (1971) used the Color Distraction Task developed by Santostefano and Paley (1964) to study the effects of the presence of black-and-white peripheral pictures and contradictory

TABLE I

Distraction Studies with Hyperactive Children

Authors	Subjects	Task	Task-irrelevant stimuli	Results
Bremer & Stern, 1976	Hyperactives Normal controls	Reading stories (eye movements recorded)	Telephone ringing, flashing oscilloscope display, and calculator noises	No distraction effect for on-task performance; more off-task behavior for hyperactives during distraction
Browning, 1967	Minimally brain-damaged Normal controls	Form discrimination learning	Flashing multicolored lights	Distraction effect for controls only
Campbell et al., 1971	Hyperactives Normal controls	Naming colors of pictures of fruit	(a) Peripheral line drawings (b) Contradictory colors	Distraction effect; no differential effect
Cohen et al., 1972	Hyperactives Normal controls	Stoop Color-Word Test	Contradicting colors	Distraction effect; no differential effect
Peters, 1977	Hyperactives Normal controls	1. Naming colors 2. Report and recall of words spoken by male voice presented binaurally through earphones 3. Recall of position of animal pictures	1. Object associated with color 2. Words spoken simultaneously by female voice 3. Pictures of household objects appearing adjacent to animal pictures	1. Distraction effect; no differential effect 2. Distraction effect; no differential effect 3. No distraction effect in either group

183

				Enhanced performance of hyperactives
Scott, 1970	Hyperactives	Arithmetic problems	Recorded music	Enhanced performance of hyperactives
Steinkamp, 1974	Minimally brain-damaged Normal controls	Four different visual tasks	(a) Stationary visual stimuli (b) Visual stimuli available for manipulation (c) Examiner present	No distraction effect on task performance measures: minimally brain-damaged group spent more "time-off" arithmetic task when visual stimuli available for manipulation; examiner's presence enhanced performance of minimally brain-damaged group on arithmetic test
Sykes et al., 1971	Hyperactives Normal controls	Vigilance task (C.P.T.) with letters as stimuli	Intermittent white noise	No distraction effect either group
Sykes et al., 1973	Hyperactives Normal controls	Choice reaction time using forms	Colors of forms	Distraction effect; no differential effect
Worland et al., 1973	Hyperactives Normal controls	1. Coding 2. Tone discrimination 3. Dot joining	Assorted attractive visual stimuli and recorded sounds	1. Distraction effect; no differential effect 2. Differential distraction effect; hyperactives more distracted 3. Enhanced performance of controls
Zentall & Zentall, 1976	Hyperactives	Letter circling	Assorted attractive visual stimuli and recorded music	Hyperactives moved less, performed nonsignificantly better with distractors present

colors (that is, colors differing from the natural colors of the fruits) on the child's ability to name the colors of fruits as rapidly as possible. Naming times were compared with those required to name the fruits with no distracting stimuli or contradictory colors present. The extraneous and contradictory stimuli resulted in longer naming times for both hyperactives and normals, but the hyperactive children were not more susceptible than the controls to their effect.

Cohen, Weiss, and Minde (1972) followed up the Campbell *et al.* investigation with a group of adolescent hyperactive children using another naming task, the Stroop Color Word Test (Stroop, 1935), on which the Santostefano-Paley Distraction Test was based. The test consists of three cards containing 100 stimuli; the first contains color names printed in black, the second, patches of color, and the third, color names printed in contradictory colors (e.g., the word *red* printed in green ink. The subject's task on the first card was to read the color names; on the second card, he was required to name the colors of the patches; and on the third, his task was to read the color names while ignoring the contradictory colors in which the names were presented. The investigators report that task difficulty increased from the first to the third card for both subject groups, but again, there was no evidence that the hyperactive children were more disrupted than the controls by the effect of the contradictory colors on the third card.

Peters (1977) recently completed a study in which he compared the performance of hyperactive and normal children on three tasks designed to assess susceptibility to distraction. Because two of the tasks, a selective listening task and a picture order task, also yield measures of incidental learning, which is the topic of a later section of this chapter, discussion of these two tasks and the results obtained from them will be delayed until later. However, for the sake of completeness, a summary of the distraction findings from all three tasks is included in Table I.

Peters's first task, a color-naming task, was a modified version of the Santostefano-Paley Color Distraction Test used by Campbell *et al.* (1971). Peters used the card containing colored fruit from the Campbell *et al.* task and added an additional control card containing only color patches. Since the form cue provided by the pictures of the fruits on the first card was not relevant to the task of naming the *colors* of the fruits, Peters expected that the form cue would act as a distracting or interfering stimulus and would, therefore, increase naming time and errors made while naming the colors. Although the results show that the presence of the irrelevant form cue produced the expected distraction effect, once again the hyperactive children were not more susceptible than the controls to the effects of the distracting stimuli.

On the other hand, another finding from this task does support the hypothesis that hyperactive children have difficulty *sustaining* attention when they are required to repeat a task. Peters found that the performance of the hyperactives was equivalent to that of the control children when they took the task for the first time, regardless of whether it was first given in the nondistraction or the distraction condition. However, their naming time was greater than that of the controls, and they also made more errors than the controls when the task was given a second time. Further evidence that hyperactives have difficulty sustaining performance over time on this task was obtained from an analysis of scores over successive blocks of the task. During the first half of the task the performance of experimental and control groups was equivalent but, during the latter half, the hyperactives made more errors. Peters (1977) used these findings to point to design problems in the original study by Campbell *et al.* (1971) and in other studies to be discussed later. He stressed that it is impossible to separate the effects of distractibility and inability to sustain attention unless the distracting and nondistracting conditions are counterbalanced.

As can be seen in the summary provided in Table I, attempts by other investigators to demonstrate high distractibility in hyperactive children also have been largely unsuccessful. An early study by Scott (1970) was limited to four hyperactive children and did not have a control group. The children were required to solve arithmetic problems in either a normal classroom, a normal classroom with background music, a three-sided cubicle, or a cubicle with background music. Scott concluded that the introduction of the task-irrelevant music *enhanced* the arithmetic performance of the hyperactive children.

Zentall and Zentall (1976) investigated the performance of hyperactive children on a letter-circling task, under conditions of either minimal or high amounts of task-irrelevant stimulation, consisting of assorted attractive visual stimuli and loud recorded music. Again, no control group of normal children was included. Although the performance of the hyperactive children did not differ significantly in the two experimental conditions, the authors report a tendency for the hyperactives to perform better in the presence of the task-irrelevant stimuli. Also of interest is the fact that concomitant measures of wrist activity demonstrated that the hyperactives moved more in the low stimulation condition.

Worland, North-Jones, and Stern (1973) compared the performance of hyperactive and normal children on three different tasks under a minimally distracting condition and under a condition in which the children were being exposed to a large number of visual and auditory task-irrelevant stimuli, consisting of objects, books, toys, and tape-recorded sounds. On a coding task, baseline differences between the two groups were found: The hyperactive children received lower scores than the controls under both the distraction and nondistraction conditions. However, although the presence of the task-irrelevant stimuli led to a reduction in performance for both hyperactive and normal children, the effect was not greater for hyperactives. On a task that required the children to connect dots to make a picture, scores of the hyperactive children were not influenced by the presence of the extraneous stimulation; somewhat surprisingly, however, the performance of the children in the control group was improved. On the remaining measure, a tone discrimination task, Worland et al. do report a distraction effect that occurred only in the hyperactive group. It must be noted, however, that this study was not designed to control for order effects. The testing session for each child lasted approximately 2½ hours, and the children were given a number of other tasks. In addition, the tasks used to study distraction (which lasted approximately ¾ of an hour) were always administered with the nondistraction condition first. As Peters's results on the color-naming task discussed above demonstrate, differences obtained between the nondistraction and distraction conditions could be due to differences in ability to maintain performance over time, that is, to a deficit in sustained attention.

Bremer and Stern (1976) administered reading tasks to hyperactive and nonhyperactive boys under a "quiet" condition and under a "distracting" condition, which consisted of a telephone that rang and contained flashing lights, and an oscilloscope display that was accompanied by the sound of a calculating machine. Like Worland et al., they failed to counterbalance the order of the nondistraction and distraction conditions, although they did minimize repetition by having the children read different stories under the two conditions. Bremer and Stern report that the distractors did not interfere with the hyperactive children's reading performance on any of the measures. On the other hand, the hyperactive boys were significantly more responsive to the distractors, as measured by number of looks toward the stimulus display. This finding is reminiscent of some of our own descriptions of the behavior of hyperactive boys during testing sessions (Freibergs & Douglas, 1969; Sykes et al., 1973); sometimes they seem to be looking away from a task and toward other available stimuli, while still maintaining levels of task performance that do not differ significantly from those of normal children.

Two other investigators, Browning (1967) and Steinkamp (1974) have studied distraction in groups of children whom they labeled as minimally brain-damaged (MBD) but whom they describe as demonstrating hyperactivity and related symptoms. Browning (1967) reported on a series of three experiments. In the first, it was determined that the presence of flashing multicolored lights interfered with discrimination learning in normal children; in the second, the presence of the same stimuli disrupted the performance of normal controls but failed to disrupt the performance of a minimally brain-damaged group. In a third experiment with an older MBD group, Browning again found no evidence that the presence of task-irrelevant visual stimuli disrupted their performance.

Steinkamp (1974) used four different tasks—the Bender-Gestalt Test, the picture completion subtest of the WISC, a coloring task, and an arithmetic task—to compare the performance of an MBD and normal control group under four conditions: (1) no distractions, (2) stationary visual stimuli and recorded classroom noises present, (3) visual stimuli available for manipulation, and (4) examiner present. Performance of the MBD and normal subjects on three of the four tasks was found to be similar, regardless of experimental condition. On the comparatively difficult arithmetic task, the MBD group did spend more time off-task when the manipulable stimuli were present, but, as in the Bremer and Stern (1976) study, there was no evidence that this resulted in inferior task performance. On the other hand, there was evidence that the examiner's presence resulted in improved performance on the difficult arithmetic task, a finding that we interpret as suggesting that the presence of an authoritative adult helped the children achieve better concentration, or sustained attention, on this demanding task.

We also wish to note briefly that, in addition to the studies just reviewed, Peters (1977, pp. 34–37) summarized 17 other distraction studies with retarded and/or brain-damaged children, some of whom may have been hyperactive. Rather surprisingly, these data provide no support for the popular belief that brain-damaged children are highly distractible. Five of the 17 studies provide some evidence of distractibility in the retarded groups, but even here, the evidence is often weak; 2 of the 5 studies included no control groups, and in 2 others, significant differences were found on some tasks but not on others.

Studies of Distractibility with Learning-Disabled Children

Although it is not possible to review in detail here the rapidly expanding literature on the effects of distraction in learning-disabled children, we refer the reader to Table II, which provides a summary of these investigations and facilitates comparison with the studies on hyperactives summarized in Table I.

In contrast to the negative findings generally obtained with hyperactive samples, investigators seem to have had considerable success in demonstrating that the task performance of learning-disabled children, particularly those in the reading-disabled category, can be disrupted by the presence of task-irrelevant stimuli.

TABLE II
Distraction Studies with Learning-Disabled Children

Authors	Subjects	Task	Task-irrelevant stimuli	Results
Alwitt, 1966	Reading-disabled Normal controls	Naming colored pictures	Inappropriate colors	Distraction effect; no differential effect
Atkinson & Seunath, 1973	Learning-disordered Normal controls	Vigilance task with colored forms as stimuli	Varying position of forms	Differential distraction effect; learning-disordered more distracted
Dykman et al., 1971	Learning-disabled Normal controls	Reaction time	Loud noise paired with reaction stimulus	Differential distraction effect; learning-disabled more distracted
Lasky & Tobin, 1973	Learning-disabled Normal controls	1. Verbal response to auditory instructions 2. Written response to auditory instructions 3. Written response to written stimuli	(a) Intermittent white noise (b) Linguistic competing messages	(a) No distraction effect of white noise on all tasks (b) Differential distraction effect of linguistic competing messages on all tasks; learning-disabled more distracted
Nober & Nober, 1975	Learning-disabled Normal controls	Wepman Auditory Discrimination Task	Classroom noises (taped)	Distraction effect; no differential effect

Study	Groups	Task	Distracting stimuli	Results
Pereslini, 1972	Learning-disabled / Normal controls	Reaction time	Recorded noise, music, or story	Differential distraction effect; learning-disabled more distracted
Sabatino & Ysseldyke, 1972	"Learning-disabled" group divided into good and poor readers	Bender Gestalt	Extraneous background stimuli	Differential distraction effect; poor readers more distracted
Samuels, 1967	Poor readers / Good readers	Learning new words	Pictures representing words	Differential distraction effect; poor readers more distracted
Santostefano et al., 1965	Reading-disabled / Normal controls	Naming colors of pictures and fruit	(a) Peripheral line drawings (b) Contradictory colors	(a) No distraction effect of peripheral line drawings in either group (b) Differential distraction effect of contradictory color; reading-disabled more distracted
Willows, 1974	Poor readers / Good readers	Reading story	Colored words printed between lines read	Differential distraction effect; poor readers more distracted
Willows, 1975	Poor readers / Good readers	Reading words	Pictures representing words	Differential distraction effect; poor readers more distracted

Summary and Critique of Distractibility Studies with Hyperactive and Learning-Disabled Children

The distraction studies with hyperactive children summarized in Table I provide no evidence to support the hypothesis that hyperactives are "stimulus driven" (Goldstein & Scheerer, 1941) or suffer from "forced responsiveness to stimuli" (Cruickshank, 1966, 1977). If these descriptions were accurate, then we would expect the hyperactive child to be indiscriminately responsive to a wide range of task-irrelevant stimuli; more important, we would expect this hyperresponsiveness to interfere seriously with performance. The fact that there are many kinds of extraneous stimuli to which hyperactives are no more vulnerable than normal children also weakens arguments suggesting that hyperactive children cannot discriminate between task-relevant and task-irrelevant stimuli, or that they have a defective filter mechanism, which fails to screen out extraneous stimulation.

On the other hand, a few of the studies summarized in Table I (Browning, 1967; Scott, 1970; Zentall & Zentall, 1976) have been interpreted by some investigators (Zentall, Zentall, & Booth, in press) as suggesting that hyperactives sometimes perform better when extraneous stimulation is present. In addition, two of the studies (Bremer & Stern, 1976; Steinkamp, 1974) demonstrate that hyperactives may spend more time than normal control children looking at or manipulating task-irrelevant stimuli without impairing their task performance significantly. These findings, together with the previously discussed evidence that the activity level of hyperactive children sometimes increases when they are subjected to stimulus-reduced environments, provide some support for the hypothesis that hyperactives may have unusual need for stimulation and, as a consequence, may also have an unusual inclination to seek heightened levels of stimulation.

When we consider the distraction studies with LD children summarized in Table II, a pattern very different from the one obtained with hyperactives emerges. In the case of LD children there does appear to be considerable evidence of a distractibility problem. Certain cautions should be observed, however, in interpreting and comparing the studies reviewed in Tables I and II. First, there are no studies in which carefully defined groups of LD, hyperactive, and normal children have been compared directly, using the same tasks and the same distracting and nondistracting conditions. Some authors (Hallahan, 1975; Zentall *et al.,* in press) have suggested, for example, that distractors that are extraneous or peripheral to a task may be much less disrupting than ones that are embedded within the task. Although the studies with both hyperactive and LD children reviewed in Tables I and II include a fairly good representation of several kinds of distractors, the disruptive effects of different types of task-irrelevant stimuli should be investigated more thoroughly in studies using well-matched samples of hyperactive, LD, and normal subjects.

A second problem in interpreting the results presented in Tables I and II involves the possible effect of statistical artifacts such as may arise, for example, if the scores in hyperactive samples are unusually variable as compared with the scores of other groups (Douglas, 1972; Stewart, 1970). It also is essential to eliminate errors in design resulting from failure to counterbalance distraction and nondistraction conditions; this becomes particularly important when studying hyperactive children, since, as we have shown, they appear to be unusually sensitive to the effects of having to repeat a task. Because fatigue and boredom seem to be critical factors in these children, careful account also must be taken of the time they are required to work at a task or on a battery of tests.

Another problem in interpreting the distraction studies with hyperactive and LD children results from the fact that investigators frequently fail to consider differences in baseline levels in task performance among the groups to be compared. As mentioned in our review of distraction studies with hyperactives, the predistraction scores of the hyperactive group sometimes are lower than those of normals. In the case of investigations comparing normal and LD children, we have been impressed even more by the number of studies in which LD children have been subjected to distraction while they were engaged in reading, or other tasks closely associated with academic skills in which they would be expected to be inferior. Certainly, an analysis of covariance design should be used in distraction studies of this kind, and we recommend employing this technique, even when predistraction differences between groups fail to reach statistical significance. Even when this precaution is taken, however, the presence of different baseline levels makes clear interpretation of distraction effects impossible. If a child is attempting to cope with a task that overtaxes his ability, then we might expect any manipulation that places an extra burden on his information-processing capacity to interfere with performance. Even if the LD group were processing the task-irrelevant stimuli in exactly the same way as normal children, we would expect this extra burden to disrupt their performance more seriously. To appreciate the truth of this argument, the reader need only consider his own reaction to distractions that occur while he is attempting to master a new skill.

Before leaving the issue of baseline differences on task performance, it is important to consider another possible explanation for the apparent susceptibility of LD children to the effects of extraneous stimuli. If distraction studies with these children employ tasks on which the LD child has great difficulty, it is possible, as Ross (1976) has suggested, that their history of failure may prompt them to turn to distractors as a means of escaping the discomfort and frustration they have come to associate with such tasks. If this were the case, then their apparent distractibility would stem from an unwillingness to cope with such tasks, rather than an inability to ignore extraneous stimuli.

In the past few years, other investigators who study distraction also have begun to point to the problem of differentiating between distractibility and difficulties children may be having with other aspects of information processing, and as we shall see in later sections of this chapter, the same problem currently is becoming apparent in the incidental learning literature. Denton and McIntyre (1978), for example, report a study in which they investigated spans of apprehension of hyperactive and normal boys, using a letter-recognition task. They found that the span was the same for both groups when no irrelevant letters (visual "noise") were present. As the number of noise letters increased, however, the apprehension span of the hyperactives decreased significantly more than that of the normal boys. Since their task was designed to be relatively insensitive to memory or motivational influences, Denton and McIntyre argued that the increasing reduction in span size in the hyperactive group represented "a true deficit in attention" (p. 19). They suggested three possible explanations for this deficit, one of which was that "the noise letters may act as more potent distractors for the hyperactive boys" (p. 24).

In a later study, however, McIntyre, Blackwell, and Denton (1978) sought further evidence on the cause of the deficit they had found in the hyperactive group. This time they investigated the effects of variations in the amount of signal-noise similarity and noise redundancy on the spans of apprehension of hyperactive and normal boys. Their results indicated that the apprehension spans of hyperactive and normal boys were affected equivalently by variations in signal-noise similarity and noise redundancy. McIntyre *et al.* took this as evidence that both hyperactive and normal boys are "capable of making several analyses concurrently, and they do not have to devote an equal amount of analytic power to each letter to decide if it is signal or noise" (p. 491). Consequently, they rejected the distractibility hypothesis as an explanation for the decrease in apprehension span in the hyperactive group when the noise letters were introduced. Instead, they intend to pursue two other possible explanations. Either the hyperactive boys pick up information from the decaying afterimage of the letters more slowly than do normal boys, or the decaying afterimage fades more rapidly for the hyperactives than for the normals. In future sections of this review, we shall be discussing other studies in which alternative explanations for apparent distractibility in hyperactive or LD samples must be considered.

Incidental Learning Studies with Hyperactive Children

In recent years, the study of incidental learning has become an increasingly popular method of evaluating children's ability to ignore irrelevant information (Hagen & Hale, 1973; Maccoby & Hagen, 1965; Ross, 1976). Like the distraction studies, work in the area of incidental learning was very much influenced by filter theories of attention. The incidental learning approach was thought to be an improvement over distraction studies, however, because the incidental learning method is designed to yield a direct assessment of "the acquisition of information that is extraneous or irrelevant to task performance" (Hagen & Hale, 1973, p. 117). Incidental learning scores usually are judged in relationship to measures of central learning, or learning on an assigned task, and interpretation of both central and incidental scores is strongly influenced by the belief that there is a necessary "trade-off" between the acquisition of information the examiner designates as relevant and that designated as irrelevant. To quote Ross (1976): "Where selective attention is high, incidental learning would be low, and vice versa" (p. 52).

Postman (1964) provides the following general definition of incidental learning: "When the instructions do not prepare the subject for a test on a given type of material, it is convenient to designate the learning of these materials as incidental" (p. 185). However, as Postman reminds us, interpretations of incidental learning studies can be complicated by the different instructions an investigator may give to his subjects.[1]

In the past few years, researchers in the area of childhood psychopathology have been strongly influenced by findings from developmental studies of incidental learning. Some reviewers (e.g., Hagen & Hale, 1973; Ross, 1976) have taken these findings as evidence that improved skill in ignoring irrelevant information leads to an increase in central learning and a decrease (or lack of change) in incidental learning as children mature. After reviewing some of the early studies, Hagen and Hale (1973) concluded that central learning improves "throughout childhood" while incidental learning "either increases or remains stable up to about 12–13 years and then it declines" (p. 122). Results such as these prompted researchers to expect that clinical samples, such as hyperactive and LD children, would demonstrate more incidental learning and less central learning on incidental learning tasks than normal children.

The only investigation of incidental learning involving children clearly diagnosed as hyperactive of which we are aware is the study of Peters (1977) mentioned earlier in our review of distraction studies. It will be recalled that, along with the color-naming task already discussed, Peters used two incidental learning tasks in his study. One of these was based on a popular test of incidental learning, which was developed by Hagen (1967). Peters's modified version of Hagen's task consisted of a series of six cards,

[1]We would add, in addition, that interpretation of these scores can be complicated by the care with which the child listens to the instructions, his willingness to obey the instructions to ignore some stimuli, and his willingness to report remembering stimuli that he was instructed to ignore.

each of which contained a picture of an animal (placed in the center of the card), paired with a picture of a household object (placed adjacent to the animal picture). In each trial, a set of cards was exposed in a particular sequence, and the child was instructed to remember the positions of the animals in the sequence. The child was told that only the animals were important and that he need not "look at these other things." The cards were then concealed, the child was shown a cue card containing a picture of one of the animals, and he was instructed to indicate the position of that picture in the original sequence. The number of trials on which he was correct constituted the measure of central learning. After the central learning trials were completed, he was asked which of the various household objects had been paired with each of the animals; the number of pairs correctly remembered constituted the measure of incidental memory.

Unlike most previous investigators, Peters (1977) included in his design a nondistraction condition in which only pictures of animals (without household objects) were present. Comparison of this condition with the distraction (two-picture) condition produced a surprising finding. Central memory scores obtained in the distraction and nondistraction conditions were not significantly different; that is, there was no evidence that the addition of pictures of household objects impaired central memory performance. A comparison of incidental memory scores in the hyperactive and normal control samples revealed that the two groups did not differ on this measure. In addition, Peters failed to find a significant interaction between subject diagnosis and task condition on his central memory measure, reflecting the fact that the distraction condition did not differentially affect memory for the central task in the two subject groups. Thus, there was no evidence of a selective attention deficit in the hyperactive children on either the central or the incidental memory measure on Peters's version of the picture order task.

Peters also used a selective listening (or shadowing) task to assess central and incidental memory in his hyperactive and normal control samples. The task was adapted from those used by Doyle (1970, 1973). In the distracting condition the child was required to repeat and try to remember target words spoken by a man binaurally through earphones, while a woman's voice simultaneously delivered irrelevant words that the child was instructed to ignore. This was compared with a nondistracting condition in which the child heard the man's voice alone.

Performance measures were derived from two different aspects of the task. First, in both the distraction and nondistraction conditions, the subject was simply required to repeat (shadow) each target word immediately after hearing it; measures from the shadowing task included number of target words correctly reported and (in the distracting condition) number of "intrusive errors" (an intrusive error was scored when the child substituted or added a phoneme to the target word that was present in the distracting word paired with it). Second, following the presentation of the 34-word list, in both the distraction and nondistraction conditions, memory for the target words spoken by the man (that is, central memory) was assessed by a recognition task in which the child was asked to identify target words from among four alternatives. In addition, in the distraction condition, a second recognition task was used to test memory for nontarget words (incidental memory); again, the child was asked to choose which word he heard before from among four alternatives.

Peters found that his hyperactive and control groups did not differ in the number of words correctly reported (shadowed) in the presence of the distracting voice. However, the hyperactives did make more intrusive errors while shadowing the target words; this finding will be discussed in more detail later. Central memory measures from the recognition section of the task revealed that children in the hyperactive group remembered fewer target words than the normal controls in *both* the distraction and nondistraction conditions. There was no evidence, however, that the ability of the hyperactive children to remember the target words was more susceptible than that of the controls to the distracting influence of the task-irrelevant stimuli. Perhaps it is not surprising, therefore, that the hyperactive and control children did not differ on the measure of incidental memory.

Incidental Learning Studies with Learning-Disabled Children

There have been considerably more studies of incidental learning with LD samples than with hyperactives. Again, space does not permit a detailed review of this literature. We do wish to stress, however, that only a few investigators have been successful in showing that LD children process more task-irrelevant information than controls (Santostephano, Rutledge, & Randall, 1965). A large number of studies have yielded results that have been taken as evidence for the incidental learning hypothesis (Hallahan, Kauffman, & Ball, 1973; Kirkbride, 1978; Pelham & Ross, 1977;[2] Siegel, 1968; Tarver, Hallahan, Kauffman, & Ball, 1976; Hallahan, Gajar, Cohen, & Tarver, n.d.), although we question the validity of this conclusion. A frequent finding is that normal children recall more relevant information than LD children but that the two groups do not differ on amount of irrelevant information remembered (Hallahan et al., 1973; Tarver et al., 1976; Hallahan et al., n.d.). When this occurs, investigators frequently resort to

[2]The study by Pelham and Ross (1977) raises several questions because their results differ considerably from the usual pattern. First, these investigators obtained significant differences between poor readers and controls on their incidental learning measure but not on their central measure. Second, the proportion of incidental stimuli remembered by both poor readers and controls was *higher* than the proportion of central stimuli remembered.

statistics based on the proportion of central and incidental material retained, or on patterns of correlations between central and incidental scores, to argue for poorer selective attention in the LD children, but as we shall argue shortly, these procedures may be misleading. In addition to the doubts raised by these ambiguous findings and questionable procedures, the most recent and comprehensive study comparing distraction and incidental learning in LD children of which we are aware (Pelham, 1977) casts further doubt on an incidental learning interpretation of the LD child's difficulties. Pelham's study yielded no evidence of a high degree of incidental learning or distractibility in a reading-disabled group.

Summary and Critique of Incidental Learning Studies with Hyperactive and Learning-Disabled Children

As was the case with the distraction studies with hyperactives reviewed earlier, the one existing study of incidental learning with hyperactive children produced essentially negative results. Thus, there is no evidence at this time to suggest that hyperactive children are more likely than controls to process and remember irrelevant information.[3]

It could perhaps be argued that the revisions made by Peters in the Hagen (1967) picture order task precluded the possibility of finding hyperactive–control differences on the incidental memory measure. Certainly it is most disturbing to discover that the presence of the irrelevant pictures did not result in decreased central memory scores. This finding should alert investigators to the fact that many researchers have not bothered to test the most basic assumption underlying the Hagen task, namely, that the presence of the incidental pictures interferes with memory for the target pictures. Hagen (1967) did test this assumption and succeeded in demonstrating a difference between the distraction (target plus nontarget picture) and nondistraction (target picture only) conditions. Since that time, however, several researchers have modified the task in various ways and have used it with subject samples substantially different from those of Hagen. Frequently, these modified versions of the task have been employed in experimental designs that did not include a nondistraction condition, and so there

---

[3]It should be mentioned that there have been three incidental memory studies with children diagnosed as impulsive using Kagan's (1966) Matching Familiar Figures Test. Since impulsives share some symptoms with hyperactives, these findings are of interest here. Although all three investigations yielded some evidence of lower central memory scores among the impulsive samples (Hallahan *et al.*, 1973; Heins, Hallahan, Tarver, & Kauffman, 1976; Weiner & Berzonsky, 1975), only Weiner and Berzonsky obtained higher incidental memory scores in their impulsive group. Furthermore, this finding was limited to their older, grade six group; there were no differences on either the incidental or the central memory measures in grades two or four.

is no way of knowing whether the presence of the incidental pictures actually interfered with central memory.

It is interesting to note that the changes that have been made in the task seem relatively minor; they include, for example, using six pictures instead of the seven originally employed by Hagen (1967) and changing exposure intervals from 5 to 6, 8, or 10 seconds (Druker & Hagen, 1969; Hagen & Sabo, 1967; Peters, 1977; Weiner & Berzonsky, 1975). Nevertheless, it appears that, although these changes appear minimal, they can strongly affect the results obtained. We were able to find only one other investigator (Kirkbride, 1978) who made minor revisions of this kind and also used the revised version under both distraction and nondistraction conditions. Like Peters, Kirkbride found no differences between the performances of her subject in the two conditions.[4]

The results obtained by Peters on the incidental memory measure from his selective listening task also fail to support the hypothesis that hyperactive children process task-irrelevant information to a greater degree than normal children. In addition, the central memory scores from this test provide no evidence that the interfering effect of the competing voice was greater for hyperactives than for control children.

On the other hand, the significant difference obtained on the intrusive error score of the shadowing task does point to one kind of difference in the reaction of normals and hyperactives to the presence of the competing voice. Although the two groups did not differ on number of words shadowed correctly, the hyperactive children apparently were unable to inhibit interference from the competing voice when they were reporting the target words. This finding is analogous to results obtained by Doyle (1973) in a study of developmental changes on this same task: Doyle reports that her younger subjects made more intrusive errors than her older children. In attempting to interpret this finding, Doyle stressed the fact that she failed to find age differences on her incidental memory measure; she argues, therefore, that the difference on intrusive errors cannot be due to the fact that the younger children were processing more information from the distracting voice than were the older children. She believes, rather, that the younger children could not both attend to the distracting information and

[4]In addition, a study by Hallahan et al. (1974b) may be relevant to this issue. These investigators were interested in studying the effects on central memory of attenuating the visual impact of the incidental pictures in the Hagen task. They accomplished this by drawing the incidental stimuli with a mixture of black and white ink. Two ratios of black to white ink were used: a ratio of one black to two white and a ratio of one black to six white. Hallahan et al. concluded that these manipulations had no effect on selective attention in their subjects. Unfortunately, the authors did not include a condition in which the incidental stimuli were eliminated completely, but extrapolation from their findings suggest that this, too, may have no effect.

refrain from allowing it to intrude upon their vocalizations during the shadowing task. Peters takes a similar approach in discussing his findings. He emphasizes that his hyperactive and control subjects were equally aware of the distracting stimuli, as indicated by the lack of group differences on incidental measures, and he suggests that the intrusive errors made by the hyperactive children result from an inability to inhibit responding with the distracting information when reporting the target words. In support of this argument, Peters reports significant correlations between scores from the Matching Familiar Figures Test of Reflection-Impulsivity (Kagan, 1966) and the intrusive error score on his listening task. Thus, Peters is suggesting that the impulsivity of his hyperactive subjects may have been responsible for their tendency to make intrusive errors.

The findings that were briefly reviewed from the incidental learning studies with LD children raise a number of methodological and theoretical problems. Many of these problems are similar to ones currently becoming evident in the developmental studies of incidental learning, which, as we stated earlier, provided the empirical and theoretical base for the work with clinical samples. Because we believe that further research on incidental learning in hyperactive and LD children will result in wasted effort until these issues are resolved, we wish to touch briefly on some of the major difficulties currently associated with the incidental learning approach.

As we already have mentioned, a major cause of our concern is the failure of many investigators to test the underlying assumption of incidental learning studies, that is, that the processing of task-irrelevant stimuli must interfere with the processing of task-relevant stimuli. Neisser (1976) has shown that human subjects sometimes demonstrate an impressive ability to process and react to information reaching them from different sources. Occasionally, too, normal subjects in the incidental learning studies remember *more* incidental material than LD children (Deikel & Friedman, 1976). This, apparently, is most likely to occur when the incidental stimuli are intrinsically related to the central task, but it does show that when normal subjects adopt a set to pay attention to incidental stimuli, they can sometimes do so and still maintain good performance on the central task.

Second, even when distraction effects are established, we question the assumption that low scores on central memory measures are solely or even mainly attributable to an inability to ignore irrelevant information. This point becomes more clear when we consider what kinds of developmental or LD–normal differences would be predicted if the task-irrelevant stimuli were simply omitted from incidental learning tasks. Note that Hagen's (1967) picture order task now becomes a straightforward test of memory for serial position, and Doyle's (1973) selective listening task becomes a recognition task assessing memory for rather lengthy lists of words. Since both tasks place relatively heavy information-processing demands on a child, the performance of older children would be expected to surpass that of younger children and, similarly, normal children would probably perform better than LD children.

Consequently, if findings from incidental learning studies are to be interpreted in terms of distractibility and the processing of irrelevant information, the onus is on investigators in this area to prove (1) that they are assessing processes that can be isolated from the processes being tapped by their central tasks, and (2) that group differences obtained on their measures reflect differences in the ability to disregard extraneous information.

We believe that the evidence fails to support these assumptions. First, as we argued in our discussion of distraction studies (p. 191), it is impossible to separate the effects of task difficulty from the effects of distractors; if a central task is difficult for a particular child, either because he is young or because he has learning disabilities, then we would expect any extraneous or incidental stimuli associated with the task to disrupt that child's performance seriously.

In addition, it appears to us that a large proportion of the significant findings in incidental learning studies have been due to central, rather than incidental, measures. As we already have mentioned, many of the studies with LD children have yielded normal–LD differences on central scores but have failed to establish differences between normal and LD groups on incidental scores. A similar pattern has emerged rather frequently in the developmental studies. Most investigators have shown an increase in central learning scores within the age range of approximately 6 to 14 years (e.g., Druker & Hagen, 1969; Hagen & Huntsman, 1971; Hallahan et al., 1974a; Hale & Piper, 1973; Weiner & Berzonsky, 1975). In the case of incidental learning measures, however, the findings have been inconsistent and generally disappointing. Although a decline after 12–13 years has been reported by some investigators, (e.g., Hale, Miller, & Stevenson, 1968; Hallahan et al., 1974b; Maccoby & Hagen, 1965; Siegel & Stevenson, 1966), a significant decrease was not found by Doyle (1973), Druker and Hagen (1969), Fraas (1973), Hagen (1967), Hagen and Sabo (1967), or Siegel (1968). Moreover, the fact that a decline in incidental learning, even when obtained, does not occur until sometime between ages 12 and 14 makes it clear that improvement on central learning before this age cannot be accounted for by an improved ability to filter out extraneous stimuli.

Some investigators have attempted to deal with these findings by developing measures based on the relative proportion of task-relevant and task-irrelevant stimuli remembered correctly by their subjects. It should be noted, however, that it is possible for this kind of measure to yield age differences, even if incidental learning remains constant across ages, so long as central task performance increases. Presumably, advocates of this approach reason that if subjects at all ages were attending equally to both task-relevant and task-irrelevant information, there should be a developmental increase in memory for both types of stimuli; consequently, when increases occur only on the central measure, they take this as evidence that, relatively speaking, older subjects are somehow ignoring the incidental information. A similar argument is applied when differences are found between LD and normal children on central memory scores, but not on incidental memory. In the absence of evidence to prove otherwise, however, we would have to argue that two groups that obtain equivalent incidental memory scores must have paid equal attention to the irrelevant information and processed it to the same degree.

An additional source of concern about the interpretation of incidental learning scores arises from patterns of correlations that have been obtained among these measures. Since Pelham's (1977) study involved several tasks, including an auditory incidental learning task, a visual incidental learning task, a speeded classification task containing distractors, and a dichotic listening task, he was able to study correlations among distraction and incidental learning scores derived from these various measures. Pelham reports a median correlation among his measures of .11 and concludes that his results suggest that "these tasks do not measure the same underlying cognitive ability" (p. 39). Correlations obtained by Peters (1977) among scores derived from the three tasks used in his study (the Color Naming Test, the Picture Order Task, and the Selective Listening Task) also revealed few significant relationships.

In view of these negative results, we must conclude that many of the investigators whose studies we have reviewed have overemphasized the importance of the selective aspects of attention and underemphasized the importance of other cognitive processes tapped by their tasks. This is not surprising when we consider the major impact of filter theories of attention on the psychological literature and the relative dearth, until the last few years, of other theoretical approaches to attentional processes. Indeed, since very early days, psychologists seem to have been fascinated with man's ability to ignore some events in his environment in favor of others. As early as 1890, William James was telling us: "Everyone knows what attention is. It is the taking possession by the mind, in clear and vivid form, of one out of what seem several simultaneous possible objects or trains of thought. Focalization, concentration of consciousness are its essence. It implies withdrawal from some things in order to deal effectively with others . . ." (pp. 403–404). In a similar vein, Hagen and Kail (1975), in a recent review of the role of attention in perceptual and cognitive development, state: "The major question concerns how the individual selects the important information and ignores the unimportant from the vast amount of input that is available to the individual at any given time" (p. 165).

In the remainder of this chapter, we shall take the position that distractibility does *not* represent the major problem in the attentional disabilities manifested in childhood hyperactivity. Instead, we shall argue that the hyperactive child's attentional problems are more concerned with "the concentration of consciousness," a phrase that tends to be neglected in James's definition quoted above. By reviewing the various tasks on which hyperactive children perform poorly, we shall attempt to show that their major disability involves a failure to apply sufficient strategic effort to the task of thoroughly processing and using the information available to them.

Interestingly, several investigators who study either developmental changes in attention or attention in LD children appear to be moving toward a somewhat similar point of view. In the review article by Hagen and Kail (1975) just quoted, for example, the authors speak of "significant developmental changes in the efficiency with which attention is deployed" (p. 188), and they also emphasize their view that "the child becomes an increasingly active participant in the attentional process with development . . ." (p. 165). The kinds of attentional strategies discussed by Hagen and Kail in this paper include: exhaustive and efficient visual scanning, detailed analysis of features differentiating stimuli, and the consistent testing of hypotheses during discrimination learning trials. In a similar vein, Pelham (1977) interprets findings from his incidental learning and distraction tasks as suggesting that the important differences between his LD and normal groups involved such factors as rate of information processing, the use of rehearsal as a memory strategy, and focused visual scanning. Finally, a recent paper by Tarver *et al.* (1976) demonstrates that LD children employ rehearsal strategies less efficiently than normals on Hagen's Incidental Learning Task.

Sustained Attention as Defined in Vigilance Studies

Some investigators (e.g., Berlyne, 1970; Kahneman, 1973) have drawn a distinction between the *selective* and the *intensive* aspects of attention. As our discussion thus far already has demonstrated, this differentiation sometimes is difficult to make; nevertheless, we believe that the distinction is fundamental for an understanding of attentional processes. Berlyne (1970) uses the term *intensity* in referring to how much attention the organism is giving to the stimulus field as a whole; he uses a related term, *attentiveness*, to refer to the individual's momentary readiness to receive and process stimuli.

Several theorists (e.g., Berlyne, 1970; Kahneman, 1973; Posner & Boies, 1971; Pribram & McGuiness, 1975) have pointed to the relationship between the intensive aspects of attention and the physiological processes of alertness or arousal. Arousal is a hypothetical construct and can only be inferred indirectly from an individual's behavior and from such psychophy-

siological measures as heart rate, skin conductance, cortical evoked responses, and electronic pupillography.

Arousal is thought to have both general and specific components. The
general component reflects the "background" state of excitability or wakefulness of the individual and is usually portrayed as an inverted U function,
varying from sleep through increasing stages of wakefulness to extreme
alertness and disorganization. Optimal psychological functioning is considered to occur in moderate states of arousal, that is, between the two extremes of sleep and disorganization (Hebb, 1955). Arousal levels above
optimal interfere with execution of a task, while lower levels are insufficient
for adequate performance (Bindra, 1959; Yerkes & Dodson, 1908). In addition, optimal level of arousal is related to task complexity. If an individual is
performing a difficult task, optimal level is lower than for a less demanding
task. Generally speaking, moderate levels of arousal are experienced as
more pleasurable than either extremely low or extremely high levels and,
accordingly, an individual attempts to achieve moderate levels through
either seeking or avoiding stimulation (Berlyne, 1967, 1971).

Kahneman (1973) describes a similar inverted-U-shaped relationship
between arousal level and attention. Central to his model is the notion that
attention depends on the individual's capacity to invest effort in the attentional process; this ability, in turn, is linked to arousal level. If arousal is
too high, attention becomes unstable and unduly narrow. Also, at either the
high or the low extreme, an individual becomes incapable of taking a task
set or of evaluating his own performance.

Among the more *specific* components of arousal, the one of most interest to us here is the phasic orienting response (OR). The OR is a brief
response, lasting only a few seconds, that is superimposed upon the more
long-lasting shifts in arousal. It appears following the perception of a stimulus and is thought to reflect psychophysiological changes that improve the
organism's capacity for extracting information from the environment and
for making an appropriate response. Sokolov (1963) describes the OR as a
reflexive response to a potentially informative and relatively novel stimulus.
With repeated elicitation of the OR, an internal neural model of the stimulus
is developed, and autonomic responsivity to the stimulus gradually
declines.

The intensive aspects of attention traditionally have been measured by
tests requiring sustained attention, such as vigilance, monitoring, or watch-
keeping tasks. Moray (1969) describes a vigilance task as "a situation
where nothing much is happening, but the observer is paying attention in
the hope of detecting some event whenever it does happen" (p. 6).

Reaction time tasks in which a warning signal is followed by a preparatory interval, which is terminated by the onset of a reaction signal, also
have been used to assess vigilance or alertness. As Posner and Boies (1971)

have argued, "the fore-period of a reaction time task may be considered as a miniature vigilance situation where alertness must be developed rapidly and maintained over a relatively brief interval" (p. 391); we would add that this state of preparedness must be produced repeatedly, often over a substantial period of time. Posner and Boies (1971) also have reviewed evidence indicating that the autonomic and central changes that occur during the foreperiod of a reaction time task are similar to those involved in vigilance tasks. In addition, Douglas (1972) has reported a substantial correlation between children's scores on vigilance and reaction time tasks, thus offering further support for the belief that the two tasks are tapping similar processes.

It should be noted that some theorists attribute poor performance on vigilance measures to defects in *selective* attention. Broadbent (1958) speaks of a failure to the filter to remain locked on the channel containing task-relevant input. Some recent investigators in the area of childhood disorders (Dykman et al., 1971; Ross, 1976) also believe that errors occur on these tasks because of the child's failure to ignore irrelevant stimuli. We have been impressed, however, by the fact that hyperactive children, in the studies we shall be reviewing, perform poorly on vigilance tasks even when they are working alone in environments designed to be as distraction-free as possible. Furthermore, as we already have discussed, studies in which we have attempted to distract them from these tasks by introducing task-irrelevant stimuli have shown their performance to be no more disrupted than that of normal controls. Nor do we believe that it is fruitful to introduce the notion that the hyperactive children are being distracted by "internal stimuli." Their deficiency appears, rather, to involve an inability to mobilize the sustained effort and control required to meet the demands of these relatively dull and repetitive tasks.

Vigilance Studies with Hyperactive Children

Vigilance Measures. Several of the vigilance studies with hyperactive children at McGill have employed visual or auditory forms of the Continuous Performance Test (adapted from Rosvold, Mirsky, Sarason, Bransome, & Beck, 1956). The stimuli usually have consisted of 12 letters, which appeared on a screen (or over earphones) one at a time; the significant stimulus to which the subject was instructed to respond was the letter X, but only when it was immediately preceded by the letter A. Using the visual form of the task, Sykes (1969) and Sykes et al. (1971) found that hyperactive children made fewer correct detections (i.e., more errors of omission) and more incorrect responses (i.e., more errors of commission) than normal controls. Sykes et al. (1973) replicated these findings on errors of omission and errors of commission using both the auditory and visual versions of the task; in addition, they found that the performance of the hyperactive group deteriorated markedly with time on the task, while that of the control group did not. As we shall discuss shortly, Anderson, Doyle, and their associates (Doyle, Anderson, & Halcomb, 1976; Dykman *et al.*, 1971) also replicated the Sykes *et al.* findings in a vigilance study with LD children, which included a hyperactive subsample.

Three studies have been completed at McGill using a delayed reaction time task (DRTT), consisting of a warning signal followed by a preparatory interval and a reaction signal to which the child is required to respond as quickly as possible (Cohen & Douglas, 1972; Firestone & Douglas, 1975; Parry, 1973). In each of the three studies, mean reaction time was slower and variability of reaction time was greater for hyperactives than for normal controls. Where the task has been administered over longer periods, a trend toward a steeper drop in the performance of hyperactives than controls also has been reported (Cohen & Douglas, 1972). A recent study by Zahn, Abate, Little, and Wender (1975) has replicated the finding that hyperactives have slower reaction times and more variable response latencies than do controls.

Measures of Impulsivity. Although we have been discussing vigilance and reaction time tests as measures of sustained attention, these tasks also provide evidence of behaviors that we consider to be impulsive. In discussing errors of commission on their vigilance task, Sykes *et al.* (1973) report that hyperactives showed a greater tendency than controls to respond to the letter *A* on the CPT before the next letter arrived; this suggests that they were anticipating an *X* but could not hold back responding until it appeared. They also made more "random" responses (responses to nonsignificant letters), as well as more "multiple" or "redundant" responses (pressing more than once to a single letter). In a follow-up study of adolescent hyperactives, Hoy *et al.* (1978) report that, relative to normal controls, their adolescent hyperactive group made more errors of commission on a monitoring task that involved responding to particular words among a series of words recorded on an 18-minute tape. (Also, in agreement with findings from the distraction studies discussed earlier, the addition of distracting voices on the tape did not disrupt the performance of hyperactives any more than that of normal children.)

Evidence of similar impulsive behaviors also was found on the DRT task. Cohen (1970) and Firestone and Douglas (1975) report that redundant responses were more frequent in their hyperactive subjects, and Firestone and Douglas found that the hyperactives also made more "interstimulus" responses (responses occurring after the warning signal but before the onset of the reaction signal). Again, responses of this kind suggest that once hyperactive children are primed to respond, they are less able than normals to inhibit premature or repetitive responding.

Vigilance Studies with Learning-Disabled Children

There have been several studies using vigilance or reaction time tasks with children labeled learning-disabled, reading-disabled, or "under-achievers" (Ackerman, Dykman, & Peters, 1977; Anderson, Halcomb, & Doyle, 1973[5]; Dykman et al., 1971; Keogh & Margolis, 1976; Noland & Shuldt, 1971; Ricks & Mirsky, 1974; Sroufe, Sonies, West, & Wright, 1973). These investigations will not be reviewed in detail here; however, it does appear that errors of omission have been found rather frequently in children with learning problems, although evidence of errors of commission (impulsive responses) is less clear.

It should be noted that some of these investigators worked with very mixed samples of subjects, and their findings underline the point we made in our introduction about the importance of trying to differentiate between LD and hyperactive children when choosing research subjects. After dis-covering differences between a mixed LD group and normal controls on a visual vigilance task, Anderson et al. (1973) and Doyle et al. (1976) took the additional step of dividing their LD sample into hyperactive and nonhy-peractive subsamples. In both studies, it was found that children in the hyperactive subsample made fewer correct detections and more false re-sponses than LD children who were not hyperactive. Indeed, graphs depict-ing "false alarm rate" (errors of commission) in the Doyle et al. (1976) study show that the distribution of these impulsive responses was so high in the hyperactive subsample that the distribution failed to overlap with those of normoactive or hypoactive subsamples of LD children or with a sample of normal controls. Ackerman et al. (1977) and Dykman et al. (1971) also divided their LD samples into subgroups based on activity level and found that sustained attention deficits were much more prevalent in their hyperac-tive subgroup.

Keogh and Margolis (1976) also divided an "educationally handi-capped" group into subgroups that were relatively high or low on hyperac-tivity ratings. Although these authors failed to find significant differences between the subgroups on their vigilance task, they point out that selection practices in the educationally handicapped classes in the school district

---

[5]Doyle et al. (1976) placed visual distractors in the corner of the screen on which the target stimuli of the vigilance task were to appear. Unfortunately, they did not include a "distrac-tion-absent" condition in their design, and so there is no way of evaluating the effects of the distraction on omission or commission errors. They do report, however, that their hyperactive subsample showed much more eye contact with the distracting stimuli than did the nonhyper-active subsample. This finding is in agreement with two studies reported earlier (Bremer and Stern, 1976; Steinkamp, 1974) in which hyperactives were found to spend more time than normals looking at task-irrelevant stimuli.

where they obtained their subjects may have resulted in overselection of hyperactive pupils. Thus, a relatively high level of hyperactivity in both subgroups might have made it unlikely that differences would be obtained.

Studies with Hyperactives on Reaction Time Tasks Making Less Stringent Demands on Sustained Attention

In order to specify the nature of the hyperactive child's attentional deficit more accurately, Sykes et al. (1973) studied the performance of a hyperactive and a normal control group on two tasks that differed in essential ways from the vigilance tasks we have been discussing.

The first, a Choice Reaction Time task (CRT), required the child to press buttons corresponding to geometric figures as these figures appeared on a screen. Trials were discrete, and before a new figure appeared, the experimenter redirected the child's attention to the task. Sykes et al. (1973) report that the mean reaction times for hyperactive and control children did not differ on this task. Thus, the attentional deficits of hyperactive children did not become apparent when the task was divided into discrete trials and the children were helped to redirect their attention to the task at the beginning of each trial.

Stimuli in the Serial Reaction Task (SRT) consisted of five lights, each associated with an individual push button. As each light went on, in random order, the child was instructed to tap the button corresponding to that light, thus turning it off. Another light did not appear until he had switched off the previous one. Again, the hyperactive children seem to have had somewhat less difficulty on this task than on the Continuous Performance Task (CPT); they did not differ from controls with respect to mean number of correct responses, although they did make more errors. Their success on the correct response measure can probably be attributed to the fact that the appearance of stimuli is paced automatically on the CPT, whereas stimuli in the SRT do not disappear until the child has made his response. This method of pacing the task guarantees that the test stimuli remain in front of the subject until he has paid at least some attention to them. Again, as in the case of the CRT, demands on sustained attention are reduced.

Psychophysiological Concomitants of Vigilance Task Performance in Hyperactive Children

There have been numerous studies attempting to relate performance on vigilance tasks to a wide variety of measures of tonic and phasic arousal. In a review of some of the relationships that have been found, Raskin (1973) reports evidence that high tonic skin conductance is associated with an ability to maintain detection accuracy over time on task, that faster reaction times are related to higher conductance levels, that phasic skin responses occur more frequently just prior to correct signal detections, and that subjects who have larger amplitude skin responses when they detect a signal produce fewer "false alarms" (that is, responses in the absence of signals). Since hyperactives are inferior to normals on several of the behavior measures used in these studies, it is of interest to look at their performance on the concomitant psychophysiological measures.

Cohen and Douglas (1972) monitored skin conductance while hyperactive and normal children were performing on the delayed reaction time task, when they were in a resting state, and while they were responding to nonsignal stimuli (i.e., stimuli to which they were not required to make a behavioral response). They found no significant differences between groups on resting skin conductance levels. Onset and habituation of the skin conductance orienting response (OR) to nonsignal stimuli also were similar for normal and hyperactive children. However, while responding to the *signal* stimuli of the DRTT, controls exhibited a significantly greater increase than hyperactives in both tonic and phasic ORs. Thus, the poor behavioral performance of the hyperactives on the DRTT reported earlier was paralleled by a lack of physiological responsivity.

The findings of Firestone and Douglas (1975), who used a slightly modified version of the DRTT, essentially replicated the results obtained by Cohen and Douglas. The authors report no differences between their hyperactive and normal groups during a resting period, but hyperactives produced fewer specific responses to the warning signal of the DRTT. These results suggest to us that any notions about unusual arousal levels in hyperactives will have to emphasize the fact that arousal levels in these children often are insufficiently modulated to meet specific task demands at specific times.

No attempt will be made to review in detail the numerous studies of autonomic and central indices of arousal in hyperactive children that have been carried out in the past few years. As Douglas (1976b) has commented, almost limitless differences in the measures and methodology used in different laboratories make comparison from study to study extremely difficult. However, Hastings and Barkley (1978) have recently completed an exhaustive review of this literature, and their analysis suggests that the overall thrust of findings by other investigators agrees with the McGill studies in some major aspects. For example, they conclude from investigations using electrodermal measures that "random groups of hyperactive children do not differ from normal children on basal electrodermal measures." In addition, after reviewing seven studies that compared hyperactive and normal children on specific skin conductance response measures, they concluded that the data suggested "*diminished electrodermal responsiveness* to specific stimuli" in hyperactive children.[6] It should be noted that this conclusion was not limited to skin conductance studies; Hastings and Barkley's review of a large number of investigations using many other autonomic and electroencephalic measures led them to the same conclusion.

The Effects of Stimulant Drugs on Vigilance Task Performance of Hyperactive Children

There is considerable evidence that the performance of hyperactive children on vigilance tasks improves when they are receiving stimulant drug medication. The favorable response of hyperactives to the stimulants frequently is taken as "proof" that the children normally are functioning at suboptimal levels of arousal, although a recent study showing that the stimulants produce similar improvements in normal children has made this argument somewhat less compelling (Rapoport, Buchsbaum, Zahn, Weingartner, Ludlow, & Mikkelsen, 1978).

In our own laboratory, Sykes et al. (1973) found that treatment with methylphenidate resulted in an increase in correct responses, a decrease in incorrect (or impulsive) responses, and less decrement in performance over time on the CPT. Cohen, Douglas, and Morgenstern (1971) found that hyperactives receiving methylphenidate demonstrated faster and less variable response times and made fewer redundant (multiple) responses on the DRTT. Thus, the drug affects both the ability to sustain attention and the tendency to respond impulsively on these two vigilance-type tests. Several other investigators have reported similar findings (Barkley & Jackson, 1977; Conners & Rothschild, 1968; Knights & Hinton, 1969; Porges, Walter, Korb, & Sprague, 1975; Sprague, 1970; Sroufe et al., 1973).

There have been several attempts to understand the mechanism linking the effects of stimulant drugs on attentional mechanisms with their effects on arousal indices. Some investigators hoped to find unusual levels of arousal in hyperactive children who responded particularly well to the stimulants, and then to show that these psychophysiological abnormalities could be "corrected" (or would become more like the patterns of normal children) when these children were placed on medication. However, as Barkley's (1976) review of these studies shows, attempts to isolate psycho-

[6]The one point of possible disagreement between Hastings and Barkley's conclusions and our own is that they report diminished responsiveness to *both* signal and nonsignal stimuli, whereas our significant differences in the Cohen and Douglas (1972) study were obtained only in the signal condition (i.e., when the children were responding to the signals on the DRTT). However, as Cohen has reported (1970), she did find differences in a nonsignal paradigm in an earlier pilot study; she suggested that methodological changes (such as presenting the stimuli through earphones instead of speakers and limiting the movement of her subjects) may have contributed to the different findings in her two studies.

physiological indices that are capable of identifying favorable drug responders have been largely unsuccessful. Somewhat more encouraging have been the studies seeking to show that the drugs produce changes in psychophysiological indicators that are thought to accompany attentional processes. In their recent review, Hastings and Barkley (1978) conclude somewhat cautiously that the findings from these investigations suggest that the stimulants "energize or increase the 'arousal' of these children and enhance the impact of stimulation on the nervous system" (p. 413).

The Effects of Reinforcement on Vigilance Task Performance of Hyperactive Children

Studies on the response of hyperactives to reinforcement contingencies delivered during vigilance task performance also are relevant to hypotheses regarding arousal patterns in these children. Wender (1972) has suggested that hyperactives are less responsive than normals to reinforcement, apparently basing this opinion on complaints from parents that discipline is ineffective in controlling them. We believe, however, that discipline problems can be more validly attributed to the hyperactive child's impulsivity and, as we shall discuss, to his unique reactions to reinforcement contingencies.

We have found considerable evidence that judiciously applied positive reinforcement helps hyperactives perform better on vigilance-type tasks. Cohen (1970), Firestone and Douglas (1975), and Parry (1973) all have demonstrated that contingent and continuous reward enhances performance on the DRTT in a manner similar to that of the stimulant drugs; that is, reaction times become both faster and less variable. Worland et al. (1973) found that rewarding hyperactive boys for each item correctly completed on a coding task resulted in more correct items, less time off task, and less "wiggling" behavior. Worland et al. interpret these changes as demonstrating an increase in "intrinsic motivation" (p. 375) in their hyperactive subjects.

Sometimes, however, reinforcement fails to have the desired effect, or even produces negative results. One reason for this seems to be that the reinforcers become a highly salient aspect of the learning situation for the hyperactive child. Consequently, he may be paying more attention to the reinforcers themselves (or to the reinforcing person) than to the particular behavior being reinforced or to the specific stimuli associated with it. In addition, hyperactive children appear to be unusually sensitive to the loss of reinforcement and to the failure of expected reinforcers to appear. Both Cohen (1970) and Parry (1973) report that hyperactives returned to baseline performance more quickly than normals when extinction trials were introduced, and Parry (1973) also found that performance on the DRTT task was more variable when the children were receiving partial, as opposed to continuous, reinforcement.

Parry found, as well, that noncontingent reinforcement ("praising" statements delivered randomly rather than after particularly good trials) produced reaction times in their hyperactive subjects that were both slower and more erratic than baseline (prereinforcement) levels. In the case of a normal control group, on the other hand, the noncontingent reinforcement had a positive effect on performance. We might speculate that the noncontingent reinforcers created heightened general arousal in the hyperactive subjects without providing the guiding cues they needed to focus their attention on the specific demands of the task. In the case of the normal children, however, even randomly directed praise seems to have been sufficient to increase motivation. Apparently the normal children did not require the additional help of being redirected repeatedly to the specific demands of the task, possibly because they had "internalized" the instructions to respond as quickly as possible more completely than the hyperactives.

The study by Firestone and Douglas (1975) included a comparison of the effects of positive and negative feedback on DRTT performance. Like reward, punishment was effective in improving reaction times and reducing variability in the hyperactive group. However, another finding from the study points to the complexities involved in assessing the effects of reinforcement on the performance of hyperactive children. Firestone and Douglas report that impulsive responses on the DRTT increased in their hyperactive boys over baseline levels when positive reinforcement was introduced; interestingly, this did not occur with negative reinforcement or with a combination of positive plus negative reinforcement.

Since Firestone and Douglas monitored skin conductance while their subjects were performing on the DRTT, they were able to show that their three reinforcement conditions (reward, punishment, and reward plus punishment) affected tonic skin conductance differentially, with only reward producing an increase in tonic conductance from baseline level. Thus, it appears that the high number of impulsive responses by the hyperactives in the reward condition was related to high tonic arousal level. This is perhaps not surprising when we consider the "inverted-U function" of arousal, described earlier. Presumably, the reward condition pushed the hyperactives to a higher-than-optimal level, which made it difficult for them to control impulsive responding. It also should be noted that no reinforcement contingencies were included in the Firestone and Douglas study to discourage impulsive responding; possibly this is another kind of specific direction hyperactive children may require.

A recent study by Worland (1976) also demonstrates that reinforcement sometimes affects the performance of hyperactives in complex ways. On both a coding and a spelling correction task, punishment for off-task behavior resulted in greater time on task than did positive reinforcement for on-task behavior in the hyperactive group. On the other hand, the negative reinforcement condition also led to decreased accuracy in the hyperactive group on the spelling correction task, apparently because the hyperactive children became more careless. The fact that hyperactives were more sensitive to the quality of feedback than the normal control group is demonstrated by the fact that controls were equally responsive to the positive and negative conditions throughout the study. In considering Worland's findings, it is important to note that reinforcement was given for on-task behavior and not on the basis of the correctness of the work being performed. Thus, as in the Parry and Firestone and Douglas studies, the reinforcers may not have provided sufficient cues to guide the child's attention toward the specific demands of the task.

The Cohen (1970) study mentioned earlier also suggests that it may be necessary to invest unusual effort in setting up reinforcement contingencies so as to direct the hyperactive child's attention to specific task requirements. Cohen monitored skin conductance in order to assess the impact of rewards administered while the children were performing on the DRTT. She reports that tonic skin conductance (general alertness) increased in both hyperactive and normal children when reward was introduced. However, although frequency of ORs to the warning signal changed from baseline to reward in the normal group, OR frequency did not change across these conditions in the hyperactive group. Cohen speculates that the hyperactives were not learning the conditions of reinforcement as well as the normals. She draws on the theorizing of Sokolov (1963), which we discussed earlier, and suggests that the hyperactives had not yet formed a "stable internal model" of the stimulus situation, which would have enabled them to predict the occurrence of the signals and thus adjust their behavior to the task demands.

Summary and Critique of Vigilance Studies with Hyperactive and Learning-Disabled Children

It is difficult to draw any firm conclusions from available data regarding the prevalence of sustained attention problems in LD children. As we have noted, LD samples in some of the vigilance studies cited contained children whom the investigators considered to be hyperactive. The demonstration of dramatic differences between hyperactive and nonhyperactive subgroups in the Doyle *et al.* study (1976) suggests that hyperactive children may be accounting, at least partially, for the poor vigilance scores obtained by LD groups. In addition, some experimenters choose their LD samples in ways that greatly increase the likelihood of finding attentional deficits. Ricks and Mirsky (1974), for example, asked teachers to select children for their poor reading groups who were "inattentive in school and six months below their grade level in reading achievement" (p. 7).

Thus, it seems that some children in LD samples (and in LD class-rooms) are probably mislabeled hyperactives. Others may be LD children who possess good, or even excellent, concentration skills. Still others may have learning disabilities combined with an inability to sustain attention and, finally, some may have "pseudoconcentration problems." By this, we mean that their apparent inability to sustain attention derives from their original learning deficit. This could occur in two possible ways: their learning disability might make it particularly difficult for them to process the information conveyed by the vigilance task stimuli effectively,[7] or their history of failure in academic and other activities might discourage them from persevering on unappealing tasks. It will be recalled that we advanced similar reasons for suggesting that LD children may, sometimes, be "pseudodistractible."

In the case of hyperactive children, on the other hand, the evidence for sustained attention deficits is quite compelling, although it should be recognized that the hyperactive label often is assigned on the basis of a cluster of symptoms that include attentional problems. The circularity inherent in this approach to choosing samples arises from the fact that a constellation of symptoms involving hyperactivity, attentional problems, and impulsivity appears to exist in both phenomenological reports and empirical findings. This is demonstrated, for example, by the high loading of activity, attentional, and impulsivity items on the Hyperactivity Factor of the Conners Teacher Rating Scales (Conners, 1969, 1970) and also, we believe, by the experimental evidence presented in this review.

Indeed, as we mentioned in our introductory remarks, we believe that these findings support the adoption of a new diagnostic label, such as "attentional-impulsivity disorder" or "attention-impulsivity-hyperactivity disorder" to replace the term *hyperactive* (or *hyperkinetic*) *syndrome.* In the vigilance studies we have just reviewed, the close relationship between concentration problems and poor inhibitory control is revealed in several ways. Although considerably more speculative, there also is some reason to believe that a relationship exists between these two symptoms and peculiarities in arousal patterns of hyperactive children.

Certainly, on both the CPT and the DRTT indices of lapses in alertness (e.g., in correct detections on the CPT and slow reaction times on the DRTT) and indices of impulsive responding (e.g., errors of commission and premature and "repetitive" responses) tend to be high and to occur together in hyperactive samples. It is interesting to note, as well, that the

---

[7]The study by Blank, Berenzweig, and Bridger (1975) suggests that slower reaction times in LD children may sometimes be attributed to difficulties in processing the information contained in the task stimuli, particularly if the stimuli are of a complex nature.

incidence of these responses increases more sharply in hyperactives than in controls as the child is required to remain working on these rather dull tasks. Equally interesting, Sykes *et al.* (1971) report that "wiggling behavior," which was measured by a stabilometric cushion placed on the child's chair, increased more sharply in hyperactives than in controls from the children's first to second session on the CPT. A possible explanation is that this extraneous movement represents stimulus-seeking behavior, as defined earlier in this chapter. Similarly, errors of commission on the CPT and impulsive responses on the DRTT may partially reflect the youngsters' need to "make something happen" and to derive stimulation from moving their own bodies.

Additional evidence of the close relationship involving concentration, impulsive responding, and arousal in hyperactives derives from the fact that improvement occurs simultaneously on vigilance and impulsivity measures when the children are placed on stimulant medication and also when they are receiving rewards. Since the stimulant drugs and reward are both known to enhance arousal, these results seem, once again, to implicate the arousal system in attending and inhibiting behaviors.

The specific manner in which arousal and these behaviors are related, however, is still unclear. Certainly, many of the experimental findings from the vigilance studies point to an underlying mechanism considerably more complex than a chronic state of underarousal, and the recent psychophysiological literature seems to agree with the behavioral data on this point. The fact that positive reinforcement increased the incidence of impulsive responding in the Firestone and Douglas (1975) study indicates that hyperactive children can be triggered rather readily (and sometimes inadvertently) from low to excessively high arousal levels. Similarly, Parry's finding that the performance of hyperactives on the DRTT deteriorated when noncontingent reward was introduced suggests that manipulations that increase arousal level but fail to direct the child's attention to how well he is meeting the specific demands of the task may actually be disruptive.

A consideration of the inverted-U arousal function discussed earlier suggests several possible explanations for this phenomenon. It may be that the range of arousal levels within which hyperactive children can function effectively is unusually narrow. Thus, relatively small shifts toward either the high or the low end of the arousal curve would result in impaired performance. We also might speculate that arousal patterns are particularly labile in hyperactive children or, alternately, that hyperactives are less capable than normals of modulating their own states of activation in order to achieve levels that are optimal for dealing with particular tasks or situations. If this were true, then the inhibitory influence of the mild negative feedback provided by Firestone and Douglas may have helped their hyperactive subjects "settle down" to meet task demands.

In their review of psychophysiological studies with hyperactive chil-

dren, Hastings and Barkley (1978) remark that there has been some disagreement in the psychophysiological literature about whether hyperactives
are typically under- or overaroused. It is interesting to note that any of the
three hypothetical mechanisms we have postulated here would help explain
why investigators have experienced so much difficulty studying level of
arousal in hyperactive children. Slight changes in the child's state of fatigue
or in the stimulation provided by events in the laboratory and in the experimental tasks could produce highly unpredictable shifts in activation levels.

It appears that the clearest and most consistent evidence of arousal
deficits in hyperactive children occur when they are required to remain alert
for the appearance of specific stimuli, or when they are required to respond
differentially to different task demands. This was suggested in our own
findings of diminished electrodermal responsiveness to the signal stimuli of
the DRTT (Cohen & Douglas, 1972; Firestone & Douglas, 1975) and by
several other demonstrations of the impact of a variety of stimuli on autonomic or central indices of specific alertness or arousal (Hastings & Barkley, 1978). Parry's (1973) study demonstrating the negative effects of
noncontingent reinforcement on the DRTT performance of hyperactives
underlines the necessity of using reinforcement schedules with these children that help cue them in to the specific demands of a task. However,
Cohen's (1970) findings, derived from galvanic skin response measures
recorded during reinforcement trials, suggest that even contingent, continuous reward increases OR frequency to the warning signal of the DRTT less
effectively in hyperactives than in normal children. This finding was paralleled by the behavioral data, which showed that, although the performance
of hyperactives on the DRTT improved during reinforcement, it did not
reach the level of the normal group. Cohen speculates that it may be necessary to take additional measures to focus the child's awareness on the
relevant cues and the quality of his own responses in a task situation;
alternatively, the hyperactive child may require more exposure to the relevant stimuli, so that stimulus-response contingencies become overlearned.

Sustained Attention as Defined in Studies of More Complex
Perceptual and Conceptual Processes: A Brief Review

Thus far, we have been discussing the sustained attention, inhibitory,
and arousal deficits of hyperactive children as they are manifested on relatively simple vigilance and reaction time tasks. Much more important for
the child's cognitive development and social adjustment, however, is the
impact of these deficits on more complex perceptual and conceptual tasks
and on his responses in social situations. Since this topic is extremely
complex and involved, we can only summarize here a few of the major

points discussed by Douglas in a recent paper dealing with higher order mental processes in the hyperactive child (Douglas, in press-a).

Studies with Hyperactives Using Tasks Requiring Perceptual and Logical Search Strategies

Table III has been adapted from a table appearing in the Douglas paper. It is presented here to give the reader an overview of the perceptual, conceptual, and social tasks on which significant differences have been found between hyperactive children and matched control groups. Included in the table is a description of the facilatory and inhibitory behaviors assessed by each task. We believe that these descriptions demonstrate rather convincingly the pervasiveness of a number of common requirements throughout the wide range of tasks listed. In each case, the child must exert sustained, careful, and organized effort if he is to cope successfully with the task; as a corollary to this, successful performance almost invariably involves an ability to inhibit any tendency to respond in a careless or superficial manner. As we shall discuss shortly, some of the tasks involve a carefully organized, perceptual search through several alternatives, while others require logical search strategies. In some cases, the alternatives from which the child must choose are presented to him; in others he must produce his own possible solutions before choosing one of them.

In order to document the nature of the hyperactive child's difficulties more clearly, Douglas also has prepared a list of tasks on which hyperactives have been shown to perform relatively well (see Table IV). Included in Table IV are descriptions of the behaviors tapped by each of these tasks and a comment regarding factors within the task or the task situation that reduce the demands for organized and self-initiated concentration and effort.

We believe that the findings in Table IV help rule out several possible explanations for the children's inability to cope with the tasks in Table III. We already have discussed factors that can improve the reaction time performance of hyperactives. In addition, the Parry (1973) study of simple reaction times in a continuous reinforcement condition makes it clear that in some circumstances (e.g., 100% reinforcement) hyperactives are capable of reacting just as quickly as normals. Similarly, the good performance of hyperactives on some tasks requiring visual discrimination (e.g., the Choice Reaction Time Task and the Picture Completion subtest of the WISC) rules out visual discrimination problems as a likely explanation of the children's failure on tasks like the Matching Familiar Figures Test or the Embedded Figures Test. Following the same line of reasoning, we believe that hyperactives are able to cope with some kinds of tasks requiring conceptual and abstracting skills (e.g., the Concept Identification Task) under

TABLE III

Tasks on Which Hyperactives Perform Poorly

Task	Facilitory behaviors	Inhibitory behaviors
Continuous Performance Test: Vigilance Task (Anderson et al., 1973; Doyle et al., 1976; Dykman et al., 1971; Sykes et al., 1973)	Establish response set for designated stimuli Concentrate on responding quickly Maintain response set (vigilance) over time	Inhibit responding to inappropriate stimuli
Reaction Time Tasks with Preparatory Interval (Cohen & Douglas, 1972; Firestone & Douglas, 1975; Parry, 1973; Zahn et al., 1975)	Establish response readiness on basis of warning signals Concentrate on responding quickly to reaction signals Establish response readiness repeatedly over time	Inhibit responding at inappropriate times
Kagan's Matching Familiar Figures Test: Reflection–Impulsivity (Campbell et al., 1971; Cohen et al., 1972; Juliano, 1974; Parry, 1973; Peters, 1977; Schleifer et al., 1975)	Concentrate on finding exact match to target picture Conduct exhaustive, organized search of all alternatives in a visual array Systematically compare standard and alternatives on critical perceptual features	Inhibit choosing pictures only superficially like standard
Embedded Figures Test: Field Dependence (Campbell et al., 1971; Cohen et al., 1972)	Concentrate on forming clear visual image of target figures Conduct exhaustive, organized search for correct figures embedded within a visual array	Ignore embedding context Inhibit responding to superficially similar figures
Porteus Mazes (Parry, 1973)	Concentrate on finding safe route to goal Conduct careful search at critical points to discover consequences of taking alternate routes	Avoid entering blind alleys Inhibit cutting corners, crossing lines, etc.
Tests with Multiple Choice Format (Hoy et al., 1978)[a]	Concentrate on finding correct logical choice among several alternatives Conduct exhaustive logical search of all alternatives	Inhibit responding to superficially correct answers

Task		
Wisconsin Card Sorting Task (Parry, 1973)[b]	Concentrate on finding all possible legitimate categories for sorting Systematically examine patterns on cards for common features Abstract class concepts from patterns (e.g., color, form, number)	Inhibit responding with salient but unacceptable categories Inhibit idiosyncratic responses
Matrix Solution Tasks (Tant, 1978)	Concentrate on finding strategies that will eliminate most cards Scan and analyze visual display Classify stimuli into groups and label each group Choose questions that will elicit most information Make correct deductions from feedback provided Remember which possibilities previous questions eliminated Coordinate a series of questions into a planful approach	Avoid being misled by salient but less informative cues
Rule Learning Tasks (Tant, 1978)	Concentrate on finding the rule connecting stimulus attributes that will enable correct sorting Conduct careful perceptual analysis of stimuli appearing on cards Code stimuli logically, depending on the presence or absence of key attributes Use feedback to assign classes of stimuli to positive and negative categories Remember logical implications of feedback	Avoid responding only to *perceptual* aspects of stimuli (as opposed to *logical* classes they represent)
Memory for Paired Associates: Arbitrary Associations (Benezra, 1978)	Concentrate on finding best way of remembering paired associates Consider possible strategies, mnemonic devices Choose most effective strategy	Inhibit choosing readily available but less effective strategies
Story Completion Task: Frustrating Stories (Parry, 1973)	Concentrate on understanding a social situation from several perspectives Consider possible motives of frustrator Consider consequences of own behavior Consider possible substitutes for lost object or event	Inhibit aggressive responses

[a]Hyperactives did not show deficit when number of choices was limited to two.
[b]Hyperactives have no problem with shifting set.

TABLE IV

Tasks on Which Hyperactives Perform Relatively Well

Task	Task requirements	Factors minimizing demands on attention and effort
Simple Reaction Time Task: Continuous Reinforcement (Parry, 1973)[a]	Concentrate on reaction signal Concentrate on reacting quickly	Child receives reinforcement for every response
Choice Reaction Time Task (Sykes et al., 1971)	Concentrate on pushing buttons corresponding to geometric figures on screen Concentrate on responding quickly	Trials are discrete E elicits child's attention before each trial
Serial Reaction Time Task (Sykes et al., 1971)	Concentrate on pushing buttons corresponding to particular lights as lights appear Concentrate on responding quickly	Stimuli are self-paced Stimuli remain in review until child responds
Picture Completion Subtest: Wechsler Intelligence Scale for Children (Douglas, 1972)	Concentrate on finding missing part on individual pictures Conduct visual search of picture for missing part	E elicits child's attention before presenting each picture Pictures are presented one at a time Only one item must be found in each picture
Concept Identification Task: Continuous Reinforcement (Freibergs & Douglas, 1969; Parry, 1973)[b]	Concentrate on discovering the "correct" concept from series of visual stimuli presented in pairs Abstract stimulus dimensions from the task stimuli Assign stimuli to nominal categories (e.g., "bird," "flower") Modify response strategies on basis of information feedback	Equipment is novel, interesting Test stimuli are colorful Child receives immediate and consistent reinforcement for every correct response Concepts to be discovered are very familiar

[a]Significant hyperactive–normal differences do occur on partial reinforcement schedule.
[b](1) Hyperactives performed very poorly on same task on a partial reinforcement schedule. (2) In the continuous reinforcement condition hyperactives showed excellent transfer to a second concept. (3) Hyperactives also were able to reverse concepts when feedback changed—i.e., no evidence of perseveration.

some conditions (continuous reinforcement). Finally, Table V (adapted from Benezra, 1978) contains a long list of tasks on which hyperactives have no memory problems. Difficulties are not apparent except in tasks requiring that the children develop rather sophisticated rehearsal strategies in order to commit the material to memory, as in the Paired Associates Task involving *arbitrary* associations.

In considering the essential qualities of the tasks on which hyperactive children do badly, it should be mentioned that other writers occasionally have referred to a few of the tasks listed in Table III as assessing *selective* attention. These writers usually have been referring to tasks like the Matching Familiar Figures Test or the Embedded Figures Test, in which the child must resist aspects of the stimulus materials that are salient but incorrect in order to focus on the correct features. We prefer, however, to label this process "sustained" attention because we believe that emphasis should be placed on the *facilatory, focusing* behaviors involved and the effort required to carry them out. We wish, also, to make it clear that the inhibitory behaviors to which we refer in Table III do *not* involve filtering or screening out salient or superficially correct aspects[8] of the problem situation; the term refers, rather, to the necessity of inhibiting a tendency to *respond* or base one's actions on these misleading aspects. To state the point differently, we expect that the child does process these more salient aspects of stimuli; however, if he is to solve the tasks successfully, he must *continue processing beyond* these aspects in order to give proper consideration to more subtle or more abstract cues that are present.

Arousal and Performance on More Complex Problem-Solving Tasks

We wish now to return briefly to consideration of the role of arousal in the deficits found in hyperactive children. In our earlier discussion of vigilancelike tasks, we showed that manipulations thought to increase arousal level in hyperactives (i.e., reinforcement and the administration of stimulant drugs) frequently improve their performance on these tasks. We also pointed out, however, that in some circumstances these manipulations prove to be disruptive, and we suggested that investigators may sometimes unintentionally push tonic levels of arousal beyond optimal limits. We suggested further that hyperactive children may be unusually prone to these arousal shifts, and we also emphasized the importance of taking care to set

---

[8]This point is similar to the one made by Peters (1977) when he was attempting to explain intrusion errors made by hyperactive children during the "shadowing" condition of the selective listening task (see our discussion on pages 197 and 198). Peters argued that both normal and hyperactive children were processing information from the second voice. However, the hyperactives made more intrusive errors because they could not inhibit saying aloud the words they were processing.

up reinforcement contingencies so as to alert the hyperactive child to the specific demands of a task.

Similar considerations also have begun to emerge from studies involving more complex problem solving. Indeed, if theories regarding the inverted U-shaped function of arousal are correct, we would expect performance on complex tasks to be even more sensitive to arousal level than performance on the simple tasks that we discussed earlier in this chapter. Several authors have argued that the stimulants do not improve hyperactives' academic achievement or performance on tasks requiring relatively high levels of information processing (Barkley & Cunningham, 1978; Rie, Rie, & Stewart, 1976; Rie, Rie, Stewart, & Ambuel, 1976; Sroufe, 1975). On the other hand, we have known for some time that stimulants improve the performance of hyperactive children on the Matching Familiar Figures Test (Campbell *et al.,* 1971) and the Porteus Mazes (Conners, 1972; Sroufe, 1975). In addition, Dalby, Kinsbourne, and Swanson (in press) report that methylphenidate improves the hyperactive child's use of re-

TABLE V
Verbal Memory Tasks on Which Hyperactives Perform Well

Tasks	Tested by	Process involved
Digits forward	Recall	Immediate recall (2–9 digits) (4 consonant letters)
Digits backward	Recall	Immediate recall & operation on material to be recalled
Consonant trigrams with delay	Recall	Recall after delay of 3, 6, 12, 18, 30 seconds (3 consonant letters)
Consonant trigrams with delay & counting task	Recall	Recall after delay of 3, 6, 12, 18, 30 seconds filled with competing activity
Series of words (with pictures)	Recall and recognition	Recall and recognition of series of words (12 per list)
Paired associates: meaningful pairs	Recall and recognition	Recall and recognition of lists of word pairs (17 pairs per list—3 trials per list)
Paired associates: meaningful pairs	Recall and recognition after long delay	Recall and recognition of lists of word pairs after 45 minutes delay

hearsal time on a paired-associates task involving arbitrary associations. Sprague and Berger (in press) also have reported preliminary evidence showing that the performance of hyperactives on arithmetic computations improved when they were receiving methylphenidate.

In another study, Sprague and Sleator (1977) have demonstrated complex and interesting dose response curves in hyperactives. These investigators report improvement on a memory recognition task when hyperactives were receiving a relatively low dosage of methylphenidate; at a higher dosage level, however, there was a performance decrement. Moreover, teachers' reports of behavioral improvement followed a different dose response pattern, with reports of improvement occurring at the *higher* dosage level. Consequently, if teachers' reports were accepted as the criterion for assigning drug dosage, it appears that this would result in dosage levels that would impair hyperactive children's performance on more complex tasks. It is unfortunate that there are no comparable data on the drug response curves of normal children; it is quite possible that there are important differences in the way normal and hyperactive children respond to different dosage levels.

Recently, a few authors (Margolin, 1978; Sahakian & Robbins, 1977) have predicted that stimulant drug medication should impair performance on tasks that require a flexible approach to problem solving. They base their reasoning on animal studies that have shown that animals receiving the stimulants focus narrowly on particular aspects of a stimulus situation and respond in a repetitive manner; the extreme of this response is represented by stereotyped behaviors. Similarly, they refer to clinical reports that describe hyperactive children on high dosages of the stimulants as showing perseveration as well as a "fixation" on performing tasks assigned to them. Indeed, they argue that it is this effect of the stimultants that produces improvement on simple vigilancelike tasks. Thus, the need for more data on the effects of the stimulants on a variety of tasks and behaviors becomes evident.

Findings from studies by Freibergs and Douglas (1969) and Parry (1973) using the Concept Identification Task described in Table III demonstrate that *reinforcement* also can affect the performance of hyperactives for better or for worse, depending on the reinforcement contingencies used. When the children were receiving positive reinforcement for every correct response, there was no significant difference between hyperactive and normal groups on the number of trials taken to solve the concept problems. In contrast, when a partial reinforcement schedule was implemented, a large proportion of hyperactives failed to reach a solution, and the mean number of trials to solution in the hyperactive group was much higher than in normal controls. Parry (1973) demonstrated that providing continuous information feedback did not compensate for the effects of partial reinforcement. Consequently, she agreed with Freibergs and Douglas's (1969) suggestion that the hyperactive children were demonstrating a unique reaction to what Amsel (1962) and Ryan and Watson (1968) have labeled the "partial reinforcement effect," that is, the reaction to the frustrative aspects of nonreward in the reinforcement condition. Parry provided further evidence for this interpretation from her findings on the simple reaction time task. As well as performing more poorly on the task, hyperactive children in her partial reinforcement group were more likely to leave the task during extinction trials when given an option to do so. In addition, the hyperactives showed a more "undifferentiated" reaction to nonreward than did normals during extinction trials, continuing to pull the lever harder than controls regardless of the reward schedule they had received. Findings of this kind support our contention that reinforcement frequently becomes an unusually salient aspect of the learning situation for hyperactives.

In a more recent study, Zentall, Zentall, and Booth (in press) unintentionally demonstrated that stimulating teaching materials can sometimes interfere with learning in hyperactive children. They added arousal-enhancing aspects, such as color and movement, to materials used for teaching spelling and, contrary to their expectations, they found that the learning of hyperactives was more impaired than when they were taught with regular teaching methods. In contrast, normal children performed better when the stimulating materials were used. As Douglas (in press-a) has noted, however, the novel materials used by Zentall *et al.* were not always designed to focus the children's attention on the essential aspects to be learned (sometimes, for example, color was used in the background rather than in the letters themselves). In addition, Zentall *et al.* report that after several exposures to the stimulating materials, the hyperactive children began to benefit from the high stimulation condition.

This tendency of hyperactives to react poorly to stimulating or challenging tasks initially and then to improve their performance with repeated exposure also was noted by Freibergs (1965). Of interest also is the fact that they often show excellent transfer on tasks that are challenging and absorbing (Freibergs & Douglas, 1969; Juliano, 1974; Tant, 1978). It should be noted that this improvement over time on repeated administrations of interesting tasks is exactly opposite to the deterioration in performance over time or with repetition that we reported for hyperactives on dull, repetitive tasks. Again, it appears that complex relations between arousal levels and task difficulty must be considered in attempting to understand the performance patterns of hyperactive children.

Higher Order Schemata, Search Strategies, and Meta Processes

We mentioned earlier that filter theories of attention have been of little help in understanding the cognitive and behavioral deficits of hyperactive children. On the other hand, we suggested that theories that stress the *effort* involved in attention (e.g., Kahneman, 1973; Pribram & McGuiness, 1975) seem somewhat more relevant because they attempt to relate the modulation of arousal to the successful deployment of effort during the attentional process. We believe, however, that several of the attentional theories that emphasize the role of experience in developing "expectancies" or a readiness to respond to particular aspects of a situation (e.g., Bindra, 1976; Hebb, 1949, 1976; Neisser, 1976) are likely to contribute most to our understanding of how the facilatory and inhibitory behaviors described in Table III develop.

As Douglas (in press-a) has discussed, these theories emphasize two related aspects of perceptual and cognitive development that appear, from our review, to be central to the impaired functioning of the hyperactive child. The first aspect involves the extent to which an individual's perceptions and cognitions of a current event are guided by prior learning, as opposed to the salience or incentive value of the event; the second involves the extent to which current perceptions and cognitions are under intentional or voluntary control, as opposed to involuntary control.

Each of these theories describes a process whereby an individual develops a hierarchy of neural representations of his perceptual experiences. Bindra uses the term *contingency organizations* to describe the central neural representations of predictive relations between the occurrence of events. Hebb speaks of "higher order cell assemblies" to refer to highly abstract and complex representations of perceptions and ideas, and Neisser talks in a similar manner about "schemata" that operate at different levels of abstraction and complexity.

In all of these theories, the quality of perception and cognition and the efficiency of the perceptual and logical strategies available to guide attentional processes are strongly influenced by these developing neural representations. Neisser describes "perceptual cycles" that involve continuous interactions between the perceiver's schemata and the objects of perception. As the child continues to interact with his environment, the schemata become increasingly subtle, complex, and abstract; as a result, they are able to guide perception in increasingly sophisticated ways, enabling the child to appreciate both distinctive features and complex structures and patterns in events that he experiences. Similarly, Bindra posits a progressive refining and elaboration of the predictive function of the individual's contingency organizations, and Hebb describes the development of higher order cell assemblies as enriching an individual's ideas and making his perceptions more meaningful.

If one accepts these assumptions, it becomes obvious that anything that interferes with the establishment of higher order schemata is likely to have profound and long-lasting effects on cognitive development. Unfortu-

nately, most of the attentional theorists have not given detailed consideration to the kinds of abnormality within an individual that are likely to
interfere with the establishment of complex and effective schemata. Hebb
(1976), however, has suggested that some children may have suffered from
selective loss of inhibitory neurons, which are believed to be particularly
vulnerable to toxins and nutritive lack, especially anoxia. As a result of this
loss, cell assemblies would be more likely to remain active after their function has been served, and perception, thought, and cognitive learning
"would be less effective, less capable of the maintained selectivity that we
know as concentration on one topic" (p. 374). Interestingly, Bindra also
emphasizes the role of inhibitory processes in the establishment of contingency learning. He believes that inhibitory-neural discharges are responsible for the delay component of contingency organizations, and he points to
the relationship between hyperactivity and damage to the frontal lobes,
which are known to be associated with inhibition. He also mentions that
inhibitory processes in the brain "mature slowly and are not effectively in
operation until fairly late in the maturational period" (p. 134); thus, it is
possible that the development of these processes is particularly retarded in
the hyperactive child.

These are only a few of the current speculations about the etiology of
the hyperactives' original deficits. In any case, we know that, for whatever
reason, these children demonstrate very early in life a disinclination to
involve themselves in a careful and reflective way with the objects and
events in their environment. To use Neisser's terminology, their "perceptual cycles" are unusually brief, or, in Bindra's terms, their "determining sets" fluctuate too rapidly. Consequently, the expectancy theories
of attention all would predict that this original tendency must inevitably
lead to a spiraling effect on the children's perceptual and cognitive development. Their inclination against looking and listening carefully or reflecting
upon their experiences in a thoughtful manner would impede the establishment of rich, subtle, and complex schemata, which, in turn, would impair
the effective deployment of perceptual and cognitive operations, and the
cycle would be continuously repeated.

Hebb (1976) provides an additional reason for predicting serious long-
term consequences from a disability that impairs the richness of early perceptual learning. He argues that the ability to become intensely involved in
a cognitive event occurs when one set of mental activities is able to maintain
itself in spite of "noise" from irrelevant sensory stimulation and spontaneous activity in other neurons in the brain; he believes that the development of higher order cell assemblies makes this possible through a recruit-
ing process that incorporates "extra" neurons into the current activity:

> Development of normal ability to concentrate and keep attention fixed on an
> assigned task, I propose, is a matter of first developing those higher-order cell-

assembly activities, and secondly, enriching them with associative connections interwoven like a tapestry so that the core process of a given mental activity may reduce conflict, not by inhibiting other activity but by co-opting and imposing its own order widely throughout the brain. When this can happen, we speak of the learning task as "interesting" which clearly means that it is one that engages the thought processes fully. (p. 313)

Thus, the expectancy theories would predict that an original disability involving poor inhibitory control or impaired ability to sustain attention would lead to the impoverishment of conceptual development, a failure to learn effective strategies for extracting information from the environment, and an inability to commit oneself totally to complex intellectual tasks. On the other hand, the child should perform reasonably well on tasks that do not emphasize these demands. As Hebb (1976) has argued, we would not expect S-R learning to be impaired in these children, and the effect on perception, thought, and cognitive learning could sometimes be relatively subtle; these processes would not be eliminated but would simply be less effective.

We believe that the nature of the tasks listed in Tables III, IV, and V support this kind of interpretation of the strengths and weaknesses of the hyperactive child's perceptual and logical processes. There is considerable evidence from studies using the tasks listed in Table III that the "search strategies" of hyperactives are defective. We use the term *search strategy* here as it has been defined by Wright and Vlietstra (1975). These authors argue that there are two basic modes of organizing observing behaviors: "exploration" and "search." In the very young child, attention is "exploratory"; that is, it is controlled by salient, curiosity-producing features of stimuli, such as intensity, contrast, change, incongruity, novelty, complexity, and surprise (Berlyne, 1960). In view of our previous discussion of the sensitivity of hyperactive children to reinforcement, it is important to note that Wright and Vlietstra stress that reinforcement-correlated features of the environment also possess salience and, as a result, they, too, exert strong control over the young child's attentional processes. The child's response to these features is spontaneous, unorganized, and short-lived. Gradually, however, as he has repeated experience with particular stimuli and situations, the youngster's propensity to explore habituates to noncritical aspects of those stimuli, while his attention to more critical aspects is strengthened because they serve to make the environment less ambiguous and thus lead to reinforcement (Gibson, 1969). Thus, familiarization with the environment facilitates a shift from diffuse, exploratory behaviors to search strategies, which are based on the relevance and informativeness of available cues. In contrast to exploratory behaviors, search strategies are deliberate, goal-oriented, purposeful, organized, and logically programmed.

As Wright and Vlietstra point out, there is considerable agreement between the development stages they describe and those posited by other theorists. For example, Berlyne (1960) differentiates between "diversive" and "explicit" exploration, while White (1965) distinguishes between an "associative" and a "cognitive" level of response. Similarly, Piaget (1961) describes an early developmental stage in which young children focus their attention on one salient feature in a situation and a later stage when they are able to "decenter" their attention in order to extract information from other available cues.

Wright and Vlietstra present evidence linking the cognitive style of reflection-impulsivity (Kagan et al., 1964) to the child's use of either exploratory or search strategies. The most popular measure of reflection-impulsivity (and the one used in most of the studies cited by Wright and Vlietstra) is the Matching Familiar Figures Test (MFFT). The MFFT was designed to assess a child's habitual speed of decision making in situations with high response uncertainty. The subject is shown a picture of a common object and is asked to choose from a group of very similar pictures the one that is identical to the standard. Time to the first response and total number of errors are recorded. Among school-age children, there is typically a substantial negative correlation between response time and errors. Children classified as impulsive are those who score below the median for their group on response time and above the median on errors; reflectives score above the median on response time and below the median on errors.

Several investigators have demonstrated that impulsive and reflective children employ different strategies on the MFFT. Studies of scanning behavior have revealed that, in general, impulsives direct fewer glances at the standard and variants and make fewer comparisons between them (Drake, 1970; Kagan, Pearson, & Welch, 1966; Siegelman, 1969). Impulsives also engage in fewer sophisticated strategies, such as comparing pairs of stimuli consisting of the standard and an alternative and searching for distinctive features in a systematic manner. In our laboratory, Garson (1977) has shown that children who engage in careful visual search on the MFFT also are more likely to engage in careful auditory and haptic search on auditory and haptic matching tasks. Thus, it appears that individuals demonstrate some generality in search patterns across different modalities.

As can be seen from Table III, several investigators have found significant differences between hyperactive children and matched control groups on the MFFT.[9] These differences now have been reported in preschool

---

[9]In some of these studies the differences found between hyperactive and normal groups on the latency measures of the MFFT have been significant only when one-tailed tests were used. As Douglas (in press-a) has suggested, this does not necessarily mean that Kagan's theorizing about cognitive tempo is wrong. She points out that measures of "looking time" tend to be unreliable when used with impulsive or hyperactive children. This problem results from the fact that it sometimes is difficult to know whether such a child is using the time to actually attend to the stimuli.

(Schleifer, Weiss, Cohen, Elman, Dvejec, & Kruger, 1975) and adolescent samples (Cohen *et al.*, 1972) as well as in school-age groups (Juliano, 1974; Parry, 1973; Peters, 1977). As mentioned earlier, Wright and Vlietstra have reviewed a number of studies that demonstrate that performance on the MFFT is related to performance on a wide range of other measures that are thought to reflect the maturity of children's search behaviors. In addition, a substantial number of investigators have found relationships between the MFFT and the Embedded Figures or Porteus Mazes Tests, two of the other "perceptual search" tasks on which hyperactive children perform poorly (see Messer, 1976, for a review of these studies). Finally, there have been a few correlational or factor-analytic studies with normal, hyperactive, or educationally handicapped children that have yielded evidence of significant relationships between these measures of perceptual search and scores on vigilance or reaction time tasks (Douglas, 1972; Douglas & Marton, 1974; Garson, 1977; Keogh & Margolis, 1976). As Keogh and Margolis emphasize, these correlations account for only a small proportion of the variance in these tests. Nevertheless, the consistency with which these relationships have been found, particularly in studies where the effects of age and IQ have been carefully controlled, suggests that the tests are tapping some common skills. To state the point more exactly, it appears that in order to apply the strategies required for successful performance on the perceptual search tests, a child must possess the more simple attentional and inhibitory skills tapped by the vigilancelike tasks. This interpretation also is strengthened by the fact that the stimulant drugs enhance performance on both the vigilance tasks and the MFFT and Porteus Mazes.

Wright and Vlietstra also discuss tasks involving logical search rather than perceptual search. They review several studies demonstrating that as children mature, they become capable of approaches to problem solving that are designed to produce the systematic information needed for task solution, as opposed to engaging in strategies that attempt to maximize reinforcement directly. Miller, Galanter, and Pribram (1960) have labeled the first of these approaches "algorithmic plans," while they label the more reinforcement-oriented approaches "heuristic plans." Wright and Vlietstra cite a number of studies to demonstrate that older children use more systematic and logical strategies than younger children on a variety of complex problem-solving tasks. In summarizing the approaches used by the younger children, Wright and Vlietstra state that they "appear to be more determined by salient characteristics of the stimulus array or by direct attempts to maximize reinforcement, a logically salient feature of such tasks" (1975, p. 232).

In the past few years, there have been several studies comparing the problem-solving efficiency of reflective and impulsive children (as defined by the MFFT) on tasks similar to the ones used in the developmental studies discussed by Wright and Vlietstra. The tasks or "diagnostic games" were inspired by the "20 Questions" game (Mosher & Hornsby, 1966; Neimark & Lewis, 1967). In a typical game of this sort, the child is presented an array or matrix of pictures and is told that the experimenter is thinking of just one of them: the subject's task is to ask questions that are answerable by a simple "yes" or "no" in order to arrive at the answer with the fewest possible questions. Thus, he must both produce and test hypotheses about the correct answer. The strategies chosen by the child can vary in sophistication from ones that eliminate half of the possible alternatives remaining at any point during solution (or "focusing" strategies) to "guessing" or "gambling" strategies that eliminate only one alternative at a time. Intermediate between these are "constraint-seeking" strategies that eliminate more than one but less than half of the alternatives with each question asked.

Cameron (1977) has reviewed several studies in which the efficiency of task strategies of children classified as impulsive or reflective have been evaluated. The majority of these (8 out of 10) have found that impulsives are less likely than reflectives to employ focusing or constraint-seeking strategies. Cameron also reports on a study of his own in which he used a task-analysis approach to explore possible reasons for the poor performance of impulsive children. He found that impulsives had no difficulty understanding or retaining instructions, but that they were less likely than reflectives to choose strategies that would eliminate a large number of alternatives and thus enable them to solve the problems more efficiently. They also were more likely to approach the task in a random fashion, apparently having no task-relevant rule in mind. Thus, the impulsive children failed to discover available logical clues, which would have enabled them to extract the required information in a few steps. Instead, they either guessed at the answer or focused too narrowly on a particular stimulus or class of stimuli. Cameron also reports that even when his impulsive subjects had discovered and verbalized the more efficient strategies, a substantial proportion of them later made moves that were inconsistent with their own chosen plans.

In a recent study at McGill, Tant (1978) administered three matrix solution tasks similar to those used in the above studies to matched groups of normal, hyperactive, and nonhyperactive reading-disabled children (see Table III). She found that several different measures of problem-solving efficiency differentiated the hyperactives from both the normal and the nonhyperactive reading-disabled groups. Questioning her subjects about dimensions within the stimulus arrays revealed that compared with children in the other groups, the hyperactive children failed to mention the presence of some dimensions more frequently. Thus, it appears that the hyperactives had conducted a less thorough perceptual analysis of the arrays than the other children. This finding agrees with Parry's (1973) report that hyperactives used fewer of the possible dimensions on the Wisconsin

Card Sorting Task than normals (see Table III). As Tant points out, however, careless scanning of the arrays could not account completely for the smaller number of efficient questions asked by the hyperactives. This is indicated by the fact that the hyperactives perceived many dimensions that they did not use in forming their questions. Tant also showed that the failure of hyperactives to use efficient strategies resulted from a true "mediational" deficiency rather than a "production" deficiency (Flavell, 1970). She presented the children with choices between good and poor questions and found that the hyperactives were not capable of recognizing the more efficient questions, even when such questions had been formulated for them.

Wright and Vlietstra (1975) also argue that search strategies play an important role in memory and recall tasks, another type of task represented in Table III. They believe that improvement in memory as children mature may result from "the increasing selectivity and systematicity of observing behavior found in the development of perceptual search." They also point to the growing body of research that has demonstrated that, in somewhat older children, "mature, logical search, often dependent on verbal processes or imagery, contributes to effective rehearsal and retrieval" (p. 225). These authors remind us that young children are virtually as good as adults at short-term iconic storage, provided they are required to process only one item at a time or are helped to focus on one item at a time. However, if these conditions are not present, their inability to organize attention in order to cope with multiple cues sets limits to the amount of information they can process and thus retain. This emphasis on perceptual analysis and organization of material to be learned occurs in several recent theories of memory. Craik and Lockhart (1972), for example, speak of "levels of processing" on memory tasks. According to them, "trace persistence is a positive function of the depth to which the stimulus has been analyzed" (p. 671).

The reader may recall that Peters (1977) found memory differences between hyperactives and normal controls on his selective listening task, which had been designed to study incidental memory. His hyperactive group recognized fewer of the target words than control subjects in *both* the distraction and the nondistraction condition of the task. This surprised us somewhat because, as Douglas (1972) has reported, previous studies at McGill had revealed no memory difficulties in hyperactives on several memory tasks, including the digits forward and digits backward subtest of the WISC and memory tests involving meaningful sentences and unrelated lists of words. However, Peters's task made rather heavy demands on the analytic and organizational skills mentioned by Wright and Vlietstra. After listening to 34 target words (or 34 pairs of target and nontarget words) the child had to choose each of the words that he had heard before from among four alternatives. It should also be noted that, besides requiring considerable rehearsal skills, Peters's task used a multiple-choice recognition format. A recent study by Hoy *et al.* (1978) suggests that multiple-choice tasks place hyperactives at a disadvantage (see Table III). Using both a spelling and a word-knowledge test, they found that the performance of hyperactives was *not* inferior to that of normal controls, so long as the children had to pick their answer from only two alternatives. However, when a five-choice format was used, significant differences between the groups emerged. Thus, it seems likely that careless, incomplete scanning of alternatives may produce lower scores in hyperactives on any task using a multiple-choice format.

To return to the memory issue, recent data collected by Benezra (1978) at McGill confirms our early impression that hyperactives cope very successfully with a large number of memory tasks (see Table V). Even when they are required to perform operations on the material to be remembered (e.g., rearranging digits backwards or reorganizing letters in alphabetical order), their performance does not differ from that of normals. Similarly, they can hold material (consonant trigrams) over both "filled" or "unfilled" delay intervals, and once they have learned material (meaningful paired associates), they retain it 45 minutes later as well as normals do. The one difficulty Benezra found in the hyperactives on her verbal memory tasks occurred when the children were required to learn and remember rather long lists of word pairs in which there was no obvious meaningful association between the words in the pairs.

In discussing her results, Benezra draws on Flavell's (1970) concept of *metamemory*. This term has been used by Flavell and other theorists (e.g., Brown, 1975, 1977; Torgesen, 1977) to refer to our introspective knowledge about the functioning of our own memory system. The researchers have demonstrated developmental differences in children's awareness of their own memory limitations. In addition, they have shown that older children are more likely to approach difficult memory tasks in a deliberate and active manner, first evaluating task requirements and then choosing strategies for transforming the material to be remembered in order to deal with it more effectively. As Benezra points out, her Paired Associates Task with meaningful associations makes rather minimal demands on the child's processing capacity because the associations that link the word pairs are provided by the experimenter. In the case of the "nonmeaningful pairs," on the other hand, the child must make a self-conscious and deliberate effort to find strategies for relating each pair of words. Questioning Benezra's subjects about how they had tried to remember the unrelated word pairs revealed that, compared with hyperactives, children in the normal group report using mnemonic strategies and elaborative rehearsal with much greater frequency. The hyperactives, on the other hand, tended to "just listen" or to use simple, repetitive rehearsal.

Although our discussion of "meta" processes thus far has been limited to metamemory, we agree with Brown's (1975) emphasis on the general problem of metacognitive development, which she defines as "the child's knowledge of his own knowledge." Tutors in our training programs constantly complain that hyperactive children seem to be unaware of their own role as problem-solvers. They report that it is difficult to get the youngsters to define problems accurately or to give adequate consideration to knowledge or strategies they already possess that might contribute to a solution. It is important to note that this difficulty often occurs in children with well-above-average IQs. Thus, the distinction that Brown (1975) and Vygotsky (1962) make between knowledge that can be acquired in a relatively automatic, unconscious way and knowledge that must be self-consciously and deliberately sought may be very relevant for an understanding of these children's cognitive strengths and weaknesses. (It is interesting to mention here that one of the "simple" tasks on which hyperactives perform poorly, the CPT, correlates significantly with academic performance but does not correlate with IQ [Gale & Lynn, 1972; Margolis, 1972; Sykes *et al.*, 1973].) Brown describes a process of "executive decision making" in which the individual must both carry out cognitive operations and oversee his own progress. She lists several requirements of such a control system, including an ability (1) to predict one's own capacity limitations, (2) to be aware of one's repertoire of problem-solving strategies, (3) to identify and characterize the problem at hand, (4) to plan and schedule appropriate problem-solving routines, and (5) to monitor the effectiveness of the routines tried. As Tant (1978) has pointed out, two types of tasks used in Tant's study, Matrix Solution Tasks, which were discussed earlier, and Rule Learning Tasks (see Table III), confront the child with several of these demands. Both involve contrived, arbitrary problems that must be analyzed in a thoughtful, self-conscious way. Successful solution requires both perceptual and logical search strategies, and these must be organized by the child into an overall problem-solving approach that must be modified as feedback is given. It should be noted that the performance of hyperactives was significantly worse than that of controls on both of these tasks, in spite of the fact that Tant matched her groups on verbal IQ and made considerable effort to keep motivation and interest high.

Brown emphasizes the importance of skills of this kind for successful academic achievement in our culture. Many school exercises are highly artificial and have no obvious purpose from the child's perspective. They simply have to be mastered for their own sake. Thus, the information involved is not likely to be learned spontaneously; the child must develop a conscious, deliberate set in order to cope with it. In view of the difficulty hyperactive children have with tasks of this kind, it is not surprising that most hyperactive children develop school problems early and continue to experience difficulty throughout their academic lives (Hechtman *et al.*, 1976; Hoy *et al.*, 1978; Mendelson, Johnson, & Stewart, 1971; Minde *et al.*, 1971; Weiss *et al.*, 1971). What *is* surprising is that so many of these children receive relatively high scores on IQ tests, particularly when the tests are administered individually. Torgesen (1977) has suggested that many items appearing on intelligence tests, particularly at the early levels, tap knowledge that can be picked up unintentionally. In addition, we would expect some learning to occur in hyperactives when conditions within the task (e.g., interest level) and within the child (e.g., arousal level) happen to be optimal. If our pessimistic description of a spiraling effect resulting from the children's original deficits is correct, however, IQ ultimately would have to be impaired. Recent data suggest that this is so (Loney, 1974; Prinz & Loney, 1974; Wikler, Dixon, & Parker, 1970). Interestingly, the study by Loney (1974) failed to reveal IQ differences between hyperactives and normal control groups in grade two but did show significant differences at the grade six level.

Summary and Critique: An Attempt to Conceptualize the Development and Consequences of Attentional Problems in Hyperactive and Learning-Disabled Children

It is interesting to note that authors have attributed to LD children some of the difficulties we have just been describing in hyperactives. As in the case of distractibility and concentration difficulties, however, it often is difficult to know whether hyperactive children were included in the LD samples and also whether the deficits described are of a primary nature or are secondary to the children's specific learning disabilities. Several investigators have reported that LD children are impulsive (Kagan, 1965; Keogh & Donlon, 1972; Messer, 1970; Nadelman & Wallace, 1973). In our own laboratory, Benezra (1978) and Tant (1978) found that a group of nonhyperactive reading-disabled children obtained higher error scores than normal controls on the MFFT, thus suggesting that LD–normal differences exist, at least on the error measure, even when hyperactive children are carefully excluded from LD samples. Evidence of a memory deficit in LD children also is beginning to emerge, and several investigators (Bauer, 1977 a,b; Kluever, 1971; Tarver *et al.*, 1976) point to ineffective rehearsal strategies as the cause.

In addition, after reviewing a large number of studies, Torgesen (1977) recently suggested that many of the failures of LD children may be due to defective meta processes. Interestingly, several of the terms he uses to describe their problem-solving strategies are extremely similar to our own descriptions of how hyperactives approach tasks. Again, it is possible that similarities in these descriptions can be attributed to poorly differentiated samples. We believe, however, that hyperactive and LD children probably do share some of these characteristics. However, as in the case of attention problems, we believe that the characteristics have developed for quite different reasons in the two groups of children.

Figure 1 represents our tentative conceptualization of the origins and consequences of the symptoms that have been reported in the two groups. We believe that it may help explain and clarify some of the confusion in the literature about the relationships among attentional problems, hyperactivity, and learning disabilities. A major assumption of the model is that hyperactive children are born with a constitutional predisposition involving poor impulse control, an inability to sustain attention, and poorly modulated arousal levels, which result in a tendency to seek stimulation and salience. Unlike some theorists (e.g., Keogh, 1971; Ross, 1976), we are unwilling to speculate about whether one of these symptoms is more "basic" or "primary" than the others. We see them as being intricately related and believe that it is quite impossible, within the limits of present knowledge, to designate any one of the three as the most "critical" and to attribute the development of the others to it. Although the hypothesized arousal abnormality of hyperactives is the most speculative of the three proposals, we feel that there is enough indirect evidence supporting this notion to make it worthy of further research and theoretical interest.

The three disabilities we have attributed to hyperactives would be expected to interfere with the development of meta processes and thus would impair the children's ability to assume and maintain a problem-solving set. In addition, they would limit higher order schema development. As a result, the children would experience repeated failure on complex tasks and on tasks requiring self-sustained effort. Consequently, they would fail to develop a sense of competence in problem-solving situations and would be likely to indulge in avoidance behaviors and to become disturbed when faced with problem-solving tasks. Thus, the original concentration, impulsivity, and arousal problems would become enhanced, and the cycle would continue with a "snowballing" effect.

In the case of the LD child, on the other hand, we assume that his primary deficit involves a constitutional predisposition toward one or more specific learning disabilities. This might include, for example, a receptive language problem or an inability to process visual symbols. It is impossible to say at this time whether or not LD children also have a primary distractibility problem or a concentration problem; only further research involving tasks on which the children are reasonably proficient will answer these questions.

However, even if no original deficits of these kinds are present, the LD child's learning disabilities could lead to pseudo- or secondary attentional problems, along with impulsivity and restlessness (or apparent hyperactiv-

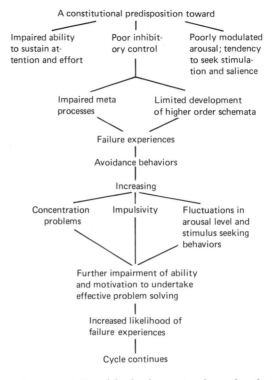

FIGURE 1. A schematic representation of the development and sequelae of attentional problems in hyperactive and learning-disabled children.

ity) through creating failure experiences. As Ross (1976) has suggested, impulsivity, restlessness, and a search for distracting stimuli may develop as ways of escaping the discomfort created by vain attempts to deal with learning situations that are beyond a child's capabilities. These avoidance behaviors, together with the original learning disability, would then result in impaired meta processes and limited development of higher order schemata: The likelihood of failure experiences would be increased and, as in case of the hyperactive child, the cycle would continue.

This conceptualization of the nature and progressive development of LD and hyperactive children's deficits may prove helpful in arriving at a differential diagnosis between children in the two groups. For example, if we are correct in our belief that the attentional, impulsivity, and arousal characteristics of hyperactives have a constitutional basis, then we might expect these symptoms to appear at a very early age. There is evidence that this is so: both Peters (1977) and Stewart, Pitts, Craig, and Dieruf (1966) found that a large proportion of mothers of hyperactives report that they

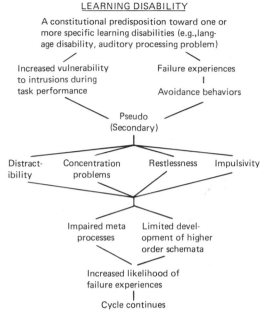

LEARNING DISABILITY
A constitutional predisposition toward one or
more specific learning disabilities (e.g.,lang-
age disability, auditory processing problem)

Increased vulnerability
to intrusions during
task performance

Failure experiences

Avoidance behaviors

Pseudo
(Secondary)

Distract-
ibility

Concentration
problems

Restlessness

Impulsivity

Impaired meta
processes

Limited devel-
opment of higher
order schemata

Increased likelihood of
failure experiences

Cycle continues

FIGURE 1. *Continued.*

became aware of their child's symptoms very early in the child's life, either during infancy or at the time he began school; that is, when he was required to conform to classroom demands for concentration and relative immobility. In the case of LD children, since distractibility, impulsivity, and restlessness are viewed as reactions to the learning deficit, these symptoms should not become as evident until the child has been in school long enough to experience academic difficulty, although language problems could create serious communication problems sooner and thus constitute an exception to this rule.

In addition, if the three major characteristics being attributed here to hyperactive children have a constitutional basis, we would expect them to permeate most aspects of the child's life, including his social relationships. In the case of LD children, although some generalization would probably occur, their impulsivity, restlessness, and distractibility should be more limited to tasks and situations involving their defective learning skills. There is considerable evidence that the hyperactive child's symptoms do have far-reaching consequences. On a Story Completion Task (see Table III) administered by Parry (1973), hyperactives demonstrated a serious inability to cope with frustrating situations. They tended to focus almost completely on the frustrating event as opposed to the motives of the people involved and also chose more endings in which the frustrated child acted aggressively. This inability to inhibit impulsive behavior in social situations becomes disturbingly evident as the children reach adolescence and come into conflict with authority figures and the courts (Ackerman *et al.*, 1977; Mendelson *et al.*, 1971; Weiss, Kruger, Danielson, & Elman, 1975).

Our proposed conceptualization also has important implications for designing treatment programs for the two groups. Most important, although secondary symptoms cannot be ignored, major emphasis should be placed on each child's original deficits. For the hyperactive child, this means directing treatment toward modifying or taking special account of his impulsive, attentional, and stimulus-seeking behaviors. Douglas (in press-b) has presented some ways in which this could be accomplished. As we have discussed, the stimulant drugs appear to be helpful in combating some of the hyperactive child's primary symptoms, although the effects of these drugs on higher mental processes and academic functioning is still in question (Barkley & Cunningham, 1978). We have somewhat more confidence in the effectiveness of cognitive training methods for dealing with the hyperactive child. This confidence is based, in part, on our own experience with this approach (Douglas *et al.*, 1976) and also on our belief that some of the major ingredients of the cognitive approach, such as self-verbalization, modeling, and self-reinforcement, are particularly appropriate for working with attentional and impulsivity problems. As Douglas (in press-b) has suggested, the cognitive approach could be extended to deal more adequately with the arousal and metacognition deficits discussed in this chapter.

In considering treatment for LD children, on the other hand, we believe that it would be most unwise to emphasize attentional and related symptoms at the expense of neglecting the children's original learning deficits. Thus, we find ourselves in strong disagreement with Ross (1976) on this point. Although cognitive training aimed at improving attention may be valuable in alleviating some of the LD youngsters' secondary symptoms, if our conceptualization is correct, there is no reason to believe that it can have any direct impact on the more basic cognitive processing deficits of these children. Ways must be found to either strengthen the defective skills or to enhance the children's learning through modalities less affected by their impairment. Clearly, considerable research effort should be invested in developing a better understanding of the nature of the various kinds of learning disabilities. There are genuine signs of progress in this extremely difficult area (e.g., Corkin, 1974; Satz, in press; Shankweiller & Liberman, 1976; Tallal, 1976; Wittelson, 1976), and the leads that have been achieved should be energetically pursued.

When we consider drug treatment, however, we see no theoretical reason for believing that the stimulants should be helpful with LD children, and the empirical evidence has not supported their use with nonhyperactive children demonstrating learning disabilities (Rie, Rie, Stewart, & Ambuel, 1976). Whether contingency management techniques elicit the somewhat unusual responses in LD samples that we have described in hyperactives is a matter for further research. On one hand, the LD child's history of failure might make him particularly dependent on external reinforcement, but on the other hand, we would not expect him to be as vulnerable as the hyperactive child to the arousing or salient qualities of reinforcers. In any case, if these methods are employed, they should be used to supplement or strengthen teaching directed toward the child's original learning deficit.

Acknowledgments

Dr. Douglas wishes to thank her current graduate students, Marilyn Ain, Esther Benezra, Maureen O'Neill, and Judy Tant, who helped in the development of many of the ideas expressed here. Thanks also are due to Mrs. Pat Jenkins, who exhibited endless skill and patience in the preparation of the manuscript.

References

Ackerman, P. T., Dykman, R. A., & Peters, J. E. Teenage status of hyperactive and nonhyperactive learning disabled boys. *American Journal of Orthopsychiatry*, 1977, 47(4), 577–596.
Alwitt, L. F. Attention in a visual task among non-readers and readers. *Perceptual and Motor Skills*, 1966, 23, 361–362.
Amsel, A. Frustrative nonreward in partial reinforcement and discrimination learning: Some recent history and a theoretical extension. *Psychological Review*, 1962, 69, 306–328.
Anderson, R. P., Halcomb, C. G., & Doyle, R. B. The measurement of attentional deficits. *Journal of Learning Disabilities*, 1973, 6, 534–539.
Atkinson, B. P., & Seunath, O. H. The effects of stimulus change on attending behavior in normal children and learning disorders. *Journal of Learning Disabilities*, 1973, 6, 569–573.
Ault, R. L., Crawford, D. E., & Jeffrey, W. E. Visual scanning strategies of reflective, impulsive, fast-accurate, and slow-inaccurate children on the Matching Familiar Figures Test. *Child Development*, 1972, 43, 1412–1417.
Barkley, R. A. Predicting the response of hyperkinetic children to stimulant drugs: A review. *Journal of Abnormal Child Psychology*, 1976, 4, 327–348.
Barkley, R. A., & Cunningham, C. E. Do stimulant drugs improve the academic performance of hyperkinetic children? *Clinical Pediatrics*, 1978, 17, 85–92.
Barkley, R. A., & Jackson, T. L., Jr. Hyperkinesis, autonomic nervous system activity, and stimulant drug effects. *Journal of Child Psychology and Psychiatry*, 1977, 18, 247–357.
Bauer, R. H. Memory processes in children with learning disabilities: Evidence for deficient rehearsal. *Journal of Experimental Child Psychology*, 1977, 24, 415–430. (a)
Bauer, R. H. Short term memory in learning disabled and nondisabled children. *Bulletin of the Psychonomic Society*, 1977, 10(2), 128–130. (b)

Benezra, E. *Learning and memory in hyperactive, reading disabled, and normal children.* Unpublished manuscript, McGill University, Montreal, 1978.

Berlyne, D. E. Arousal and reinforcement. In D. Levine (Ed.), *Nebraska Symposium on Motivation* (Vol. 15). Lincoln: University of Nebraska Press, 1967.

Berlyne, D. E. Attention as a problem in behavior theory. In D. I. Mostofsky (Ed.), *Attention: Contemporary theory and analysis.* New York: Appleton-Century-Crofts, 1970.

Berlyne, D. E. *Aesthetics and psychobiology.* New York: Appleton-Century-Crofts, 1971.

Bindra, D. *Motivation, a systematic reinterpretation.* New York: Ronald, 1959.

Bindra, D. *A theory of intelligent behavior.* New York: Wiley, 1976.

Blank, M., Berenzweig, S. S., & Bridger, W. H. The effects of stimulus complexity and sensory modality on reaction time in normal and retarded readers. *Child Development,* 1975, *46,* 133–140.

Boring, E. G. A short historical perspective. In D. I. Mostofsky (Ed.), *Attention: Contemporary theory and analysis.* New York: Appleton-Century-Crofts, 1970.

Bremer, D. A., & Stern, J. A. Attention and distractibility during reading in hyperactive boys. *Journal of Abnormal Child Psychology,* 1976, *4,* 381–387.

Broadbent, D. E. *Perception and communication.* New York: Pergamon, 1958.

Broadbent, D. E. *Decision and stress.* New York: Academic, 1971.

Brown, A. L. The role of strategic behavior in retardate memory. In N. R. Ellis (Ed.), *International review of research in mental retardation* (Vol. 1). New York: Academic, 1974, pp. 55–111.

Brown, A. L. The development of memory, knowing, knowing about knowing and knowing how to know. In H. W. Reese (Ed.), *Advances in child development and behavior* (Vol. 10). New York: Academic, 1975.

Brown, A. L. Development, schooling, and the acquisition of knowledge about knowledge. In R. C. Anderson, R. J. Spiro, & W. E. Montague (Eds.), *Schooling and the acquisition of knowledge.* Hillsdale, N.J.: Lawrence Erlbaum, 1977.

Browning, R. B. Hypo-responsiveness as a behavioral correlate of brain damage in children. *Psychological Reports,* 1967, *20,* 251–259.

Cameron, R. *Source of problem solving inefficiency in relation to conceptual tempo.* Paper presented at the biennial meeting of the Society for Research in Child Development, New Orleans, March 17–20, 1977.

Campbell, S. B. *Cognitive styles in normal and hyperactive children.* Unpublished doctoral dissertation, McGill University, 1969.

Campbell, S. B. Hyperactivity: Course and treatment. In A. Davids (Ed.), *Child personality and psychopathology* (Vol. 3). New York: Wiley-Interscience, 1976.

Campbell, S. B., Douglas, V. I., & Morgenstern, G. Cognitive styles in hyperactive children and the effect of methylphenidate. *Journal of Child Psychology and Psychiatry,* 1971, *12,* 55–67.

Cleland, C. C. *Severe retardation: Program suggestions.* Paper read at the Regional Council on Exceptional Children, Austin, Texas, 1961.

Cohen, N. J. *Psychophysiological concomitants of attention in hyperactive children.* Unpublished doctoral dissertation, McGill University, 1970.

Cohen, N. J., & Douglas, V. I. Characteristics of the orienting response in hyperactive and normal children. *Psychophysiology,* 1972, *9,* 238–245.

Cohen, N. J., Douglas, V. I., & Morgenstern, G. The effect of methylphenidate on attentive behavior and autonomic activity in hyperactive children. *Psychopharmacologia,* 1971, *22,* 282–294.

Cohen, N. J., Weiss, G., & Minde, K. Cognitive styles in adolescents previously diagnosed as hyperactive. *Journal of Child Psychology and Psychiatry,* 1972, *13,* 203–209.

Conners, C. K. A teacher rating scale for use in drug studies with children. *American Journal of Psychiatry*, 1969, *126*, 884–888.

Conners, C. K. Symptom patterns in hyperkinetic, neurotic, and normal children. *Child Development*, 1970, *41*, 667–682.

Conners, C. K. The effect of pemoline and dextroamphetamine on evoked potentials under two conditions of attention. In C. Conners (Ed.), *Clinical use of stimulant drugs in children*. Amsterdam: Excerpta Medica, 1972.

Conners, C. K., & Rothschild, G. Drugs and learning in children. In *Learning Disorders* (Vol. 3). Seattle: Special Child, 1968.

Conners, C. K., & Rothschild, G. H. The effects of dextroamphetamine on habituation of peripheral vascular response in children. *Journal of Abnormal Child Psychology*, 1973, *1*, 16–25.

Corkin, S. Serial-ordering deficits in inferior readers. *Neuropsychologia*, 1974, *12*, 347–354.

Craik, F. I. M., & Lockhart, R. S. Levels of processing: A framework for memory research. *Journal of Verbal Learning & Verbal Behavior*, 1972, *11*, 671–684.

Crinella, F. M. Identification of brain dysfunction syndromes in children through profile analysis: Patterns associated with so called "minimal brain dysfunction." *Journal of Abnormal Psychology*, 1973, *82*, 33–45.

Cromwell, R., Baumeister, A., & Hawkins, W. Research on activity level. In N. R. Ellis (Ed.), *Handbook of mental deficiency*. New York: McGraw-Hill, 1963.

Cruickshank, W. M. The learning environment. In W. M. Cruickshank & D. F. Hallahan (Eds.), *Perceptual and learning disabilities in children: Psychoeducational practices*. Syracuse: Syracuse University Press, 1975.

Cruickshank, W. M. *The brain injured child in home, school and community*. Syracuse: Syracuse University Press, 1977. (Rev. 1966, as, *Learning disabilities in home, school and community*.)

Cruickshank, W. M., Bentzen, F. A., Ratzeburg, F. H., & Tannhauser, M. T. *A teaching method for brain-injured and hyperactive children*. Syracuse: Syracuse University Press, 1961.

Dalby, J. T., Kinsbourne, M., & Swanson, J. M. Hyperactive children's underuse of learning time: Corrections by stimulant treatment. *Child Development*, in press.

Dardano, J. E. Relationships of intermittent noise, intersignal interval, and skin conductance to vigilance behavior. *Journal of Applied Psychology*, 1962, *46*, 106–114.

Deikel, S. M., & Friedman, M. P. Selective attention in children with learning disabilities. *Perceptual and Motor Skills*, 1976, *42*, 675–678.

Denton, C. L., & McIntyre, C. W. Span of apprehension in hyperactive boys. *Journal of Abnormal Child Psychology*, 1978, *6*, 19–24.

Deutsch, J. A., & Deutsch, D. Attention: Some theoretical considerations. *Psychological Review*, 1963, *70*, 80–90.

Douglas, V. I. Stop, look and listen: The problem of sustained attention and impulse control in hyperactive and normal children. *Canadian Journal of Behavioral Science*, 1972, *4*, 259–282.

Douglas, V. I. Sustained attention and impulse control: Implications for the handicapped child. In J. A. Swets & L. L. Elliott (Eds.), *Psychology and the handicapped child*. Washington, D.C.: U.S. Office of Education, 1974, pp. 149–168.

Douglas, V. I. Effects of medication on learning efficiency—research findings: Review and synthesis. In R. P. Anderson & C. G. Halcomb (Eds.), *Learning disability/minimal brain dysfunction syndrome*. Springfield, Ill.: Charles C Thomas, 1976, pp. 139–148. (a)

Douglas, V. I. Perceptual and cognitive factors as determinants of learning disabilities: A review chapter with special emphasis on attentional factors. In R. M. Knights & D. J.

Bakker (Eds.), *The neuropsychology of learning disorders: Theoretical approaches.* Baltimore: University Park Press, 1976, pp. 413–421. (b)

Douglas, V. I. Higher mental processes in hyperactive children: Implications for training. In R. M. Knights & D. J. Bakker (Eds.), *Rehabilitation, treatment and management of learning disorders.* Baltimore: University Park Press, in press. (a)

Douglas, V. I. Treatment approaches: Establishing inner or outer control? In C. K. Whalen & B. Henker (Eds.), *Hyperactive children: The social ecology of identification and treatment.* New York: Academic, in press. (b)

Douglas, V. I., & Marton, P. *Variables underlying hyperactive behaviour: A correlational study with normal children.* Unpublished manuscript, McGill University, 1974.

Douglas, V. I., Parry, P., Marton, P., & Garson, C. Assessment of a cognitive training program for hyperactive children. *Journal of Abnormal Child Psychology,* 1976, *4,* 389–410.

Doyle, A. *A developmental study of memory for the distractor in selective listening.* Unpublished doctoral dissertation, Stanford University, 1970.

Doyle, A. Listening to distraction: A developmental study of selective attention. *Journal of Experimental Child Psychology,* 1973, *15,* 100–115.

Doyle, R. B., Anderson, R. P., & Halcomb, C. G. Attention deficits and the effects of visual distraction. *Journal of Learning Disabilities,* 1976, *19,* 48–54.

Drake, D. M. Perceptual correlates of impulsive and reflective behavior. *Developmental Psychology,* 1970, *2*(2) 202–214.

Druker, J. F., & Hagen, J. W. Developmental trends in the processing of task-relevant and task-irrelevant information. *Child Development,* 1969, *40,* 371–382.

Dykman, R. A., Ackerman, P. T., Clements, S., & Peters, J. E. Specific learning disabilities: An attentional deficit syndrome. In H. R. Myklebust (Ed.), *Progress in learning disabilities* (Vol. 2). New York: Grune & Stratton, 1971.

Egeth, H., & Bevan, W. Attention. In B. B. Wolman (Ed.), *Handbook of General Psychology.* Englewood Cliffs, N. J.: Prentice-Hall, 1973, pp. 8–102.

Farley, F. H., & Farley, S. V. Impulsiveness, sociability, and the preference for varied experience. *Perceptual and Motor Skills,* 1970, *31,* 47–50.

Farnham-Diggory, S., & Gregg, L. W. Short-term memory function in young readers. *Journal of Experimental Child Psychology,* 1975, *19,* 279–298.

Firestone, P. *The effects of reinforcement contingencies and caffeine on hyperactive children.* Unpublished doctoral dissertation, McGill University, 1974.

Firestone, P., & Douglas, V. I. The effects of reward and punishment on reaction times and autonomic activity in hyperactive and normal children. *Journal of Abnormal Child Psychology,* 1975, *3,* 201–215.

Flavell, J. H. Developmental studies of mediated memory. In H. W. Reese & L. P. Lipsitt (Eds.), *Advances in child development and behavior* (Vol. 5). New York: Academic, 1970.

Flavell, J. H., & Wellman, H. M. Metamemory. In R. V. Kail & J. W. Hagen (Eds.), *Perspectives on the development of memory and cognition.* Hillsdale, N.J.: Laurence Erlbaum, 1975.

Forehand, R., & Baumeister, A. A. Effects of variations in auditory-visual stimulation on activity levels of severe mental retardates. *American Journal of Mental Deficiency,* 1970, *74,* 470–474.

Fraas, L. A. Intentional and incidental learning: A developmental and comparative approach. *Journal of Mental Deficiency Research,* 1973, *17,* 129–137.

Freibergs, V. Concept learning in hyperactive and normal children. Unpublished doctoral dissertation, McGill University, 1965.

Freibergs, V., & Douglas, V. I. Concept learning in hyperactive and normal children. *Journal of Abnormal Psychology*, 1969, *74*, 388–395.

Gale, A., & Lynn, R. A developmental study of attention. *British Journal of Educational Psychology*, 1972, *42*, 260–266.

Gardner, W. I., Cromwell, R. L., & Foshee, J. G. Studies in activity level: II. Effects of distal visual stimulation in organics, familials, hyperactives and hypoactives. *American Journal of Mental Deficiency*, 1959, *63*, 1028–1033.

Garson, C. *Cognitive impulsivity in children and the effects of training.* Unpublished doctoral dissertation, McGill University, 1977.

Gibson, E. J. *Principles of perceptual learning and development.* New York: Prentice-Hall, 1969.

Goldstein, K., & Scheerer, M. Abstract and concrete behavior: An experimental study with special tests. *Psychological Monographs*, 1941, *53*, 1–151.

Hagen, J. W. The effect of distraction on selective attention. *Child Development*, 1967, *38*, 685–694.

Hagen, J. W., & Hale, G. A. The development of attention in children. In A. D. Pick (Ed.), *Minnesota symposium on child psychology* (Vol. 7). Minneapolis: University of Minnesota Press, 1973.

Hagen, J. W., & Huntsman, N. J. Selective attention in mental retardates. *Developmental Psychology*, 1971, *3*, 151–160.

Hagen, J. W., & Kail, R. V., Jr. The role of attention in perceptual and cognitive development. In W. M. Cruickshank & D. P. Hallahan (Eds.), *Perceptual and learning disabilities in children* (Vol. 2) *Research and theory.* Syracuse: Syracuse University Press, 1975.

Hagen, J. W., & Sabo, R. A. A developmental study of selective attention. *Merrill-Palmer Quarterly*, 1967, *13*, 159–171.

Hale, G. A., & Piper, R. A. Developmental trends in children's incidental learning: Some critical stimulus differences. *Developmental Psychology*, 1973, *8*. 327–335.

Hale, G. A., & Taweel, S. S. Children's component selection with varying degrees of training. *Journal of Experimental Child Psychology*, 1974, *17*, 229–241.

Hale, G. A., Miller, L. K., & Stevenson, H. W. Incidental learning of film content: A developmental study. *Child Development*, 1968, *39*, 69–77.

Hallahan, D. P. Distractibility in the learning disabled child. In W. M. Cruickshank & D. P. Hallahan (Eds.), *Perceptual and learning disabilities in children* (Vol. 2). Syracuse: Syracuse University Press, 1975, pp. 195–218.

Hallahan, D. P., Gajar, A. H., Cohen, S. B., & Tarver, S. G. *Selective attention and locus of control in learning disabled and normal children.* Unpublished manuscript, n.d.

Hallahan, D. P., Kauffman, J. M., & Ball, D. W. Selective attention and cognitive tempo of low achieving and high achieving sixth grade males. *Perceptual and Motor Skills*, 1973, *36*, 579–583.

Hallahan, D. P., Kauffman, J. M., & Ball, D. W. Developmental trends in recall of central and incidental auditory material. *Journal of Experimental Child Psychology*, 1974, *17*, 409–421. (a)

Hallahan, D. P., Kauffman, J. M., & Ball, D. W. Effects of stimulus attenuation on selective attention performance in children. *Journal of Genetic Psychology*, 1974, *125*, 71–77. (b)

Hallahan, D. P., Tarver, S. G., Kauffman, J. M., & Graybeal, N. L. A comparison of the effects of reinforcement and response cost on the selective attention of learning disabled children. *Journal of Learning Disabilities*, in press.

Hastings, J. E., & Barkley, R. A. A review of psychophysiological research with hyperkinetic children. *Journal of Abnormal Child Psychology*, 1978, *6*, 311–324.

Hebb, D. O. *Organization of behavior.* New York: Wiley, 1949.

Hebb, D. O. Drives and the CNS (conceptual nervous system). *Psychological Review*, 1955, *62*, 413–448.

Hebb, D. O. *Textbook of psychology* (3rd ed.). Toronto: W. B. Saunders, 1972.

Hebb, D. O. Physiological learning theory. *Journal of Abnormal Child Psychology*, 1976, *4*(4), 309–314.

Hechtman, G., Weiss, J., Finkelstein, J., Weiner, D., & Benn, R. Hyperactives as young adults: A preliminary report. *Canadian Medical Association Journal*, 1976, *115*, 625–630.

Heins, E. D., Hallahan, D. P., Tarver, S. G., & Kauffman, J. M. Relationship between cognitive tempo and selective attention in learning disabled children. *Perceptual and Motor Skills*, 1976, *42*, 233–234.

Hoy, E., Weiss, G., Minde, K., & Cohen, N. The hyperactive child at adolescence: Emotional, social, and cognitive functioning. *Journal of Abnormal Child Psychology*, 1978, *6*, 311–324.

James, W. *The principles of psychology* (Vol. I). New York: Holt, 1890, pp. 404.

Juliano, D. B. Conceptual tempo, activity, and concept learning in hyperactive and normal children. *Journal of Abnormal Psychology*, 1974, *83*(6), 629–634.

Kagan, J. Reflection-impulsivity and reading ability in primary grade children. *Child Development*, 1965, *36*, 609–628.

Kagan, J., Pearson, L., & Welch, L. Modifiability of an impulsive tempo. *Journal of Educational Psychology*, 1966, *57*(6), 359–365.

Kagan, J., Rosman, B. L., Day, B., Albert, J., & Phillips, W. Information processing in the child: Significance of analytic and reflective attitudes. *Psychological Monographs*, 1964, *78*(1, Whole No. 578).

Kahneman, D. *Attention and effort*. Englewood Cliffs, N.J.: Prentice-Hall, 1973.

Keogh, B. K. Hyperactivity and learning disorders: Review and speculation. *Exceptional Child*, 1971, *38*, 101–110.

Keogh, B. K., & Donlon, G. Field dependence, impulsivity and learning disabilities. *Journal of Learning Disabilities*, 1972, *5*, 331–336.

Keogh, B. K., & Margolis, J. S. Learn to labor and wait: Attentional problems of children with learning disorders. *Journal of Learning Disabilities*, 1976, *9*, 276–286.

Kirkbride, A. J. *An investigation of some aspects of memory and selective attention in achieving and learning disabled children*. Paper presented at the Canadian Psychological Association Annual Meeting, Ottawa, Ontario, June 1978.

Kluever, R. Mental abilities and disorders of learning. In H. R. Myklebust (Ed.), *Progress in learning disabilities* (Vol. 2). New York: Grune & Stratton, 1971.

Lasky, E. Z., & Tobin, H. Linguistics and nonlinguistic competing message effects. *Journal of Learning Disabilities*, 1973, *6*, 243–250.

Knights, R. M., & Hinton, G. G. The effects of methylphenidate (Ritalin) on the motor skills and behavior of children with learning problems. *Journal of Nervous and Mental Diseases*, 1969, *148*, 643.

Loney, J. The intellectual functioning of hyperactive elementary school boys: A cross sectional investigation. *American Journal of Orthopsychology*, 1974, *44*, 754–762.

Maccoby, E. E., & Hagen, J. W. Effects of distraction upon central versus incidental recall: Developmental trends. *Journal of Experimental Child Psychology*, 1965, *2*, 280–289.

Margolin, D. I. The hyperkinetic child syndrome and brain monomines: Pharmacology and therapeutic implications. *Journal of Clinical Psychiatry*, 1978, *39*(2), 127–130.

Margolis, J. S. Academic correlates of sustained attention. Unpublished doctoral dissertation, University of California at Los Angeles, 1972.

McIntyre, C. W., Blackwell, S. L., & Denton, C. L. Effect of noise distractibility on the spans of apprehension of hyperactive boys. *Journal of Abnormal Child Psychology*, 1978, *6*, 483–492.

Mendelson, W., Johnson, N., & Stewart, M. A. Hyperactive children as teenagers: A follow-up study. *Journal of Nervous and Mental Disease*, 1971, *153*, 273–279.

Messer, S. B. Reflection-impulsivity: Stability and school failure. *Journal of Educational Psychology*, 1970, *61*, 487–490.

Messer, S. B. Reflection-impulsivity: A review. *Psychological Bulletin*, 1976, *83*(6), 1026–1052.

Miller, D. J., Galanter, E., & Pribram, K. H. *Plans and the structure of behavior*. New York: Holt-Dryden, 1960.

Minde, K., Lewin, D., Weiss, G., Lavigeur, H., Douglas, V. I., & Sykes, E. The hyperactive child in elementary school: A five-year controlled follow-up. *Exceptional Children*, 1971, *38*, 215–221.

Minde, K., Webb, G., & Sykes, D. Studies on the hyperactive child: VI. Prenatal and paranatal factors associated with hyperactivity. *Developmental Medicine and Child Neurology*, 1968, *10*, 355–363.

Moray, N. *Attention: Selective processes in vision and hearing*. London: Hutchison Educational, 1969.

Mosher, F. A., & Hornsby, J. R. On asking questions. In J. S. Bruner, R. R. Olver, & P. M. Greenfield (Eds.), *Studies in cognitive growth*. New York: Wiley, 1966.

Nadelman, L., & Wallace, E. *The relationship of self-concept, conceptual tempo and intelligence to reading achievement*. Unpublished manuscript, University of Michigan, Ann Arbor, 1973.

Neimark, F. D., & Lewis, N. The development of logical problem-solving strategies. *Child Development*, 1967, *38*, 107–117.

Neisser, U. *Cognition and reality: Principles and implications of cognitive psychology*. San Francisco: W. H. Freeman, 1976.

Nober, L. W., & Nober, E. H. Auditory discrimination of learning disabled children in quiet and classroom noise. *Journal of Learning Disabilities*, 1975, *8*(10), 57–60.

Noland, E., & Schuldt, W. J. Sustained attention and reading retardation. *Journal of Experimental Education*, 1971, *40*, 73–76.

Parry, P. The effect of reward on the performance of hyperactive children. Unpublished doctoral dissertation, McGill University, 1973.

Pelham, W. *Selective attention in poor readers: Dichotic listening, speeded classification and incidental learning tasks*. Unpublished manuscript, 1977.

Pelham, W. E., & Ross, A. O. Selective attention in children with reading problems: A developmental study of incidental learning. *Journal of Abnormal Child Psychology*, 1977, *5*, 1–8.

Peresleni, L. I. Nekotorye osobennosti vnimaniia udetes s otkonemiiami v razvitii. (Some aspects of attention among children with developmental deficiencies.) *Defektologiia*, 1972, *4*, 23–28.

Peters, K. G. Selective attention and distractibility in hyperactive and normal children. Unpublished doctoral dissertation, McGill University, 1977.

Piaget, J. *Les mécanismes perceptifs*. Paris: Presses Universitaires de France, 1961.

Piaget, J. *The moral judgment of the child*. London: Routledge & Kegan Paul, 1968. (Originally published, New York: Harcourt Brace, 1932.)

Porges, S. W., Walter, G. F., Korb, R. J., & Sprague, R. I. The influence of methylphenidate on heart rate and behavioral measures of attention in hyperactive children. *Child Development*, 1975, *46*, 727–733.

Posner, M. I., & Boies, S. J. Components of attention. *Psychological Reports*, 1971, *78*, 391–408.

Postman, L. Short-term memory and incidental learning. In A. W. Melton (Ed.), *Categories of human learning*. New York: Academic, 1964, pp. 145–201.

Pribram, K. H., & McGuiness, D. Arousal, activation, and effort in the control of attention. *Psychological Review*, 1975, *82*, 116–149.

Prinz, R., & Loney, J. Teacher-rated hyperactive elementary school girls: An exploratory study. *Child Psychiatry and Human Development*, 1974, *4*, 246–257.

Quay, H. C. Psychopathic behavior: Reflections on its nature, origins, and treatment. In F. Weizman & I. Uzgiris (Eds.), *The structuring of experience*. New York: Plenum, 1977, pp. 371–383.

Rapoport, J. L., Buchsbaum, M. S., Zahn, T. P., Weingartner, H., Ludlow, C., & Mikkelsen, E. J. Dextroamphetamine: Cognitive and behavioral effects in normal prepubertal boys. *Science*, 1978, *199*, 560–563.

Raskin, D. C. Attention and arousal. In W. F. Prokasy & D. C. Raskin (Eds.), *Electrodermal activity in psychological research*. New York: Academic, 1973.

Ricks, N. L., & Mirsky, A. F. Sustained attention and the effects of distraction in under-achieving second grade children. *Journal of Education*, 1974, *156*(4), 4–17.

Rie, H. E., Rie, E. D., & Stewart, S. Effects of methylphenidate on underachieving children. *Journal of Consulting and Clinical Psychology*, 1976, *44*, 250–260.

Rie, H. E., Rie, E. D., Stewart, S., & Ambuel, J. P. Effects of methylphenidate on under-achieving children. *Journal of Consulting and Clinical Psychology*, 1976, *44*, 250–260.

Ross, A. O. *Psychological aspects of learning disabilities and reading disorders*. New York: McGraw-Hill, 1976.

Rost, K. J., & Charles, D. C. Academic achievement of brain-injured and hyperactive children in isolation. *Exceptional Children*, 1967, *34*, 125–126.

Rosvold, H. E., Mirsky, A. F., Sarason, I., Bransome, E. D., & Beck, L. H. A continuous performance test of brain damage. *Journal of Consulting Psychology*, 1956, *20*, 343–352.

Ryan, T. J., & Watson, D. Frustrative nonreward theory applied to children's behavior. *Psychological Bulletin*, 1968, *2*, 111–125.

Sabatino, D. A., & Ysseldyke, J. E. Effect of extraneous "background" on visual-perceptive performance of readers and non-readers. *Perception and Motor Skills*, 1972, *35*, 323–328.

Sahakian, B. J., & Robbins, T. W. Are the effects of psychomotor stimulant drugs on hyperac-tive children really paradoxical? *Medical Hypotheses*, 1977, *3*(4), 154–158.

Samuels, S. J. Attentional process in reading: The effects of pictures on the acquisition of reading response. *Journal of Educational Psychology*, 1967, *58*, 337–342.

Santostefano, S., & Paley, E. Development of cognitive controls in children. *Child Develop-ment*, 1964, *35*, 939–949.

Santostefano, S., Rutledge, L., & Randall, D. Cognitive styles and reading disability. *Psy-chology of the Schools*, 1965, *2*, 57–62.

Satterfield, J. H., & Dawson, M. E. Electrodermal correlates of hyperactivity in children. *Psychophysiology*, 1971, *8*, 191–197.

Satterfield, J. H., Antonian, G. C., & Brashears, G. C. Electrodermal studies in minimal brain dysfunctional children. In C. K. Conners (Ed.), *Clinical use of stimulant drugs in chil-dren*. Amsterdam: Excerpta Medica, 1974.

Satz, P. Some developmental and predictive precursors of reading disabilities: A six year follow-up. In D. Pearl & A. Benton (Eds.), *Dyslexia: An appraisal of current research*. NIMH, in press.

Schleifer, M. *Moral judgments of children*. Unpublished doctoral dissertation, McGill Univer-sity, 1971.

Schleifer, M., & Douglas, V. I. Moral judgments, behaviour, and cognitive style in young children. *Canadian Journal of Behavioural Science*, 1973, *5*(2), 133–144.

Schleifer, M., Weiss, G., Cohen, N., Elman, M., Dvejec, H., & Kruger, E. Hyperactivity in preschoolers and the effect of methylphenidate. *American Journal of Orthopsychiatry*, 1975, *45*, 38–50.

Scott, T. J. The use of music to reduce hyperactivity in children. *American Journal of Orthopsychiatry*, 1970, *40*, 677–680.

Shankweiller, D., & Liberman, I. Y. Exploring the relations between reading and speech. In R. K. Knights & D. J. Bakker (Eds.), *The neuropsychology of learning disorders*. Baltimore: University Park Press, 1976, pp. 297–314.

Shores, R. E., & Haubrich, P. A. Effect of cubicles in educating emotionally disturbed children. *Exceptional Children*, 1969, *36*, 21–24.

Siegel, A. W. Variables affecting incidental learning in children. *Child Development*, 1968, *39*, 957–968.

Siegel, A. W., & Stevenson, H. W. Incidental learning: A developmental study. *Child Development*, 1966, *37*, 811–818.

Siegelman, E. Reflective and impulsive observing behavior. *Child Development*, 1969, *40*, 1213–1222.

Skrzypek, G. V. Effect of perceptual isolation and arousal on anxiety, complexity preference, and novelty preference in psychopathic and neurotic delinquents. *Journal of Abnormal Psychology*, 1969, *74*, 321–329.

Sokolov, Ye. N. *Perception and the conditioned reflex*. New York: Macmillan, 1963.

Solley, C. M., & Murphy, G. *Development of the perceptive world*. New York: Basic, 1960.

Somervill, J. W., Jacobsen, L., Warnberg, L. S., & Young, W. Varied and environmental conditions and task performance by mentally retarded subjects perceived as distractible and non-distractible. *American Journal of Mental Deficiency*, 1974, *79*, 204–209.

Somervill, J. W., Warnberg, L. S., & Bost, D. E. Effects of cubicles versus increased stimulation on task performance by first grade males perceived as distractible or non-distractible. *Journal of Special Education*, 1973, *7*, 169–185.

Sprague, R. L., & Berger, B. D. Drug effects on learning performance: Relevance of animal research to pediatric psychopharmacology. In R. M. Knights & D. J. Bakker (Eds.), *Rehabilitation treatment and management of learning disorders*. Baltimore: University Park Press, in press.

Sprague, R. L., & Sleator, K. Methylphenidate in hyperkinetic children. Differences in dose effects on learning and social behavior. *Science*, 1977, *198*, 1274–1276.

Sprague, R. L., Barnes, K. R., & Werry, J. S. Methylphenidate and thioridazine: Learning, reaction time, activity and classroom behavior in disturbed children. *American Journal of Orthopsychiatry*, 1970, *40*, 615–628.

Spring, C., Greenberg, L., Scott, J., & Hopwood, J. Electrodermal activity in hyperactive boys who are methylphenidate responders. *Psychophysiology*, 1974, *11*, 436–442.

Sroufe, L. A. Drug treatment of children with behavior problems. In F. D. Horowitz, M. Hetherington, S. Scarr-Salapatek, & G. Siegel (Eds.), *Review of child development research* (Vol. 4). Chicago: University of Chicago Press, 1975.

Sroufe, L., & Stewart, M. A. Treating problem children with stimulant drugs. *New England Journal of Medicine*, 1973, *289*, 407–413.

Sroufe, L. A., Sonies, W. D., West, W. D., & Wright, F. S. Anticipatory heart-rate deceleration and reaction time in children with and without referral for learning disability. *Child Development*, 1973, *44*, 267–275.

Steinkamp, M. W. *Relationships between task-irrelevant distractions and task performance of normal, retarded hyperactive, and minimal brain dysfunction children*. Unpublished doctoral dissertation, University of Illinois, 1974.

Stewart, M. A. Hyperactive children. *Science*, 1970, *222*, 94–98.

Stewart, M. A., Pitts, F. N., Craig, M. B., & Dieruf, W. The hyperactive child syndrome. *American Journal of Orthopsychiatry*, 1966, *36*, 861–867.

Stine, O. C., Saratsiotis, J. B., & Mosser, R. S. Relationship between neurological findings and classroom behavior. *American Journal of Disease of Children*, 1975, *129*, 1036–1040.

Strauss, A. A., & Lehtinen, L. *Psychopathology and education of the brain-injured child* (Vol. 1). New York: Grune & Stratton, 1947.

Stroop, J. R. Studies of interference in serial verbal reactions. *Journal of Experimental Psychology*, 1935, *18*, 643–661.

Surwillo, W. W., & Quilter, R. E. The relation of frequency of spontaneous skin potential responses to vigilance and age. *Psychophysiology*, 1965, *1*, 272–276.

Swanson, J. M., & Kinsbourne, M. Stimulant-related state dependent learning in hyperactive children. *Science*, 1976, *192*, 1354–1357.

Swets, J. A., & Kristofferson, A. B. Attention. *Annual Review of Psychology*, 1970, *21*, 339–366.

Switzky, H. N., & Haywood, H. C. Conjugate activity of motor activity in mentally retarded persons. *American Journal of Mental Deficiency*, 1973, *77*, 567–570.

Sykes, D. H. Sustained attention in hyperactive children. Unpublished doctoral dissertation, McGill University, 1969.

Sykes, D. H., Douglas, V. I., & Morgenstern, G. Sustained attention in hyperactive children. *Journal of Child Psychology and Psychiatry*, 1973, *14*, 213–220.

Sykes, D. H., Douglas, V. I., Weiss, G., & Minde, K. K. Attention in hyperactive children and the effect of methylphenidate (Ritalin). *Journal of Child Psychology and Psychiatry*, 1971, *12*, 129–139.

Tallal, P. Auditory perceptual factors in language and learning disabilities. In R. K. Knights & D. J. Bakker (Eds.), *The neuropsychology of learning disorders*. Baltimore: University Park Press, 1976, pp. 315–332.

Tant, J. L. Problem solving in hyperactive and reading disabled boys. Unpublished doctoral dissertation, McGill University, 1978.

Tarver, S. G., Hallahan, D. P., Kauffman, J. M., & Ball, D. W. Verbal rehearsal and selective attention in children with learning disabilities: A developmental lag. *Journal of Experimental Child Psychology*, 1976, *22*, 375–385.

Torgesen, J. K. The role of nonspecific factors in the task performance of learning disabled children: A theoretical assessment. *Journal of Learning Disabilities*, 1977, *10*, 27–34.

Treisman, A. Strategies and models of selective attention. *Psychological Review*, 1969, *76*, 282–299.

Vygotsky, L. S. *Thought and language*. Cambridge, Mass.: M.I.T. Press, 1962.

Weiner, A. S., & Berzonsky, M. D. Development of selective attention in reflective and impulsive children. *Child Development*, 1975, *46*, 545–549.

Weisen, A. Differential reinforcing effects of onset and offset of stimulation on the operant behavior of normals, neurotics and psychopaths. Unpublished doctoral dissertation, University of Florida, 1965.

Weiss, B., & Laties, V. G. Enhancement of human performance by caffeine and the amphetimines. *Pharmacological Reviews*, 1962, *14*, 1–36.

Weiss, G., Kruger, E., Danielson, U., & Elman, M. Effect of long-term treatment of hyperactive children with methylphenidate. *Canadian Medical Association Journal*, 1975, *112*, 159–165.

Weiss, G., Minde, K., Werry, J., Douglas, V. I., & Nemeth, E. Studies on the hyperactive child: VIII. Five-year follow-up. *Archives of General Psychiatry*, 1971, *24*, 409–414.

Wender, P. H. The minimal brain dysfunction syndrome in children. *Journal of Nervous and Mental Disease*, 1972, *155*, 55–71.

Werry, J. S., Sprague, L., Weiss, G., & Minde, K. Some clinical and laboratory studies of psychotropic drugs in children—an overview. In W. L. Smith (Ed.), *Drugs and cerebral functions.*: CIBA Symposium, 1970.

Werry, J. S., Weiss, G., Dogan, K., Minde, K., & Douglas, V. I. *Studies on the hyperactive child. VII. Comparison of neurological findings between hyperactive, normal and neurotic children*. Paper read at the Canadian Psychiatric Association Annual Meeting, Toronto, June 1969.

Werry, J., Weiss, C., & Douglas, V. I. Studies on the hyperactive child I: Some preliminary findings. *Canadian Psychiatric Association Journal*, 1964, *9*, 120–130.

White, S. H. Evidence for a hierarchical arrangement of learning processes. In L. P. Lipsitt & C. C. Spiker (Eds.), *Advances in child development and behavior* (Vol. 2.). New York: Academic, 1965, pp. 187–220.

Whitehill, M., DeMyer-Gapin, S., & Scott, T. J. Stimulation seeking in antisocial preadolescent children. *Journal of Abnormal Psychology*, 1976, *85*, 101–104.

Wikler, A., Dixon, J., & Parker, J., Jr. Brain function in problem children and controls: Psychometric, neurological and electroencephalographic comparison. *American Journal of Psychiatry*, 1970, *127*, 634–645.

Willows, D. M. *Influences of background pictures on children's decoding of words*. Paper presented at the biennial meeting of the Society for Research in Child Development, Denver, Colorado, April 1975.

Wittelson, S. Abnormal right hemisphere specialization in developmental dyslexia. In *Proceedings of NATO: An international conference, The neuropsychology of learning disorders: Theoretical approaches*. Baltimore: University Park Press, 1976.

Worland, J. Effects of positive and negative feedback on behavior control in hyperactive and normal boys. *Journal of Abnormal Psychology*, 1976, *4*, 315–326.

Worland, J., North-Jones, M., & Stern, J. A. Performance and activity of hyperactive and normal boys as a function of distraction and reward. *Journal of Abnormal Child Psychology*, 1973, *1*, 363–377.

Wright, J. C., & Vlietstra, A. G. The development of selective attention: From perceptual exploration to logical search. In H. W. Reese (Ed.), *Advances in child development and behavior* (Vol. 10). New York: Academic, 1975, pp. 196–235.

Yerkes, R. M., & Dodson, J. D. The relation of strength of stimulus to rapidity of habit formation. *Journal of Comparative Neurology*, 1908, *18*, 459–482.

Zahn, T. P., Abate, F., Little, B., & Wender, P. MBD, stimulant drugs and Ans activity. *Archives of General Psychiatry*, 1975, *32*, 381–387.

Zentall, S. Optimal stimulation as theoretical basis of hyperactivity. *American Journal of Orthopsychiatry*, 1975, *45*(4), 549–563.

Zentall, S., & Zentall, T. R. Activity and task performance of hyperactive children as a function of environmental stimulation. *Journal of Consulting and Clinical Psychology*, 1976, *44*, 693–697.

Zentall, S., Zentall, T. R., & Booth, M. E. Within-task stimulation: Effects on activity and spelling performance in hyperactive and normal children. *Journal of Educational Research*, in press.

9 The Cognitive Effects of Stimulant Drugs on Hyperactive Children

James M. Swanson and Marcel Kinsbourne

Hyperactivity is now the most common psychiatric disorder of childhood. It is so commonly encountered and the problems it creates for the individual, the family, and the school are so serious that it demands treatment. Fortunately, there are several treatments that are effective in reducing hyperactive behavior. The most commonly used (yet still controversial) treatment is with stimulant drugs (amphetamine, methylphenidate, and pemoline). Recently, behavior modification techniques (e.g., the home-based reward system of O'Leary & Pelham, 1978, and cognitive training by Douglas, in press-a) and dietary intervention (e.g., removal of artificial food additives, as suggested by Feingold, 1974) have been used as alternatives to drug treatment.

Unfortunately, only short-term benefits for all of these treatments have been shown. Despite extensive work in the area, no long-term benefits have been documented for any treatment for hyperactivity. This suggests to us that current treatments must be improved before any long-term benefit can be expected.

We will discuss our research program, the purpose of which has been to evaluate and improve one of the treatment procedures mentioned above—treatment with stimulant drugs. But before discussing our research, some background information on the disorder called "hyperactivity" will be presented.

Definition of the Disorder

The term *hyperactivity* has limited value as a descriptive label because the condition is more of a cognitive disorder than a motor disorder. The

James M. Swanson and Marcel Kinsbourne • Neuropsychology Research Unit, Hospital for Sick Children, Toronto, Ontario M5G 1X8 Canada.

generally applied definitions of hyperactivity (e.g., see Fish, 1971, or the DSM-II, 1968, of the American Psychiatric Association) emphasize the activity (e.g., restlessness, overactivity) and conduct (e.g., fighting, classroom disruptions) components of hyperactivity. A recent emphasis has been on the attentional or cognitive dysfunctions associated with the disorder. Apparently, the American Psychiatric Association (DSM-III, in preparation) now proposes a classification using the label "attentional problem, with or without hyperactivity," which will minimize the activity component of the disorder. However, it must be realized that at the present time, the term *hyperactivity* is used by clinicians to label not only children who are overactive but also children who have attentional problems and children who have conduct problems. Thus, "hyperactivity" should be taken as a label for a basic symptom-complex, not as a descriptive label.

In our discussion, we will review a concept of attention and a definition of hyperactivity that we have found to be useful in a clinical setting. Over the past 3 years we have encountered a large number of children with the classical symptoms of hyperactivity who were referred to a learning clinic (located in a hospital) for medical evaluation and treatment. In addition to providing clinical service, we have engaged in a program of research that has made both practical and theoretical contributions toward helping us understand and treat this disorder. Our patients receive standard physical, psychometric, and neurological assessments, and in addition, they are tested in the laboratory as part of our ongoing research. Usually, if symptoms of hyperactivity are confirmed, treatment with stimulant medication is tried. Our approach has been to select well-established procedures from experimental psychology for measuring performance in the laboratory and to apply them in assessing objectively the *cognitive effects* of stimulant drugs on our patients. Before describing our laboratory evaluations, we will describe the clinical population we have investigated in our research.

The Clinical Population

A variety of problems other than hyperactivity are encountered in a learning clinic. Some learning failures are selective (e.g., in reading), some are neurological handicaps, some are due to impoverished social circumstances and poor emotional climate of the family, some are due to specific psychiatric disorders other than hyperactivity. Initial screening by an experienced pediatrician and psychologist usually identifies children belonging to these groups, who are then appropriately treated or referred for specialized treatment elsewhere (Kinsbourne, 1975). We consider only the children who pass this initial screening as being behaviorally hyperactive. What are their symptoms?

An extensive list of symptoms of hyperactivity is given in the Diagnostic and Statistical Manual (DSM-II) of the American Psychiatric Association (1968), which provides three classifications labeled DSM 308.0 (Immature), DSM 308.2 (Overanxious), and DSM 308.4 (Unsocialized-Aggressive). Wender (1971) has suggested three similar classes of hyperactive children, and his labels for the subsyndromes are "hyperkinetic," "neurotic," and "sociopathic." Lists of the symptoms of hyperactivity generally include overactivity, short attention span, restlessness, anxiety, distractibility, impulsiveness, aggressiveness, lack of effort, disruptiveness, and many others. The variety of behavioral symptoms presents an initial problem of diagnosis. No one symptom definitely establishes the diagnosis of hyperactivity, and not all symptoms are present in each case. Also, each symptom calls for an evaluation of degree, because almost any child will manifest each symptom at some time in the course of normal life experiences. The behavior is considered abnormal only when it occurs constantly and in situations when it is clearly inappropriate. We have suggested elsewhere (Swanson & Kinsbourne, 1978) that since hyperactivity is now so well known to the public, yet still so vaguely interpreted even by specialists, *overdiagnosis* is likely to occur. We have developed procedures to help prevent possible overdiagnosis (Swanson, Kinsbourne, Roberts, & Zucker, 1978; Swanson & Kinsbourne, 1978; Kinsbourne, Swanson, & Herman, in press), which we have described in some detail elsewhere.

Considering a hypothetical individual in whom all symptoms are present, the symptom complex breaks down into three components: the motor component, the attentional component, and the social component. Kinsbourne (1977) has suggested that each of these components assumes particular importance at a different phase of the developmental process. The motor component is most prominent early in life between birth and 5 years, and overactivity is usually among the symptoms noted when the parent is interviewed and a history is obtained describing the child's early years. However, as the hyperactive child grows older and reaches school age, the cognitive component assumes importance. At that time it is recognized that task orientation cannot be maintained long enough to accomplish what is expected in school, so problems occur. The inability to maintain task orientation often leads to disruptiveness in group situations, in both academic and play settings. Poor student–teacher and peer relationships are common. As the hyperactive child matures, a pattern of school failure and poor peer relationships understandably leads to problems during the teen-age years, when the social component assumes prominence.

Most of the patients we see in the clinic are over 5 years old, so the prominence of the motor component of hyperactivity has declined. Most are also under 13 years old, so the prominence of the social component has not yet peaked. In this age range (5 to 12), the cognitive problems are most prominent, but certainly they are not the only ones that demand treatment. However, the cognitive component of hyperactivity will be the focus of this chapter.

Magnitude of the Problem

Hyperactivity is a serious and may be a growing mental health problem. It was once thought to be a very rare disorder that affected perhaps 1% of the school-age population. But a recent survey in the United States (Werry & Quay, 1971) indicated that 30% of an urban school-aged population had symptoms of hyperactivity. In Canada, Trites (in press-b) used the 39-item Conners Teacher Rating Scale (Connors, 1973), a widely used instrument to assess the symptoms of hyperactivity, and found that 15% of a stratified sample of Ottawa school children obtained an average rating of over 1.5 per item on the hyperactivity subscale. When the Conners Rating Scale had been developed in 1969, a score of 1.5 per item was the point that cut off the upper 2.5% of the normal school-aged population. Thus, a score of 1.5 per item identified an "abnormal" condition, and that score has been used as the criterion to identify a serious condition that requires clinical treatment (Sprague & Sleator, 1973). But Trites's (in press-b) data seem to indicate that a score of 1.5 per item is no longer abnormal, since it demarcates 15% of the population rather than 2.5%.

Is hyperactivity increasing as these studies suggest? Or is the disorder now just recognized more often? Or is hyperactivity overdiagnosed? We (Swanson & Kinsbourne, 1978) have previously discussed some problems that could lead to overdiagnosis of the disorder, which we will not repeat here, and we do not believe hyperactivity affects more than 3% of the school-aged population. Even at that level, hyperactivity represents a major mental health problem.

Etiology. While the magnitude and seriousness of the disorder are generally accepted, the causes of the disorder remain obscure. Early hypotheses suggested "minimal brain damage" as a unitary cause, but this view has not received support in subsequent research and is not widely accepted today. Subtle brain dysfunction due to imbalance in neurotransmitters has also been suggested as a cause of hyperactive behavior, but this hypothesis has not been substantiated by adequate research. A variety of environmental pollutants (including lead and artificial food additives) have been indirectly implicated. Parental consumption of tobacco and alcohol have been linked to increased hyperactivity in their offspring. Even individual variation on a personality dimension (impulsivity-reflectivity) has been suggested as the underlying cause of hyperactivity. We will discuss a few of these possibilities in detail.

The role of brain damage in generating hyperactive behavior was proposed because, in children who have demonstrable brain damage, a pattern of hyperactive behavior is often observed. For example, during the early 1900s it was noted that the postencephalitic behavior of children was characterized by restlessness, inattentiveness, impulsivity, antisocial behavior, and irritability (Ebaugh, 1923; Kahn & Cohen, 1934). A similar pattern of behavior was noted by Strauss and his associates (Strauss & Lehtinen, 1948; Strauss & Kephart, 1955) in studies of the psychological characteristics of a group of children who were retarded due to brain injury. Many individuals in whom brain damage was not apparent also have similar patterns of hyperactive behavior. It has been proposed (Kahn & Cohen, 1934; Strauss & Lehtinen, 1948; Strauss & Kephart, 1955) that these individuals, too, probably have brain damage but that routine neurological examination simply fails to detect its presence. It has often been suggested that this is because the brain damage occurs at birth, after which the neurological symptoms dissipate rapidly, and only when the child starts school does the behavioral consequence become apparent (see Strother, 1973).

It is clear that brain damage can be the cause of hyperactive behavior. However, the view that all hyperactive behavior is caused by brain damage is not based on sound logic. Two conferences have been held on the question of "minimal brain damage," the first in 1962 at Oxford (Bax & MacKeith, 1963) and the second in Washington in 1963 (Clements, 1966). In both cases, the consensus was that brain damage should not be inferred from behavioral signs. The term *minimal brain damage* is seldom used these days, but the term *minimal brain dysfunction* (MBD) is often used (Clements, 1966; Wender, 1971) to satisfy those who favor medical models.

Hyperactivity has also been regarded as a neurodevelopmental lag. Some observations by physicians in a particular child are called soft neurological signs of MBD, but these findings are considered abnormal only with reference to that child's age. If the child were younger, the finding would be considered normal (Kinsbourne, 1973). Viewed in this way, the behavior of the hyperactive child, whether it reflects motor immaturity, failure to focus attention, or cognitive deficiencies, is assumed to represent behavior typical of younger normal children. It is well established that activity level is highest in the youngest children and undergoes a regular developmental decline. Thus, one might regard a hyperactive child as retaining the activity level of a younger normal child. The apparent resolution of hyperactivity at adolescence would then be regarded as a final closing of the gap between the lagging individual and others. However, it has become clear that at least in some cases hyperactivity persists into the adult years. This presents a serious difficulty for the lag model.

Thomas and Chess (1968) noted that children seem to express the same temperamental patterns at different ages despite dramatic developmental changes in abilities and behavior. Perhaps hyperactivity is due to an inherited temperament and the disorder represents an extreme placement on dimensions of personality or cognitive style, such as those suggested by Buss and Plomin (1975)—emotionality, activity, sociability, or impulsivity. Kinsbourne (1977) has discussed this possibility in detail elsewhere.

In this chapter we will advocate a model that appears to combine the merits of these various approaches. Hyperactive behavior will be regarded as differing only in degree from comparable behavior manifest in the general population. We will suppose a continuum of individual difference between the extreme of underfocused attention and concentration, manifested as hyperactivity, and its opposite, the extreme of overfocused attention, which may be manifested as anxious behavior. We will assume that the cognitive and behavioral style of any one individual is determined by his placement on this continuum, which we regard as representing the resultant of opposing influences from several sources. We consider an individual's placement to be subject to bias, through brain damage, because of a developmental lag, or as the result of individual differences in temperament, determined by genetic diversity. Thus, there can be functional convergence in terms of the pattern of behavior due to more than one pathogenesis. Furthermore, we consider it possible that episodes of hyperactive behavior could arise on the basis of adverse environmental circumstances (e.g., experiences that lead a child to feel powerless and to regard his own actions as inconsequential) or on the basis of certain chemical agents that might occur in the diet (e.g., artificial colors), as suggested by Feingold (1974), rather than on the basis of constitutional factors.

According to this view, hyperactivity has a diverse etiology and it is unlikely that one cause of the disorder will ever be identified. We agree with Douglas (in press-b), who suggested that even if a hyperactive behavior is produced by different etiologies, it is likely that a common treatment will be appropriate in most cases, despite the diversity of causes. The treatment we will discuss is the most common treatment for hyperactivity—treatment with stimulant drugs, e.g., amphetamine (Dexedrine), methylphenidate (Ritalin), or pemoline (Cylert).

Background Information on Drug Treatment

Bradley (1937) initially described this treatment for hyperactivity. He gave small doses of amphetamine (Dexedrine or Benzedrine) to "problem" children in a group home, and he noticed increased attention, cooperation, and goal-directed activity in some (but not all) of his patients. He later described his use of stimulants in the treatment of a large number of children with learning and behavior problems (Bradley, 1950). Laufer and Denhoff (1957) emphasized that not all children with symptoms of hyperactivity responded favorably to stimulant drugs. Their emphasis remains with us today (Fish, 1971).

Laufer and Denhoff (1957) renamed "hyperactivity" as the "hyperkinetic impulse disorder" in an attempt to emphasize its cognitive component. They hypothesized that the disorder was due to subcortical brain damage, specifically in the reticular activating system, and thus had an organic etiology. However, they reasoned that psychological problems could produce anxiety in children, which could result in similar symptoms and thus could complicate the diagnosis. They suggested that if the symptoms of the hyperkinetic-impulse disorder were present, a provisional diagnosis should be made and a *diagnostic drug trial* should be given with either a stimulant drug (amphetamine) or a depressant drug (phenobarbitol). If the stimulant drug had a favorable effect and decreased the symptoms of hyperactivity, or if the depressant drug had an adverse effect and aggravated the symptoms, the provisional diagnosis (implicating brain damage) was confirmed. But if the stimulant drug had an adverse effect, or the depressant drug a favorable effect, then the provisional diagnosis of hyperkinetic impulse disorder was abandoned and psychological reasons for the symptoms were implicated.

Use of the diagnostic drug trial has become a standard practice in the medical treatment of hyperactivity. Wender (1971), Eisenberg (1972), Solomons (1971), Cantwell (1975), and Safer and Allen (1976) all describe the usefulness of this procedure and consider it necessary for competent treatment of hyperactive children. However, a favorable response to stimulant drugs is no longer taken as evidence for brain damage.

Wender (1971, 1973) has reviewed the rationale behind use of the diagnostic drug trial to evaluate possible CNS abnormalities of hyperactive children. Following Laufer and Denhoff (1957), he noted that a favorable response to stimulant drugs could be based on an assumption of an abnormally low activation level of the central nervous system (possibly due to subcortical brain damage) that was corrected by the drug treatment. A drug-induced normalization of behavior would then be expected only if this particular abnormal state of "underarousal" existed before the drug was given. Wender (1973) also noted that a state of overarousal (an abnormally high CNS activation level) may produce behavioral symptoms of hyperactivity. It may be that only symptoms due to a low arousal level (see Satterfield, Cantwell, Lesser, & Podosin, 1972) respond favorably to stimulant medication, and that a high arousal level characterizes those persons who have an adverse response to stimulant drugs.

Rapoport, Buchsbaum, Zahn, Weingartner, Ludlow, and Mikkelsen (1978) have recently questioned the basic assumption of the diagnostic drug trial. They suggest that even nonhyperactive individuals (both normal adults and normal children) respond in a beneficial way to stimulant drugs, and it is therefore "important that no diagnostic significance be inferred from a beneficial drug effect" (Rapoport *et al.*, 1978, p. 562). As we will discuss below, we believe that Rapoport *et al.* ignored the well-established task-specificity of response to stimulant drugs (Weiss & Laties, 1962) and that their wholesale indictment of the diagnostic drug trial is unwarranted.

For example, Burns, House, Fensch, and Miller (1967) and Smith (1967) have clearly shown that normal adults have an adverse response to stimulant drugs on standard laboratory learning tests. In addition, Rapoport *et al.* clearly ignored the consistent finding that a significant minority of children with symptoms of hyperactivity respond *adversely* to stimulant drugs. Even in Bradley's (1937, 1950) initial work, it was clear that not all individuals in the relevant clinical population had a beneficial response to stimulant drugs. These findings alone contradict the assertion that everyone has a beneficial response to stimulant drugs and that the diagnostic trial is useless for that reason.

The Rapoport *et al.* (1978) report, however, is correct in emphasizing the warning so clearly stated by Smith, Weitzner, Levenson, and Beecher (1963) concerning the use of certain laboratory tests to measure response to stimulant drugs. Smith *et al.* pointed out that "low level" intellectual tasks, even though they might be the most *sensitive* to the presence or absence of the drug effects, seriously overestimate the favorable response to stimulant drugs. This overestimation of the favorable response must be carefully avoided in the clinical use of the diagnostic drug trial. In addition, we (Swanson & Kinsbourne, 1978) have noted the same danger associated with the use of rating scales to evaluate drug trials. Sprague and Sleator (1977) have provided the most detailed treatment of this topic by comparing dose-related effects on teacher ratings and memory tests. It is clear that the manner in which one evaluates a response to stimulant drugs assumes a primary importance in any discussion of a diagnostic drug trial, and we will emphasize that point in the next section.

Evaluation of Diagnostic Drug Trials

In our research we systematically classify patients referred with symptoms of hyperactivity according to their response to stimulant drugs in order to label each patient as a "favorable responder" or an "adverse responder." In this way, our definition is not much different from the early definition offered by Laufer and Denhoff (1957); but the advance is in the *way we measure the response to medication.* Laufer and Denhoff (1957) emphasized the cognitive component of the disorder relative to the motor component, in addition to formally proposing the use of a diagnostic drug trial, but they did not suggest how to determine the effect of a diagnostic drug trial on cognition. The usual procedure then, as it still is now, was to ask interested adults (teacher and parents) how the medication was working. We have pointed out a serious problem with this method of evaluation (Swanson & Kinsbourne, 1978). The effect of the drug on the "conduct" of both favorable and adverse responders is often the same—it has a controlling effect, initially thought to be a paradoxical "calming" effect, that is now generally attributed to an attention-focusing effect of the drug. This attention-focusing effect apparently occurs in all humans, but in normal situations (e.g., in an academic setting in school) it should help only those who start in an underfocused state. Thus, while the drug might act to "calm" most patients and reduce their disruptive behavior, it should improve the ability to concentrate for only some of the patients (Swanson & Kinsbourne, 1978). Also, the dose that has the optimal effect on concentration may be different from the dose that optimally affects social interaction (Sprague & Sleator, 1977).

How does one determine whether stimulants work? Eisenberg (1972) and Safer and Allen (1976) give detailed descriptions of how drug trials can be evaluated by the pediatrician. The typical suggestion is that small doses should be tried initially, and that increases should be made if no improvement is noted. Over an extended period of time following initiation of stimulant therapy, one of two outcomes will occur: At some level of medication, either an apparent improvement in behavior will result (a favorable response) or behavior will deteriorate (an adverse response). If the adverse response occurs at the initial (small) dose, or a favorable response does not occur before an adverse response emerges, then the child can be classified as an adverse responder. If a favorable response emerges at a lower dose level than that at which an adverse response occurs, then the adverse response can be interpreted as an overdose effect, and the child can be classified as a favorable responder (at the lower dose). Solomons (1971) has suggested that this method can be used to determine the optimum level of medication for an individual child, and that the process takes about 2 *months*. He suggests that telephone contact with parents is sufficient for monitoring response to medication, but others believe that parent and teacher questionnaires are more objective and desirable means of eliciting subjective impressions of a child's response to medication (Sprague & Sleator, 1973; Conners, 1973).

Subjective Evaluation of Response to Questionnaire

Questionnaires for quantifying clinical impressions of hyperactive behavior were developed following the early investigations of hyperactive children. On the basis of over a decade of work on the population of children initially investigated by Bradley (1937, 1950) and Laufer and Denhoff (1957), Davids (1971) developed a rating scale for assessing seven key characteristics of the "hyperkinetic impulse disorder." Conners (1969) developed a teacher rating scale during his extensive research in this area, and his questionnaire is now widely used. The questionnaires are similar in purpose; by having an involved observer, usually a teacher or parent, rate a child after Placebo and Drug conditions, it has been shown that these instruments are useful in detecting a favorable response to drugs (Conners, 1973; Denhoff, Davids, & Hawkins, 1971). Safer and Allen (1976) have incorporated a questionnaire in their proposed method of determining a response to stimulant therapy in a clinical rather than a research setting. However, Schain and Reynard (1975) have commented on the weakness of questionnaires for evaluating response to medication, and Sprague and Sleator (1977) have also emphasized their limitations.

Over the last 40 years, thousands of children have received stimulant medication as a treatment for hyperactivity. Hundreds of research studies have been performed to investigate this treatment. Despite its extensive clinical use and the intense research in the area, *no clear demonstration of a beneficial long-term effect of this treatment has been reported in the literature.* Why might this be the case? Barkley (1976) has pointed out that in most studies of the effect of stimulant drugs, the favorable effects documented are in cognitive functioning rather than in conduct, but that it is the conduct or social interaction of children that leads to the diagnosis of hyperactivity. Furthermore, when medication is tried, usually subjective evaluations by questionnaires are used that monitor changes only on the dimension of social interaction. This may be the wrong dimension of behavior to use in order to establish the optimal dose, and use of this dimension may lead to selection of high levels of medication, which impair cognitive functioning (Sprague & Sleator, 1977). If this occurs in a significant number of cases, it could mask a long-term beneficial effect that might occur at a different dose.

Also, it is possible that reliance on subjective evaluations of drug trials may result in an inappropriate treatment of some children (e.g., those we call adverse responders) in addition to the overdosing of favorable responders. If a heterogeneous group of children including both the favorable and the adverse responders is evaluated to determine the long-term benefit of treatment with stimulant drugs, any long-term benefit for the favorable responders may be masked by a long-term impairment in the adverse responders.

Before an adequate test of the long-term benefit of stimulant medication can be made, it is necessary to separate the favorable from the adverse responders, and to maintain each favorable responder on his optimal dose. In order to do this, objective evidence that the medication improves rather than impairs the ability to concentrate must be obtained, in addition to subjective impressions of the effect of medication on conduct. We have developed several laboratory tests for this purpose, and we will describe our procedures in detail below.

Laboratory Tests

Once a laboratory test is chosen, the measurement of the effect of a short-acting stimulant drug [e.g., d-amphetamine (Dexedrine) or methylphenidate (Ritalin)] is a simple matter. However, the choice of an appropriate laboratory task to measure the effects of stimulant drugs is *not* a simple matter. In order for a test to have diagnostic significance in the way proposed by Laufer and Denhoff (1957), the normal drug-induced response as measured by it must not be a beneficial one (Rapoport *et al.*, 1978). If everyone shows a drug-induced benefit, then the basis for the diagnostic trial does not exist.

What responses do "normal" people have to stimulant drugs? In their comprehensive and excellent review, Weiss and Laties (1962) noted that in normal adults, even though a wide range of behavior (including physical endurance, athletic performance, motor coordination, and monitoring) could be enhanced by stimulants, enhancement of performance on intellectual tasks was a "notable exception." They further emphasized that stimulants do not possess "properties which lead to improved intellectual performance except, perhaps, when normal performance has been degraded by fatigue or boredom" (p. 21). Thus, the literature suggests that an intellectual task such as one involving learning should be chosen as a diagnostic test, since only on such a task is the normal response to stimulant drugs not a drug-induced facilitation of performance.

Apparently, the effect of stimulant medication on complex learning tasks is still misunderstood, because some (e.g., Kolata, 1978) still assert that stimulant drugs improve the performance of normal adults on laboratory tests of learning. The studies by Burns *et al.* (1967) and Smith (1967), however, have provided clear evidence that the laboratory learning task is specifically one that documents the adverse response of normal adults to stimulant drugs. When our research was started, it was noted that the same learning paradigms that had been used to show a drug-induced *impairment in performance of normal adults* (Burns *et al.*, 1967; Smith, 1967) had been used to show a drug-induced *improvement of performance in hyperactive children* by Conners and his colleagues (Conners, Eisenberg, & Sharpe, 1968; Conners & Rothschild, 1968; Conners, Rothschild, Eisenberg, & Schwartz, 1969).

Unfortunately, many of the early studies on hyperactive children apparently were done merely to demonstrate the presence or absence of an effect of a stimulant drug treatment. For this reason, tasks were chosen (such as the continuous performance task or CPT, see Sykes, Douglas, Weiss, & Mende, 1971) that were considered to be *sensitive* to drug effects, without adequate concern for the task-*specificity* of response to the drug. Barlow (1977) has shown that while the CPT is probably the task most sensitive to drug effects, it overestimates the favorable response to the drug treatment. Thus, it is not an appropriate test to evaluate a diagnostic drug trial. What laboratory test is appropriate? Our experience suggests that the paired-associate paradigm provides an appropriate test for a diagnostic drug trial. We believe that the important feature of this laboratory test is that it requires acquisition of new associations through repeated practice.

What effects do stimulant drugs have on performance of normal children on the paired-associate learning test? As we have pointed out above, normal adults and hyperactive children differ in their response to stimulants in terms of their performance on laboratory *learning* tests. Thus, the following two possibilities exist: (1) Normal children, like hyperactive children, could show *improved* learning on stimulants. This outcome would suggest that children *in general* respond differently from adults; (2) normal children, like normal adults, could show *impaired* learning on stimulants. This outcome would suggest that only hyperactive children have an abnormal response to stimulants. Unfortunately, not much work has been done on normal children, and that which has (e.g., Rapoport *et al.*, 1978) did not use a learning test. Thus, the evaluation of these two possibilities must await further research. We have, however, done considerable research on the clinical group of hyperactive children, using a learning test, which we will review in the next section.

Experiments Using Paired-Associate Learning

We have used the paired-associate learning test to evaluate over 400 children referred with symptoms of hyperactivity. In our initial paired-associate task, color slides of animals in naturalistic settings were used as stimuli, and the four directions (north, south, east, and west) were used as responses. Since there were more stimuli than responses, the task involved assigning stimuli (animals) to classes (directions). We now use the digits as response items, and pictures of animals affixed to cards as stimuli. Two stimuli are assigned to each response. A learning session consists of presenting a list of stimulus items (animal pictures) one at a time in a random sequence, for the patient to study. The length of the list is varied from 4 to 20 items, depending on the patient's age. During the initial presentation, the patient is told to associate each animal with a hypothetical "zoo," designated by a direction in our old procedure and a number in our new procedure. Starting on the second time through the list, a patient is asked to say in which "zoo" each animal lives. If the patient's response is correct, he is reinforced ("That's right; good"). If the response is incorrect, the patient is corrected ("That's wrong") and the correct response is provided verbally to reinstruct the patient as to which association was appropriate. The list is presented 10 times, each time in a random order, or until a criterion of two perfect recitations of the list is met. To accomplish this, the patient must concentrate on the task for about 15 to 25 minutes. He must sit in the same place (a chair) and listen to an adult (the experimenter/teacher) provide information regarding new associations to be made between old and familiar items. The cognitive skills necessary for much of the learning that occurs in the traditional classroom are necessary to perform this task, including the ability to persevere at a task imposed by an adult.

A task was chosen on which little transfer would occur from list to list. From the study of human learning, "transfer" characteristics of different list structures have been determined. In the terminology of verbal learning research, the list sequence utilized in this experiment is labeled "A-B," "C-B" to denote that the stimulus items change across lists but the response items do not. As suggested in a review by Kausler (1974), the stimulus aspects of the list structure (common zoo animals, which change from list to list) should produce slight negative transfer, but the unchanging response set should produce slight positive transfer. The two transfer effects, which are opposite in direction, are thought to be equal in magnitude, so no overall transfer from list to list is to be expected (Kausler, 1974). Other list structures are expected to result in either overall positive or overall negative transfer.

In the research described below, we tried to evaluate the maximum response to an *acute administration* of stimulant medication. Methylphenidate is short-acting; it starts to exert its effect within 1 hour after administration and its effect is virtually gone 4 to 6 hours after a single administration. This characteristic of the drug was utilized to set up drug and placebo conditions within a single day. In the initial paradigm, medication (usually methylphenidate) was given either in the morning (at 9:00 A.M.) or in the afternoon (12:15 P.M.) and placebo at the other time. Tests to measure the drug's effects were given at 2 hours after each administration, because it is at this time that the drug has its largest behavioral effect.

In the first experiment (Swanson & Kinsbourne, 1976) we demonstrated state-dependent learning in a group of hyperactive children who had been on stimulant medication for extended periods of time and had been reported to have had a favorable clinical response. In addition, one of the most important results of that study was the replication of Conners's (Conners et al., 1968, 1969; Conners & Rothschild, 1968) previous work with paired-associate learning. As shown in Figure 1, under the double-blind conditions of our laboratory tests, the hyperactive patients' performance in the drug condition was superior to performance in the placebo condition. A mixed "control" group was also tested, composed of children in whom hyperactivity had been disconfirmed ($N = 10$) and normal children ($N = 6$). In this mixed control group, a nonsignificant trend toward a

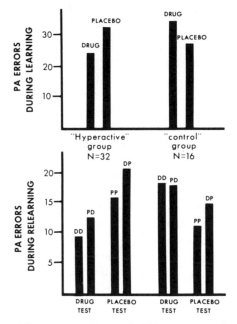

FIGURE 1. Performance of hyperactive and control children on a paired-associate learning test, at 2 hours after administration of drug (methylphenidate) or placebo. At the top, acquisition performance on Day 1 is shown; at the bottom, retention performance on Day 2 is shown. Adapted from Swanson and Kinsbourne (1976).

drug-induced impairment was observed. This differential response to stimulant drugs confirmed the belief that the paired-associate learning test had "diagnostic significance" in the sense proposed by Laufer and Denhoff (1957).

Other indirect evidence supported this view. Stevenson (1972) had earlier noted that the paired-associate learning paradigm is the laboratory task with the highest correlation with school performance. This suggested that it met the criterion of "maximum transfer" (Vellutino, Steger, Moyer, Harding, & Niles, 1977), which requires that the evaluation of a learning disability should rely on performance in units that closely approximate the ability in question. An important study by Gittelman-Klein and Klein (1975) showed that the drug-induced improvement in performance on paired-associate learning was the only measure (of several they took) that correlated positively with overall evaluations by teachers ($r = .68$) and psychiatrists ($r = .48$) of methylphenidate-treated hyperactive children in a 12-week follow-up study.

As discussed before, it is well known that not all children referred with symptoms of hyperactivity respond favorably to a clinical trial on stimulant drugs; at least 25% show no effect or get worse on stimulants. Thus, a critical requirement of a diagnostic laboratory test is that *not all* children referred with symptoms of hyperactivity should show a drug-induced facilitation of performance on it. The next study (Swanson *et al.,* 1978) was designed to provide information about the percentage of children who would be classified favorable and adverse responders on the basis of the paired-associate task. The time response characteristics of a single administration of methylphenidate were measured in children who had the clinical symptoms of hyperactivity on the basis of history and behavior at home and at school. The same procedure was used for administering drug and placebo as described before, and an initial day of practice was used to determine what size stimulus list to use for the testing on the subsequent day.

The list length determined on the 1st day was adhered to when eight different lists of the same length were presented on the 2nd day. The eight tests were distributed across the 8 hours of testing between 8:30 A.M. and 4:30 P.M., so as to sample performance throughout the periods of expected drug action. All testing was conducted under double-blind conditions. The testing times were:

a. 8:45 A.M.–before Administration I
b. 9:00 A.M.–Medication I
c. 9:30 A.M.–½ hour after Administration I
d. 11:00 A.M.–2 hours after Administration I
e. 12:00 M.–3 hours after Administration I
f. 12:15 P.M.–Medication II
g. 12:45 P.M.–½ hour after Administration II
h. 2:15 P.M.–2 hours after Administration II
i. 3:15 P.M.–3 hours after Administration II
j. 4:15 P.M.–4 hours after Administration II

In the published article, we presented data "adjusted for baseline." Here we present the data without baseline adjustments. As shown in Figure 2, two types of responses were clearly defined. The favorable responses consisted of a decrease in errors on the learning task by 2 hours after medication, and the adverse response consisted of an increase in errors on the learning task by 2 hours after the drug treatment. Approximately two-thirds of the patients had a favorable response to the drug on the basis of this laboratory test, which is the same percentage as that reported in the literature on the basis of clinical judgment.

How do these favorable and adverse effects hold up over time? This question was investigated in the third experiment, in which we recalled the patients from the first and second experiments for retesting (Dalby, Kinsbourne, Swanson, & Sobol, 1977). Again the paired-associate learning paradigm and the double-blind drug–placebo administration was used.

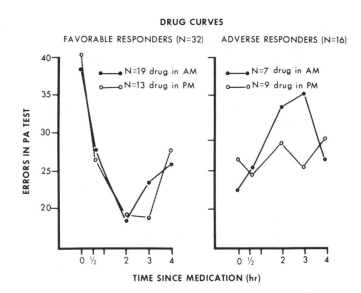

FIGURE 2. The time response characteristics of response to methylphenidate (Ritalin) in terms of performance on the paired-associate learning test. At the left, the pattern of response that leads to a classification as a "favorable responder" is shown; at the right, the pattern of response that leads to a classification of an "adverse responder" is shown. Adapted from Swanson, Kinsbourne, Roberts, and Zucker (1978).

Different conditions within both the drug and placebo conditions were also established to investigate the "total-time hypothesis." According to this hypothesis, a few long intervals of stimulus exposure (e.g., 4 12-second presentations) would result in the same amount of learning as many short intervals (e.g., 12 4-second presentations). The experimental conditions allowed 4, 8, or 12 seconds per item for learning. By thus varying the amount of time allowed for each presentation of an item to be learned, we could then determine if hyperactive children fail to take advantage of long time intervals as effectively as they take advantage of short time intervals.

The results are shown in Figure 3. In an unmedicated state (placebo), the hyperactive patients did not take advantage of the long time intervals effectively, and thus for a given total amount of time (e.g., after 24 sec or 48 sec) they performed worse when each trial was long (e.g., 12 sec) than when it was short (e.g., 4 sec). This pattern of performance (shown in the placebo conditions in Figure 3) is abnormal because the total-time hypothesis has been shown to hold for both normal adults and normal children in a variety of settings (see Dalby *et al.*, 1977). As Figure 3 also indicates, the effect of the drug treatment was to improve the favorable responders' utilization of the long intervals, bringing their performance in line with the total-time principle. Regardless of the presentation rate, a given amount of time (e.g., 24 sec or 48 sec) resulted in about the same performance on the learning test. With regard to utilization of time, this reflects a normalization of the hyperactive child's behavior.

What can be learned from this test? It confirmed in a laboratory setting what has been suggested by clinical experience—that is, the hyperactive child finds it hard to maintain concentration for more than brief periods of time. Our data show that the "concentration span" (defined as the length of time effectively employed to study a stimulus-response pair) of the child in the placebo state was under 8 seconds, since there was a deficit at that presentation rate compared with the 4-second rate (see Dalby et al., 1977). The data also show that the effect of the drug was to increase the concentration span of our patients to over 12 seconds. However, these effects do not occur in every patient. In about 40% of the patients referred to us with symptoms of hyperactivity (our adverse responders), performance (and "concentration span") in the medicated state actually declines when medication is given.

If only those patients who demonstrate a favorable *cognitive* response are given long-term trials on stimulant medication, will a long-term benefit be observed? That is the question we are addressing in our current research.

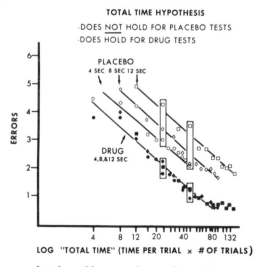

FIGURE 3. Performance of 28 favorable responders on the paired-associate learning test, at 2 hours after administration of drug (methylphenidate) or placebo. In each condition, three tests were given to determine the effect of presentation rate (4 sec, 8 sec, or 12 sec). If the total-time hypothesis holds, performance from all three presentation rates would fall on the same linear regression line relating error scores to total time. This occurs in the drug condition but not in the placebo condition. Adapted from Dalby, Kinsbourne, Swanson, and Sobol (1977).

Other Laboratory Tests

It is clear that only 60 to 70% of our patients with symptoms of hyperactivity respond favorably to stimulant medication on the paired-associate learning task, and on the basis of our research we have proposed an operational definition of stimulant responsive hyperactivity (Swanson *et al.*, 1978; Swanson & Kinsbourne, 1978).

How do our favorable and adverse responders (on the learning test) respond on other laboratory tests? Recently in our laboratory, children have been tested on the Continuous Performance Task (Barlow, 1977), the Matching Familiar Figures test (Mock, Swanson, & Kinsbourne, 1978), the Lykken maze test (Freeman, 1978), a pursuit tracking task (Kapelus, Swanson, & Kinsbourne, 1979), a button press and eye movement reaction time task (Swanson, Ledlow, & Kinsbourne, in preparation), uncued and cued free recall task (Swanson, Eich, & Kinsbourne, 1978), and an incidental learning task (Thurston, 1977). In all cases, we divided the referred patients (all of whom had symptoms of hyperactivity documented by a pediatrician in the learning clinic) into groups of favorable and adverse responders to stimulant medication on the basis of their performance on the paired-associate learning test in drug and placebo conditions. One basic question we have asked in this research program is: Do these two subgroups of hyperactive children have the same response pattern or a different response pattern to stimulant medication when other laboratory tasks are used to measure performance? We will review our findings (which are as yet unpublished), below.

Tasks That Overdiagnose Stimulant Responsivity

On some tasks, we have found that both of our subgroups (favorable and adverse responders on the paired-associate test) show improved performance in the drug condition relative to the placebo condition. Using the Continuous Performance Task (CPT), Barlow (1977) found that all subjects made faster responses and committed fewer errors when on drug than when on placebo. Kapelus *et al.* (1979) found that both the favorable and adverse responder groups performed better on a computer-controlled tracking task in the drug condition. Thurston (1977) used a one-trial free-recall task in an incidental learning paradigm and found that both favorable and adverse responders showed reduced incidental recall and increased central recall when treated with stimulant medication. In the context of a choice reaction time task (manual button press response to a light stimulus), Swanson *et al.* (1978) monitored saccadic eye movement latency in drug and placebo conditions. In both groups of subjects, the manual RT was reduced significantly (85 msec) by the drug, but eye movement latency was unaffected (214 msec on placebo and 213 msec on drug).

Since all of our patients show a drug-induced improvement in performance on these tasks (and since we know from the literature that not all of them will respond favorably to the drug in a clinical sense), we believe that these tests overdiagnose the favorable response pattern to the drug treatment. Using these tests, then, one could be led to classify adverse responders as favorable responders, and thus to mistreat a significant minority of the patients (up to 40%) with stimulant drugs. Using the same reasoning as Rapoport et al. (1978), we do not think that the tests mentioned above have any diagnostic significance. As suggested by Smith et al. (1963), these tests may be more sensitive than others to drug effects, but they will seriously overestimate the beneficial response to stimulant drugs.

Tasks with Complex Response Patterns

Freeman (1978) used the Lykken maze test with favorable and adverse responders (as defined above) in drug and placebo conditions. In that test, several rows of four lights made up a maze. At each choice point (e.g., row of the maze), one of the four alternatives was arbitrarily designated as the "correct" path, one was designated as an incorrect choice and "punished" (e.g., followed by a noxious tone), and two were designated as incorrect choices but were not associated with punishment. Children were required to find the correct path through the maze by trial and error, and to demonstrate their learning by negotiating the maze without making an error. The number of errors made during learning (both punished and unpunished errors) was then taken as the measure of performance on the task.

There were several ways in which favorable and adverse responders differed on this task. First, in the placebo condition, adverse responders avoided punished locations in the maze, but favorable responders did not. Next, the drug corrected this avoidance learning decrement in the favorable responders, but it had no effect on the avoidance of learning of adverse responders. Finally, the overall learning of the adverse responders was impaired by the drug (from 68.91% correct in placebo to 62.65% correct in drug), but the overall learning of the favorable responders was unaffected (68.66% correct on placebo and 69.40% correct on drug). The Lykken maze test thus shows several differences between favorable and adverse responders, and it may have some diagnostic significance.

Mock et al. (1978) tested favorable and adverse responders using the Matching Familiar Figures (MFF) test, which required children to match a standard figure with one of several alternatives. Only one of the alternatives exactly matched the standard, but all the others were similar to the standard. In this test, the two subgroups did not differ overall in terms of the time taken to inspect the figures before a choice was made, and the drug treatment did not affect this measure of performance. However, the favorable responder group yielded a bimodal distribution of times. When the children were classified as either impulsive-hyperactive children or distractible-hyperactive children, it was clear that the impulsive group had abnormally short response latencies and the distractible group had abnormally long response latencies. Inspection of the drug effect in these two groups separately showed that the drug normalized the average response latency in both groups—by *increasing* it in the impulsive group and *decreasing* it in the distractible group. In both cases, error scores tended to be lower in the drug condition than in the placebo condition, but due to the restricted range of the possible number of errors, the difference was not significant.

The MFF test, then, may have some clinical relevance if the group of favorable responders is subdivided on the basis of symptom type. Also, this test has some diagnostic significance if only the error scores are used to measure the drug effect. However, the primary dependent variable (response latency) is difficult to use diagnostically because a drug-induced effect in either direction can be interpreted as a favorable response, depending on the type of patient.

Which tests, then, are useful in diagnosing stimulant responsiveness in hyperactive children? Our experience indicates that the tests that require the child to acquire new information through practice (e.g., a paired-associate learning task or the Lykken maze) are the best for diagnostic purposes, because on these tests some patients' performance is impaired by the drug. These children, then, can be identified as adverse responders and can be protected from possible mistreatment with stimulant drugs. On the other hand, tasks that require prolonged monitoring (the CPT or pursuit tracking) or repetition of a simple response (a choice reaction time task) seem to induce a "state" in all individuals that makes them respond favorably to stimulant drugs. Thus, those tests have no diagnostic significance. Reliance on them will result in false positive decisions, which could lead to misuse of stimulant drugs in a significant minority of those children referred with recognizable symptoms, since it is clear from experience that roughly 25% to 40% of those children will not have a beneficial clinical response to the drug.

Problems with Drug Treatment

One objective of our research program has been to find tests that will *exclude* some children with symptoms of hyperactivity from an extended treatment with stimulant drugs. We believe that learning tests can be used for this purpose. However, our research with laboratory learning tests has demonstrated several serious weaknesses of current drug treatments, even after a favorable response has been established. First, we have documented the short time course of the effect of medication (Swanson *et al.*, 1978). This short length of action represents a severe clinical weakness, because it means that medication must be administered at least three times per day to have an adequate coverage. Increases in dose do not increase the length of coverage but produce overdose effects that impair rather than improve cognitive functioning. Longer acting agents would significantly improve the treatment of favorable responders to stimulant medication.

The second problem we have identified associated with stimulant medication concerns state dependent learning. We (Swanson & Kinsbourne, 1976) have demonstrated that when new material is learned in a drug state established in the laboratory, performance during acquisition is improved relative to the placebo state. However, if recall of material is required later, and the drug state is *not* established again, then retention of the information (acquired in the drug state) is actually *impaired* relative to material that was acquired in a placebo state earlier (see Figure 1). Similar impairment occurs when material is initially learned in a placebo state and retention is tested later in a drug state. This type of impairment associated with a drug-induced change in state (from drug to placebo or placebo to drug) has been called state-dependent learning. It is possible that the beneficial effects of stimulant medication are state-dependent, and for that reason, short-term favorable effects are not translated into a long-term benefit. We have recently replicated our earlier experiment in which we observed state-dependent learning, and are investigating state-dependent effects in free recall (cued and uncued), spelling, and reading comprehension. This type of research is necessary in this area and in any instance in which a psychotropic drug is used for a clinical purpose, because long-term benefit of the treatment is expected only in the *absence* of a state-dependent effect.

A third problem with drug treatment concerns the dose of medication required to produce an optimal behavioral effect. We have shown (Swanson et al., 1978) that even when a favorable cognitive response to a low dose of medication (e.g., 10 to 15 mg of methylphenidate) is documented in a group of patients, a higher dose of the same drug (e.g., 20 mg) will have an adverse effect in the same individuals. This adverse effect on cognition may occur in the absence of common side effects (e.g., heart rate changes, insomnia, crying) and thus may be overlooked in the method of titration to optimal dose.

Sprague and Sleator (1973) have recommended dosing on a mg-per-kg (of body weight) basis and recommend .3 mg/kg as the optimal dose. However, Schain and Reynard (1975) found that dosing on a mg/kg basis did not solve the dosage problems. In our experience, we have found that dosing on a mg/kg basis is *not* useful in the treatment of hyperactive children. Across the age range of 5 to 15 years, the need for medication does not seem to increase as the child's body size increases. This effect may occur because intellectual maturation occurs over the same age range, which decreases the need for medication, or it may occur for some other as yet undiscovered reason. However, dosing on a mg/kg basis logically requires increasing the dose for children as they age, which may result in overdosing older children. We have found (for a group of favorable responders) that when their established doses are expressed as mg/kg figures, the heavier children require a lower mg/kg dose than the lighter children according to our behavioral indices.

One possible solution to the problem of selecting the dose is to rely on measures of the serum level of the drug after a standard dose, rather than body weight, to estimate the optimal dose level. It is possible that a narrow range of serum levels delineate the minimally effective and toxic levels of the drug, and that different oral doses are necessary to get different individuals within this effective range, due to individual differences in absorption and metabolism of the drug. At the Hospital for Sick Children, we (Soldin, Hill, Chan, Swanson, & Hill, 1979) have developed a method for measuring serum level of methylphenidate (and its active metabolites), and we are currently investigating the feasibility of using serum level measures to establish optimal dose.

Directions for Future Research

In this chapter, we have discussed our procedures for identifying the significant minority of children with behavioral symptoms of hyperactivity who do not benefit from stimulant medication. We believe that our procedures can be used as a screening device that can help prevent the overdiagnosis of hyperactivity. We have also described several experiments that point out how stimulant medication works when it does have a favorable effect. Specifically, we have documented the short time course and the state-dependent effects of methylphenidate. Thus our research has been directed at identifying problems with the clinical use of stimulant drugs.

Enough studies have been conducted to establish that stimulant drugs are useful in the treatment of hyperactivity. Such studies have confirmed the clinical opinions that led to the widespread use of stimulant therapy. However, even though the use of stimulant medication is a widespread and a proven effective treatment, there are many problems with it. We believe that research should be directed toward identifying the problems with stimulant drug treatment, in order to encourage the improvement of current treatment procedures, and perhaps to point the way for the development of better forms of medication for hyperactivity.

We have not discussed alternative methods for treating hyperactivity in this chapter. Recently, dietary treatments and behavior modification techniques have been used as alternatives to medication. Feingold (1974) initiated a treatment in which artificial food additives are removed from the diets of hyperactive children, and some who have tried this treatment claim success with it. Others are skeptical (e.g., Wender, 1977). We are currently investigating this possibility in an inpatient study at the Hospital for Sick Children, and our preliminary results indicate that high doses of color do impair concentration (Swanson & Kinsbourne, in press). Treatments with behavior modification techniques have emerged that may be effective (O'Leary & Pelham, 1978; Douglas, in press-a; O'Leary & O'Leary, in press). Considerable work is being conducted in both of these areas and up-to-date summaries of the status of behavior modification techniques, as well as of dietary treatments and other forms of therapy for hyperactivity, will soon be available as published reports of two international conferences on hyperactivity (Trites, in press-a; Knights & Bakker, in press).

References

Barkley, R. A. Predicting the response of hyperkinetic children to stimulant drugs: A review. *Journal of Abnormal Child Psychology*, 1976, *4*, 327–348.

Barlow, A. *A neuropsychological study of a symptom of minimal brain dysfunction: Distractibility under levels of high and low stimulation.* Doctoral dissertation, University of Toronto, 1977.

Bax, M., & MacKeith (Eds.). *Minimal cerebral dysfunction.* In *Little club clinics in developmental medicine* (Vol. 10). London: William Heineman, 1963.

Bradley, C. The behavior of children receiving benzedrine. *American Journal of Psychiatry,* 1937, *94*, 577.

Bradley, C. Benzedrine and dexedrine in the treatment of children's behavior disorders. *Pediatrics,* 1950, *5*, 24.

Burns, J. T., House, R. F., Fensch, F. C., & Miller, J. G. Effects of magnesium pemoline and dextroamphetamine on human learning. *Science,* 1967, *152*, 849–851.

Buss, A. H., & Plomin, R. *A temperament theory of personality development.* New York: Wiley, 1975.

Cantwell, D. P. *The hyperactive child: Diagnosis, management, current research.* New York: Spectrum, 1975.

Clements, S. D. *Minimal brain dysfunction in children—terminology and identification.* Washington, D.C.: Public Health Service Publication No. 1415, 1966.

Conners, C. K. A teacher rating scale for use in drug studies with children. *American Journal of Psychiatry,* 1969, *126*, 884.

Conners, C. K. Rating scales for use in drug studies with children. *Psychopharmacology Bulletin,* Special Issue, 1973, 24–41.

Conners, C. K., & Rothschild, G. Drugs and learning in children. In J. Helmuth (Ed.), *Learning disorders* (Vol. 3). Seattle: Special child, 1968.

Conners, C. K., Eisenberg, L., & Sharpe, L. Effects of methylphenidate (Ritalin) on paired-associate learning and Porteus maze performance in emotionally disturbed children. *Journal of Consulting Psychology,* 1968, *28*, 14–22.

Conners, C. K., Rothschild, G., Eisenberg, L., & Schwartz, L. S. Dextroamphetamine sulphate in children with learning disorders: Effects on perception, learning and achievement. *Archives of General Psychiatry,* 1969, *21*, 182–190.

Dalby, T., Kinsbourne, M., Swanson, J. M., & Sobol, M. Hyperactive children's under-use of learning time: Correction by stimulant treatment. *Child Development*, 1977, *48*, 1448–1453.

Davids, A. An objective instrument for assessing hyperkinesis in children. *Journal of Learning Disorders*, 1971, *4*, 35.

Denhoff, E., Davids, A., & Hawkins, R. Effects of dextroamphetamine on hyperkinetic children: A controlled double-blind study. *Journal of Learning Disabilities*, 1971, *4*, 27.

Diagnostic and statistical manual of mental disorders (2nd ed.). Washington, D.C.: American Psychiatric Association, 1968.

Diagnostic and statistical manual of mental disorders (3rd ed.). Washington, D.C.: American Psychiatric Association, in preparation.

Douglas, V. I. Higher order processing in hyperactive children: Relevance for training. In R. Knights & D. Bakker (Eds.), *Rehabilitation, treatment and management of learning problems* (An international NATO-sponsored conference), Baltimore: University Park Press, in press. (a)

Douglas, V. I. Hyperactivity: Where do we stand? In R. Trites (Ed.), *Hyperactivity in children*. Baltimore: University Park Press, in press. (b)

Ebaugh, F. G. Neuropsychiatric sequelae of acute epidemic encephalitis in children. *American Journal of Diseases of Childhood*, 1923, *25*, 89–97.

Eisenberg, L. The clinical use of stimulant drugs in children. *Pediatrics*, 1972, *49*, 709.

Feingold, B. *Why your child is hyperactive*. New York: Random House, 1974.

Fish, B. The one-child, one-drug myth. *Archives of General Psychiatry*, 1971, *25*, 193.

Freeman, R. *An avoidance learning deficit in hyperactive children*. Doctoral dissertation, University of Waterloo, 1978.

Gittelman-Klein, R., & Klein, D. F. Are behavioral and psychometric changes related in methylphenidate treated, hyperactive children? *International Journal of Mental Health*, 1975, *4*, 182–212.

Kahn, E. & Cohen, L. H. Organic drivenness: A brain stem syndrome. *New England Journal of Medicine*, 1934, *210*, 748–756.

Kapelus, G. J., Swanson, J. M., & Kinsbourne, M. *Effects of stimulant drugs on the performance of hyperactive children in a computer controlled tracking task*. Unpublished manuscript, 1979.

Kausler, D. H. *Psychology of verbal learning and memory*. New York: Academic, 1974.

Kinsbourne, M. Minimal brain dysfunction as a neurodevelopmental lag. *Annals of the New York Academy of Sciences*, 1973, *205*, 268–273.

Kinsbourne, M. The hyperactive and impulsive child. *Ontario Medical Review*, 1975, December, 657–660.

Kinsbourne, M. The mechanism of hyperactivity. In M. Blau, I. Rapin, & M. Kinsbourne (Eds.), *Topics in child neurology*. New York: Spectrum, 1977.

Kinsbourne, M., Swanson, J. M., & Herman, D. Laboratory measurement of hyperactive children's response to stimulant medication. In E. Denhoff & L. Stein (Eds.), *Minimal brain dysfunction: A developmental approach*. New York: Masson, in press.

Knights, R., & Bakker, D. *Rehabilitation, treatment and management of learning problems* (An international NATO-sponsored conference). Baltimore: University Park Press, in press.

Kolata, G. B. Childhood hyperactivity: A new look at treatment and causes. *Science*, 1978, *199*, 515–517.

Laufer, M., & Denhoff, E. Hyperactive behavior symptoms in children. *Journal of Pediatrics*, 1957, *50*, 463.

Mock, K., Swanson, J. M., & Kinsbourne, M. *Stimulant effect in matching familiar figures:*

Changes in impulsive and distractible cognitive styles. Paper presented at the American Educational Research Association Annual Meeting, Toronto, 1978.

O'Leary, S., & O'Leary, D. Behavior therapy with hyperactive children. In R. Knights & D. Bakker (Eds.), *Rehabilitation, treatment and management of learning problems* (An international NATO-sponsored conference). Baltimore: University Park Press, in press.

O'Leary, S. G., & Pelham, W. E. Behavior therapy and withdrawal of stimulant medication with hyperactive children. *Pediatrics, 1978, 61,* 211–217.

Rapoport, J. L., Buschbaum, M. S., Zahn, T. P., Weingartner, H., Ludlow, C., & Mikkelsen, E. J. Dextroamphetamine: Cognitive and behavioral effects on normal prepubertal boys. *Science, 1978, 199,* 560–563.

Safer, D. S., & Allen, R. P. *Hyperactive children: Diagnosis and management.* Baltimore: University Park Press, 1976.

Satterfield, J. H., Cantwell, D. P., Lesser, L. I., & Podosin, R. L. Physiological studies of the hyperactive child. *American Journal of Psychiatry, 1972, 128,* 1418.

Schain, R. J., & Reynard, C. L. Observations and effects of a central stimulant drug (methylphenidate) on children with hyperactive behavior. *Pediatrics, 1975, 55,* 709.

Smith, G. M., Weitzner, M., Levenson, S. R., & Beecher, H. K. Effects of amphetamine and decobarbitol on coding and mathematical performance. *Journal of Experimental Pharmacology and Therapeutics, 1963, 141,* 100–104.

Smith, R. G. Magnesium pemoline: Lack of facilitation in human learning, memory and performance tests. *Science, 1967, 152,* 603–605.

Soldin, S. J., Hill, B. M., Chan, Yang-Pui M., Swanson, J. M., & Hill, J. E. A liquid-chromatographic analysis for ritalinic acid [α-Phenyl-α'-(2-piperidyl) acetic acid] in serum. *Clinical Chemistry, 1979, 25,* 51–54.

Solomons, G. Guidelines on the use and medical effects of psychostimulant drugs in therapy. *Journal of Learning Disabilities, 1971, 4,* 6.

Sprague, R. L., & Sleator, E. K. Effects of psychopharmacologic agents on learning disorders. *Pediatric Clinics of North America, 1973, 20,* 719.

Sprague, R. L., & Sleator, E. K. Methylphenidate in hyperkinetic children: Differences in dose effects on learning and social behavior. *Science, 1977, 198,* 1274–1276.

Stevenson, H. W. *Children's learning.* New York: Appleton-Century-Crofts, 1972.

Strauss, A. A., & Kephart, N. C. *Psychopathology and education of the brain injured child* (Vol. 2). New York: Grune & Stratton, 1955.

Strauss, A. A., & Lehtinen, L. E. *Psychopathology and education of the brain injured child* (Vol. 1). New York: Grune & Stratton, 1948.

Strother, R. C. Minimal cerebral dysfunction: A historical overview. *Annals of the New York Academy of Sciences, 1973, 205,* 6–17.

Swanson, J. M., & Kinsbourne, M. Stimulant-related state-dependent learning in hyperactive children. *Science, 1976, 192,* 1754.

Swanson, J. M., & Kinsbourne, M. Should you use stimulants to treat the hyperactive child? *Modern Medicine, 1978, 46,* 71–80.

Swanson, J. M., & Kinsbourne, M. Artificial colors and hyperactive behavior. In R. Knights & D. Bakker (Eds.), *Rehabilitation, treatment and management of learning problems* (An international NATO-sponsored conference). Baltimore: University Park Press, in press.

Swanson, J. M., Eich, J., & Kinsbourne, M. *Stimulant-related state-dependent retrieval in free recall.* Paper presented at the Psychonomic Society Meeting, San Antonio, November 1978.

Swanson, J. M., Kinsbourne, M., Roberts, W. & Zucker, K. A time response analysis of the effect of stimulant medication on the learning ability of children referred for hyperactivity. *Pediatrics, 1978, 61,* 21–29.

Swanson, J. M., Ledlow, A., & Kinsbourne, M. *The effect of methylphenidate on eye movement latencies and manual response times of hyperactive children.* In preparation.

Sykes, D. H., Douglas, V. I., Weiss, G., & Mende, K. K. Attention in hyperactive children and the effect of methylphenidate (Ritalin). *Journal of Child Psychology and Psychiatry,* 1971, *12,* 155–159.

Thomas, B., & Chess, A. *Temperament and behavior disorders in children.* New York: New York University Press, 1968.

Thurston, C. *Effects of methylphenidate (Ritalin) on selective attention in hyperactive children.* Master's thesis, University of Guelph, 1977.

Trites, R. *Hyperactivity in children.* Baltimore: University Park Press, in press. (a)

Trites, R. Epidemiological study: Hyperactivity in urban Canada. In R. Trites (Ed.), *Hyperactivity in children.* Baltimore: University Park Press, in press. (b)

Vellutino, F. R., Steger, B. M., Moyer, S. C., Harding, C. J., & Niles, J. A. Has the perceptual deficit hypothesis led us astray? *Journal of Learning Disabilities,* 1977, *10,* 54–64.

Weiss, B., & Laties, V. G. Enhancement of human performance by caffeine and the amphetamines. *Pharmacological Reviews,* 1962, *14,* 1–36.

Wender, E. Food additives and hyperkinesis. *American Journal of Diseases of Children,* 1977, *131,* 1204–1206.

Wender, P. *Minimal brain dysfunction in children.* New York: Wiley-Interscience, 1971.

Wender, P. Some speculations concerning a possible biochemical basis of minimal brain dysfunction. *Annals of the New York Academy of Sciences,* 1973, *205,* 18–28.

Werry, J. G., & Quay, H. C. The prevalence of behavior symptoms in younger elementary school children. *American Journal of Orthopsychiatry,* 1971, *41,* 136–140.

10 *Attention and Cognitive Style in Children*

Tamar Zelniker and Wendell E. Jeffrey

Introduction

Invariably, whether growing out of the psychoanalytic concept of ego functions (Klein, 1958; Gardner, Holtzman, Klein, Linton, & Spence, 1959), the Wernerian construct of psychological differentiation (Witkin, Dyk, Faterson, Goodenough, & Karp, 1962), or Kagan's notion of conceptual tempo (Kagan, Rosman, Day, Albert, & Phillips, 1964), research on cognitive styles is based on perceptual tasks that reflect individual differences in some aspect of perceptual selectivity. Most influential in determining the direction of current research were Kagan (Kagan, Moss, & Sigel, 1963; Kagan *et al.*, 1964) and Witkin (Witkin *et al.*, 1962). Initially, Kagan and his colleagues were concerned primarily with the development of children's categorizing behavior, and this work led to the Conceptual Style Test. It is probably not too unfair to say that this test has not proved as useful as might have been expected given its intuitive appeal.

Kagan's research on cognitive tempo, however, has been the source of a tremendous amount of subsequent research activity. In spite of a number of measurement problems regarding validity (Block, Block, & Harrington, 1974, 1975; Kagan & Messer, 1975) and reliability (Ault, Mitchell, & Hartmann, 1976; Egeland & Weinberg, 1976), cognitive tempo has been shown to be a rather consistent and pervasive trait. Thus, the classification of subjects as reflective or impulsive on the basis of their speed and accuracy on a Matching Familiar Figures Test (MFFT) has been found to remain stable over time (Kagan, 1965; Yando & Kagan, 1970). Furthermore, the tendency to perform impulsively, i.e., fast and inaccurately, or reflectively,

Tamar Zelniker • Department of Psychology, Tel Aviv University, Ramat Aviv, Israel. Wendell E. Jeffrey • University of California, Los Angeles, California 90024. The preparation of this chapter was facilitated by a grant from the Research Committee of the University of California, Los Angeles, and by grants MH6639 and MH25076 from the United States Public Health Service.

i.e., slowly and accurately, has been observed across various tasks from visual discrimination (Heider, 1971; Kagan, 1966a) to concept formation (Nuessle, 1972).

Other than impulsivity-reflectivity, the dimension of cognitive style most extensively investigated has been field dependence/independence or field articulation (Witkin *et al.*, 1962; Witkin, Moore, Goodenough, & Cox, 1975). Though by no means identical, the two dimensions of style seem to have certain common denominators, as indicated by the consistent yet moderate overlap between them (Campbell & Douglas, 1972; Keogh & Donlon, 1972; Massaro, 1975). For example, both field articulation (Witkin *et al.*, 1975) and cognitive tempo (Zelniker & Jeffrey, 1976) have been characterized by global versus analytic information-processing tendencies. In the area of selective attention, performance of field-dependent subjects (Dargel & Kirk, 1971; Davis, 1972), as well as of impulsives (Hartley, 1976), was reported to be more influenced by the salience of stimulus attributes than that of field-independent and reflective subjects. In spite of some basic similarities, however, the two styles are not highly correlated. This is not necessarily paradoxical. It is quite conceivable that there are several dimensions of cognitive style and that some pairs of dimensions are orthogonal while other pairs are correlated to different extents due to common factors.

Judging from research in the last decade, the most celebrated aspect of cognitive style seems to be its relationship to quality of performance. Within the dichotomy defining a cognitive style, one style group (e.g., impulsives or field-dependents) is typically associated with poor performance (inaccurate, hasty, inappropriate, and inflexible), while the second style group (e.g., reflectives or field-independents) is associated with superior performance (accurate, analytic, and adaptable). As data supporting such a differential association have been accumulating it has become increasingly popular to equate differences in cognitive style with differential rates of development. Specifically, it is suggested that impulsivity and field dependence reflect a developmental lag or "arrest." However, a basic assumption underlying the study of cognitive style is that of homogeneity of intelligence. Indeed, with but few exceptions, cognitive styles have not been found to be closely related to intelligence (Kagan, 1965; Messer, 1976; Witkin *et al.*, 1975; Wright & Vlietstra, 1977). Since a generalized developmental lag is not likely to occur without a concomitant deficiency in intelligence, it seems necessary to evaluate carefully the developmental lag hypothesis.

The Confounding of Cognitive Style and Development

Many of the individual differences in cognitive style identified by the various measures of information processing parallel the age differences observed with these measures. Relevant to this issue, Wright and Vlietstra (1977) highlight various instances of correspondence between the performance of impulsive children and the performance typical of younger children. For example, passive visual exploration versus directed search behavior seems characteristic of both younger as compared to older children, and impulsive as compared to reflective children. Furthermore, developmental trends are found in the performance measures defining cognitive styles. That is, children become more field-independent and more reflective as they grow older (Kagan, 1965, 1966b; Kagan et al., 1964; Witkin, Goodenough, & Karp, 1967).

While we are completely aware that parallels between cognitive style and developmental trends indeed exist, one of our main objectives is to challenge the conclusion favored by many researchers in the field, namely, that cognitive style differences represent nothing more than differences in rates of maturation. One argument against the developmental lag interpretation is that, carried to its logical conclusion, this interpretation would imply that in adulthood individual differences in information processing cease to exist. This is an assumption that no serious observer of human cognitive behavior would entertain. In fact, the existence of substantial individual differences in diverse aspects of information processing by adults is well documented. For example, several studies have demonstrated individual differences in speed of information coding (Hunt, Frost, & Lunneborg, 1973; Hunt, Lunneborg, & Lewis, 1975). Furthermore, consistent individual differences in speed and efficiency of iconic storage (Sperling, 1960), in readout from short-term acoustic store (Moore & Massaro, 1973), and in other memory-related functions (Hunt et al., 1973) tend to be so large that experiments on general processing principles in these areas necessitate careful design to control for interindividual variation.

Some individual differences in processes related to cognitive style do parallel different developmental levels for these processes. One cannot automatically assume, however, that such processes would develop eventually along the same "normal" lines. Rather, processing differences may endure and others may interact with environmental-social factors to produce permanent differences. According to this line of reasoning, another argument against the developmental lag hypothesis is that, in spite of age-related trends in most cognitive style measures, individual differences in cognitive style may prevail through adulthood. Indeed, several longitudinal projects (Kagan, 1971; Kagan & Moss, 1962; Witkin et al., 1967) provide evidence that some aspects of individual differences in cognitive style remain stable from childhood through adolescence and early adulthood, or at the very least, that some early differences in cognitive style predict later differences of a similar nature.

Developmental trends in various measures of cognitive style suggest that as they grow older, children who lag in some aspect of processing tend

to perform in a manner increasingly similar to those who are more developmentally advanced. However, what we might be observing is a ceiling effect
that obscures individual differences in performance. As children grow older
they become more competent processors. The variability in performance on
many tasks is, therefore, reduced, and thus differences between cognitive
styles appear deceptively attenuated. Furthermore, we assert that even if
children of different cognitive styles may eventually meet the same problem-solving criterion on some tasks, they do not necessarily reach that point
by the same route. Therefore, the main purpose of the present chapter is to
demonstrate that cognitive style differences in attention and performance
may exist independent of maturation. It is argued that in certain instances,
differences in performance may be due to an interaction between style and
specific task demands rather than to differences in general ability, tempo-
rary or permanent, in problem-solving competence.

   An extensive review of the cognitive style literature is neither feasible
nor appropriate within the scope of the present chapter. Instead, we have
chosen to focus on a small, yet representative, sample of works within the
reflection-impulsivity area, notably, those dealing directly or indirectly
with differences in attentional processes. For a broader and more detailed
coverage, the reader may refer to comprehensive reviews of reflection-impulsivity (Kagan & Kogan, 1970; Messer, 1976; Wright & Vlietstra, 1977)
and to several excellent reviews of field dependence/independence (Goodenough, 1976; Witkin et al., 1975). For a discussion of methods of assessing
individual differences in cognitive style in relation to developmental
changes, see Kagan (1969, 1971) and Wohlwill (1973).

Attention and Cognitive Style: A Developmental Lag Approach

   The role of attention as a critical first step in problem solving and
learning has been clearly documented (Gibson, 1969; Hagen & Hale, 1973;
Odom & Guzman, 1972; Wright & Vlietstra, 1977; Zeaman & House,
1963). Therefore, quite naturally, much of the work on individual differences in information processing has also focused on attention, most specifically on visual attention.

   Receptor orientation is an obvious aspect of attention that is fairly
easily measured. In the visual scanning procedure, the child's direction-of-
gaze is monitored via either continuous filming of the eye (Ault, Crawford,
& Jeffrey, 1972; McCluskey & Wright, 1975; Wright, 1971) or discrete
photographs taken in quick succession (Drake, 1970). The general tenor of
the findings of visual scanning studies with the MFFT and similar match-
to-sample tasks has been that reflective children perform a more exhaustive
and systematic search than impulsive children. Furthermore, reflective chil-

dren were more analytic than impulsives as evidenced by a larger number of homologous comparisons, i.e., successive fixations on corresponding components of different figures. When different age groups were included, older children and adults were in general more systematic and exhaustive in their scanning, and they engaged in homologous comparisons more than younger subjects. Given these data, the popularity of the developmental lag interpretation is not surprising.

Investigations of style differences in information processing on tests other than the MFFT included various forms of visual matching tasks (Odom, McIntyre, & Neale, 1971), incidental learning (Weiner & Berzonsky, 1975), and concept formation (Nuessle, 1972; Ault, 1973; Denney, 1973; McKinney, 1973; Zelniker, Renan, Sorer, & Shavit, 1977). A training and transfer procedure designed by Pick (1965) was employed by Odom et al. (1971) in an attempt to discern what aspects of the stimuli in a matching task were processed by impulsive and reflective children. Subjects were presented with a line drawing of a standard geometric form and five comparison stimuli: two identical to the standard and three varying from it in some feature. Initially, subjects were trained to identify the stimuli that were identical to the standard form. A subsequent transfer test was administered to assess the type of perceptual learning that had occurred during the initial discrimination learning. One condition, designed to identify prototype learning, used the same standard forms as in the training condition, but new variants. A second condition, designed to identify distinctive feature learning, used new standard forms but the features distinguishing the variants from the standard were the same as in the training condition. A control condition included both new standards and new variants.

Overall, impulsive children made more discrimination errors than reflective children in the transfer task. Reflective children made fewest errors in the distinctive feature condition, indicating that their dominant processing strategy involved learning of features differentiating the stimuli in the array. Neither prototype nor distinctive feature learning characterized processing of impulsive children: their performance in the experimental conditions was not significantly better than in the control condition. Inasmuch as the distinctive features learning strategy had been found most efficient for successful discrimination (Pick, 1965), and the number of discrimination errors that children make as a result of overlooking distinctive feature differences decreases with age (Gibson, Gibson, Pick, & Osser, 1962), it could be argued that the impulsives' poorer performance was due to a developmental lag.

Particularly relevant to the analysis of the role of attention in cognitive style is a study by Weiner and Berzonsky (1975) employing an incidental learning paradigm designed by Hagen (1972) and developed by Hale and

Piper (1973). There were two different sets of stimulus cards. One set included six *pictorial* stimulus cards. On each card, a line drawing of an animal was paired with a drawing of a household object. The animal represented the central (relevant) component of each stimulus, and the household object was the incidental (irrelevant) component. Central learning required that for each set of cards, children learn the location of relevant components within the array. In a subsequent phase, the extent of incidental learning that had taken place during central learning was assessed. In this phase, children were asked to indicate which household object had been paired with each animal in the central learning phase. In the second set of stimuli, a colored geometric figure (e.g., red circle or blue square) appeared on each of six stimulus cards. The task was analogous to that just described. In this case, shape was the central component of each stimulus and color was the incidental component. In the central phase, children learned the location of the stimuli according to their shape, then, in the incidental learning test, were asked to indicate which color had been associated with each shape.

There were no differences between impulsive and reflective second- and fourth-graders in any of the conditions, nor between impulsive and reflective sixth-graders with shape stimuli. With pictorial stimuli, reflective 6th-graders displayed significantly less incidental learning and more central learning than impulsives. Analyses within cognitive style groups were performed to examine the relationship between central and incidental learning. It should be noted that in the shape stimuli, color was superimposed on shape and the two dimensions were, therefore, considered to be integral components of the total stimulus. In the pictorial stimuli, however, the central and incidental components were separate and were, therefore, considered to be nonintegral.

A positive correlation between central and incidental learning scores was regarded as indicating that the two components were in fact processed as integral parts of the total stimulus. Not surprisingly, both groups processed as integral the superimposed dimensions of shape stimuli. As noted by the authors, it is difficult to attend selectively to a relevant dimension when it is superimposed on an irrelevant one. The separate dimensions of pictorial stimuli were processed as nonintegral by reflectives, as shown in the negative correlation between central and incidental scores. According to the authors, such processing involved selective attention to central features during initial learning. By contrast, the positive correlation between central and incidental scores of impulsive sixth-graders indicated that they processed pictorial stimuli as integral, and, therefore, that they had not attended selectively to central stimulus features. Their poor attention to central features explains their inferior central learning performance in comparison to same-age reflective children. Inasmuch as the efficiency of selective attention increases with age, processing of pictorial stimuli by sixth-grade impulsive children was interpreted to reflect a developmental lag in the onset of effective utilization of selective attention.

With impulsives performing in general less accurately than reflectives, and with the recurring parallel between developmental trends and individual differences, it is not surprising that the various investigators found it appealing and parsimonious to resort to a developmental lag interpretation. As an alternative to the developmental lag hypothesis, however, we propose that individual differences in performance in many instances reflect age-independent differences in style of processing.

Style: Individual Differences in Attention Deployment

Problem solving is a multistage, complex, sequence of information processing. The critical question is what aspects of information processing vary across individuals yet are consistent within individuals and can thus be considered dimensions of style. Odom has demonstrated quite clearly how individual differences in attention may affect subsequent processing stages. For example, he has shown that selective attention determines whether or not one performs successfully not only on a simple matching task (Odom & Guzman, 1972; Odom & Mumbauer, 1971) but also on tasks that presumably reflect the individual's stage of cognitive development (Odom, 1977; Odom, Astor, & Cunningham, 1975).

At a more general level, individuals may differ in the degree to which they attend to the detail contained in visual stimuli. For example, a stimulus may be processed globally as a gestalt, or alternatively, it may be broken down into component details or dimensions, with each component attended to separately. The complexity and structure of a stimulus are highly relevant to this discrimination. The more complex a stimulus and the more distinguishable, or salient, its components, the greater the extent to which those components are likely to be analyzed.

A theoretical analysis corroborated by empirical evidence on the role of the stimulus in determining types of information processing has been offered by Garner (Garner, 1970, 1974). Garner proposes that stimulus components or dimensions may be integral (e.g., brightness and saturation), or separable (e.g., size of circle and orientation of its diameter). Integrality versus nonintegrality in processing has been assessed by examining speed of sorting on the basis of stimulus dimensions under three conditions. Sorting of stimuli varying on a single dimension serves as the baseline to which sorting on two dimensions that are redundant or orthogonal is compared. With nonintegral dimensions, performance in all three conditions is approximately equal. With integral dimensions, there is facilitation of performance with redundant dimensions and interference with orthogonal dimensions as compared to performance in a single-dimension condition.

Garner cites evidence demonstrating that, depending on task and conditions, nonintegral dimensions may be processed as integral and, furthermore, that when two dimensions are processed as integral, they are in effect combined by the processor into a single, new stimulus dimension.

According to Garner, processing depends on the nature of the stimulus and the manner in which it interacts with the specific task or response required. We would go one step further and propose that both the stimulus characteristics and the task requirements in turn interact with the individual's spontaneous processing tendency. It may be expected, therefore, that the same stimulus dimensions may be processed as integral by some individuals and as nonintegral by others.

Data in Support of Individual Differences in Attention Deployment

In order to demonstrate differences in style of attending we would first need to identify the same individual differences in processing of complex stimuli in different age groups. A developmental study on the effect of irrelevant information on speeded classification (Strutt, Anderson, & Well, 1975) is a case in point. Six-, 9-, and 12-year-olds, as well as adults, were administered a sorting task. Stimulus information was defined according to three binary dimensions: form (circle or square), line within the form (horizontal or vertical), and star (above or below the form). A stimulus card consisted of one relevant dimension that served as the basis for sorting, and zero, one, or two irrelevant dimensions. Although the study focused on developmental trends in selective attention, pertinent to the present analysis is the report of individual differences in processing that cut across ages. In all age groups the majority of the subjects processed orthogonal dimensions as integral; cards containing irrelevant orthogonal dimensions were sorted more slowly than cards containing no irrelevant information. However, a small percentage of the subjects in each age group sorted cards with orthogonal dimensions as fast as cards with a single dimension. These results indicate that individuals differ in the way they process dimensions of complex stimuli; while many subjects processed these dimensions as integral, some individuals, regardless of age, processed the dimensions as nonintegral.

Additional evidence pertaining to individual differences in information processing comes indirectly from developmental research on breadth of attention. Various experimental paradigms have been employed to assess the number of stimulus dimensions attended to by children of different ages. Major paradigms include optional shift following discrimination learning (Adams & Shepp, 1975), concept learning (Rydberg & Arnberg, 1976), incidental learning (Hagen, 1972; Hagen & Hale, 1973; Hale & Piper, 1973), and stimulus matching (Odom & Guzman, 1972; Odom & Mumbauer, 1971).

In the experiment by Adams and Shepp (1975) the number of dimensions attended to (one or two) was determined on the basis of test trials following optional shift learning of nursery school and second-grade children. The main finding of the study was that various overtraining manipulations had differential effects on breadth of attention of nursery school and second-grade children. However, performance of control groups following optional shift without overtraining indicated that the distribution of children attending to two dimensions (60%) and to one dimension (40%) was the same in the two age groups. On the basis of this evidence one might conclude that there are age-independent individual differences in preferred manner of attention deployment.

A more direct measure of attention deployment was obtained by Rydberg and Arnberg (1976), who investigated breadth of attention in haptic (active touch) concept learning. With each of four items exemplifying values of a different tactile dimension, the subjects' breadth of attention was monitored by recording the number of objects examined (by touch alone) on each trial. The task was designed such that problems could be solved by attending either to a single dimension or to several dimensions on each trial. The larger the number of dimensions examined per trial, the greater the memory load.

All adults and all 11-year-olds solved the problems, but only half of the 8-year-olds arrived at correct solutions. Dimensional scanning data indicated that the number of dimensions scanned during a given trial increased with age: the scanning of four dimensions constituted 26% of the 8-year-olds' precriterion trials and 77% of the adults', whereas single-dimension scanning accounted for 47% of the 8-year-olds' and only 8% of the adults' precriterion trials. The most likely interpretation of these data would have been that the developmental increase in breadth of attention contributed to the larger proportion of subjects who could solve the problems. However, precriterion analysis of spontaneous attentional tendencies indicated that 8-year-old nonsolvers attended to more dimensions per trial than did 8-year-old solvers. This finding is discordant with the above interpretation, which relates broader attention to successful solution. Since broader attention in this task led to a greater memory load, it is reasonable to assume that for the 8-year-old nonsolvers, broad attention resulted in memory overload, which increased task difficulty beyond their capacity.

Although a direct assessment of individual differences in breadth of attention in this study is not available, rough calculations suggest that the same trend in attention deployment appeared in different ages. Precriterion performance indicated that 77% of the adults' trials involved four-dimension scanning. According to additional analyses, 55% of the 8-year-olds were nonsolvers and were observed to employ a broad attention strategy. Further, 26% of the trials of 8-year-old solvers were characterized by four-dimension scanning. Together, these data suggest that most of the trials of 8-year-olds, like those of the adults, involved broad attention deployment. The reported increase with age in breadth of attention and number of subjects who solve the problems correctly may be given a new interpretation based on an interaction between age-independent individual differences in breadth of attention and developmental changes in memory capacity. With the increase in memory capacity with age, older subjects find the task easy enough so that those who prefer to attend to several dimensions are able to do so without a loss in proficiency.

More direct support for the existence of individual differences in breadth of attention comes from a similar study that provides detailed analysis of processing strategies in adult subjects (Bruner, Goodnow, & Austin, 1956). A visually presented concept attainment test included geometrical figures varying on different dimensions such as shape, color, number, etc. In the course of each problem, the subject was presented with a set of stimulus cards, one at a time, and asked to identify a preselected concept that constituted either one specific dimension, such as "red" or "circles," or a specific combination of dimensions, such as "red circles" or "two squares." With the presentation of each card, the subject was told whether the card did or did not include the concept and was asked to state what he thought the concept was.

Adults were found to vary in the number of dimensions they included in their hypotheses. Some adults included several dimensions while others included only a single dimension. In light of considerable within-subject consistency, lack of uniformity in performance could not be viewed in terms of error-variance. Instead, Bruner *et al.* (1956) coined the terms *whole-scanning* and *detail-scanning* to describe the extremes of a hypothetical processing strategy continuum. Whole-scanning refers to a strategy characterized by hypotheses that include a large number of stimulus dimensions, while detail- or part-scanning is characterized by hypotheses that include only a few or a single stimulus dimension. Even though detail-scanning entailed a greater memory load, both strategies led to correct solutions. Thus, with sufficient mental capacity, quality of performance does not distinguish between broad and narrow attention strategies insofar as both lead to successful performance.

Attention Deployment and Task Demands

The term *breadth of attention* presumably pertains to how a stimulus is processed. Narrow attention, for example, is indicative of focusing or analytic strategy whereby the individual's tendency is to break a stimulus into its dimensions or components and attend to, or assess, each component separately. Broad attention suggests a global strategy of attention deployment whereby a complex stimulus is processed as a whole or stimulus dimensions are processed as integral (see Garner, 1970, 1974). Evidence reflecting this tendency is particularly strong in cases where broad attention is employed even if it increases task difficulty beyond the individual's ability to perform successfully, as was evident in the performance of Rydberg and Arnberg's 8-year-old nonsolvers. Just as striking, perhaps, is the predisposition to employ broad attention even when, in principle (regardless of memory capacity), only narrow attention can lead to a correct solution. For example, a task like the MFFT requires analysis of stimuli into component details and careful examination of each detail across several stimuli. Although broad attention in this case does not entail memory overload, processing the stimuli globally or as gestalts simply does not permit a correct solution. It would appear, therefore, that an individual who prefers to employ broad or global attention with tasks that require analysis of stimuli into components is not likely to perform the tasks successfully. Such tasks should, however, be conducive to good performance by individuals with narrow attention deployment. Conversely, a task requiring more global analysis would be compatible with broad attention but incompatible with narrow attention deployment.

Breadth of Attention and Cognitive Style

Assessing the various tasks on which impulsive children have consistently performed more poorly than reflective children, it appears that by and large, successful performance required an analytic approach or, in terms of the preceding discussion, narrow attention. This requirement and the absence of impulsives' inferiority in general intelligence raises the possibility that the impulsives' apparently deficient performance stems from the incompatibility between their preference for broad attention deployment and the narrow attention required by the tasks. Furthermore, in most of those tasks, stimulus details relevant for correct solutions were not readily discriminable or salient. Consequently, the difficulty of the required analysis was magnified, particularly for individuals with broad attention tendency.

The hypothesis of an association between cognitive style and breadth of attention maintains that reflectives have a greater tendency to use narrow attention or analytic processing, whereas impulsives have a greater tendency to use broad attention or global processing. To test this hypothesis, 12-year-old children classified as impulsive or reflective on the basis of their performance on the MFFT, were administered the Bruner et al. (1956) concept attainment task (Zelniker & Jeffrey, 1976). The results demonstrated that these cognitive style groups indeed differed in their attention strategies. Impulsives employed a larger number of dimensions in their hypotheses than did reflectives, indicating that impulsives used mostly a whole-scanning strategy, whereas reflectives used a detail- or part-scanning strategy. Clearly, impulsives showed greater breadth of attention than did reflectives. Yet, impulsive and reflective children did not differ in number of problems solved or efficiency of solution scores. Unlike Rydberg and Arnberg's 8-year-olds, 12-year-olds in the Zelniker and Jeffrey (1976) study had memory capacity sufficiently large to accomodate either strategy with equal proficiency. The results, therefore, reflect individual preferences in breadth of attention that correspond to cognitive styles rather than differences in problem-solving competence in this task.

Taken together, the observation of a difference in attention strategies of impulsives and reflectives and the notion that there should be compatibility between attention deployment and task demands suggest the following hypotheses. If by changing either instructions or stimuli, breadth of attention required by a particular task can be varied, individuals in each cognitive style group should perform better when the requirements are compatible with their preferred attention strategy. Specifically, impulsives should perform better when the task requires broader attention or more "global" analysis than when the task requires analysis of details. Reflectives should show the opposite trend and perform more poorly when "global" rather than "detail" analysis is required.

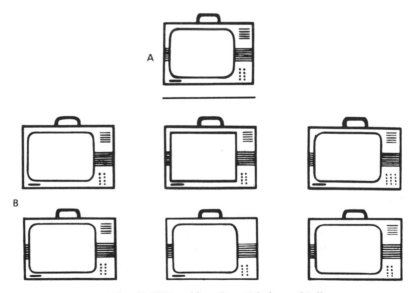

FIGURE 1. A detail MFFT problem. From Zelniker and Jeffrey, 1976.

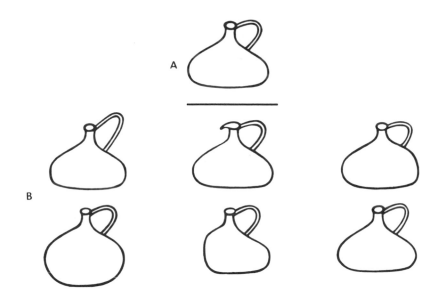

FIGURE 2. A global MFFT problem. From Zelniker and Jeffrey, 1976.

To test this hypothesis, Zelniker and Jeffrey (1976) manipulated the level of stimulus analysis (detail vs. global) necessary for problem solution. For this purpose they designed two sets of match-to-standard problems similar to the MFFT. In one set, the variants differed from the standard in some detail inside the figure, thus requiring analysis of details (see Figure 1). In the second set, the differences were in the contour of the variants, thus requiring global analysis (see Figure 2). As can be seen from Figure 2, the global items can be most readily processed as an integral figure or a gestalt and do not lend themselves easily to detail analysis. Moreover, the figures in the global problems were drawn such that a comparison of the whole figure with the standard would be most efficient for executing the match. Breaking those figures down to small components was expected to interfere with, or at least decrease, the efficiency of the comparisons. According to the principles proposed above, it was expected that impulsives would perform better and reflectives more poorly on global than on detail MFFT problems.

The results indicated that overall, global and detail problems were of equal difficulty level, as reflected by the error scores. As predicted, impulsives were significantly more accurate on global than on detail problems, whereas reflectives were significantly more accurate on detail than on global problems. In addition, impulsives were less accurate than reflectives on both the standard MFFT and the detail MFFT but not on the global

MFFT. These findings suggest that the standard MFFT indeed requires analysis of stimuli into small details and that impulsives may be inferior on that task due to their global attention strategy.

Attention and Cognitive Style: The Developmental Lag Interpretation Reevaluated

As we have seen in the previous sections, inferior performance of impulsive as compared to reflective children of the same age often has been assumed to indicate that impulsives were lagging behind reflectives developmentally. However, analyses of the interaction between attention strategies and task demands suggest that such a conclusion may not be justified. These two types of children may simply differ in their characteristic approach to stimuli, and the particular tasks employed in research have tended to favor the approach taken by reflective subjects.

The matching procedure in the standard MFFT as well as the distinctive features learning task (Odom *et al.*, 1971) require attention to details. Similarly, in a concept formation study (Nuessle, 1972), in which impulsives performed more poorly than reflectives, correct solutions could be attained only by forming successive hypotheses, each based on only one of four simultaneously presented stimulus dimensions. In their study on incidental learning, Weiner and Berzonsky (1975) ascribed inferior central learning of impulsive children to a developmental lag in their attention deployment mechanism. However, efficient central learning in this task required exclusive attention to central features, which is incompatible with the global processing strategy impulsives tend to use.

A task often employed to investigate problem solving of impulsive and reflective children is based on the "20 Questions" test, developed by Mosher and Hornsby (1966). Reflectives tend to ask proportionally more constraint-seeking questions than do impulsives (Ault, 1973; Denney, 1973; McKinney, 1973), and thus, the latter have been labeled less mature and less efficient problem-solvers. Paradoxically, however, the assessment of actual effectiveness of solutions, as reflected by either number of questions to solution (Denney, 1973) or removal of incorrect pictures (Ault, 1973), has revealed no differences between impulsive and reflective children.

The above paradox can be resolved if we assume that the higher proportion of constraint-seeking questions asked by reflectives indicates their tendency to isolate stimulus details or dimensions rather than a more mature cognitive strategy of problem solving. According to this assumption, what appears to be a constraint-seeking question (e.g., "Is it red?") may be in effect a question about a detail of a particular picture rather than about a dimension relevant to the whole array of pictures.

To examine this interpretation, impulsive and reflective second-graders were asked to solve the 20 Questions problems via a sorting procedure (Zelniker *et al.*, 1977). Pictures were sorted into as many groups as the subject wished to form. The subject then selected one of the groups and asked the experimenter whether the correct picture was in that group. By further sorting of the appropriate group and subsequent feedback from the experimenter, the subject proceeded to narrow down the size of the relevant group until the appropriate picture was identified. Sorting based on a single dimension, e.g., color (red vs. blue), yields two groups. Sorting based on two dimensions, e.g., color (red vs. blue), and size (small vs. large), yields four groups: small-red, small-blue, large-red, large-blue. Thus, the larger the number of dimensions employed simultaneously as the basis for sorting, the larger the number of groups.

Impulsive children, who are likely to attend to several dimensions simultaneously, were expected to sort the pictures into a large number of groups than reflective children, who tend to focus on a single dimension at a time. The results were in line with these expectations. At the same time, there was no difference in number of questions to solution asked by impulsives and reflectives, indicating that children in the two groups were equally efficient. The data suggest that the types of questions asked by reflective and impulsive children reflected their preferred perceptual processing rather than problem-solving maturity.

We have shown here how, by analyzing task demands in cognitive style research, one finds that various tasks emerge as being biased in favor of an analytic processing strategy used typically by reflective children. We have demonstrated that the influence of attention strategy on problem solving becomes evident when stimuli or task characteristics are varied within a specific experimental paradigm (Zelniker & Jeffrey, 1976; Zelniker *et al.*, 1977). In support of the proposed interaction between cognitive style and task demands we also have shown that with a mere change of stimuli or mode of solution in the tasks we have used, problem-solving deficiency of impulsive children disappeared.

Cognitive Styles: Separate but Unequal?

In the foregoing analysis, we have delineated how the difficulty impulsive children encounter with various tasks may stem from the incompatibility between task demands and their global processing tendency rather than an inferior problem-solving competence. If this is true, each cognitive style group should perform better when task demands are compatible than when they are incompatible with their preferred tendencies. Accordingly, children in each cognitive style group should be equally successful when task demands are compatible with their attention strategy.

Within-group comparisons in the study by Zelniker and Jeffrey (1976), supported this contention. Impulsives performed better on tasks requiring global analysis than on tasks requiring detail analysis, whereas reflectives showed the opposite trend. Yet, between-groups comparisons indicated that the proposed interaction between cognitive style and task demands lacked complete symmetry. That is, reflectives were superior to impulsives on analytic tasks but impulsives were not superior to reflectives when global attention was required. This lack of symmetry deserves special attention.

From a methodological point of view, these trends may reflect a built-in bias of "global" tasks. Stimuli such as the global MFFT problems (see Figure 2) employed by Zelniker and Jeffrey (1976) may not lend themselves readily to detail analysis. Thus, while allowing impulsives to use their preferred global mode of processing, these stimuli also facilitate or even enhance global processing in reflectives. By contrast, the analytic MFFT problems (Figure 1), which require detail analysis for successful solution, nevertheless allow both analytic and global processing. By virtue of their structure, then, these analytic problems provide for greater divergence of performance than do global problems, permitting impulsives to employ the inappropriate, global mode of stimulus processing and thus enhancing the likelihood that reflectives will manifest superior performance.

Cognitive style differences may also be evaluated in the context of cerebral hemisphere specialization. Recent findings suggest that the right hemisphere performs mainly gestalt, global, parallel processing, whereas the left hemisphere performs mainly analytic, detail, sequential processing (Bogen, 1975; Gazzaniga, 1975; Nebes, 1975). Modes of processing associated with the left and the right hemisphere thus correspond, respectively, to reflective and impulsive processing strategies. Because research has shown that individuals differ in their reliance on one or the other hemisphere, one might hypothesize that reflectives rely more on a left hemisphere and impulsives on a right hemisphere mode of processing. Given that our culture and educational system are biased in favor of detail, analytic processing, children with global processing strategies are at a disadvantage (Bogen, 1975; Gazzaniga, 1975). With this bias, the impulsives' inclination to use more global processing is not likely to be encouraged and consequently, their preferred global strategy may not develop as well as the reflectives' analytic strategy. Cognitive style asymmetry may thus be attributed to Western hemisphere cultural bias in favor of left hemisphere, analytic processing strategies.

An alternative interpretation of cognitive style asymmetry may be found in a model formulated by Broadbent (1977), which maintains that processing of global and detail aspects of stimuli is hierarchically and sequentially organized. He posits two separate visual processing systems

tuned to different spatial frequencies with high and low frequency designat-
ing, respectively, smaller and larger distances between receptor-stimulated
regions. A detail, high-frequency system detects small, sharply defined
spots and a second, global, low-frequency system, detects large, ill-defined
shapes. The high-frequency system is assumed to be nested within the low-
frequency system and to process stimuli more slowly. According to the
model, initial processing that provides general information is performed by
the low-frequency system. This processing is quick, relatively passive, and
effortless. The second stage of processing involves analysis of details. This
is an active, effortful, and more time-consuming process performed by the
high-frequency system.

Within this model, the impulsive child would be seen as less likely to
advance to the second stage of processing and thus to respond globally,
fast, and inaccurately where detail analysis is required. The reflective child,
on the other hand, may be assumed to proceed readily from the first to the
second stage and to expend considerable time and effort on analysis of
details. Broadbent's model suggests that reflective children, who tend to
focus on stimulus details, begin the analysis with global processing. Accordingly, the fact that reflectives engage in stage I processing, albeit
briefly, may account for their ability to solve problems requiring global
processing as accurately as do impulsives.

The fact that reflectives perform global tasks more slowly than impulsives (Zelniker & Jeffrey, 1976) suggests, however, that processing strategies of the two cognitive style groups differ even when the two groups
perform equally accurately. For example, reflectives may go through the
initial processing stage relatively fast and, regardless of task demands,
activate the second stage in order to perform high-frequency analysis. Only
after this strategy is determined to be inappropriate do they revert to responding on the basis of stage I processing, hence the extra time they
require for low-frequency analysis.

An Effort Dimension of Cognitive Style

In addition to relating breadth of analysis to speed of processing,
Broadbent's model proposes a correlation between processing systems and
the amount of effort expended by the processor. Quick, low-frequency
(global) processing is suggested to be rather effortless, whereas high-frequency (detail) processing is seen as an activity that requires considerable
effort. It may be assumed, therefore, that impulsives, who tend to engage in
more global analysis, expend less effort than reflectives, who tend to perform more detail analysis.

Several possible patterns of relationships may exist between variations
in effort mobilization and the individual's preference for detail versus global

processing. One such possibility is that the amount of effort committed by an individual may influence the strategy that the individual would be likely to employ. Alternatively, the amount of effort expended may be a function of the requirements of the information-processing strategy the individual tends to employ. Another factor that might effect the amount of effort invested in information processing is the individual's total available capacity and level of arousal (Kahneman, 1973). Low total capacity or suboptimal arousal may lead to suboptimal mobilization of effort, which may, in turn, underlie the impulsives' tendency for global processing.

Other potential sources of variance in effort mobilization include motivational-cognitive and metacognitive factors. One variable is the individual's causal attribution of success and failure in learning and problem-solving. As a result of repeated failure experience, a child may learn to attribute failure to enduring poor ability, and success to an external cause such as luck. If impulsives maintain such a pattern of causal attribution, they would tend to mobilize minimal effort. Another factor that has a potentially important role in the mobilization of sufficient effort for the performance of a particular task is the realistic estimation of task difficulty (Brown, 1977). Assessment of task difficulty is one of several cognitive controls commonly referred to as metacognitive processes (Brown, 1975, 1977; Flavell, Friedrichs, & Hoyt, 1970; Kreutzer, Leonard, & Flavell, 1975). A problem may stem from either under- or overestimation of difficulty. Impulsives may underestimate task difficulty due to low criterion for accuracy and, therefore, mobilize insufficient effort. Alternatively, an impulsive child, as a result of a history of failures, is likely to perceive moderately difficult or even easy tasks as beyond his capability. As findings based on pupillary dilation (Peavler, 1974) and behavioral measures (Shulman & Greenberg, 1971) indicate, when a task is perceived as exceeding one's capability, effort mobilization is likely to be suspended.

The capacity-arousal hypothesis suggests that there may be a built-in limitation in the information-processing system of impulsive children. However, the hypothesis based on cognitive and metacognitive variables do not espouse a general deficiency in problem-solving competence. Further, there is evidence indicating that it is possible to alter children's subjective causal attribution of success and failure (Dweck, 1975), and to improve performance of impulsive children by providing training in appropriate use of metacognitive processes (Meichenbaum & Goodman, 1971). Such modifications in metacognitive processes should enable impulsive children to realize their partially hidden potential. It would appear, therefore, that the identification of sources of variation in cognitive style is necessary for a better understanding of style asymmetry and for constructing optimal learning conditions for children having different styles of information processing.

A Word of Caution

In this chapter we have rejected the developmental lag interpretation of cognitive style in favor of an approach that focused primarily on the role of attention and considered secondarily the role of effort and metacognition in individual differences in information processing. The global–detail distinction was shown to be particularly useful in analyzing not only processing tendencies but also stimulus characteristics and task demands, as well as sources of bias resulting from specific interactions between processor and task variables. In those instances where global processing does not lead to a satisfactory response, we feel that the role of effort and metacognition deserves considerable attention as it is probably through the manipulation of these variables that we can most readily alter processing strategies.

We do not presume, however, that there are no other dimensions of individual variation, nor do we believe we have categorically invalidated the developmental lag position. Nevertheless, we would emphasize that the developmental lag hypothesis is primarily descriptive and tends to lead to both a theoretical and a practical dead end. What is needed is a theory that accounts for individual differences evident in children as well as in adults and that recognizes the positive qualities of a source of variance in human cognition that contributes so greatly to the variety of human accomplishment in art, science, and technology.

References

Adams, M. J., & Shepp, B. Selective attention and the breadth of learning: A developmental study. *Journal of Experimental Child Psychology,* 1975, *20,* 168–180.

Ault, R. L. Problem-solving strategies of reflective, impulsive, fast-accurate and slow-inaccurate children. *Child Development,* 1973, *44,* 259–266.

Ault, R. L., Crawford, D. E., & Jeffrey, W. E. Visual scanning strategies of reflective, impulsive, fast-accurate, and slow-inaccurate children on the Matching Familiar Figures test. *Child Development,* 1972, *43,* 1412–1417.

Ault, R. L., Mitchell, C., & Hartmann, D. P. Some methodological problems in reflection-impulsivity research. *Child Development,* 1976, *47,* 227–231.

Block, J., Block, J. H., & Harrington, D. M. Some misgivings about the Matching Familiar Figures test as a measure of reflection-impulsivity. *Developmental Psychology,* 1974, *10,* 611–632.

Block, J., Block, J. H., & Harrington, D. M. Comment on the Kagan-Messer reply. *Developmental Psychology,* 1975, *11,* 249–253.

Bogen, J. E. Educational aspects of hemisphere specialization. *Educator,* 1975, *17*(2), 24–32.

Broadbent, D. E. The hidden preattentive processes. *American Psychologist,* 1977, *32,* 109–119.

Brown, A. L. The development of memory: Knowing, knowing about knowing, and knowing how to know. In H. W. Reese (Ed.), *Advances in child development and behavior* (Vol. 10). New York: Academic, 1975.

Brown, A. L. Development, schooling and the acquisition of knowledge about knowledge. In R. C. Anderson, R. J. Spiro, & W. E. Montague (Eds.), *School and the acquisition of knowledge*. Hillsdale, N. J.: Lawrence Erlbaum, 1977.

Bruner, J. S., Goodnow, J. J., & Austin, G. A. *A study of thinking*. New York: Wiley, 1956.

Campbell, S. B., & Douglas, V. I. Cognitive styles and responses to the threat of frustration. *Canadian Journal of Behavioral Science*, 1972, *4*, 30–42.

Dargel, R., & Kirk, R. E. Manifest anxiety, field dependency, and task performance. *Perceptual and Motor Skills*, 1971, *32*, 383–393.

Davis, J. K. *Cognitive style and conditional concept learning*. Paper presented at the annual meeting of the American Educational Research Association, Chicago, April 1972.

Denney, D. R. Reflection and impulsivity and determinants of conceptual strategy. *Child Development*, 1973, *44*, 614–623.

Drake, D. M. Perceptual correlates of impulsive and reflective behavior. *Developmental Psychology*, 1970, *2*, 202–214.

Dweck, C. S. The role of expectations and attributions in the alleviation of learned helplessness. *Journal of Personality and Social Psychology*, 1975, *31*, 674–685.

Egeland, B., & Weinberg, R. A. The Matching Familiar Figures test: A look at its psychometric credibility. *Child Development*, 1976, *47*, 483–491.

Flavell, J. H., Friedrichs, A. G., & Hoyt, J. D. Developmental changes in memorization processes. *Cognitive Psychology*, 1970, *1*, 324–340.

Gardner, R. W., Holtzman, P. S., Klein, G. S., Linton, H. B., & Spence, D. P. Cognitive control: A study of individual consistencies in cognitive behavior. *Psychological Issues*, 1959, *1*. (Monograph 4)

Garner, W. R. The stimulus in information processing. *American Psychologist*, 1970, *25*, 350–358.

Garner, W. R. The processing of information and structure. New York: Lawrence Erlbaum, 1974.

Gazzaniga, M. S. Review of the split brain. *Educator*, 1975, *17*(2), 9–12.

Gibson, E. J. *Principles of perceptual learning and development*. New York: Appleton-Century-Crofts, 1969.

Gibson, E. J., Gibson, J. J., Pick, A. D., & Osser, H. A. A developmental study of the discrimination of letter-like forms. *Journal of Comparative and Physiological Psychology*. 1962, *55*, 897–906.

Goodenough, D. R. The role of individual differences in field dependence as a factor in learning and memory. *Psychological Bulletin*, 1976, *83*, 675–695.

Hagen, J. W. Strategies for remembering. In S. Farnham-Diggory (Ed.), *Information processing in children*. New York: Academic, 1972.

Hagen, J. W., & Hale, G. A. The development of attention in children. In A. D. Pick (Ed.), *Minnesota symposium on child psychology* (Vol. 7). Minneapolis: University of Minnesota Press, 1973.

Hale, G. A., & Piper, R. Developmental trends in children's incidental learning: Some critical stimulus differences. *Developmental Psychology*, 1973, *8*, 327–335.

Hartley, D. G. The effect of perceptual salience on reflective-impulsive performance differences. *Developmental Psychology*, 1976, *12*, 218–225.

Heider, E. R. Information processing and the modification of an "impulsive conceptual tempo." *Child Development*, 1971, *42*, 1276–1281.

Hunt, E. G., Frost, N., & Lunneborg, C. L. Individual differences in cognition: A new approach to intelligence. In G. Bower (Ed.), *Advances in learning and motivation* (Vol. 7). New York: Academic, 1973.

Hunt, E., Lunneborg, C. L., & Lewis, J. What does it mean to be high verbal? *Cognitive Psychology*, 1975, *7*, 194–227.

Kagan, J. Impulsive and reflective children: Significance of conceptual tempo. In J. D. Krumboltz (Ed.), *Learning and the educational process*. Chicago: Rand McNally, 1965.

Kagan, J. Reflection-impulsivity: The generality of dynamics of conceptual tempo. *Journal of Abnormal Psychology*, 1966, *7*, 17–24. (a)

Kagan, J. Developmental studies in reflection and analysis. In A. H. Kidd & J. L. Rivoire (Eds.), *Perceptual development in children*. New York: International Universities Press, 1966. (b)

Kagan, J. The three faces of continuity in human development. In D. A. Goslin (Ed.), *Handbook of socialization theory and research*. Chicago: Rand McNally, 1969.

Kagan, J. *Change and continuity in infancy*. New York: Wiley, 1971.

Kagan, J., & Kogan, N. Individual variation in cognitive processes. In P. H. Mussen (Ed.), *Carmichael's manual of child psychology* (3rd ed., Vol. 1). New York: Wiley, 1970.

Kagan, J., & Messer, S. B. A reply to "Some misgivings about the Matching Familiar Figures test as a measure of reflection-impulsivity." *Developmental Psychology*, 1975, *11*, 244–249.

Kagan, J., & Moss, H. A. *Birth to maturity: A study in psychological development*. New York: Wiley, 1962.

Kagan, J., Moss, H. A., & Sigel, I. E. Psychological significance of style and conceptualization. In J. C. Wright & J. Kagan (Eds.), *Basic cognitive processes in children. Monographs of the Society for Research in Child Development*, 1963, *28*(2, Serial No. 86).

Kagan, J., Rosman, B. L., Day, L., Albert, J., & Phillips, W. Information processing in the child: Significance of analytic and reflective attitudes. *Psychological Monographs*, 1964, *78*(1, Whole No. 578).

Kahneman, D. *Attention and effort*. Englewood Cliffs, N.J.: Prentice-Hall, 1973.

Keogh, B. K., & Donlon, G. Field dependence, impulsivity, and learning disabilities. *Journal of Learning Disabilities*, 1972, *5*, 15–21.

Klein, G. S. Cognitive control and motivation. In G. Lindzey (Ed.), *Assessment of human motives*. New York: Rinehart, 1958.

Kreutzer, M. A., Leonard, C., & Flavell, J. H. An interview study of children's knowledge about memory. *Monographs of the Society for Research in Child Development*, 1975, *40*(1, Serial No. 159).

Massaro, D. J. The relation of reflection-impulsivity to field dependence-independence and internal-external control in children. *Journal of Genetic Psychology*, 1975, *126*, 61–67.

McCluskey, K. A., & Wright, J. C. *Reflection-impulsivity and age as determinants of visual scanning strategy and preschool activities*. Paper presented at the meeting of the Society for Research in Child Development, Denver, April 1975.

McKinney, J. D. Problem solving strategies in impulsive and reflective second graders. *Developmental Psychology*, 1973, *8*, 145.

Meichenbaum, D. H., & Goodman, J. Training impulsive children to talk to themselves: A means of developing self-control. *Journal of Abnormal Psychology*, 1971, *77*, 115–126.

Messer, S. B. Reflection-impulsivity: A review. *Psychological Bulletin*, 1976, *83*, 1026–1053.

Mitchell, C., & Ault, R. L. *The relationship of some problem solving variables to cognitive tempo*. Paper presented at the meeting of the Society for Research in Child Development, New Orleans, March 1977.

Moore, J., & Massaro, D. Attention and processing capacity in auditory recognition. *Journal of Experimental Psychology*, 1973, *99*, 49–54.

Mosher, F. A., & Hornsby, J. R. On asking questions. In J. S. Bruner, R. R. Olver, & P. M. Greenfield (Eds.), *Studies in cognitive growth*. New York: Wiley, 1966.

Nebes, R. D. Man's so-called "minor" hemisphere. *Educator*, 1975, *17*(2), 13–16.

Nuessle, W. Reflectivity as an influence on focusing behavior of children. *Journal of Experimental Child Psychology*, 1972, *14*, 265–276.

Odom, R. D. *The décalage from the perspective of a perceptual salience account of developmental change*. Paper presented at the meeting of the Society for Research in Child Development, New Orleans, March 1977.

Odom, R. D., & Mumbauer, C. C. Dimensional salience and identification of the relevant dimension in problem solving: A developmental study. *Developmental Psychology,* 1971, *4,* 135–140.

Odom, R. D., Astor, E. C., & Cunningham, J. G. Effects of perceptual salience on the matrix task performance of four- and six-year-old children. *Child Development,* 1975, *46,* 758–762.

Odom, R. D., & Guzman, R. D. Development of hierarchies of dimensional salience. *Developmental Psychology,* 1972, *6,* 271–288.

Odom, R. D., McIntyre, C. W., & Neale, G. The influence of cognitive style on perceptual learning. *Child Development,* 1971, *42,* 883–891.

Peavler, W. S. Pupil size, information overload and performance differences. *Psychophysiology,* 1974, *11,* 559–566.

Pick, A. D. Improvement of visual and tactual form discrimination. *Journal of Experimental Psychology,* 1965, *69,* 331–339.

Rydberg, S., & Arnberg, P. W. Attention and processing broadened within children's concept learning. *Journal of Experimental Child Psychology,* 1976, *22,* 161–177.

Shulman, H. G., & Greenberg, S. N. Perceptual deficit due to division of attention between memory and perception. *Journal of Experimental Psychology,* 1971, *88,* 171–176.

Sperling, G. The information available in brief visual presentations. *Psychological Monographs,* 1960, *74*(11, Whole No. 498).

Strutt, G. F., Anderson, D. R., & Well, A. D. A developmental study of the effects of irrelevant information on speeded classification. *Journal of Experimental Child Psychology,* 1975, *20,* 127–135.

Weiner, A. S., & Berzonsky, M. D. *Development of selective attention in reflective and impulsive children.* Paper presented at the American Educational Research Association Annual Meeting, Washington, D.C., 1975.

Witkin, H. A., Dyk, R. B., Faterson, H. F., Goodenough, D. R., & Karp, S. A. *Psychological differentiation.* New York: Wiley, 1962.

Witkin, H. A., Goodenough, D. R., & Karp, S. A. Stability of cognitive style from childhood to young adulthood. *Journal of Personality and Social Psychology,* 1967, *7,* 291–300.

Witkin, H. A., Moore, C. A., Goodenough, D. R., & Cox, P. W. *Field-dependent and field-independent cognitive styles and their educational implications.* Research Bulletin 75-24. Princeton, N.J.: Educational Testing Service, 1975.

Wohlwill, J. F. The study of behavioral development. New York: Academic Press, 1973.

Wright, J. C. *Reflection-impulsivity and associated observing behaviors in preschool children.* Paper presented at the meeting of the Society for Research in Child Development, Minneapolis, April 1971.

Wright, J. C., & Vlietstra, A. G. Reflection-impulsivity and information processing from three to nine years of age. In M. Fine (Ed.), *Intervention with hyperactivity.* Springfield, Ill.: Charles C Thomas, 1977.

Yando, R. M., & Kagan, J. The effects of task complexity on reflection-impulsivity. *Cognitive Psychology,* 1970, *1,* 192–200.

Zeaman, D., & House, B. J. The role of attention in retardate discrimination learning. In N. R. Ellis (Ed.), *Handbook of mental deficiency: Psychological theory and research.* New York: McGraw-Hill, 1963.

Zelniker, T., & Jeffrey, W. E. Reflective and impulsive children: Strategies of information processing underlying differences in problem solving. *Monographs of the Society for Research in Child Development,* 1976, *41*(5, Serial No. 168).

Zelniker, T., Renan, A., Sorer, I., & Shavit, Y. Effect of perceptual processing strategies on problem solving of reflective and impulsive children. *Child Development,* 1977, *48,* 1436–1442.

11   *Attention in the Classroom*

DOROTHY PIONTKOWSKI AND ROBERT CALFEE

Introduction

Trying to observe instruction in an active first-grade classroom can be a humbling experience. So much is going on and the distractions are so many, the wonder is that teacher and student make any sense of the situation. Yet they generally do—instruction and learning go on with a fair degree of success. The critical factor is attention. When the observer's attention is properly focused, when he has learned what to look for and what to ignore, significant patterns become clear to him. Likewise, teacher and student work together effectively when each attends to the situation in an active, selective fashion.

Our purpose in this chapter is to discuss psychological components of attention as these apply to classroom instruction and learning. Experimental research provides an understanding of how attention operates in laboratory settings. Our responsibility as educational psychologists is to build an interpretive bridge between basic research and practical classroom application. This has been attempted infrequently in the area of attention. In our review, we will rely on basic and applied research, we will turn to illustrations where these seem to help, and when research is lacking we will fall back on common sense.

Our base of operations will be the concept of an information-processing model. We will use this method of inquiry to organize our thoughts about what attracts and holds the attention of the teacher and his students. We believe that teachers can profitably adapt the information-processing approach for understanding how a student thinks, and for examining their own ways of thinking. This approach forces one to spell out in detail the mental steps that a person goes through while performing a task. Such an analysis is useful for both diagnosis and instruction—for discovering where

DOROTHY PIONTKOWSKI AND ROBERT CALFEE • School of Education, Stanford University, Stanford, California 94305.

the student experiences difficulty in the task and for helping him learn to handle it more successfully.

In this chapter we first discuss attention in a general sense and then consider three psychological components of the concept. We review the research on each component and relate it to the practical needs of teachers, to instruction, and to individual differences in students. We discuss techniques for assessing inattentiveness, and strategies the teacher may find effective for promoting more adaptive attention.

Commonsense Ideas of Attention

Educators often talk about attention as a general mental state in which the mind focuses on some special feature of the environment. As such, attention is considered essential for learning. It is hard to believe that the student who disregards instruction will benefit from it. Thus, the teacher needs reliable signs of the student's state of attention.

From an early time, educational research has touched on attention, on measures of attention, and on the relation between attention and school learning. As long ago as the turn of the century, Ribot (1898) noted that attention is not a mere "phantom" of the mind but can be inferred from an individual's physical actions when he directs himself toward information. The first studies of students' physical "attentiveness" were not designed to measure attention *per se*. Morrison (1925) used three student behaviors— eye expression, physical attitude, and motor activity—to evaluate teachers' control over students. He found substantial variability among teachers in the control they maintained over their students, as measured by the number of students who were physically attentive. In this study, the teacher was considered to be in control of his students when they were sitting quietly and visually focusing on the instructional task. This concept of relating control to observed attentiveness is provocative. What does the student do who is not paying attention to instruction? There are few hard data on this point, but we suspect that the student who is inattentive to instruction finds something else to attend to. Moreover, we suspect that this student is more likely identified as "the disruptive one." In any event, the nature of this study shows that attention is more than an unobservable "psychological" concept.

Morrison's physical cues were later used to evaluate the relation between attention and achievement. Shannon (1942) reported positive correlations between degree of attentiveness as measured by Morrison's cues and student achievement—higher for boys ($r = .67$) than for girls ($r = .34$). More recent studies have confirmed this general relation. Lahaderne (1968) reports significant correlations between fifth-graders' achievement and attention, again slightly higher for boys (r about .5) than for girls (*r* about .4). The data showed no relationship between attention and students' attitude toward school, indicating that the inattentive students were not necessarily "turned off." In two other studies (Cobb, 1972; Meyers, Attwell, & Orpet, 1968) that examined the relationship between behavioral ratings and achievement, the most powerful predictor of achievement in both cases was attention. Samuels and Turnure (1974) contrasted first-graders' attention to reading instruction with their word-recognition skills. Again, the results indicate that as attention increased, early reading skills increased.

Many teachers recognize the importance of gaining and holding students' attention in order to foster learning. In a recent survey of elementary teachers in compensatory reading programs (Rubin, Trismen, Wilder, & Yates, 1973), two items referred to students' attention span. One item asked the teacher to estimate the amount of time he worked with students on various activities; another asked the teacher to indicate agreement or disagreement with various statements about the problems of disadvantaged students (Figure 1). Most teachers in compensatory reading programs assigned "some" or "a great deal" of time to activities intended to increase attention span. Over half (58%) of the teachers believed that a "shorter attention span" was a source of difference in academic capabilities of the disadvantaged students. However, as can be seen in the figure, attentional deficits and time spent remedying these have somewhat lower priority than other categories presented to the teachers. We suspect that teachers find attention in this general sense to be a serious problem for only a few students, but for these students it is a serious problem indeed.

"Attention span" is most often used in a general way by teachers. One can imagine the teacher saying: "This was a great hour! The students really paid attention—except for Henry. His problem is that he has a short attention span." One can form a picture of the situation—most of the students are focused on the teacher. Whenever a question is asked, several students raise their hands and offer answers. Expressions are serious and intent. However, Henry is not behaving like the other students in some way or another—he may be looking out the window or poking his neighbor or laughing at the wrong times or doodling or sleeping.

Unfortunately, such a general characterization of attention lacks precision about the students' behavior or thought, and provides no insight about how to change either. Are the students focused on the relevant dimensions of instruction? Are they merely feigning attentiveness? Perhaps Henry focused on the task at first but then lost interest. Has he really "tuned out," or is he listening but not looking? Does he already know the material so well that he can attend with only "part of his mind"?

Answers to such questions require a careful analysis of the role of attention in the classroom. General descriptions of attentiveness do not

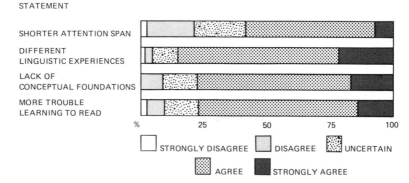

FIGURE 1. Teachers' estimates of time spent on various activities and degree of relationship of attributes of students in compensatory reading classes. Data from Rubin, Trismen, Wilder, and Yates (1973).

pinpoint behavior that needs to be changed if students are to profit from instruction. "Pay attention!" serves to arouse the students for a while. However, for consistent, long-term inprovement in attention the teacher must identify precise problems and try specific remedies.

Components of Attention

Experimental research on attention is readily sorted into two areas of investigation—psychophysiological and psychological. Pribram and

McGuinness (1975) recently reviewed the psychophysiological data on attention and found evidence for three distinct but interacting neural systems that operate as control mechanisms:

Arousal. The "What is it?" reaction, a phasic physiological response to changes in intensity, timing, or figure–ground relationship of the sensory input.

Activation. The "What's to be done?" reaction, a tonic physiological readiness to respond by activation of the "go" mechanisms.

Effort. The measure of attention "paid" to stimuli, the coordinating activity of arousal and activation that produces a change in a person's information-processing capacity.

Posner and Boies (1971), in their review of psychological research on attention, also isolate three major categories of mental activity:

Alertness. The development and maintenance of optimal sensitivity to the environment.

Selectivity. The act of scanning the environment in order to select the most salient dimensions and to focus on those features while excluding others.

Central Processing. The focal point of "thinking" where the selected elements are brought together for identification, comparison, recording, interpretation, or the like. Central processing has a sharply limited capacity.

Physiological control systems can be put into reasonable correspondence with psychological processes. Arousal is an orienting, reflexive reaction and is more or less the same as alertness—sensitivity to available information, readiness to respond to sensory input. For example, a person is least alert or mentally responsive when drugged or asleep, and highly sensitive when riding a roller coaster. Selective attention would probably be described by the psychophysiologists as the coordination of arousal to available cues by way of adaptive responses developed through previous experience (activation). For instance, consider two people observing a work of art. The two will attend selectively to different features of the work, depending on their experience, skills, and purpose for observing. The critic appreciates the flow of color and form; the naturalist notices the apples on a tree with persimmon leaves. Central processing capacity is important when two or more events require processing but is not involved when the response is automatic. Pribram and McGuiness describe such behavior by saying that contingencies between input and mental representations are direct and no *effort* is required for reaction. Effort thus reflects the amount of attention "paid" to maintain active processing of information. The experienced driver can listen to the radio, carry on a conversation, or enjoy the scenery while reacting in a smooth and flexible manner to the changing circumstances of the highway. For the less skillful driver, the basic task absorbs his total attentional capacity, and any additional information load leads to a rapid deterioration in performance.

Future research may provide a more complete analysis of attention, but for the purpose of this chapter we will focus on the psychological components identified by Posner and Boies—alertness, selectivity, and central processing capacity. We will examine each of these components as it comes into play in the classroom and discuss training strategies for correcting dysfunction in that component. Learning suffers if the student is sleepy, is looking at the wrong picture on the page, or hasn't mastered fundamental skills. Each of these reflects a kind of failure in attention, but the proper remedial action by the teacher differs from one case to another.

Alertness

For some time we have known how the level of sensitivity to stimulation, as measured by physiological indicators like muscle tone, is related to performance (Yerkes & Dobson, 1908). Increases in alertness from a stuporous condition are accompanied by improved performance, but beyond a certain point increased sensitivity causes deterioration of performance. It is thought that the curvilinear relationship between alertness and performance occurs as the person increases his focus on the specific task at hand. Narrowed focus helps him to do the task better up to a point. However, when the focus becomes too restricted important relevant details are ignored and performance suffers (see Easterbrook, 1959, for a review of early work).

The optimal level of alertness depends on task difficulty (Fitts & Posner, 1967). An easy task can be performed efficiently at a lower level of alertness than a hard task. Supporting evidence comes largely from studies of industrial tasks (Welford, 1968), but the generalization probably holds for many educational situations. Task difficulty depends on the person's training as well as features of the task itself (Posner, 1973). The cliché about doing something "in your sleep" means that the person is so skilled in performing that task he does not need to be wide-eyed and alert during its execution.

In turn, the task influences alertness. Some jobs are inherently monotonous, such as scanning a radar screen or a panel of dials. For long periods of time nothing happens, but the operator is supposed to respond whenever an unusual event occurs. Under these conditions, level of alertness drops rapidly over 10 to 30 minutes, more quickly when the operator is tired or under the influence of a drug such as alcohol (Buckner & McGrath, 1963). The instructor asks too much when he expects the student to respond to the "pearls of wisdom" that come in the middle of a boring lecture. The student may be literally half asleep.

Maintaining Alertness in the Classroom

Two specific ways of maintaining alertness are to introduce variety to the task and to provide feedback about performance on the task (Keele, 1973). Even the most intriguing task becomes boring if it is repeated often without change. Short tasks built around concrete, personally relevant problems keep the student alert and active. If things are happening and the student is busy, interest in the task itself keeps the student alert. When students are kept informed about how well they are doing on a task, the job at hand seems more important and worth doing.

The typical classroom atmosphere has been judged by some observers to be repetitious and dull (Silberman, 1970). Such generally boring conditions lead the student to become stuporous or to turn his attention elsewhere. The teacher need not create a carnival atmosphere, but a certain level of activity and vitality is needed to maintain the students' level of alertness. Moderate levels of music and other background noise help the student stay alert, especially if he is tired or sleepy (Keele, 1973).

Students and teacher remain alert when the classroom situation is interesting in its own right. Variety is the spice of life, including life in the classroom. Novelty—totally new elements or familiar events in unexpected contexts—has a strong effect on arousal level (Berlyne, 1960). Some teachers are judged by classroom observers to be unusually stimulating and creative; their students are considered more alert and interested. The elements of this teaching style include humor, "human interest," novelty, and a personal approach (Ryans, 1960). Livening a lecture with humor, posing a cut-and-dried problem in a new way, confronting students with unexpected questions, changing the art work on the walls, introducing variety into the schedule—all these make the classroom situation more interesting, novel, and stimulating.

Group activities pose special problems in maintaining levels of alertness and in spotting students whose alertness has lapsed. Placement in the group matters. Most classrooms contain an "action zone" where the teacher spends most time and where interactions are most frequent (Brophy & Good, 1974). The higher achieving students tend to migrate into this zone, the poorer students to leave it. A practical strategy for the teacher is to arrange seat assignments so that the student who has trouble staying alert to the lesson is placed in the action zone.

One study evaluated students' work habits when seating assignments were changed (Schwebel & Cherlin, 1972). Observations showed whether students sat in the front, middle, or back row in the classroom. The students in each row were then reassigned so that one-third remained in the original row, and one-third were relocated into each of the other two zones. New observations were carried out 2 to 3 weeks after the move. Figure 2 shows the mean change scores for two of the observed behavioral categories —"own work" and "inactivity or unassigned activity." Although behavior in every group changed in the desired direction, the students placed at the front of the classroom showed the greatest decrease in percent of time inactive or on task-irrelevant behavior.

A frequent tactic in classroom instruction is to arouse interest in a topic through discussion. But it is risky to rely on any single procedure, as Zivin (1974) illustrates in "How to Make a Boring Thing More Boring." How can an object (or task) be made more attractive and interesting so that a youngster pays more attention to it? Zivin reasoned that one answer was to "entice a child to start thinking about something . . . [and then] his attention will often sustain itself" (p. 232). The idea sounds good, but it didn't work.

The investigator first measured which of several toys was least inter-

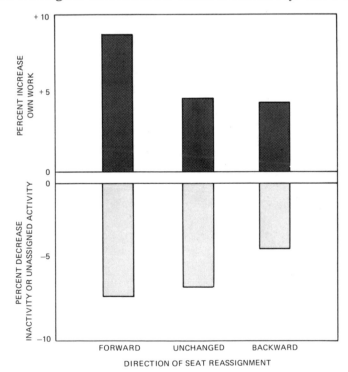

FIGURE 2. Changes in work-related behavior after some students were reassigned to seats in other parts of the classroom. Data from Schwebel and Cherlin (1972).

esting to a student (kindergarten through second grade). The students in the experimental group then met with the tester, who said, "Let's talk about this toy. Tell me everything you think of that you could do with this toy. Use your wildest imagination." The purpose of the discussion was to alert attention to details of the toy. Control students talked with the investigator about their favorite TV shows. Afterwards the students could play with any toy they chose. Compared with the control group, the experimental group consistently *avoided* the critical toy, as if they had talked it to death. Zivin's results do not mean that discussion always lessens interest. But this can happen, and teachers should be aware that although familiarity can lessen the information-processing load through easier encoding, it can also breed contempt.

Selectivity

An adequate level of arousal is a *sine qua non,* but it is equally critical for a student to focus on the relevant features in the array of information. Selective attention includes three elements: (a) picking out a designated object or event from a larger set, (b) paying special notice to certain features of this stimulus, and (c) disregarding other features of the same stimulus.

Consider these elementary processing demands within selectivity as a teacher observes students working math problems at the blackboard. He focuses on David, who is adding two-place numbers. He notices that David has written the problems so that the numbers are not properly aligned and now is having trouble deciding which numbers to add. The teacher ignores the fact that David has written "3" backwards. The important point here is that the object and feature selected by the teacher determine his thoughts and his actions—he will instruct David to place numbers in appropriate columns, and, at least for now, not correct the figure reversal.

Selective attention is influenced by both external and internal sources of information. On the one hand, external information is picked up by the sense organs from the environment in a data-dependent or "bottom-up" sequence. Simultaneously, internal sources of information organize and transform incoming data within a concept-driven or "top-down" system (Norman, 1976). The person is most likely to notice aspects of a situation that are perceptually salient and distinctive, and that fit in with what past experience tells him is important.

External Sources of Influence on Selectivity

A feature of the stimulus often grabs a person's attention by its natural prominence. Bright colors, loud sounds, sharp contrasts, novelty that is unexpected within familiar contexts—all these attract attention. A classroom teacher plays a loud chord on the piano, the coach blows the whistle—these events stand out naturally against the backgrounds and thereby capture the students' attention. In other cases, perceptual salience is learned. Students soon learn to attend selectively to the teacher's sudden change in tone of voice, which gives warning that he "means business."

People are pretty good at picking out salient stimuli. The occasional visitor to the classroom is confused and distracted by the activity and babble, but the situation is much like a cocktail party. People all around are talking loudly, yet you hear the person talking to you. The distinctive characteristics of each person's voice allow you to attend selectively to the message you want to hear and to disregard the surrounding noise (Cherry, 1953). If someone is particularly loud, if two conversations develop along similar themes, if a familiar or pertinent message comes along (someone mentions your name *sotto voce* or drops a line of particularly juicy gossip), then these messages take center stage and displace the original focus. Moderate classroom activity operates in similar fashion for most students. Background noise maintains alertness; salient stimuli are selected and the general buzz ignored.

Unfortunately, stimuli intended to maintain interest and motivation sometimes take over from those of more vital importance. Arranging learning situations that are interesting and that attract the student's focus requires careful consideration of consequences. Novelty attracts, but it also distracts, and may take attention away from matters of relevance. The brightly colored pictures that decorate first-grade books attract the student's attention to the book. But the pictures sometimes distract from the printed symbols that are critical in reading (Samuels, 1967).

A problem exists when the background is more attractive than the task, or when the distinction between relevant and irrelevant stimuli is unclear to the student. We spoke earlier about activity and moderate levels of background noise in order to maintain alertness. However, distinctive differences between the relevant stimuli in the classroom and those that are irrelevant background "noise" need to be maintained so that the student finds it relatively easy to select the former and disregard the latter. Achieving adequate clarity can be especially important in the open-space classroom. The conventional class (30 students seated in rows) is not necessarily a calm sea. But the number and variety of students and activities in more "innovative" schools pose special challenges. In their study of open-space schools, Roper and Nolan (1976) found that the single greatest concern of teachers in these schools was the distractive effects of noise on both students and teachers.

Two sources of external influence on selectivity need to be controlled by the teacher—the specific elements of the stimuli relevant to the learning task, and the general activity level in the learning situation. What can the teacher do to make critical elements of the stimulus more noticeable? The answer is to make stimulus characteristics prominent. The teacher can take advantage of natural perceptual salience so that relevant dimensions stand out:

1. Emphasize critical features of a stimulus. The different parts of a chart on blood circulation become distinct when each is given its own bright color.
2. Eliminate irrelevant features. In Britten's *Young Person's Guide to the Orchestra* each musical instrument has its solo moment in the concerto, when its unique sound is emphasized and all other instruments are muted.
3. Put an old stimulus into a new context. The rubbish in a local stream goes unnoticed normally, but collected and piled at the front of the classroom it becomes impressive.

The teacher needs to be sensitive to the delicate balance between a situation that is stimulating and one in which relevant stimuli are "drowned out." For example, if teachers share an open area, they need to work together in coordinating specific time periods for quiet and for noisy activities. Teachers can also control noise levels by systematic variation in the arrangement of space—self-contained rooms can serve to contain distracting activities or can serve as quiet retreats, free of visual and social distraction. The noise that accompanies different activities provides the basis for dividing open pods into areas so that activities are assigned according to "acceptable noise levels" (Roper & Nolan, 1976).

Forcing everyone to be quiet all the time is a high price for eliminating distraction. Permitting anyone to raise a hubbub whenever and wherever he wishes is equally unreasonable. Planning effective use of time and space achieves a compromise between these extremes and allows each student's special needs to be met according to the task demands.

Internal Influences on Selectivity

Selective attention requires a decision about which information in the stimulus to take in and which to ignore. What the person thinks about when confronted with information depends not only on the situation but on his background as well. An immediate memory search tells how the stimulus resembles stored knowledge, and determines what is meaningful in the situation. For example, if you know something about South Seas artifacts, you may "see" Fiji Island statues in Figure 3. An entirely different set of experiences is aroused if you are asked what word you see in the figure.

A person's mental set reflects the way he has organized his experi-

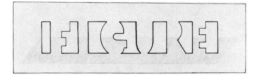

FIGURE 3. An ambiguous figure that changes depending on what you expect to see. From Hochberg (1964).

ences, and how these meet the needs of the moment. Expectations "selectively sensitize" one to personally important aspects of the environment (Bruner, 1973). As William James (1890) noted:

> [Others] have, then, utterly ignored the glaring fact that subjective interest may, by laying its weighty index-finger on particular items of experience, so accent them as to give to the least frequent associations far more power to shape our thought than the most frequent ones possess. The interest itself, though its genesis is doubtless perfectly *natural, makes* experience more than it is made by it. (p. 402, italics in original)

Broadbent (1977) has recently described two cognitive processes in selective attention—filtering and pigeonholing. Filtering is the selection of a stimulus feature on the basis of possible interpretations. Pigeonholing is a subsequent process that matches the filtered input with information stored in the "pigeonholes" of long-term memory. Thus, it is in this second stage that the factors of meaning and motive are brought into play. "The most promising of [the filtered] interpretations is then verified by active interrogation of the sensory field to check whether certain stimulus features are present which have not previously been detected" (p. 115). Navon (1975) offers other labels for a similar two-stage process: "Suggestion" is the primary action taken on the flow of sensory information, and "inquiry" occurs when the cognitive system probes the environment in order to validate the suggestion.

The relative influence of "personal frames of reference"—the cognitive factors that make up mental set—is greater in more complex situations (Forgus, 1966). With increased complexity, many features compete for selection, and the relevant characteristics of the stimulus are less likely to stand out. Hence, students faced with the abundance of information in the classroom may rely more on mental set than on the perceptual salience of the features. Thus, teachers need to remain sensitive to the aspects of the situation that the student considers personally relevant.

The ability to select relevant features also depends on a person's information-processing capacity. If the situation is unfamiliar, capacity is quickly overloaded and ability to be selective suffers. Whether the student knows what to look for or not, he will lack the processing capacity to proceed. We will discuss this matter in more detail in the next section.

What can the teacher do to influence the student's mental set—the ideas and expectations he brings to the situation? When the student is presented with a new and complex situation for the first time, the teacher can point out the significant features that require attention. If the task is to pick out the major theme played by the orchestra, it helps to know that "every time a new theme is introduced in this symphony, it is played by the clarinet." Similarly, the computer science student can be told that mistakes often occur in the INPUT FORMAT card when writing a program.

When a teacher or textbook uses words to direct attention, it is essential that the words refer to familiar concepts and relations. If a student does not know the sound of a clarinet, then advice to "listen for the clarinet theme" is no help. For the common elements in a concept to be useful, the student must be able to identify the elements with ease. For instance, "in

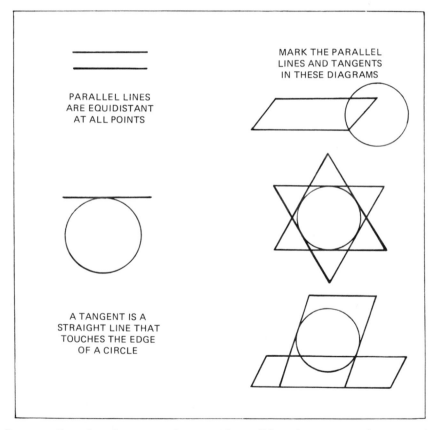

FIGURE 4. Examples of geometric figures with parallels and tangents as features to be discovered.

the products of 9 listed below, as the multiplier of 9 increased by 1, the last numeral in the product goes down by 1":

$$9 \times 1 = 9$$

$$9 \times 2 = 18$$

$$9 \times 3 = 27$$

If the student understands the terms *multiplier, product, numeral* and can quickly recognize which numbers are intended by each term, then instructions using these labels direct his attention toward useful information. Otherwise, he simply grows more confused.

Certain stimulus dimensions seem to be perceived naturally as features of an object or event. Other elements blend to form inseparable conglomerates. For these elements to become available for analysis requires considerable training and experience (Lockhead, 1972). The connoisseur directs his attention to specific features of a wine; for the less sophisticated wine-taster, a sip has a holistic quality, complex but inseparable elements woven into a single experience. Geometric diagrams like those in Figure 4 are seen at first by the students as wholes. Directing a student's attention to "parallels" or "tangents" is a test of embedded figure skill. The student's ability to profit from verbal instructions intended to help him focus on the significant elements is limited until he has had experience in analyzing and constructing geometric diagrams on his own (Elman, 1973).

Developmental and Individual Differences in Selective Attention

The young and "careless" child acts spontaneously, often missing the relevant characteristics of the stimulus. His manner of processing information is direct, fast-acting, "associative"—he responds impulsively to the stimulus as a whole by direct stimulus–response association (White, 1965, 1970). His response repertoire is limited to actions that come instantly to mind after a superficial scan of the situation. He is predominantly influenced by the external features of the environment. The older, "more attentive" person, with his greater wealth of experiences, is more logical—he reflects, weighs, thinks the situation through before reacting. White refers to this reflective manner of processing information as operating at a "cognitive level."

Wright (1977) also proposes a sequence of exploration-to-search behavior in selective attention, one in which development occurs in both a continuous and a discontinuous manner. When faced with a novel situation, a person relies on exploratory behavior—he selects aspects of the situation that stand out. Exploration leads to familiarity with the salient properties of the stimulus. When later faced with a similar situation, the person depends on what he has learned in the past, and as a consequence becomes more reflective and goal-oriented in his search—he selects the relevant, informative features according to his prior experience. With experience and familiarity in a variety of situations, the developing child gradually comes to use the reflective mode of selecting the most appropriate features. Cognitive control over selective attention is directed by familiarization—"That is, one must know where most of the landmarks are before he can make a reasoned decision to attend to particular ones" (Wright & Vlietstra, 1975, p. 234). There is a final, discontinuous stage in Wright's model, in which the prior knowledge of a situation becomes so sure and dominant that the person again responds quickly and with little reference to the environment.

With developmental changes in selective attention comes improved performance (Hagen & Hale, 1973). Perception and memory are relatively stable from age 4 onward, but the child continues to learn to make fuller use of his cognitive resources:

> . . . older children are more likely to employ selective attention and to ignore secondary stimulus features when these features are defined as incidental than when they constitute useful redundant information. Clearly, there are developmental increases not only in children's ability to attend selectively but in their ability to determine when it is most appropriate to employ selective attention. (p. 31)

Younger children *act* precipitously; older ones *think* before acting. Instruction aimed at "improving" memory and perception is probably misdirected. Rather, the need is to learn to make better use of existing perceptual and memory capabilities (Hagen, Jongeward, & Kail, 1975).

Students differ in their use of selective attention. In the Samuels (1967) study cited earlier, the effect of pictures on reading ability was not the same for all children. The availability of pictures did not interfere with the performance of the good readers, but the poor readers learned significantly less well when pictures were available. Doyle, Anderson, and Halcomb (1976) tested the ability of normal readers and learning-disabled students to respond selectively to certain events and ignore distractions on a basic vigilance task. The student was directed to identify specified events on a screen by pressing appropriate buttons. To the lower left on the task display, another screen presented numerical figures that the student was instructed to ignore. Figure 5 shows the contrasting performance of the two groups. The learning-disabled students correctly identified fewer events, responded with more false alarms, and looked more frequently at the distracting events for a longer mean contact-time, leading the authors to conclude that learning-disabled students suffer an "attentional deficit"—they do not ignore competing irrelevant stimuli. This conclusion fits with Ross's (1976) comments on the "recurring theme of selective attention" as a source of reading problems in learning-disabled students.

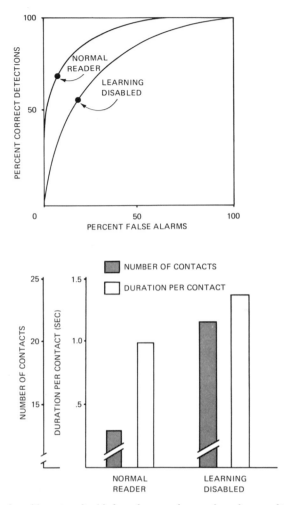

Figure 5. Results of learning-disabled students and normal readers on distractability task. Data from Doyle, Anderson, and Halcomb (1976).

Kagan (1966) has described a similar category of individual differences in problem solving by the labels of reflectivity and impulsivity. Some students respond quickly and inaccurately on tests that require fine discrimination; other children are more reflective, think longer, and make fewer mistakes. The relation to selective attention is direct. Siegelman (1969) studied the visual attention of fourth-grade boys while taking the Matching Familiar Figures test. The reflective boys spent time comparing selected parts of the stimuli; the impulsive boys tended to respond to the whole stimulus without selection of relevant features. Differences in reflectivity and impulsivity are correlated with performance on reading achievement tests, problem solving, and other tasks that require one to evaluate alternatives—to think through and select the most relevant features before taking action in a situation (Kagan, 1964).

There are striking parallels between impulsive students and those classified as hyperactive. Between 1 and 5 in 20 elementary school students are now classified as hyperactive, minimally brain-damaged, or learning-disabled (Craig & Malgoire, 1977). Diagnosis is often imprecise and is usually based on general assessments of misbehavior or failure to learn in a regular classroom. Treatment often includes stimulant drugs. The evidence indicates that such treatment produces short-term improvement—parents, teachers, and professionals report positive changes in behavior, and performance is better on "repetitious, routinized tasks requiring sustained attention. . . ." (Sroufe & Stewart, 1973). The paradoxical effect of stimulant drugs is far from understood. When the student's responsiveness to relevant information is enhanced, he might become attentive to relevant features of the task and hence less disruptive. However, drug levels often exceed those needed for improvement on cognitive tasks, and the goal of drug therapy seems more generally to be to eliminate misbehavior than to facilitate learning (Werry & Sprague, 1970).

Short-term gains from such treatment seem worthwhile in their own right, but they may prevent steps toward more lasting improvement. Once a hyperactive or impulsive child has "slowed down," the tendency is to breathe a sigh of relief and treat him as a regular member of the class. But such children often lack basic skills in selecting relevant information, possibly as a result of earlier maladjustment to schooling. Unless instructed in how to use their time, they do not benefit from school experience even after their "attention spans" have been "extended."

What kind of instruction might a teacher use to improve such a student's skills? Direct instruction is an obvious candidate—teach the student to take his time, and teach him *what to do* when he slows down. This approach seems almost too simple, but in one reasonably good study of this problem, the results were promising. Egeland (1974) identified 24 impulsive children in an inner-city school and trained them over 4 weeks in eight 30-minute training sessions with a variety of materials and exercises. A "delay-training" group of children was told that it was important to try not to make mistakes, and that one way of doing this was to "think about your answers and take your time." This suggestion was enforced by telling the child when a 10- to 15-second interval had elapsed; only then could he respond. A "strategy-training" group was given similar instructions, but was also provided with a variety of rules and strategies to try out during the delay interval.

The training method in this study has several important features—it

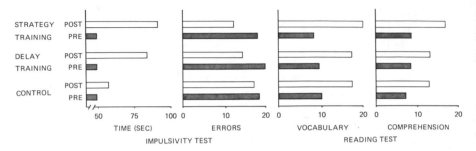

FIGURE 6. Results of Egeland study on training impulsive students to slow down and concentrate. Data from Egeland (1974).

was extensive and relatively long-term. The training extended over a variety of materials and a range of contexts. The students were provided with positive ideas about what to do to improve performance in solving a problem.

Was it worth it? The answer is shown in Figure 6. On the impulsivity test both the Delay and Strategy groups took more time after training than before and made fewer errors. There was no significant change in the performance of the control students on this test.

The impulsivity test was designed to measure the direct effects of Delay and Strategy training. What about the effects on tasks not directly related to the training? The answer was clear-cut for the two measures of reading achievement shown in Figure 6. Students in the Control and Delay groups improved about the same from pretest to posttest; students in the Strategy group gained 25% or more than the other two groups. Egeland speaks to the practical implications for classroom teaching when he states that "for the impulsive child to become efficient at processing information he must be able to use the reflective approach without having to concentrate on the mechanics of applying the strategy. Future training studies need to concentrate on ways of making the acquired reflective approach more automatic" (p. 171). It is such "automatic reflectivity" that Wright (1977) appears to describe as the final stage in the development of efficient information processing.

Central Processing

A fundamental property of human information processing is the restriction on the number of attention-demanding elements the mind can handle at the same time. The limitation is relative rather than absolute. Well-practiced responses to familiar situations demand little attention, and under these conditions a person can handle two or more noncompeting tasks simultaneously.

Consider the new English teacher faced with his first stack of student compositions. As he reads, he must work consciously to isolate the elements requiring evaluation—organization, style, grammar, punctuation, and spelling. He may reread the papers several times, each time focusing on a different aspect. With experience, he learns to shift attention swiftly from one element to another, now focusing on improper use of a semicolon, now questioning the lead sentence in a paragraph. Not only does he know which cues to select from the paper, the process requires no conscious effort. The correction process is automatic—without the need to concentrate on looking first for one kind of error, next for another, and so on. The misspelled word jumps out on the page like the flashing light at a dangerous intersection, even while the teacher is reading for overall organization and style. But this ability to process several aspects of the composition all at one time and apparently in parallel comes only after much practice.

Neisser (1967) has proposed two levels of information processing—preattentive and focal. Pribram and McGuinness (1975) make a similar distinction between automatic processing and mental effort. Preattentive or automatic processing occurs when properties of the stimulus are familiar and readily linked to experience, when they are noticed quickly and without noticeable concentration. The stimulus makes contact with past knowledge quickly, automatically, and without interruption of ongoing activity. On the other hand, focal attention takes time and intellectual effort, and often intrudes on consciousness. Only one or two tasks that require focal attention can be handled simultaneously, and anything else going on at the same time is disregarded.

What causes the limitation in central processing? Some psychologists favor the *single-channel hypothesis*—unfamiliar information must pass through a narrow gate, and the person must decide what stimuli to admit at a given time (Broadbent, 1958; Deutsch & Deutsch, 1963; Treisman, 1964, 1969). Interference occurs when incompatible operations require attention. Another explanation suggests that interference occurs when the task demands exceed the available cognitive resources (Kahneman, 1973; Norman, 1976). Attentional capacity is exceeded when information from past experience is insufficient for immediate, effortless processing, so that the person has too many things to think about.

Automaticity

LaBerge (1975) describes the development of automaticity as the "gradual elimination of attention in the processing of information" (p. 58). Norman (1976) attributes automaticity to practice: "A general rule appears to be that when a skill is highly learned—perhaps because it has been practiced for years and years—then it becomes automated, requiring little conscious awareness, little allocation of mental effort" (p. 65). Thus, the fluent reader executes complex skills automatically (LaBerge & Samuels, 1974). For instance, the eye moves unconsciously at a regular pace of one movement every quarter second, jumping a relatively fixed distance on each saccade (movement) regardless of what is printed, zipping back unerringly from the end of one line to the beginning of the next (Haber & Hershenson, 1973). Each word is assigned a particular meaning from the many it possesses. The gist is interpreted and stored in memory (Gough, 1972). All this happens with relatively little intellectual effort and no conscious awareness. The skilled reader skims the written message and attends with ease to the meaning because the elementary skills have become automatic.

However, if you reflect on your mental activities while reading this material, the process is disturbed. You experience difficulty, your reading slows, and you cannot remember what you have just read. Forcing an automatic process into awareness (i.e., into focal attention) interferes with its automaticity. Normally the task flows so easily that the reader may be almost asleep and yet the basic processes automatically continue to operate even after the search for meaning has ceased.

What has just been said does not mean that the skilled reader always has an easy time. Mental effort is involved in thoughtful reading like that described by I. A. Richards (1942) in How to Read a Page. Here each word and sentence is examined for subtlety of meaning and alternative interpretations. The thoughtful reader considers other ways to express the ideas, and traces the implications of the writer's ideas. It is hard work, and difficult to pursue more than briefly. Active participation and awareness characterize this level of concentration, both because concerted thought leads to action and also because active responding is needed to sustain the effort of thought.

The skilled reader knows when a situation demands concentration and when it is "safe" to process the information automatically. But the beginning reader has to participate and maintain an awareness much like the "thoughtful" reader (Calfee, 1975). He needs to attend selectively to critical sources of information in letters and words and to arrive at reasonable sound correspondences. Newly acquired decoding skills must be brought into play in order to reach reasonable approximations as to what pronunciation makes most sense in a given context. The beginning reader actively searches for information stored in his head—letter identification, sound-symbol correspondences, vocabulary, and syntax. Like Richards's "thoughtful reader," the individual must apply effort and hard work.

When tasks require effort there is greater susceptibility to distraction than when processing is automatic. A study of concentration among under-achieving and achieving college students (Baker & Madell, 1965) illustrates this point. Reading comprehension measures were taken in ordinary situations—quiet, no distractions—and in a condition with humorous conversation in the background. There was no difference between the groups' comprehension scores under ordinary conditions, and both groups scored less well when distraction was introduced. The significant interaction effect between achievement and condition indicates that distraction had a differential effect on the two kinds of students. When distraction was present the achievers' comprehension scores fell by one-quarter, but the underachievers' scores fell by one-half. The greater deterioration of performance in the underachieving group suggests that their reading skills were less automatic, and that they had a lower threshold for distractibility.

Practice with feedback is the key to automaticity. Once a certain level of competence has been reached, the teacher should push for speed. Students sometimes ponder over matters that no longer require deliberate consciousness. Speed reading courses press the student toward quickened, automatic reading, and development of skimming ability is certainly a useful skill (Maxwell, 1969). On the other hand, one should not confuse "nonattentive" scanning with Richards's thoughtful reading.

Monitoring and Fostering Attention in the Classroom

Attention is critical to learning. If the student isn't paying attention to instruction, he won't profit from it. Consideration of the psychological components of attention in turn focuses the teacher's attention on what the student is doing (or not doing) that stands in the way of learning. When teachers are trained to recognize and respond to deficiencies in students' behavior, the result is improved response to instruction. Dimmit (1970), investigating teachers' perception of their students' attending behavior, found that some teachers concentrated on subject matter and disregarded student reaction. Others stereotyped students' attentiveness at levels that matched the students' ability, and taught to the "able-attentive" students. Still others taught to what they perceived as the class-average level of attention. When teachers were trained to attend to individual students, and to engage those students whose alertness had lapsed, students' attention to instruction increased.

But how can a teacher best tell whether a student is maintaining attention to the critical elements of instruction? Sophisticated laboratory methods use brain waves, heart rate, and similar indices to measure attention. Fortunately, two simple methods, practical for the classroom, are also valid: (a) notice where the student's eyes are directed, and (b) ask the student immediately after the event what is on his mind.

Visual Measures of Attentiveness

Man is a visual animal, and there is a class relation between what a person is attending to and where he is looking. One way to trick a person is to look elsewhere while tossing a ball in his direction. He is totally surprised, because he doesn't expect you to throw the ball toward him when you are obviously not attending to him. The classroom teacher can use this same principle to assess the focus of the student's attention.

The idea is especially effective in a situation where visual attention is critical, as the following episode illustrates. A group of second-graders is performing dramatic readings. The teacher has instructed the students to read a page from the story to themselves before he picks two or three students to act it out. Sally opens her book and glances at the page for a moment. Her gaze wanders to the teacher who is intent on the lesson plan. Sally takes in another group that is talking loudly, notes the time on the clock, peers intently at the book for a few seconds, closes it with a snap, and looks up with a smile on her face. The other children finish reading the story. Sally is silent during a brief class discussion of the story content. The teacher picks Sally and two other children to act out the reading. Sally's role in the skit, while "creative" in spots, generally meshes with the sense of the story—even though she had clearly read none of the material, she is good at following the lead of the other students.

A person has to look at a page to read it. To the observer, it is clear that Sally did not attend to the task. The teacher missed this episode, but does express general concern afterward: "Sally is interested and motivated, and reads as well as the other students. But she scores poorly on reading comprehension." The observer shares what he has seen, and on reflection the teacher notes that Sally does have trouble maintaining attention to a task. Attention is a problem for teacher as well as student. To deal effectively with the students' needs, to deal with attentional requirements of classroom instruction, the teacher must remain alert, must select relevant indicators of student attentiveness, and must learn to do this automatically.

The importance of visual attentiveness to learning is supported by a number of studies. "Sesame Street" is an educational television program for preschoolers. It is instructional but also is designed to be attractive and entertaining. Even so, children differ in the time they spend looking at "Sesame Street" when it is available (Ball & Bogartz, 1970). Children who spend more time watching the program (actual eye contact time) do better on tests of cognitive skills before they watch the program and they learn more from the program than children for whom eye contact time is less (Figure 7). In first-grade reading instruction girls are more attentive, as measured by eye contact with teacher and workbook, than are boys, and they are also better readers at the end of first grade. Visual attentiveness

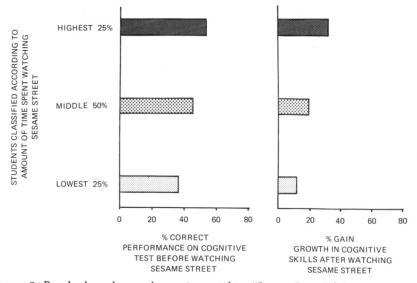

FIGURE 7. Preschoolers who spend more time watching "Sesame Street" do better on a cognitive test before they start watching the program, and learn more from watching the program. Data from Ball and Bogartz (1970).

seems to be a critical variable, however, since both boys and girls who spend more time looking at the teacher and workbook learn more (Samuels & Turnure, 1974).

Verbal Measures of Attentiveness

Although eye contact is a valid and useful index of attentive learning, there is the "horse-to-water" problem—you can get a student to look at you attentively while you are teaching, but you can't make him learn. Eye contact is an indicator. It tells the teacher what captures the students' attention and what does not. When most of the class looks out the window during a science demonstration, this signals a lack of interest or understanding. On the other hand, an entertaining lecture may keep eyes focused on the teacher, but the trick is to get the students to think and not simply to laugh. Moreover, the empty stare into space may evidence more thought than the eye riveted with boredom on the text.

Students can be clever in feigning attention to instruction. Hudgins (1967) studied the observer's ability to detect such feigning in junior high school students. He wondered about the degree to which "group-produced stimuli"—the nonverbal signals from a class—provide an accurate measure of the students' attention to instruction. An observer rated the students according to their apparent attention to the teacher's instruction, and then instruction was interrupted and students reported what they had just been thinking. The correlations between the observer's coding of student attentiveness and student self-report of attending to the lesson in nine classrooms ranged from .03 to .66 (mean $r = .27$). Among other things, some students apparently learn to appear as though they are paying attention.

Eye contact is often useful, especially in tasks like reading, but needs to be supplemented by another measure—ask the student to tell you what is on his mind. Direct questions are an excellent way to find out what the student has attended to and what features of a stimulus have proven salient for him.

To be sure, the technique has limits. It can be disruptive; the student's train of thought once interrupted may be lost and hard to recapture. The questioner needs to be sensitive and analytic. Broad questions such as "Do you understand what you are doing?" yield broad and uninformative responses, like "yes" or "no." The student may have trouble finding words to express his thoughts, or he may have little conscious awareness of how he is thinking. The teacher may need to help the student formulate alternatives by giving him cues that he can build upon to describe his thinking.

Discussion is a practical approach along these lines (Gall & Gall, 1976). The use of questions tied to the lesson content allows learning and the evaluation of learning to occur simultaneously. Reviews of the literature on the use of direct questions by teachers (Dunkin & Biddle, 1974; Rosenshine, 1976) indicate three general trends: (1) a positive correlation between use of direct questions by the teacher and achievement, (2) nonsignificant correlations between open-ended questions and achievement, and (3) negative correlations between personal-opinion questions and achievement. Two other studies also report negative correlations between open-ended questions and achievement in elementary grades (Stallings & Kaskowitz, 1974; Soar, 1973).

A combination of observation and direct questioning provides the teacher with specific information about precise difficulties a student has in performing a task. As an example, consider the following illustration of a child who is doing poorly in third-grade arithmetic. The work sheets he hands in at the end of each math period are full of mistakes, almost as if he answers at random. To understand the student's problem, the teacher spends most of one period observing the student as he works on his math work sheets. He begins each work sheet with a long and intense examination. Then he rapidly works the problems on the page, making many errors. The next day, the teacher squats beside the student as he begins his task and asks what he is thinking.

Student: "I'm trying to figure out what I'm supposed to do."
Teacher: "How do you figure it out?"

Student: "I just think about it for a while and then I either add the
           numbers or subtract them."
Teacher: "Do you read the instructions at the top of the page?"
Student: "Well, no. . . . It's kinda hard to understand them."

The student is not a facile reader, and printed text does not "grab" his
attention the way it does for others. Further conversation shows that the
student is competent in arithmetic, once he understands the task.

Questioning reaches more than attention—it engages the full range of
cognitive processes. If the student focuses on irrelevant aspects of a problem, then his best efforts will go for naught. The teacher, by careful analysis of the student's answers to questions, can often tease out those features
that most fully occupy his attention.

Special Problems of Attention

Some students are so "inattentive" that special action is called for. A
student may have acquired a behavior pattern so ill-suited to the classroom,
so habitual, and so all-encompassing, that direct steps must be taken to
change his behavior. Cobb and Hops (1973) have identified a constellation
they call "academic survival skills"—attending to the teacher, following
teacher instructions, and volunteering to answer academic questions. Students without these behaviors do poorly academically. Cobb and Hops
trained teachers to use positive reinforcement to shape students' behavior,
and the students were taught explicit strategies for using the "survival
skills." Figure 8 shows attending behavior and reading achievement for
trained first-graders and control students. The experimental students increased their attending behavior and reading scores during implementation,
and also continued to improve after the program was stopped.

The practical solutions in this example come from the tradition known
as "behavior modification." First, the teacher asks himself certain questions: (1) How would you like the student to behave? (2) What behavior
would you like to stop? (3) What reinforcers are available to you—what can
you offer the student that he finds rewarding? (4) How are you now using
those reinforcers—how must the student behave for you to reward him? (5)
How can you rearrange conditions so that reinforcement is contingent (depends) on desired behavior, and not on other unwanted acts?

Behavior modification methods (e.g., Becker, 1972) use language that
is strongly behavioristic, but many of the ideas have a long history in
psychology. While the approach sometimes seems narrow and superficial,
it gives the teacher a way of handling classroom situations where little else
helps. The emphasis on reinforcement contingencies makes the teacher

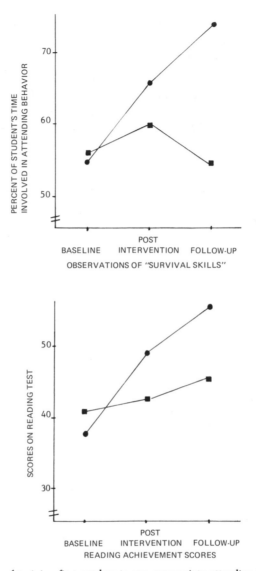

FIGURE 8. Results of training first-graders to use appropriate attending behavior (● trained students; ■ untrained students). Data from Cobb and Hops (1973).

think about his own behavior in relation to the student's—it is easy to send the student mixed messages, telling him to do one thing but rewarding him for doing something else.

How can the situation be arranged so that the student is rewarded for keeping his selective attention on relevant features of the task? This question is particularly germane for the student who switches rapidly from one task to another, who spends only a moment in one place, whose actions are disruptive, who not only fails to do his work but makes trouble for others.

Let us analyze this problem using the questions posed earlier as guidelines. First, spell out desirable and undesirable behavior. Concrete language is important. Vague statements—"He just doesn't pay attention," "He's always bothering the other students"—need to be refined. Answering a question, writing, looking at a book, looking at the speaker—all are actions that mark attention. Walking around, moving the chair to a neighbor's table, passing a note to a student during a class discussion, shouting irrelevant comments when someone else is talking—such behavior means that attention is not on the assigned task.

Next, what reinforcers are available? Some programs rely on tokens—candy, money, or markers that are redeemable for toys and other rewards. Other readily available reinforcers are of more lasting effectiveness than tokens. These include the teacher's social reactions to the student, verbal praise, smiling, recognizing him. A useful way to identify reinforcers is the Premack principle (Premack, 1965). "For any pair of responses, the more probable one will reinforce the less probable one." In plain English, find out what the student does most of the time when he has a choice, and let him do it *after* he has done what you want. The reinforcer need not be something that the teacher finds personally rewarding. If the student regularly asks to clean the chalkboard or sharpen pencils, then these are rewarding actions. "Bert, I like the way you wrote the assignment. It is really neat. You can take the report to the office for me."

Now, how are reinforcers being used in the class? This step requires concerted thought and analysis; observation by another person often helps. Teachers "give away" reinforcers through broad and imprecise praise. "John, you're going great!" can be a real morale booster to the student who hears little that is positive. "Sara, I'm pleased with how carefully you listened to what Peter was saying. Your question showed that you really understood his point" is more specific, more focused, so that the student gains knowledge and also feels good.

A problem arises when the student is rewarded for misbehaving. Disruptive, smart-alecky behavior is hard to ignore, even when you realize that your natural reaction reinforces it. For some students the only rewards that life offers are scolding and "punishment." The class bully, wise guy, or cutup has a major role in the classroom drama, and some students find this role better than being ignored.

A neutral observer, by giving the teacher immediate feedback, can foster awareness of reinforcement contingencies (Becker, 1972). In Becker's study, the observer raised one finger to signal that the student was not attending—he was doing something on the list of undesired acts. Two fingers signaled a desired behavior, and three fingers meant the teacher was giving a reinforcer. The busy-ness of teaching makes it hard to attend to all that is happening. A signal system seems simpleminded, but it can increase the teacher's awareness of his actions and how they relate to the student's behavior.

Behavior modification works well and quickly to gain students' attention when the classroom regimen is manifestly disrupted. It appears more effective than many other approaches. A typical study (Madsen, Becker, & Thomas, 1968) compared the relative effectiveness of three approaches for maintaining attention in special education classes. The students had multiple problems, and the chances were about 50–50 that the observer would spot a misbehavior every moment or so. The three approaches for maintaining appropriate attention were:

Rules. The teacher explicitly repeated the rules for appropriate classroom conduct several times a day, like "sit quietly while working; pay attention and look at me when I am talking; walk, don't run"; and so on.

Ignore. The teacher ignored disruptive behavior by acting as if the misbehavior did not occur.

Praise. The teacher showed approval for behaviors conducive to learning, e.g., for achievement, for prosocial behavior, for following rules, for concentrating on work, for paying attention.

An observer recorded behavior over several weeks while different combinations of these approaches were in effect (Figure 9). Rules did not noticeably affect behavior. Ignoring misbehavior increased it. Praising appropriate actions cut misbehavior in half within a week or two.

Judicious use of reinforcement changes behavior. Students become less disruptive and focus more on the task. The approach seems Orwellian and smacks of behavior control. But teachers (indeed, everyone) exert behavior control all the time. We try to arrange conditions so that people will do what we want them to. Behavior modification brings these actions into the open, making them more effective and, one hopes, more reasoned.

Praise does not teach a student how to handle the task, nor is there any guarantee of transfer to other situations. Madsen found that when reinforcement was stopped during Control Baseline II, misbehavior increased to almost the original level (Figure 9). The students had not learned to maintain attention on their own. For lasting effect behavior modification must be combined with other training, just as was true in methods of attentional control mentioned earlier in this chapter. Changing superficial responses without altering underlying habits and thoughts had no more lasting effect than administering a drug to calm hyperactivity. The student with a history of inattentiveness and disruptiveness needs direct guidance in how to solve problems and how to handle assigned tasks.

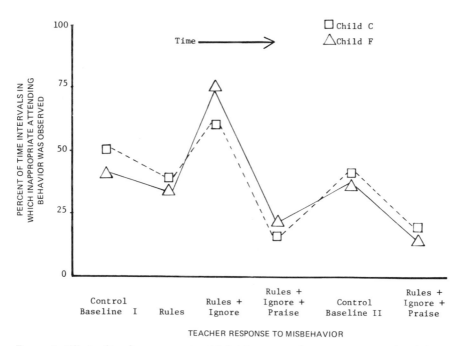

FIGURE 9. Effects of teacher response to misbehavior on rate of inappropriate attending behavior. Data from Madsen, Becker, and Thomas (1968).

Summary

Attentiveness is the gateway to successful classroom learning. The effective content of instruction depends on the focus of the students and the teacher's attention—a person thinks most fully about those aspects of a situation that he perceives as most central.

Our aim in this chapter has been to link the findings of experimental research to the activities of the classroom by describing each of the three separable components of attention—alertness, selectivity, and central processing—along with the personal and situational factors that enhance or interfere with each component.

A number of practically beneficial generalizations are supported by laboratory research. Alertness is best maintained when the task is varied, feedback is provided, and the learning situation is kept interesting to the students. Selectivity is influenced by both external and internal sources of information. The right balance is needed between novelty that maintains the students' alertness and the need to keep irrelevant stimulation in the background. Selectivity also depends immediately on what is personally relevant—what a person has learned to look for in previous, similar situations. Limited central processing prevents successful performance on more than one task requiring mental effort, but several things can be accomplished simultaneously when performance is automatic.

Research also provides some backing for practical methods of measuring and enhancing attention in the classroom. For instance, several studies show a clear relation between achievement and two straightforward methods of monitoring attention—keeping track of where the student's eyes are directed, and asking the student what he is thinking about as he performs a task. There are large individual differences in how students attend in class. Some students have learned to disregard instruction, or they continually focus on things other than instruction. The evidence suggests that direct training on attention is effective. Students can learn to pay attention to the task and can learn to slow down so that there is an opportunity to think about what they have focused on. However, attentional training is most effective when it is coupled with training on how to spend the attentive time thus gained.

The information-processing analysis of attention and other cognitive activities provides the teacher with a useful tool for more precise assessment and instruction. Broad and global conceptualization of attention leads the teacher to broad and global treatments. Attention is a complex process, but analysis of the underlying components gives the researcher and the teacher an understanding that leads to improved measurement and treatment of the attentional problems that limit learning for many students.

References

Baker, R. W., & Madell, T. O. A continued investigation of susceptibility to distraction in academically underachieving and achieving male college students. *Journal of Educational Psychology*, 1965, *56*, 254–258.

Ball, S., & Bogartz, G. A. A summary of the major findings in "The first year of Sesame Street: An evaluation." Princeton, N.J.: Educational Testing Service, 1970.

Becker, W. C. Applications of behavior principles in typical classrooms. In C. E. Thoresen (Ed.), *Behavior modification in education*. The 71st Yearbook of the National Society for the Study of Education. Chicago: University of Chicago Press, 1972.

Berlyne, D. E. *Conflict, arousal, and curiosity*. New York: McGraw-Hill, 1960.

Broadbent, D. E. *Perception and communication*. London: Pergamon, 1958.

Broadbent, D. E. The hidden preattentive processes. *American Psychologist*, 1977, *32*, 109–118.

Brophy, J. E., & Good, T. L. *Teacher–student relationships: Causes and consequences*. New York: Holt, Rinehart & Winston, 1974.

Bruner, J. S. *Beyond the information given: Studies in the psychology of knowing*. New York: Norton, 1973.

Buckner, D. N., & McGrath, J. J. *Vigilance: A symposium*. New York: McGraw-Hill, 1963.

Calfee, R. C. Memory and cognitive skills in reading acquisition. In D. Duane & M. Rawson (Eds.), *Reading, perception and language.* Baltimore: York, 1975.

Cherry, E. C. Some experiments on the recognition of speech, with one and with two ears. *Journal of the Acoustical Society of America,* 1953, *25,* 975–979.

Cobb, J. A. Relationship of discrete classroom behaviors to fourth-grade achievement. *Journal of Educational Psychology,* 1972, *63,* 74–80.

Cobb, J. A., & Hops, H. Effects of academic survival skills training on low achieving first graders. *Journal of Educational Research,* 1973, *67,* 108–113.

Craig, P. A., & Malgoire, M. A. *Analyses of the Office of Education's proposed rules for the identification of children with specific learning disabilities under the Education for All Handicapped Children Act.* Unpublished manuscript, Menlo Park, Cal.: Stanford Research Institute, 1977.

Deutsch, J. A., & Deutsch, D. Attention: Some theoretical considerations. *Psychological Review,* 1963, *70,* 80–90.

Dimmit, N. M. A study of training and photographic feedback methods for promoting accurate teacher perception of student attending behavior. Unpublished doctoral dissertation, Stanford University, 1970.

Doyle, R. B., Anderson, R. P., & Halcomb, C. G. Attention deficits and the effects of visual distraction. *Journal of Learning Disabilities,* 1976, *9*(1), 59–65.

Dunkin, M. J., & Biddle, B. J. *The study of teaching.* New York: Holt, Rinehart & Winston, 1974.

Easterbrook, J. A. The effect of emotion on the utilization and the organization of behavior. *Psychological Review,* 1959, *66,* 183–201.

Egeland, B. Training impulsive children in the use of more efficient scanning techniques. *Child Development,* 1974, *45,* 165–171.

Elman, A. *The perception of transformation in geometry drawing.* Paper presented at the American Psychological Association Convention, Montreal, 1973.

Fitts, P. M., & Posner, M. I. *Human performance.* Belmont, Cal: Brooks/Cole, 1967.

Forgus, R. H. *Perception.* New York: McGraw-Hill, 1966.

Gall, M. D., & Gall, J. P. The discussion method. In N. L. Gage (Ed.), *The psychology of teaching methods.* The 75th Yearbook of the National Society for the Study of Education. Chicago: University of Chicago Press, 1976.

Gough, P. B. One second of reading. In J. F. Kavanaugh & I. G. Mattingly (Eds.), *Language by ear and by eye: The relationships between speech and reading.* Cambridge, Mass.: M.I.T. Press, 1972.

Haber, R. N., & Hershenson, M. *The psychology of visual perception.* New York: Holt, Rinehart & Winston, 1973.

Hagen, J. W., & Hale, G. A. The development of attention in children. In A. D. Pick (Ed.), *Minnesota symposium on child psychology* (Vol. 7). Minneapolis: University of Minnesota Press, 1973.

Hagen, J. W., Jongeward, R. H., Jr., & Kail, R. V., Jr. Cognitive perspectives on the development of memory. In H. Reese (Ed.), *Advances in child development and behavior* (Vol. 10). New York: Academic, 1975.

Hochberg, J. E. *Perception.* Prentice-Hall Foundations of Modern Psychology Series, Richard S. Lazarus (Ed.). Englewood Cliffs, N.J.: Prentice-Hall, 1964.

Hudgins, B. B. Attending and thinking in the classroom. *Psychology in the Schools,* 1967, *4,* 211–216.

James, W. *The principles of psychology* (Vol. 1). New York: Holt, 1890.

Kagan, J. Reflection-impulsivity and reading ability in primary grade children. *Child Development,* 1964, *36,* 609–628.

Kagan, J. Developmental studies in reflection and analysis. In A. H. Kidd & J. L. Rivoire

(Eds.), *Perceptual development in children.* New York: International Universities Press, 1966.

Kahneman, D. *Attention and effort.* Englewood Cliffs, N.J.: Prentice-Hall, 1973.

Keele, S. W. *Attention and human performance.* Pacific Palisades, Cal.: Goodyear, 1973.

LaBerge, D. Acquisition of automatic processing in perceptual and associative learning. In P. M. A. Rabbitt & S. Dornic (Eds.), *Attention and performance.* London: Academic, 1975.

LaBerge, D., & Samuels, S. J. Toward a theory of automatic information processing in reading. *Cognitive Psychology,* 1974, *6,* 293–323.

Lahaderne, H. M. Attitudinal and intellectual correlates of attention: A study of four sixth-grade classrooms. *Journal of Educational Psychology,* 1968, *59,* 320–324.

Lockhead, G. R. Processing dimensional stimuli: A note. *Psychological* Review, 1972, *79,* 410–419.

Madsen, C. H., Jr., Becker, W. C., & Thomas, D. R. Rules, praise, and ignoring: Elements of elementary classroom control. *Journal of Applied Behavior Analysis,* 1968, *1,* 139–150.

Maxwell, M. J. *Skimming and scanning improvement: A program for self-instruction.* New York: McGraw-Hill, 1969.

Meyers, C. E., Attwell, A. A., & Orpet, R. E. Prediction of fifth grade achievement from kindergarten tests and rating data. *Educational and Psychological Measurement,* 1968, *28,* 457–463.

Morrison, H. C. *The practice of teaching in the secondary school.* Chicago: University of Chicago Press, 1925.

Navon, D. Global precedence in visual recognition. Unpublished doctoral dissertation, University of California, San Diego, 1975.

Neisser, U. *Cognitive psychology.* New York: Appleton-Century-Crofts, 1967.

Norman, D. A. *Memory and attention: An introduction to human information processing.* New York: Wiley, 1976.

Posner, M. I. *Cognition: An introduction.* Glenview, Ill.: Scott, Foresman, 1973.

Posner, M. I., & Boies, S. J. Components of attention. *Psychological Review,* 1971, *78*(5), 391–408.

Premack, D. Reinforcement theory. In D. Levine (Ed.), *Nebraska symposium on motivation.* Lincoln: University of Nebraska Press, 1965.

Pribram, K. H., & McGuinness, D. Arousal, activation, and effort in the control of attention. *Psychological Review,* 1975, *82*(2), 116–149.

Ribot, T. *The psychology of attention.* London: Open Court, 1898.

Richards, I. A. *How to read a page.* New York: Norton, 1942.

Roper, S. S., & Nolan, R. R. *How to survive in the open-space school.* Occasional paper No. 10, Stanford Center for Research and Development in Teaching, School of Education, Stanford University, 1976.

Rosenshine, B. Classroom instruction. In N. L. Gage (Ed.), *The psychology of teaching methods.* The 75th Yearbook of the National Society for the Study of Education. Chicago: University of Chicago Press, 1976.

Ross, A. O. *Psychological aspects of learning disabilities and reading disorders.* New York: McGraw-Hill, 1976.

Rubin, D., Trismen, D. A., Wilder, G., & Yates, A. *A descriptive and analytic study of compensatory reading programs.* Phase I Report Contract No. OEC-71-3715. Princeton: Educational Testing Service, 1973.

Ryans, D. G. *Characteristics of teachers: Their descriptions, comparison, and appraisal.* Washington, D.C.: American Council on Education, 1960.

Samuels, S. J. Attentional processes in reading: The effect of pictures on the acquisition of reading responses. *Journal of Educational Psychology,* 1967, *58,* 337–342.

Samuels, S. J., & Turnure, J. E. Attention and reading achievement in first-grade boys and girls. *Journal of Educational Psychology,* 1974, *66*(1), 29–32.

Schwebel, A. I., & Cherlin, D. L. Physical and social distancing in teacher–pupil relationships. *Journal of Educational Psychology,* 1972, *63*(6), 543–550.

Shannon, J. R. Measures of validity of attention scores. *Journal of Educational Research,* 1942, *35*, 623–631.

Siegelman, E. Reflective and impulsive observing behavior. *Child Development,* 1969, *40*, 1213–1221.

Silberman, C. E. *Crisis in the classroom.* New York: Random House, 1970.

Soar, R. S. *Follow through classroom process measurement and pupil growth (1970–1971): Final report.* Gainesville, Fla.: College of Education, University of Florida, 1973.

Sroufe, L. A., & Stewart, M. A. Treating problem children with stimulant drugs. *New England Journal of Medicine,* 1973, *289*, 407–413.

Stallings, J. A., & Kaskowitz, D. H. *Follow through classroom observation evaluation—1972–1973.* Menlo Park, Cal.: Stanford Research Institute, 1974.

Treisman, A. M. Verbal cues, language and meaning in selective attention. *American Journal of Psychology,* 1964, *77*, 206–219.

Treisman, A. M. Strategies and models of selective attention. *Psychological Review,* 1969, *76*, 282–299.

Welford, A. T. *Fundamentals of skill.* London: Methuen, 1968.

Werry, J. S., & Sprague, R. L. Hyperactivity. In C. G. Costello (Ed.), *Symptoms of psychopathy.* New York: Wiley, 1970.

White, S. H. Evidence for a hierarchical arrangement of learning processes. In L. P. Lipsitt & C. C. Spiker (Eds.), *Advances in child development and behavior* (Vol. 2). New York: Academic, 1965.

White, S. H. Some general outlines of the matrix of developmental changes between five and seven years. *Bulletin of the Orton Society,* 1970, *20*, 41–57.

Wright, J. C. *On familiarity and habituation: The situational microgenetics of information getting.* Paper presented at the Symposium on Attention and Cognition, Society for Research in Child Development, New Orleans, 1977.

Wright, J. C., & Vlietstra, A. G. The development of selective attention: From perceptual exploration to logical search. In H. W. Reese (Ed.), *Advances in child development and behavior* (Vol. 10). New York: Academic, 1975, pp. 195–239.

Yerkes, R. M., & Dodson, J. D. The relation of strength of stimulus to rapidity of habit-formation. *Journal of Comparative Neurology of Psychology,* 1908, *18*, 459–482.

Zivin, G. How to make a boring thing more boring. *Child Development,* 1974, *45*, 232–236.

Watching Children Watch
Television

Daniel R. Anderson, Linda F. Alwitt, Elizabeth
Pugzles Lorch, and Stephen R. Levin

The national pastime of American children is watching television. They spend perhaps 20% of their waking hours in front of TV sets, cumulatively more time than they spend in school (Lyle & Hoffman, 1972a, b). Although there has been some research interest in the social and cognitive impact of television (cf. Liebert, Neale, & Davidson, 1973; Stein & Friedrich, 1975), there have been few studies on the nature and development of TV viewing itself. There has been little information on how children watch, why they watch, or what they watch.

In this chapter we review research on children's television viewing behavior and present new analyses of visual attention to TV. We watch children watch television not simply from a desire to understand its effects but also from a conviction that systematic analyses of real-life activities can lead to new and general insights into cognitive and social development.

When Children Begin to Watch Television

A reasonable first approach to studying TV viewing is determining when children begin to watch TV. The issue, however, is somewhat more complicated than it may at first seem. When adults watch TV, not only do they presumably engage in a variety of information-processing activities ranging from primitive orienting reflexes to complex inferential thought, but they also have the larger concept of "watching TV" as something to do. A very young child may have neither the concept of "watching TV" nor the cognitive abilities to meaningfully follow the most simple cinematic conventions.

Daniel R. Anderson, Linda F. Alwitt, Elizabeth Pugzles Lorch, and Stephen R. Levin • Department of Psychology, University of Massachusetts, Amherst, Massachusetts 01002.

Consider the following visual TV sequence: a brief shot of an airplane flying; a cut to the interior of a passenger airplane; a zoom to the face of a passenger. When adults are exposed to this sequence they may be visually attracted to the TV screen by the sound of the airplane; they may then infer that the interior scene was the same airplane, and that a flight, therefore, is in progress. Being familiar with cinematic conventions, adults may assume that the zoom to the passenger indicates a central character. The sequence of mental activities, therefore, ranges from basic attentional phenomena to inferences requiring integration of perceptually disparate scenes as well as utilization of a knowledge of television technique. If such complex cognitive processing is essential to consistent and purposeful "watching TV," then one would expect a developmental progression in TV viewing behavior that to some extent parallels cognitive development. In particular, we would expect that the transition from sensorimotor representation to symbolic forms of representation (e.g., Piaget, 1952) provides the cognitive basis for the beginning of consistent TV viewing.

Until recently, only one study examined TV viewing in very young children. Schramm, Lyle, and Parker (1961) interviewed parents in two western communities as to what age their children began to make "fairly regular use" of television. The median age of children at the beginning of TV use was reported to be 3.2 years in one sample and 2.8 years in the other.

The Schramm et al. (1961) study presents several problems of interpretation. The first problem is that "use" of television is not defined. The second problem is the Schramm et al. (1961) reliance on retrospective reports of parents who must recall their children's earlier TV viewing behavior. To illustrate this problem, we asked 60 parents of 3-, 4-, and 5-year-olds (1) at what age their children "started watching TV," (2) at what age their children "first purposely (as opposed to simply glancing at it occasionally) started watching TV," (3) at what age their children "first started asking that the TV set be turned on or that the channel be changed," and (4) at what age their children "started having favorite programs" (Levin & Anderson, unpublished data). The results are indicated in Table I. Not only do the ages indicated by the parents depend on the particular TV viewing behavior but they also depend on the current age of the child.

The older the child, the greater the age estimated by a parent for the beginning of the behavior, indicating that a parent's criterion may shift upward in light of the child's more advanced TV viewing behaviors. Retrospective accounts of TV viewing must, therefore, be considered of limited validity.

Recently, we reported the first study in which very young children were directly observed viewing TV (Anderson & Levin, 1976). The 72 children, aged 12 to 48 months, were individually observed at our laboratory in

TABLE I
Age in Years Given by Parents for Initial Television Viewing Behaviors

Present age of child	"Started watching"	"Purposefully watching"	"Asking TV set turned on"	"Started having favorite programs"
3	1.19	1.62	2.18	2.36
4	1.47	2.22	2.90	2.84
5	1.81	2.62	3.33	3.44
All ages[a]	1.49	2.15	2.80	2.88

[a]All age effects significant, $p<.05$.

Amherst. The child and the parent remained in a comfortably furnished viewing room while a "Sesame Street" program was played on a video monitor. A variety of attractive toys were available for the children to play with as an alternative to TV viewing. Visual attention was measured by having an observer depress a switch when the child looked at the TV and release the switch when the child looked away. Times of onset and offset of visual attention were automatically stored in a computer, thus providing a continuous record of each child's attention to the TV.

There was a dramatic increase in visual attention from 1 to 4 years of age such that 1-year-olds attended about 12% of the time, 2-year-olds 25%, 3-year-olds 45%, and 4-year-olds 55%. The increase in attention was partly due to longer looks at the TV in older children but was primarily due to a large increase in the frequency of looking at the TV at 2½ years of age. Twelve- to 24-month-olds looked at the TV about 90 times an hour, whereas the 30- to 48-month-olds looked at the TV about 150 times an hour. We noted that

> younger than 30 months, children did not systematically monitor the TV screen but rather, had their attention "captured" for short periods of time. The younger children appeared to be far more interested in playing with toys and interacting with their mothers than watching television. Older children, on the other hand, appeared to more deliberately "watch" television; they sat oriented toward the TV, often playing with toys, but glancing up at the screen frequently. (Anderson & Levin, 1976, p. 810)

Interestingly, the parents also reported a sharp increase in amount of home TV viewing at 2½ years of age, thus corroborating the laboratory observations.

The evidence from the interview studies and from our observational research converges on the conclusion that children begin purposive, systematic TV viewing between 2 and 3 years of age. This finding is reasonably consistent with Piaget's descriptions of cognitive development at this age. Piaget suggests that children move from predominantly sensorimotor representations of the external world to internalized representations that are more symbolic in nature. At the time of this transition children should begin to use these representations in order to appreciate some continuity of the TV image from one scene to the perceptually disparate next, and thus begin a rudimentary appreciation of plot lines in short TV segments.

Amount of Television Viewing

After children begin regular, purposive TV viewing, they apparently spend considerable amounts of time in front of TV sets. Estimates of how much time is spent vary considerably from study to study. Estimates appear to depend, among other things, on the age of the child, socioeconomic status, time of year, and the type of question asked of the parents or the child. No studies have validated questionnaire responses with in-home observations of children.

Lyle and Hoffman (1972a, b) have reported the most thorough research on weekly viewing times for children ranging from preschool to high school. Estimates for preschoolers were obtained from parents, whereas estimates for the older children were obtained by asking the children themselves. They report 21.5 hours for preschoolers, 22.8 hours for 1st-graders, 30.7 hours for 6th-graders, and 27.7 hours for 10th-graders. Other studies report viewing times that vary widely from those of Lyle and Hoffman. Friedrich and Stein (1973), for example, report an average of 34.2 hours per week for preschoolers, and they suggest that this is likely an underestimate! Since most such studies do not provide detailed procedures (e.g., definitions of "watching TV"), it is often difficult to resolve discrepancies.

An even greater concern is the reliability and validity of parent and child estimates of viewing time. Bechtel, Achelpohl, and Akers (1972) directly observed the TV viewing of a small number of families by installing a camera inside the homes. They noted that adults, when asked how much they "watch TV", generally overreported from 25% to 50%, as compared to the amount of time they were actually visually oriented toward the TV set. It is possible, however, that the adult subjects interpreted "watching TV" as simply equivalent to being in a room with a TV set on. Bechtel et al. (1972) did not report the correlations between estimated and actual viewing, leaving open the possibility that adults did accurately assess their own viewing but overestimated by a constant factor.

Problems are also encountered when parents estimate their children's viewing behavior. Greenberg, Ericson, and Vlahos (1972) reported that 9- and 10-year-old children's self-reports correlated only minimally with their parents' estimates of the children's viewing (the correlation for hours/Saturday was .22, that for hours/day was .07). The children generally reported far more television viewing than did the parents. It is, of course, impossible to know which estimates are more accurate since the validity of parental reports is unknown and children are notoriously poor at time estimates.

The particular questions asked of parents also presents a problem. In a recent study, Levin (1976) asked parents of preschoolers to estimate in two different ways the amount of their children's home viewing. One technique involved asking the parents to estimate the number of hours their children viewed TV each morning, afternoon, and evening of each day of the week. They estimated an average of 24.3 hours per week with a range of 1.5 to 49 hours. The second technique presented the parents with a current list of TV programs on which they estimated weekly viewing times for each program. Using this procedure, the same parents estimated an average of 32.7 hours per week with a range of 10 to 65 hours. Although the two techniques correlate reasonably well ($r = .77$), the difference in estimated times is highly significant (52 of 59 of the program estimates were greater than the daily time estimates, $p < .001$). Until there is a thorough direct observational study that validates parent and child estimates of viewing in the home, reports of amount of children's viewing must be considered only with caution. Nevertheless, until better methods are used, it is necessary to employ these estimates in order to identify factors that influence amount of TV viewing.

Factors Related to Amount of Home Viewing

Consistent TV viewing begins between 2 and 3 years of age and remains high until the teens, when viewing declines (Robinson, 1972). Some studies have found a negative correlation between socioeconomic status and amount of TV viewing in children (Greenberg & Dervin, 1970; McIntyre & Teevan, 1972), whereas other studies have found little relationship (Friedrich & Stein, 1973; Lyle & Hoffman, 1972a; McLeod, Atkin, & Chaffee, 1972). Black children are generally reported to watch TV more than white children (e.g., Lyle & Hoffman, 1972a).

Several investigations have attempted to determine *why* children watch TV. When older school-aged children are asked, the most frequent answers are for entertainment, to relax, and to relieve loneliness (Lyle & Hoffman, 1972a). Younger children's answers are usually less enlightening (e.g., "it's fun"). Children's activities that were displaced by television when it first arrived were consumption of other entertainment media (comic books, radio), play, interaction with adults, and sleep (Himmelweit, Oppenheim, & Vince, 1958; Schramm et al., 1961).

Parents probably strongly influence the amount of TV viewing in their children. Many parents openly use TV as a "baby-sitter" (Steiner, 1963) apparently because children are considerably quieter and less active when they watch TV (Gadberry, 1974). Parents' viewing may also influence children's viewing. In a stepwise multiple-regression analysis, we (Levin & Anderson, unpublished data) found that the amount of viewing by the mother was by far the best predictor of the amount of viewing by preschoolers, accounting for 50% of the variance. Other variables, which accounted for an additional 14% of the variance were, in order of importance, parents' interest in their children's viewing, the estimated amount of time the TV was on each week, availability of a color TV, and the father's TV viewing. Friedrich and Stein (1973) and others (cf. Stein & Friedrich, 1975) report that the pattern of program preference of preschoolers is also somewhat related to parental program preference.

The amount of time children spend in front of TV sets is determined by parental TV viewing, use of TV as a baby-sitter, age, and likely a large number of other factors related to ethnicity, socioeconomic status, and so on. The research identifying these factors has been correlational, and little attempt has been made to sort out the relative contributions of each factor. Other important questions, such as the degree to which amount of TV viewing constitutes a stable individual difference characteristic, have not even been studied. Studies concerned with the impact of home television viewing on social and cognitive development typically assume that home viewing does, in fact, constitute a reliable individual difference (e.g., Frueh & McGhee, 1975). Of course, all such studies are limited by the unknown validity of parents' and children's estimates of viewing time.

Studies concerned with amount of TV viewing do not take into account children's behavior *while* they are actually in front of TV sets. Recent research, however, has begun to clarify the ways in which children watch TV.

Visual Attention to Television

When children "watch" TV, they ordinarily do not simply stare at the screen for hours on end. In fact, depending on the child and the viewing circumstances, visual attention fluctuates considerably (Anderson & Levin, 1976; Becker & Wolfe, 1960; Sproull, 1973). In two separate studies, for example, we found that preschoolers look at and away from the TV about 150 times an hour (Anderson & Levin, 1976; Levin, 1976). Logically, three factors can influence these fluctuations: environmental distractors, characteristics of the child, and attributes of the TV program.

Distractors

Although there have been no extensive investigations of the television-viewing environment of children, it is likely that distractions of various kinds are common. In laboratory viewing situations in which distractions are minimal, visual attention is typically 85% or greater. In pretesting segments of "Sesame Street," for example, Children's Television Workshop researchers found it necessary to set up a slide projector, which functioned as a distractor, in order to produce less than maximum attention.

Toys also function effectively as distractors. In a recent laboratory study, we (Lorch, Anderson, & Levin, 1977) showed 5-year-olds two "Sesame Street" programs with and without toys present. The toys were sufficient to reduce attention to 44.5% from the high level of 87.1% when no toys were available.

A potential distractor is the presence of other children. Surprisingly, however, Sproull (1973) found that the presence of peers had no effect on 4-year-olds' visual attention to "Sesame Street." The peers did, however, increase the frequency of other program-related behaviors such as laughing and imitation.

Characteristics of the Child That Affect Attention to Television

The only individual difference in children that is known to be reliably related to visual attention to television is age. As we have discussed previously, children begin purposive, systematic TV viewing at around $2^1/2$ years. Beyond that time, however, attention continues to increase to a small extent at least up to age 5 (Levin, 1976). Even when age is statistically controlled, however, reliable individual differences in visual attention and other viewing behaviors (e.g., talking during the program, bodily orientation with respect to the TV) persist from session to session over a several-week period. We were not able to find any substantial relationship between these viewing styles and a number of measures of individual differences in intelligence and personality (Levin, 1976). We did find, on the other hand, a pattern of attention to TV that appears to characterize *all* children, as well as adults.

A General Pattern of Attention to Television

Children look at a TV, look away, and look back throughout the program. We examined the manner in which these looks and pauses are elicited, maintained, and terminated. As part of this research, we discovered a previously unreported general pattern of visual attention that can be described without reference to specific fluctuations in program content or distractions.

Consider a look at the TV that has been in progress for some period of time, t. As the look progresses through time, the likelihood of continuing to look could stay the same, decrease, or increase. We will examine three corresponding hypotheses: distraction, fatigue, and inertia.

The distraction hypothesis states simply that the child continues to look at the TV until distracted or until something "boring" occurs in the TV program. Since the distractor or the boring thing cannot "know" how long the child had been looking, the conditional probability of continuing to look at some later time $t + i$, given that the look had already progressed to time t, will be a flat function as illustrated in Figure 1.

The second hypothesis, illustrated in Figure 1, suggests simply that as the look continues through time, the child's attention becomes fatigued so that the probability of continuing to look at the TV decreases as the time the look has been in progress increases. Simply stated, the longer the child has been looking, the less likely it is that she/he will keep looking.

The third simple hypothesis is that a sort of behavioral "inertia" is built up such that the child is more likely to continue looking at the TV the longer he or she has already been looking. A plot of P $(LOOK_{t+i}/LOOK_t)$ should, therefore, be an increasing function, as indicated in the third panel of Figure 1. Of course, other hypotheses could be suggested that are variants or combinations of these three simple notions, but the central issue is whether factors that serve to terminate or maintain a look do so with regard to the temporal course of the look.

Using 3-second intervals, we calculated the conditional probability of continuing to look at the TV as a function of time since the look began (Anderson, Levin, & Sanders, n.d.). The analyses were based on the data of 60 3-, 4-, and 5-year-olds from Springfield, Massachusetts, who watched nearly 3 hours of heterogeneous children's programs. To illustrate

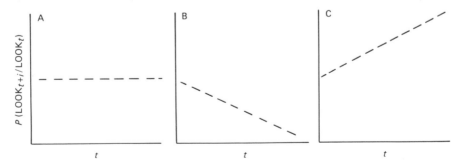

FIGURE 1. Three simple models of looking at television. (A): distraction; (B): fatigue; (C): inertia.

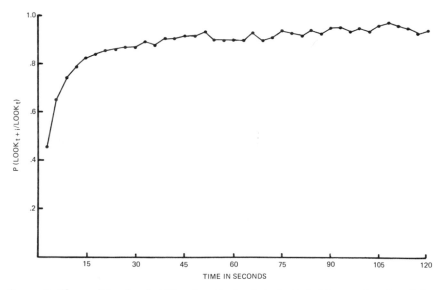

FIGURE 2. The conditional probability of continuing to look at television as a function of time since the look began. The data are based on 60 preschool children who watched nearly 3 hours of television.

the analysis, consider the calculation of the first three points in the function. There were a total of 26,664 looks at the TV over all three sessions. Of those looks, 12,162 continued beyond 3 seconds; the probability of continuing to look beyond 3 seconds, given that the look started, is 12,162 ÷ 26,664, or .456. To calculate $P(LOOK_6/LOOK_3)$, we first consider that only 12,162 looks entered the interval from 3 to 6 seconds. Of these looks, 7,806 continued beyond 6 seconds. The conditional probability of continuing to look beyond 6 seconds, given that the look has lasted 3 seconds, therefore, is 7,806 ÷ 12,162, or .642. In an identical manner $P(LOOK_9/LOOK_6)$ = 5,763 ÷ 7,806 = .738. The complete function, calculated in this manner, is illustrated in Figure 2. The figure clearly implicates the third hypothesis: A child is increasingly likely to continue to look at the TV the longer the look progresses. If a look lasts longer than about 15 seconds, the child has a strong tendency to become progressively "locked in" to the TV screen.

This "attentional inertia" may have been anecdotally and melodramatically described by Brazelton (1972):

> I have observed this in my own children and I have seen it in other people's children. As they sat in front of a set that was blasting away, watching a film of horrors of rapidly varying kinds, the children were completely quiet . . . they were hooked. If anyone interrupted, tapped a child on the shoulder to break through his state of rapt attention, he almost always would start and might even break down in angry crying. (p. 47)

In our viewing room, a child typically looked at the TV for only a short period of time before looking away (54% of all looks were less than 3 seconds long), but if a look continued beyond about 10 seconds, we often observed the child's body relax, head slouch forward, and mouth drop open. This posture might then be maintained continuously for several minutes, ending abruptly as if the child were "released" by some change on the TV (since we did not interrupt the children, we did not observe any "angry crying"). In the next section some of these "releasing factors" will be identified, but first consider an equivalent analysis of the pauses between looks. If attentional inertia characterizes the children's behavior when they are *not* looking at TV, then the conditional probability of looking back at the TV should diminish as a function of time since the end of the last look.

If a child has not looked at the TV for some period of time, t, we may, in an analogous fashion, calculate the conditional probability of looking at the TV as a function of time since the end of the last look. An increasing function would be predicted if the child has a strategy of periodically "checking" the TV screen. If, however, a child looks at the TV *only* because some aspect of the TV program attracts attention, then a flat function would be obtained. A decreasing function is predicted if the "inertia" found in looking at the TV also described the child's play behavior between looks. We calculated, therefore, $P(\text{LOOK}_{t+i} | \text{NOT LOOK}_t)$ as a function of t, for the same 60 children. Figure 3 shows very clearly that the longer the

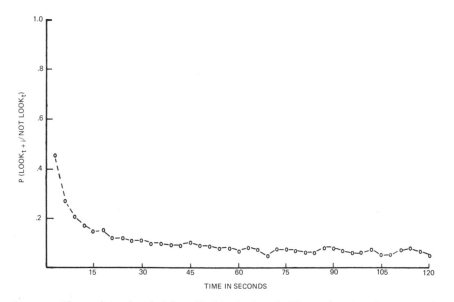

FIGURE 3. The conditional probability of looking back at the TV as a function of time since the end of the last look. The data are based on the same children indicated in Figure 1.

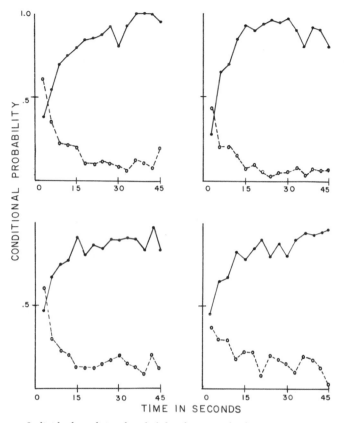

FIGURE 4. Individual conditional probability functions for four representative children.

"pause" has been in progress, the less likely it is that the child will look back at the TV. Either the children become "locked in" to their play, or the attractiveness of the TV diminishes the longer the child looks away.

In order to determine whether these inertia functions characterize the viewing behavior of individual children, we plotted the individual conditional probability functions. Each child's data showed the inertial patterns, indicating that the functions illustrated in Figures 2 and 3 are not artifacts of averaging individual curves. Examples of individual curves are given in Figure 4.

Figure 5 indicates the results of a reanalysis of the visual attention data presented by Anderson and Levin (1976). The curves again show the same inertial tendencies in these 12- to 48-month-old Amherst children as were found in the 36- to 60-month-old Springfield children. The lower overall attention of the 1-and 2-year-olds is reflected both in a lower probability of maintaining a look and in a lower probability of initiating a look. The youngest children are less likely to become locked in to the TV and are more likely to become locked into the non-TV environment than are the older children. Importantly, however, the same inertial tendencies in attention to TV were found in children as young as 12 months of age.

We are intrigued as to whether attentional inertia holds for adults. At

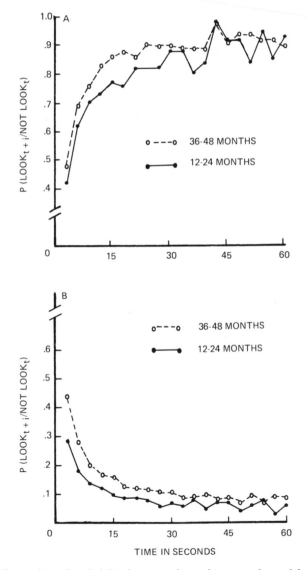

FIGURE 5. The conditional probability functions obtained in a reanalysis of the data of Anderson and Levin (1976).

the time of this writing, we have examined the visual attention of six college students who each watched 4½ hours of prime-time TV programs. The students were allowed to read novels, eat, or do homework while the TV was on (it was not difficult to get subjects). The analysis revealed inertial patterns for each adult virtually identical to those of the children. Attentional inertia holds, therefore, for people ranging in age from 1 to 23 years.

It is worth noting here that this phenomenon, which has been previously unreported, would not likely have been discovered in the context of current theories of attention based on traditional laboratory research paradigms. Television provides a dynamic, meaningful stimulus quite unlike the static stimuli, presented trial by trial, employed in most studies of attention.

Attributes of Television Programs That Influence Visual Attention

Although distractions, individual styles of viewing, and attentional inertia influence a child's attention to TV, they do so within the context of the TV program itself. It is reasonable to suppose that fluctuations of program content importantly control fluctuations of a child's attention to that program. Children's Television Workshop researchers (cf. Lesser, 1972) have hypothesized that much of the variation in the attention of young children may be directly in response to the variation of relatively simple attributes of TV programs. Similar notions are inherent in characterizations of the young child as being "stimulus bound," i.e., controlled by the concrete, immediate attributes of the stimulus environment (e.g., Bruner, 1973). Intuitive identification of these attributes, however, is not easy. Becker and Wolfe (1960) asked parents and teachers of school-aged and preschool children to identify the parts of TV programs that received the greatest attention from the children. While they found moderately good predictions of the older children's attention, they found that "neither educators trained for preschool or kindergarten work nor mothers of preschool children seem able to predict, with any high degree of reliability, the interest reactions of youngsters. We would hypothesize . . . that the ability of adults to predict the interest of children to television programs decreases with the decreasing age of the children" (pp. 212–213).

Recently we reported an attempt to identify attributes of "Sesame Street" that were associated with elevated or depressed visual attention in preschoolers (Anderson & Levin, 1976; Levin & Anderson, 1976). With the same procedure that we used to rate the continuous onsets and offsets of visual attention, observers rated "Sesame Street" Test Show 4 for the times of onset and offset of 44 different attributes. Since the times of occurrence of attention for each child were known and since we knew the times of occurr-

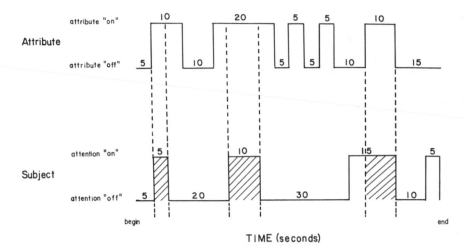

FIGURE 6. The attribute analysis of Anderson and Levin (1976).

ence of each attribute, we were able to calculate the percent attention in the exact presence of an attribute and compare it to the percent attention in the exact absence of the attribute. An illustration of this analysis, taken from Levin and Anderson (1976, p. 130), is shown in Figure 6:

> The upper time line represents the occurrence of a hypothetical attribute throughout a hypothetical 100-second television program. The numbers along the line represent the lengths of time the attribute was present or absent. Similarly, the lower time line represents the attention and non-attention of a hypothetical child throughout the program. The shaded portions indicate when the child attended *in the presence of the attribute.* From the diagram the following information can be obtained. 1. The child attended for 35 seconds or 35% of the program. 2. The attribute occurred for 50% of the program. 3. The child's attention in the presence of the attribute was 25 seconds or 50%. The child's attention in the absence of the attribute was 10 seconds or 20%. We conclude that attention is enhanced in the presence of the attribute (50%), as compared to the absence of the attribute (20%). (Levin & Anderson, 1976)

The percent attention in the presence and absence of 44 visual and auditory attributes were compared in analyses of variance. We found elevated attention in the presence of women, women's voices, children, children's voices, eye contact, puppets, animation, peculiar voices, movement, lively music, auditory changes, and rhyming, repetition, and alliteration. Depressed attention was found in the presence of adult men, men's voices, animals, inactivity, and still drawings. Camera activities such as cuts, pans, and zooms, as well as most special effects, had relatively little relationship to attention.

Although many of the attribute effects were quite large, we cautioned against too readily assuming a causal relationship between an attribute and attention. It may be that for a given TV program, the presence of a particular attribute is correlated with the presence of another, truly effective attribute. In "Sesame Street" Test Show 4, for example, adult men (both visually and auditorily) were associated with depressed attention. Adult men were, however, also associated with other attributes that received depressed attention, such as inactivity. Strictly speaking, demonstrating a causal relationship between an attribute and attention requires an experimental manipulation of the attribute while holding other factors constant. Such a demonstration with professionally produced TV material would be difficult and expensive, to say the least. In lieu of such demonstrations we examined the generality of attribute effects with a much larger heterogeneous sample of children's TV programs and advertisements and using a new and more detailed attribute analysis procedure (Anderson, Alwitt, Lorch, & Levin, unpublished data).

A New Attribute Analysis

In our initial attribute analyses we simply examined the temporal overlap between an attribute and visual attention. An attribute may, however, have an overall positive or negative relationship with attention for a number of reasons. At the time an attribute occurs, the effect on attention must be dependent on whether or not the child is looking at the TV. If the child is looking at the TV, the attribute can maintain the look, or it can lead to the termination of the look. If, on the other hand, the child is not looking at the TV, the attribute can elicit a look or inhibit it. The effect of an attribute, furthermore, may come from the change produced by its onset or by its continuation through time, or both. An attribute may have both positive and negative effects on attention depending on which combination of these factors is examined. It is possible, for example, that a given sound attribute could elicit attention if the child is not looking and terminate attention if the child is looking.

What we wish to do, in essence, is predict the onset and termination of visual attention as a function of the onset and continued presence of an attribute. If fluctuations in attention are "time locked" to fluctuations of an attribute, a case for causation is better made, although the problem of correlated attributes may still exist.

As an illustration of the analysis, consider the attribute "adult male voice." Our initial analyses of visual attention to "Sesame Street" (Anderson & Levin, 1976; Levin & Anderson, 1976) indicated that attention in the presence of an adult male voice was lower than in its absence. An analysis of the 60 Springfield children's attention to nearly 3 hours of heterogeneous children's programming (ranging from "Mister Rogers

Neighborhood" to "The Flintstones") replicated this effect in that visual attention was lower by 4% in the presence of a male voice as compared to its absence ($p < .001$). This effect could occur for four reasons: (1) If a child is not looking at the TV, the onset of a man talking keeps the child from looking, and/or (2) the continued presence of a man talking keeps the child from looking. (3) If a child is already looking at the TV, the onset of a male voice causes the child to look away, and/or (4) the continued presence, beyond the onset, of an adult male voice causes the child to look away. We will examine each of these possibilities in turn.

The first possibility required that the computer be programmed to identify all the instances, for a given child, in which the onset of an adult male voice occurred while the child was not looking. The computer then calculated the proportion of such instances in which the child then began looking within a 3-second interval following the attribute onset. Thus we calculated the probability of the child initiating a look at the TV following the onset of an adult male voice. For our 60 children, the probability is .185. This probability must be compared to a "control" value that assesses the probability of a look onset when the attribute is not present. The computer identified all successive 3-second intervals of the TV programs in which an adult male voice was not present and had not been present for at least 3 seconds. It was necessary, furthermore, to consider only those control intervals in which the child was *not* looking at the TV at the beginning of the interval. The proportion of these control intervals in which the child then initiated a look was calculated to be .171, which was not significantly different from .185. We therefore conclude that the onset of a male voice had no significant relationship to the onset of a look at the TV.

Although the onset of an adult male voice does not affect attention onset, the continued presence of a man talking could. The continued presence of an attribute was defined as its continued occurrence for each successive 3-second interval following the 3-second onset interval. An attribute occurrence that is 9 seconds long, for example, would contain one onset interval followed by two continuation intervals. For each child, the computer identified all continuation intervals for which the child was not looking at the beginning of the interval. The proportion of these intervals in which there was a look onset was then calculated to be .141 for the continuation of adult male voice and was compared to the control value of .171. This difference of .030 in the probabilities is significant [$t(59) = -6.36$, $p < .001$], and we conclude that the continued presence of an adult male voice is associated with a reduced probability of a look onset. A causal description of this result is that although the onset of adult male voice does not inhibit attention onset, its continued presence does.

Parallel analyses must be performed for the instances in which an attribute occurs while a child *is* looking at the TV. The analyses are strictly analogous except that attribute onset, continuation, and control intervals are identified in which the child is looking at the beginning of the interval, and the probability of look termination is calculated. The probability of a look ending following the onset of a male voice was calculated to be .252, where the control probability was .254. This difference is not significant, and we conclude that the onset of an adult male voice is not associated with the termination of a look. The probability of a look ending during the continuation of a male voice, however, was .291, which is significantly different from the control probability of .254. Children tend to look away from the TV in the continued presence of a man talking.

We can now reinterpret the negative relationship of visual attention and an adult male voice. Although the onset of a man talking neither elicits nor turns off children's looks at the TV, the continued presence of an adult male voice, beyond 3 seconds, reliably terminates looks and also keeps them from occurring. This set of results, and those for 30 other attributes are presented in Table II. The table indicates the results of the temporal overlap analysis illustrated in Figure 6, as well as the new analysis of attribute onset and continuation effects. For instances in which the child was not looking at the time of attribute occurrence, a significant effect ($p < .01$) is labeled as "eliciting" attention or "inhibiting" attention, as appropriate. For instances in which the child was looking, a significant effect is labeled as "maintaining" or "terminating" attention. The values given are the differences between the probabilities for the onset or continuation intervals and the appropriate control values.

Discussion of the Attribute Effects

Meaningful Units

The largest effects come from a group of attributes that tend to define meaningful units of activity and programming. "Bit change" is defined as the transition point between one segment of programming and another. At this point all ongoing attributes and producer-intended message units are terminated and others begin. If a child is not looking at the TV, a bit change strongly elicits a look, whereas if the child is looking, a bit change tends to terminate the look. This is an attribute with powerful positive *and* negative effects on visual attention.

Many of the bit changes were to, from, and between commercials. Correspondingly, commercial onset also had both eliciting and terminating effects on attention. As a commercial continued beyond its onset, however, it tended to turn off those looks it elicited. In general, we found that the children's attention to commercials was lower than that to the regular pro-

TABLE II
Attribute Analyses

| Attributes | Total | Child not looking when attribute occurs | | | | Child looking when attribute occurs | | | |
| | | Attribute onset | | Continuation | | Attribute onset | | Continuation | |
		Elicit	Inhibit	Elicit	Inhibit	Maintain	Terminate	Maintain	Terminate
Meaningful units									
Bit change	—	.184 ^{d}	—	^{a}	^{a}	—	.123 ^{d}	^{a}	^{a}
Auditory change	—	.064 ^{d}	—	^{a}	^{a}	n.s.	—	^{a}	^{a}
Cuts	—	n.s.	—	^{a}	^{a}	.040 ^{d}	—	^{a}	—
Commercials	-.04 ^{d}	.196 ^{d}	—	—	n.s.	—	.096 ^{d}	—	.052 ^{d}
Camera techniques									
Still camera	n.s. ^{c}	—	n.s.	—	n.s.	—	n.s.	—	.018 ^{c}
Zoom	-.10 ^{d}	—	n.s.	—	.033 ^{d}	—	n.s.	—	.229 ^{d}
Pan	-.03 ^{d}	—	n.s.	n.s.	—	—	n.s.	—	.108 ^{d}
People									
Adult male									
White man	-.07 ^{d}	—	.029 ^{d}	—	.038 ^{d}	n.s.	—	n.s.	n.s.
Black man	+.12 ^{d}	n.s.	—	.062 ^{d}	—	n.s.	—	.044 ^{c}	—
Male voice	-.04 ^{d}	n.s.	—	—	.030 ^{d}	n.s.	—	—	.038 ^{d}
Adult female									
White woman	n.s.	n.s.	—	n.s.	—	.040 ^{d}	—	—	n.s.
Female voice	+.04 ^{d}	.055 ^{d}	—	n.s.	—	n.s.	—	—	n.s.
Child									
White boy	n.s.	—	n.s.	—	n.s.	n.s.	—	—	.031 ^{c}
Black boy	+.106 ^{d}	n.s.	—	.040 ^{c}	—	.074 ^{d}	—	n.s.	—
White girl	n.s.	—	n.s.	n.s.	—	n.s.	—	n.s.	n.s.
Child's voice	+.06 ^{d}	.016 ^{c}	—	.057 ^{d}	—	.050 ^{d}	—	—	—
Characters									
Puppets	+.07 ^{d}	.076 ^{c}	—	.028 ^{d}	—	—	n.s.	—	n.s.

Animals	-.12^d	—	.026^c	—	.048^d	—	n.s.	—	.100^d
Animation	+.096^c	.106^c	—	.054^d	—	—	n.s.	n.s.	.083^d
Eye contact	-.06^d	n.s.	—	—	.028^c	—	.060^d	—	n.s.
Peculiar voice	+.107^d	.064^d	—	.093^d	—	—	n.s.	—	—
Visual Techniques									
Letters, numbers, script	+.02^c	.035^d	—	n.s.	—	—	n.s.	n.s.	—
Still drawings, photos	-.167^c	n.s.	—	—	.030^d	—	n.s.	—	.212^d
Activity									
Active stationary	n.s.	—	n.s.	n.s.	—	.036^c	—	n.s.	—
Moving through space	+.04^d	.029^d	—	—	.025^c	.055^d	—	n.s.	—
Sound									
Music									
Slow music	-.18^d	n.s.	—	—	.070^d	—	.108^d	—	.166^d
Lively music	-.04^d	.095^d	—	—	.032^d	n.s.	—	—	n.s.
Other sounds									
Laughing	n.s.	.037^c	—	a	a	—	n.s.	a	a
Applause	+.148^d	.087^c	—	n.s.	—	—	n.s.	n.s.	—
Rhyming, repetition, alliteration	-.07^d	.038^d	—	—	.059^d	.024^c	—	.022^c	—
Sound effects	+.16^d	.079^d	—	.031^c	—	.054^d	—	.064^d	—

[a] This attribute has no continuation intervals.
[b] Total effect based on analysis illustrated in Figure 6.
[c] $p < .01$.
[d] $p < .001$.
[e] n.s. indicates nonsignificant trend.

gramming, although attention to particular commercials specifically directed at children was quite high. Ward, Levinson, and Wackman (1972) also noted that children's attention to commercials is somewhat lower than that to regular programming.

Within a program segment, units of activity are sometimes defined by "cuts" (sudden visual scene changes) and "auditory changes" (transitions from one sound source to another, e.g., man's voice to sound effect). Auditory changes elicited looks from children who were not attending but had no effect on children who were attending. Cuts, on the other hand, maintained attention when the children were looking but, sensibly, had no effect when the children were not looking.

These results can be related to a study recently reported by Wartella and Ettema (1974). Using combinations of bit change, auditory change, cuts, and several other variables originally discussed by Watt and Krull (1974), they identified two factors of commercials, which they labeled "auditory complexity" and "visual complexity." These two factors are roughly equivalent to amount of auditory and visual change. They reported that, similar to our findings, the onset of commercials led to fluctuations in attention of their preschool and second-grade subjects. They also reported that "auditory complexity" appeared to be most strongly related to continued attention to the commercials. As will be apparent, our analyses also strongly implicate auditory attributes as most importantly related to visual attention.

Camera Techniques

It is commonly believed that in order to hold young children's attention, a TV program should include frequent camera activities such as zooms and pans. In our initial analyses of attributes of "Sesame Street," however, we noted that pans and zooms had little relationship to attention (Anderson & Levin, 1976; Levin & Anderson, 1976). The present detailed analyses, based on a larger sample of TV programming, indicates that lengthy zooms and pans actually tend to terminate looks at the TV. Notice that Table II indicates that a continued zoom is also associated with the inhibition of look onset. Since zoom is a visual attribute, we presume such an effect can occur because (1) correlated sound attributes inhibit attention; (2) the child may use peripheral vision or very brief glances at the TV not detected by the observer; or (3) since long zooms terminate looks, the effect is simply a kind of spillover effect, i.e., the child does not look back at the TV for the remainder of the zoom.

When a camera is static, not engaged in zooms, pans, or other such activities, there is a slight tendency for looks to be terminated over extended periods.

Adult Males

In our first study we found that adult men both visually and auditorily were associated with depressed attention. As we have already noted in our example of the new attribute analysis, this trend was replicated for adult male voice, in that the continued presence of a male talking (singing was not counted as part of this attribute) both inhibited and terminated looks. The results for the visual presence of adult men must, however, be qualified. Black men on the screen were associated with enhanced attention such that the continued visual presence of black men both elicited and maintained looks. White men, on the other hand, were associated with depressed attention. The negative effect of a white man on the screen was, curiously, due to both the onset and the continuation of the attribute inhibiting looks at the screen. The negative effect of this visual attribute was apparent only when the children were *not looking* at the TV. The children, who were all white, were either monitoring the presence of white men through peripheral vision or, more plausibly, were affected by the correlated presence of a sound attribute, probably an adult male voice.

Black men were present in only 5.9% of the program material, whereas white men were present 26.6% of the time, indicating a possible novelty effect for black men. In our previous work with "Sesame Street" in which both attributes were negative, white men and black men occurred frequently and nearly equally often (20% and 21%, respectively).

Women

Replicating our earlier work, women, both visually and auditorily, were associated with enhanced attention (there were only small amounts of a black woman on our tapes—the effect was, overall, positive). When children were not looking at the TV, the onset of a woman's voice elicited attention, and when children were looking at the TV, the onset of a woman on the screen tended to maintain attention. Although the effects are not large, they stand in contrast to the results for men. Women are generally less frequently seen on television than are men (e.g., Gerbner, 1972; Sternglanz & Serbin, 1974), so it is possible that a novelty effect contributes in a small way to the enhanced attention to women.

Children

Children's voices elicited and maintained attention. The visual presence of children is less reliable: The continued presence of a white boy terminated looks, whereas the onset of a black boy maintained looks. There was no effect of a white girl (black girls appeared very infrequently).

Other Characters

We again found that the overall effect of puppets on the screen was positive with respect to visual attention. The effect is, however, *not likely visual* since the onset and continuation of puppets elicited attention from children who were *not* looking at the TV. There was no effect of puppets in maintaining looking. We believe that the effect is again understandable in terms of the sounds associated with puppets. A highly correlated sound attribute is "peculiar voices," which we defined as voices a child was unlikely to hear except as part of a mass medium experience. The onset and continuation of peculiar voices reliably elicited looks at the TV, although there was no effect if the child was already looking.

Another highly positive attribute associated with peculiar voices is animation. Again, the effects of this visual attribute were on the child who was *not* looking at the TV: The onset and continuation of animation elicited looks, but did not significantly affect children who were already looking. It is quite possible, therefore, that the positive effects of these visual techniques on visual attention are in fact mediated by correlated auditory attributes.

In our initial research on "Sesame Street," we found that, contrary to intuition, the visual presence of animals was negatively related to attention. This effect was repeated in the present analyses. The continued presence of filmed animals terminated looks at the TV. Since there were also smaller effects of animals inhibiting looks at the TV, it could be that once children are "turned off" by animals, they continue to monitor the associated audio narrative, which further inhibits their looking. Levin and Anderson (1976) speculated "that this effect would not hold for animals such as Lassie or Joe (*Run, Joe, Run*) which behave in a nearly human fashion. We believe that young children's fascination for animals 'in real life' may be due to the interactive and tactual qualities that are not possibly presented on TV" (p. 132).

A finding that does not replicate our earlier work is a negative relationship of eye contact and attention. The onset and continuation of a character making eye contact with the audience reliably terminated looks. Virtually all eye contact in these tapes was made by the lead characters of "Captain Kangaroo," "Mister Rogers Neighborhood," and "Romper Room School." These characters, who generally received low attention, typically made eye contact while talking about events and topics somewhat remote in space and time from the concrete setting of the TV program.

Visual Techniques

Like animation, the visual presentation of numbers and letters was positively related to attention. But also like animation, the effect was on children who were *not* looking at the TV. Again, it appears that sound attributes (perhaps auditory change) mediate the effect of this visual attribute.

A visual technique that does affect looking with high reliability is the presentation of still photos and drawings. Visual attention drops about 16% in the presence of stills, primarily when the stills are presented longer than 3 seconds.

Activity

The onset of active stationary activity and motion (central character or object moving through space) maintains attention. Motion also elicits attention, perhaps through mechanisms of peripheral vision (Kaufman, 1974). The unlikely finding that continued motion inhibits looking gets our nomination for a probable alpha error (at a .01 significance level, one spurious result is expected).

Music

In our analysis of attention to "Sesame Street" we found no effect of slow music and a positive effect of lively music. Our new analyses reveal, however, that slow music inhibited and terminated visual attention. Lively music, on the other hand, had mixed effects: The onset of lively music elicited attention, but its continued presence inhibited looking. Our only explanation of this discrepancy between these two studies is simply that Joe Raposo's early "Sesame Street" songs may be particularly more compelling than the varieties of music we found in "Mister Rogers Neighborhood," "Captain Kangaroo," "The Flintstones," "Romper Room School," "Gilligan's Island," and "Vegetable Soup."

Other Sound Attributes

Laugh and applause tracks are quite common on children's TV programs. These attributes elicited attention from children who were not looking at the TV. Sound effects both elicited and maintained attention.

An attribute that the producers of "Sesame Street" believe is strongly related to attention is "rhyming, repetition, and alliteration" ("one, two, buckle my shoe" . . . "three, three, three," . . . "Wanda the witch lives somewhere west of Washington"). Our work with "Sesame Street" confirmed this notion. The present analyses, however, show a negative relationship due to continued rhyming, repetition, and alliteration. The onset of the attribute, on the other hand, had small eliciting and maintaining effects. Extended rhyming, repetition, and alliteration occurred primarily in

"Captain Kangaroo" in sequences such as the camera panning a storybook with still drawings while an extended children's poem was recited in a male voice-over.

Summary of Attribute Effects

The most remarkable results of our new attribute analyses are the indications of the powerful influence of sound attributes over visual attention. A number of visual attributes, in fact, appear to have a relationship to visual attention only by virtue of their association with sound attributes (e.g., white man, puppets, and animation) that elicit or inhibit attention of children who are not looking at the TV when the attribute occurs.

Other visual attributes, such as animals, have a strong tendency to terminate looks at the TV and then inhibit further looks. Such look inhibition presumably happens because the children in some way keep track of the sounds associated with the animals. When an auditory change or bit change occurs, this inhibition is released, and a look is elicited.

The new analyses, with some qualifications and a few contradictions, confirm and extend our previous findings (Anderson & Levin, 1976; Levin & Anderson, 1976). Women, women's voices, children's voices, auditory changes, peculiar voices, movement, cuts, sound effects, laughing, and applause are relatively unambiguously related to enhanced visual attention, whereas male voices, extended zooms and pans, animals, and stills are negatively related to attention. Some attributes, such as bit change and lively music, appear to have both positive and negative relationships. A few attributes were positive in one study and negative in the other. Eye contact, for example, was related to enhanced attention in the "Sesame Street" analysis but was related to depressed attention in the later analysis.

Attention to television is influenced by distractions, individual styles of attending, attentional inertia, and the vicissitudes of television content. Auditory attributes, in particular, play a major role in determining visual attention. In order to understand attention to television, therefore, we must examine auditory attention.

Auditory Attention to Television

In reviewing research on attention to television, Lyle (1972) noted that studies of visual attention to the TV screen leave unanswered "the question of whether or not 'attention time' is restricted to 'eye contact' time" (p. 26). Auditory attention to television is an area of research that has, however, been nearly unexplored. Although it is clear that auditory attributes are highly effective determinants of looking at TV, we know almost nothing about the determinants of listening to TV.

Television programming has often been described as "radio with pictures," since most intended messages are presented via the audio track. If visual attention is strongly related to auditory attention, one might expect to find a positive relationship between visual attention and comprehension of a TV program.

In testing this relationship, Friedrich and Stein (1973) time-sampled preschoolers' visual attention to "Mister Rogers Neighborhood" and "Batman." Although individual differences in attention were somewhat related to character identification, they were not related to other knowledge of content, nor were they related to any measures of behavior change. This failure to find any substantial relationship of visual attention to the children's knowledge of content may have been due to the children's prior familiarity with the programs.

Recently, we examined 5-year-olds' comprehension of two "Sesame Street" tapes as a function of visual attention (Lorch et al., 1977). One group of children was allowed to play with toys while viewing the programs, and another group viewed without toys. As discussed earlier, attention in the toys group was substantially below that of the no-toys group (44% and 87%, respectively). Immediately following the viewing session, the children were tested for their knowledge of the content of each of the 15 bits. We found no significant differences between the two groups in their knowledge of the programs. We did, however, find significant within-group correlations between visual attention and comprehension. Not only was the correlation significant for visual comprehension items but it was also significant for auditory comprehension items. The pattern of results suggests not only that variations in visual attention are produced in part by variations in the comprehensibility of the TV program but also that visual attention and auditory comprehension are positively correlated.

Bernard Friedlander and his associates have come closest to directly examining children's auditory attention to television (Bohannon & Friedlander, 1973; Friedlander, 1975; Friedlander & Cohen de Lara, 1973). Their work indicates, surprisingly, that young children may pay little attention to the audio track *at a semantic level*. In their procedure, children are presented with a TV program in which a degraded sound track is sometimes present. The children are instructed that they may receive a normal sound track by operating a switch. Among other findings, Friedlander reports an age trend such that 5- to 8-year-old children have only a minimal preference for the normal sound track, whereas older children show a consistent preference. The younger children actually preferred a meaningless sound track with "lively intonation" to a monotonous semantically sensible sound track.

Further research on auditory attention to television must, therefore, take into consideration the *level* at which children are listening. While it is quite clear from the attribute research that children listen to television even when they are not looking, Friedlander's results suggest that children may often not be attending at the level of word and sentence meaning.

A Possible Theoretical Direction for Future Research on Attention to Television

In total, the research indicates that children's attention to television is a complex interaction of the child's level of cognitive development, individual differences, environmental distractions, variations in TV program content, and attentional inertia. It is also apparent that visual attention is in large part controlled through audition.

Most of our description of children's attention has been couched in terms of concrete attributes of TV programs such as presence of music, animals on the screen, camera techniques, and so on. Such an emphasis stems, in part, from the belief that young children tend to be perceptually dominated by concrete, here-and-now stimulation. We have not addressed the very important issues of the relationship of children's attention to more abstractly defined content. When children "watch" television, their attention is surely controlled in part by concrete attributes, but it is likely that much of their attention is to action *sequences* that can be relatively concrete or perhaps more subtle and abstract. As the children's cognitive level increases, so, presumably, does the level of abstraction at which they are capable of attending.

In a study of comprehension, Collins and Westby (1975) showed second-, fifth-, and eighth-graders an action detective TV program. One group of children saw the program edited so that the scenes were randomly ordered and no sensible sequential plot line could be discerned. The control group saw the original version. In tests of comprehension and memory of the program, Collins and Westby found that second-graders performed at the same level on both versions of the program, whereas fifth- and eighth-graders were substantially confused by the randomly ordered version. Since second-graders appreciated the randomly ordered program about as much as they appreciated the normal program, one possible conclusion is that they were attending at a level considerably lower than that abstractly defined as the "plot."

If the children are attending to the TV at a level different from that intended by the producer, then a procedure to identify the boundaries of action sequences defined at successive levels of abstraction would be highly valuable. Such a procedure may be implicit in the work of Darren Newtson on adults' perception of ongoing behavior. Following Heider (1958), Newtson assumed that behavior is typically viewed as a series of discrete actions rather than continuous and undifferentiated. Pursuing this notion, Newtson asked adult subjects, who viewed a film of another person, to push a button when "one meaningful action ends and a different one begins, that is, when the person stops doing one thing and begins to do something discriminably different" (Newtson, 1976, p. 224). Newtson established that adults were not only highly reliable in identifying "breakpoints" in action sequences but were also capable of varying their level of analysis. Upon instruction, adults could identify the breakpoints between large, somewhat abstractly defined behavior sequences as readily as they could identify the smallest concretely detailed behaviors. Newtson (cf. 1976) found, furthermore, that the small and large units formed a hierarchical structure: "That is, persons marking small units were breaking down the same units employed by large-unit subjects into their component parts" (p. 225). In further research, Newtson reported evidence that the unit of perception employed by the subject was also the unit of comprehension and memory of the observed actions. Collins and Westby's finding that younger children have relatively little comprehension of the plot of a TV show is suggestive that those children were attending at the level of lower order subunits, with little conceptual integration.

Newtson's ideas can be extended to encompass visual attention to television. Assume that a look is maintained until the current conceptual unit has been processed. When the breakpoint for that current unit has been reached, the viewer (1) stops looking, (2) continues to attend at the same conceptual level, or (3) continues to attend, but at the next higher conceptual level. We hypothesize that as the look continues, the viewer tends to process units at successively higher levels. Since higher conceptual levels have breakpoints further apart in time, the possible "exit" points for attention become more infrequent, increasing the conditional probability of continuing to look. The theory is thus able to account for attentional inertia in TV viewing. The attentional inertia effect should, therefore, hold only for materials having a temporal structure that can be described at several levels of abstraction. Since it is reasonable to expect that younger children would attend to a TV program at lower levels of abstraction than older children, the theory would also predict that average look length should increase with age, which it does (Anderson & Levin, 1976; Levin, 1976).

If children's attention to television is deployed according to their units of perception, then fluctuations of attention should be related to transitions between these units. Although this notion was not directly examined in our current analyses, we did find that one kind of breakpoint—namely, the attribute "bit change"—was strongly associated with onset and termination of looking at the TV. Future research might do well, therefore, to determine whether developmental differences in variations of attention relate to variations in program content at different levels of abstraction. If such a relationship is found, we can truly begin to understand what children watch when they watch television.

Final Comments

We have devoted the bulk of this chapter to laboratory studies of children's attention to television. Television viewing behavior can, however, be studied at several levels, all of which are complexly interrelated. At a molar level are the economic and political factors that have led to the wide availability of television and the particular programming that is presented (cf. Melody, 1973). More directly acting on the child are the parents' TV viewing behaviors, socioeconomic, cultural, and even geographic factors that influence how much time a child spends in front of a TV. Finally, the child's cognitive level and other individual factors affect the child's patterns of attention to and comprehension of the TV programs. But the child's attention and comprehension are influenced by the nature of the TV programs, which are themselves the product of molar economic and political forces. An understanding of children's TV viewing behavior, therefore, cannot be divorced from a consideration of the overall social, political, and historical context in which it occurs.

A similar point has recently been made by Ulric Neisser (1976) in a critique of cognitive psychology. He deplored the proliferation of laboratory research paradigms "lacking in ecological validity, indifferent to culture, even missing some of the main features of perception and memory as they occur in ordinary life . . . cognitive psychologists must make a greater effort to understand cognition as it occurs in the ordinary environment and in the context of natural purposeful activity. We may have been lavishing too much effort on hypothetical models of the mind and not enough on analyzing the environment that the mind has been shaped to meet" (pp. 7–8). Increasingly, our children's minds meet television. We hope we have shown that watching children watch televison can lead not only to a better understanding of children's televison viewing but also, perhaps, to a better understanding of children's minds.

ACKNOWLEDGMENTS

We gratefully acknowledge the assistance of Rex Bradford, Hilary Chmielinski, Diane Field, Bruce Gordon, Rosemarie Miskiewicz, and Jeanne Sanders. Grants from the National Science Foundation and the W. T. Grant Foundation provided the financial support for the preparation of this chapter and for much of the research reported within. D. R. Anderson is supported by a Research Scientist Development Award from the National Institute of Mental Health.

References

Anderson, D. R., & Levin, S. R. Young children's attention to *Sesame Street*. *Child Development*, 1976, *47*, 806–811.

Anderson, D. R., Levin, S. R., & Sanders, J. A. *Attentional inertia in television viewing.* Unpublished manuscript, n.d.

Bechtel, R. B., Achelpohl, C., & Akers, R. Correlates between observed behavior and questionnaire responses on television viewing. In E. A. Rubinstein, G. A. Comstock, & J. P. Murray (Eds.), *Television and social behavior.* Vol. 4: *Television in day-to-day life: Patterns of use.* Washington, D.C.: U.S. Government Printing Office, 1972.

Becker, S., & Wolfe, G. Can adults predict children's interest in a television program? In W. Schramm (Ed.), *The impact of educational television.* Urbana, Ill.: University of Illinois Press, 1960, pp. 195–213.

Bohannon, J. N., & Friedlander, B. Z. The effect of intonation on syntax recognition in elementary school children. *Child Development*, 1973, *44*, 675–677.

Brazelton, T. B. How to tame the TV monster. *Redbook*, 1972, *138*, 47–51.

Bruner, J. S. *Beyond the information given: Studies in the psychology of knowing.* New York: Norton, 1973.

Collins, A., & Westby, S. *Children's processing of social information from televised dramatic programs.* Paper presented at the Society for Research in Child Development meeting, Denver, 1975.

Friedlander, B. Z. Automated evaluation of selective listening in language-impaired and normal infants and young children. In B. Z. Friedlander, G. M. Sterritt, & G. E. Kirk (Eds.), *Exceptional infant.* Vol. 3: *Assessment and interventions.* New York: Brunner/Mazel, 1975.

Friedlander, B. Z., & Cohen de Lara, H. Receptive language anomaly and language/reading dysfunction in "normal" primary-grade school children. *Psychology in the Schools*, 1973, *10*, 12–18.

Friedrich, L., & Stein, A. Aggressive and prosocial television programs and the natural behavior of preschool children. *Monographs of the Society for Research in Child Development*, 1973, *38*(4, Serial No. 151).

Frueh, T., & McGhee, P. E. Traditional sex role development and amount of time spent watching television. *Developmental Psychology*, 1975, *11*, 109.

Gadberry, S. Television as a babysitter: A field comparison of preschoolers' behavior during playtime and during television viewing. *Child Development*, 1974, *45*, 1132–1136.

Gerbner, G. Violence in television drama: Trends and symbolic functions. In G. A. Comstock & E. A. Rubinstein (Eds.), *Television and social behavior.* Vol. 1: *Content and control.* Washington: U.S. Government Printing Office, 1972.

Greenberg, B. S., & Dervin, B. *Use of the mass media by the urban poor.* New York: Praeger, 1970.

Greenberg, B. S., Ericson, P., & Vlahos, M. Children's television behaviors as perceived by mother and child. In E. A. Rubinstein, G. A. Comstock, & J. P. Murray (Eds.), *Television and social behavior.* Vol. 4: *Television in day-to-day life: Patterns of use.* Washington, D.C.: U.S. Government Printing Office, 1972.

Heider, F. *The psychology of interpersonal relations.* New York: Wiley, 1958.

Himmelweit, H., Oppenheim, A., & Vince, P. *Television and the child.* London: Oxford, 1958.

Kaufman, L. *Sight and mind.* New York: Oxford University Press, 1974.

Lesser, G. S. Learning, teaching, and television production for children: The experience of *Sesame Street. Harvard Educational Review*, 1972, *42*, 232–272.

Levin, S. R. Relationships between preschool individual differences and patterns of television viewing. Unpublished doctoral dissertation, University of Massachusetts, 1976.

Levin, S. R., & Anderson, D. R. The development of attention. *Journal of Communication,* 1976, *26,* 126–135.

Liebert, R., Neale, J., & Davidson, E. *The early window: The effects of television on children and youth.* New York: Pergamon, 1973.

Lorch, E. P., Anderson, D. R., & Levin, S. R. *Comprehending Sesame Street: The effects of visual attention.* Paper presented at the National Association of Educational Broadcasters annual meeting, Washington, D.C., October 1977.

Lyle, J. Television in daily life: Patterns of use. In E. A. Rubinstein, G. A. Comstock, & J. P. Murray (Eds.), *Television and social behavior.* Vol. 4: *Television in day-to-day life: Patterns of use.* Washington, D.C.: U.S. Government Printing Office, 1972.

Lyle, J. L., & Hoffman, H. R. Children's use of television and other media. In E. A. Rubinstein, G. A. Comstock, & J. P. Murray (Eds.), *Television and social behavior.* Vol. 4: *Television in day-to-day life: Patterns of use.* Washington, D.C.: U.S. Government Printing Office, 1972. (a)

Lyle, J. L., & Hoffman, H. R. Explorations on patterns of television viewing by preschool-age children. In E. A. Rubinstein, G. A. Comstock, & J. P. Murray (Eds.), *Television and social behavior.* Vol. 4: *Television in day-to-day life: Patterns of use.* Washington, D.C.: U.S. Government Printing Office, 1972. (b)

McIntyre, J., & Teevan, J. Television and deviant behavior. In G. A. Comstock & E. A. Rubinstein (Eds.), *Television and social behavior.* Vol. 3: *Television and adolescent aggressiveness.* Washington, D.C.: U.S. Government Printing Office, 1972.

McLeod, J., Atkin, C., & Chaffee, S. Adolescents, parents, and television use: Adolescent self-report measures from Maryland and Wisconsin. In G. A. Comstock & E. A. Rubinstein (Eds.), *Television and social behavior.* Vol. 3: *Television and adolescent aggressiveness.* Washington, D.C.: U.S. Government Printing Office, 1972.

Melody, W. *Children's television: The economics of exploitation.* New Haven: Yale University Press, 1973.

Neisser, U. *Cognition and reality.* San Francisco: W. H. Freeman, 1976.

Newtson, D. Foundations of attribution: The perception of ongoing behavior. In J. Harvey, W. Ickes, & R. Kidd (Eds.), *New directions in attribution research.* Hillsdale, N.J.: Lawrence Erlbaum, 1976.

Piaget, J. *The origins of intelligence in children.* New York: International Universities Press, 1952.

Robinson, J. P. Television's impact on everyday life: Some cross-national evidence. In E. A. Rubinstein, G. A. Comstock, & J. P. Murray (Eds.), *Television and social behavior.* Vol. 4: *Television in day-to-day life: Patterns of use.* Washington, D.C.: U. S. Government Printing Office, 1972.

Schramm, W., Lyle, J., & Parker, E. B. *Television in the lives of our children.* Stanford: Stanford University Press, 1961.

Sproull, N. Visual attention, modeling behaviors, and other verbal and nonverbal metacommunication of pre-kindergarten children viewing *Sesame Street. American Educational Research Journal,* 1973, *10,* 101–114.

Stein, A. H., & Friedrich, L. K. Impact of television on children and youth. In E. M. Hetherington (Ed.), *Review of child development research* (Vol. 5). Chicago: University of Chicago Press, 1975, chap. 4.

Steiner, G. A. *The people look at television.* New York: Knopf, 1963.

Sternglanz, S. H., & Serbin, L. A. Sex role stereotyping in children's television programs. *Developmental Psychology,* 1974, *10,* 710–715.

Ward, S., Levinson, D., & Wackman, D. Children's attention to television advertising. In E. A. Rubinstein, G. A. Comstock, & J. P. Murray (Eds.), *Television and social behavior.* Vol. 4: *Television in day-to-day life: Patterns of use.* Washington, D. C.: U. S. Government Printing Office, 1972.

Wartella, E., & Ettema, J. S. A cognitive developmental study of children's attention to television commercials. *Communication Research,* 1974, *1,* 69–88.

Watt, J. H., & Krull, R. K. An information theory measure for television programming. *Communication Research,* 1974, *1,* 44–68.

Index